Cambridge Studies in Medieval Life and Thought
Fourth Series

The series *Cambridge Studies in Medieval Life and Thought* was inaugurated by G. G. Coulton in 1921; Professor John H. Arnold now acts as General Editor of the Fourth Series, with Dr Christopher Briggs, Dr Helen Gittos, Professor Adam J. Kosto, and Dr Magnus Ryan as Advisory Editors. The series brings together outstanding work by medieval scholars over a wide range of human endeavour extending from political economy to the history of ideas.

This is book 122 in the series, and a full list of titles in the series can be found at:
www.cambridge.org/medievallifeandthought

FLEMISH TEXTILE WORKERS IN ENGLAND, 1331–1400

In the fourteenth century, with the encouragement of King Edward III, textile workers from the Low Countries – predominantly Flanders but also Brabant – settled in England. Using extensive and original resources from both sides of the English Channel, Milan Pajic argues that the exponential growth of the English textile industry was due to the skill and influence of Flemish immigrants, challenging interpretations from a section of economic historians in the latter half of the twentieth century who concluded that immigrants did not contribute to the economic development of England. The book explores the geography of immigration, the reasons behind the movement of people and the varied social encounters with local populations. In so doing it uncovers an important and vibrant history which provides essential historical context for contemporary debates on the free movement of people.

MILAN PAJIC is the Alexander von Humboldt postdoctoral fellow at Freie Universität Berlin. This is his first book.

FLEMISH TEXTILE WORKERS IN ENGLAND, 1331–1400

Immigration, Integration and Economic Development

MILAN PAJIC
Freie Universität Berlin

CAMBRIDGE
UNIVERSITY PRESS

CAMBRIDGE
UNIVERSITY PRESS

Shaftesbury Road, Cambridge CB2 8EA, United Kingdom

One Liberty Plaza, 20th Floor, New York, NY 10006, USA

477 Williamstown Road, Port Melbourne, VIC 3207, Australia

314–321, 3rd Floor, Plot 3, Splendor Forum, Jasola District Centre, New Delhi – 110025, India

103 Penang Road, #05–06/07, Visioncrest Commercial, Singapore 238467

Cambridge University Press is part of Cambridge University Press & Assessment, a department of the University of Cambridge.

We share the University's mission to contribute to society through the pursuit of education, learning and research at the highest international levels of excellence.

www.cambridge.org
Information on this title: www.cambridge.org/9781108733625

DOI: 10.1017/9781108774215

First published 2024
First paperback edition 2025

A catalogue record for this publication is available from the British Library

Library of Congress Cataloging-in-Publication data

NAMES: Pajic, Milan, 1985- author.
TITLE: Flemish textile-workers in England, 1331-1400 : immigration, integration and economic development / Milan Pajic.
DESCRIPTION: 1 Edition. | New York, NY : Cambridge University Press, 2024. | Series: Cambridge studies in medieval life and thought: fourth series | Includes bibliographical references and index.
IDENTIFIERS: LCCN 2023022922 (print) | LCCN 2023022923 (ebook) | ISBN 9781108489201 (hardback) | ISBN 9781108733625 (paperback) | ISBN 9781108774215 (epub)
SUBJECTS: LCSH: Textile industry–England–History–14th century. | Weavers–England–History–14th century. | England–Emigration and immigration–History–14th century. | Flemings–England–History–14th century. | Social integration–England–History–14th century. | Economic development–England–History–14th century.
CLASSIFICATION: LCC HD9861.7.E53 P35 2024 (print) | LCC HD9861.7.E53 (ebook) | DDC 338.4/767709362–dc23/eng/20230720
LC record available at https://lccn.loc.gov/2023022922
LC ebook record available at https://lccn.loc.gov/2023022923

ISBN 978-1-108-48920-1 Hardback
ISBN 978-1-108-73362-5 Paperback

CONTENTS

FIGURES

MAPS

TABLES

ACKNOWLEDGEMENTS

Over the past few years, I have had to be on the move and search for evidence in numerous archives across several locations in order to complete this exciting project. However, this would not have been possible without the support and help of many people who were around in these places. In the following sentences, I would like to express my gratitude to them.

First and foremost, I am grateful to my supervisors, Christophe Tournu and Marc Boone, for their guidance and support. During my MA degree, Christophe Tournu's enthusiasm was particularly inspiring for the development of my interest in immigration history, as well as for the framing of the topic for the doctoral thesis. Even though I had no prior training in medieval history, Marc Boone accepted to co-supervise this work, and his belief in me was instrumental in the eventual success. Since then, it has been almost a decade, and whenever I had any scientific, personal or administrative problem, they were more than ready to help and encourage me. In the same manner, I would also like to thank my colleagues and friends Jan Dumolyn, Nora Berend, Bart Lambert and Miri Rubin. I have benefited from many fruitful exchanges with them over the past few years, be it at work, in the library, in the archives, at dinners or lunches, or during coffee breaks. Their guidance and advice were of crucial help. I would like to single out Jan, who was my 'unofficial' supervisor and introduced me to many practical and methodological aspects of the historians' craft that actually allow me to call myself a medievalist.

I am grateful to all involved in the book's production at Cambridge University Press, and to Chris Briggs in particular for all his suggestions and comments on different versions of the manuscript. Since this work was first proposed, the editors, John Arnold, Liz Friend-Smith and Liz Hanlon, have been extremely patient and supportive. Thank you to

Chris Jackson for copyediting the material, and anonymous readers for their feedback on the draft chapters.

During my research stays in the UK, the late Mark Ormrod was always generous and helped with archival research, and provided comments on initial drafts which always pushed me to see the broader picture. His kindness and insightful advice were an inspiration for my career choices, and all I can say is that he is greatly missed. While I was in London for almost a year, I made several important findings among the documentary evidence held at the London Metropolitan Archives (LMA). This was possible only because of the availability of Professor Caroline Barron, whose suggestions were always encouraging during our numerous conversations at the Institute of Historical Research. I owe a big thanks to the personnel of different archives in London, Chelmsford, Norwich, Ghent, Bruges, Brussels and Lille, and especially to Paul Dryburgh and Jonathan Mackman from the National Archives (TNA). In the same manner, also to Catherine Otten, for providing me with good and useful paleography classes, and to Thérèse de Hemptine, who was ready to jump in whenever my paleographic skills failed me. Over the past few years I have benefited from discussions with numerous historians during seminars and conferences that I attended, and to all of them I am very grateful, in particular to John Lee, John Oldland, James Davis, Liesbeth van Houts, the late Richard Britnell, Maryanne Kowaleski, Jelle Haemers, Vedran Sulovsky, John Baker, Jean-Philippe Genet, Martha Carlin, Marcel Elias, Elodie Lecuppre-Desjardin, Sarina Kuersteiner, Thomas Ertl, Jim Bolton, Catherine Casson, Benoit Tock, Matthew Champion, the late Derek Keene, and Sarah Wroot and Davor Salihovic (both of whom also produced the maps in this book).

This research would have not been possible without financial help from various funding bodies. Thus, I am grateful to IAP (Inter-University Attraction Pole) phase VII/26 Belgian Science Policy Project: 'City and society in the Low Countries (1200–1800): Between resilience and vulnerability'; also to BOF (Bijzonderonderzoek fonds), which funded my research with the special research fund for a joint doctorate; to FWO, which funded my research stay in London; as well as to Collège Doctoral Européen, for funding my travels to conferences and for the several months needed to finalise the writing up of the dissertation. After my Ph.D., I was privileged to be elected a Junior Research Fellow at St Catharine's College at the University of Cambridge. I am grateful to the Master and Fellows not only for allowing me to conduct my research in the best possible circumstances for three years, but also for their hospitality and endlessly constructive conversations. I owe a big thank you to FSR and to the Alexander von Humboldt Foundation for funding my postdoctoral fellowships at the Université Catholique de Louvain and Freie Universität Berlin.

Parts of this book are based on research conducted for articles published in connection with the project IAP City and Society. Sections on Flemings in London and Colchester in Chapter 2 and sections on the massacre of Flemish immigrants in London during the Peasants' Revolt of 1381 in Chapter 6 draw extensively from: B. Lambert and M. Pajic, 'Drapery in exile: Edward III, Colchester and the Flemings, 1351–1367', *History: The Journal of the Historical Association*, 99:338 (2014), 733–53; M. Pajic, 'Xénophobie et intégration: Le cas de la communauté flamande de Colchester 1351–1367', *Revue du Nord* (2017), 509–31; M. Pajic, 'Flemish rebels in exile: Their perception in 14th-century London and the creation of new identities', in T. Silec and A. Stazzone (eds), *Peuples conquérants, peuples conquis: Perceptions identitaires au Moyen Âge en Europe (Ixe–XVe siècle)*, volume issu du colloque international du Centre d'Études Médiévales Anglaises Paris Sorbonne (7–8 novembre 2014), *Bulletin des Anglicistes Médiévistes* (2015), pp. 187–206; B. Lambert and M. Pajic, 'Immigration and the common profit: Native cloth-workers, Flemish exiles and royal policy in fourteenth-century London', *Journal of British Studies*, 55:4 (2016), 633–57. Several sections in Chapter 1 are taken from J. Dumolyn and M. Pajic, 'Enemies of the count and of the city: The collective exile of rebels in fourteenth-century Flanders', *The Legal History Review*, 84:3–4 (2016), 461–501. While most of the published work reused here is reinforced with additional new research and rewritten accordingly, statistical data and some examples from archival sources taken from the aforementioned articles were less subject to major adjustments.

Of course, the writing of this book was made a lot more pleasant because of the hospitality of colleagues during my stays in Ghent and Cambridge. Special thanks go to the late Philip Oliver, Hester Lees-Jeffries, Jonas Braekevelt, Koen Vanheule, Ewoud Vaerniers, Stefan Meysman, Matthew O'Farrell and Emerance Delancenserie.

Finally, I am grateful to Céline, who was there for me in the worst moments, and I owe her a special debt of gratitude for her support, affection and tolerance.

NOTE ON CURRENCY, WEIGHTS AND MEASURES

Given the nature of a study where the main subjects (artisans) under investigation moved across numerous cities in different countries, a variety of sources from these areas had to be used. Not only are these primary materials in several different languages, but they also mention a variety of currencies, weights and measures throughout the second half of the fourteenth century that deserve some clarification.

The standard unit for all currencies mentioned in the study was the pound. Three types of pound circulated in our evidence – pound sterling from England, pound groot and pound *Parisis* from Flanders (£1 groot = £12 *Parisis*, and is not to be confused with the *livre parisis* of France). One pound (£1) contained twenty shillings/*schellingen* (20s), or 240 pence/*penningen* (d). Further subdivisions included a mark (160d) for pound sterling and a mite (1d = 24 miten) for pound groot. When prices, wages or other values are recorded in Flemish currencies, this is specified by adding groot or *Parisis* to the numerals (for example, £300 groot). For English currency (pound sterling), no such additional information is provided (for example, £7 6s). As the currency exchange varied greatly over time, we can only propose indicative conversion rates between these currencies:[1]

1£ sterling = 231d or 19s 3d groot

As regards weights and measures, traditional medieval units were used across different towns. Wool was sold in sacks of 364lbs (165 kilograms) and stones of 14lb (6.5 kilograms). Cloth was measured by the yard (3 feet, or 0.9 metres) or the ell, which was often as long as a yard and a

[1] These approximate values are based on currency exchanges observed by Hans van Werveke across various financial sources in Flanders for the fiscal years 1378 and 1379. H. van Werveke, 'Westeuropese munstelsels in de tweede helft van de veertiende eeuw', *Handelingen der Maatschaapij voor Geschiedenis en Oudheidkunde te Gent*, 27 (1973), 241–7, at 247.

quarter (1.1 metres). Depending on the type of cloth, sizes fluctuated, but it is considered that throughout the second half of the fourteenth century the dimensions of a standard English broadcloth were 24 yards long and 2 yards wide, while narrower cloths such as straits or russets from Essex were 12 yards long and 2 yards wide.[2]

[2] J. H. Munro, 'Medieval woollens: The western European woollens and their struggles for international markets, c. 1100–1500', in D. Jenkins (ed.), *The Cambridge History of Western Textiles*, 2 vols. (Cambridge and New York, 2003), vol. I, pp. 240–80; R. H. Britnell, *Growth and Decline in Colchester, 1300–1525* (Cambridge, 1986), p. 60.

ABBREVIATIONS

ADN	Archives départementales du Nord.
Benham, *Court Rolls*	*The Court Rolls of the Borough of Colchester*, ed. W. G. Benham and H. I. Jeayes, 4 vols. (Colchester, 1921–41).
CCA	Canterbury Cathedral Archives.
CCR	*Calendar of the Close Rolls Preserved in the Public Record Office*, 61 vols. (London, 1892–1963).
CFR	*Calendar of the Fine Rolls Preserved in the Public Record Office*, 22 vols. (London, 1911–62).
CPMR	*Calendar of the Plea and Memoranda Rolls Preserved among the Archives of the Corporation of the City of London at the Guildhall*, ed. A. H. Thomas and Philip E. Jones, 6 vols. (Cambridge, 1926–61).
CPR	*Calendar of the Patent Rolls Preserved in the Public Record Office*, 55 vols. (London, 1891–1916).
ERO	Essex Record Office.
Espinas, Pirenne, *Recueil*	*Recueil des documents relatifs à l'histoire de l'industrie drapière en Flandre*, ed. G. Espinas and H. Pirenne, 3 vols. (Brussels, 1909).
Fenwick, *Poll Taxes*	*The Poll Taxes of 1377, 1379, and 1381*, ed. C. C. Fenwick, 3 vols. (Oxford, 1998).
HRO	Hampshire Record Office.
Letter Books	*Calendar of Letter-Books of the City of London: A–L*, ed. R. R. Sharpe (London, 1905).
LMA	London Metropolitan Archives.
NRO	Norfolk Record Office.
PROME	*The Parliamentary Rolls of Medieval England*, ed. C. Given-Wilson et al., 16 vols. (Woodbridge, 2005).

RAG	Rijksarchief Gent.
SAB	Stadsarchief Brugge.
SAG	Stadsarchief Gent.
SRO	Suffolk Record Office.
TNA	The National Archives.

INTRODUCTION

This book deals with the fundamental historical problems of migration which, still today, remain unresolved and dominate social and political debates. It will be based on a very concrete case study of the historical migration of Flemish textile workers to England which touches upon essential aspects (social, political, economic and cultural factors) behind the complex process of emigration and immigration. This historical example is drawn from one of the first well-documented policies of the English crown to encourage the immigration of skilled artisans, during one of the most dramatic periods in the history of the former Low Countries and the British Isles, in particular the county of Flanders and England, namely the fourteenth century. The Black Death, warfare, mass devaluations and production crises created a period of fundamental social, political and economic upheaval. In this book, I will focus on Edward III's (1327–77) invitation to Flemish textile workers to settle in England in 1331, and their economic and social impact on its cities. This book will have two primary aims of analysis: the migration of Flemings and their settlement. The first will be to identify systems and build models of migratory movements within a long-term perspective, that is, understanding migration paths and causes, networks, strategies and migrants' personalities. The second will focus on what is commonly known as 'integration', that is, the immigrants' settlement, acculturation and acquisition of their social, economic and political position in the host country. In addition to a detailed treatment of these two aims, the book attempts to evaluate the economic impact of the immigrant community on a specific industry. I will argue that the success of immigrants was not solely reflected in the rise of their average earnings, but also in the fact that their skills and human capital acquired prior to emigration contributed to the development of the English textile industry in the fourteenth century.

The topic of immigration has received much attention in the past three decades, and migration history has become one of the booming fields. Numerous studies focusing on the fortunes of immigrants and their interactions throughout various historical periods have come to light.[1] Some historians have pushed back the temporal boundaries of studies of this subject, and it is safe to say that our views of pre-modern societies as 'immobile' have proved to be to a large extent false.[2] However, in the ocean of studies that include 'migration', 'mobility' and other terms used to describe the movement of people, there is still no consensus amongst historians about definitions and typologies that can be used to measure and qualify migration.[3] This is certainly due to a lot of parameters related to the distance of migration and the period of stay that we must take into account in order to establish whether someone is a 'real' migrant or seasonal mover.[4] Although we might have a tendency to think that, in order to become an 'immigrant', one must travel a long distance (internationally, or intercontinentally) and have a long-term stay, migration can also be internal and include mobility between cities, regions and provinces within the same state. There are also various reasons for people to migrate, and we can distinguish between voluntary and forced migration. Labour migrants are usually associated with voluntary migration, and their mobility has economic motivations, while refugees are driven from their homes by war, natural disasters, persecution and other violence. Some historians have treated these two categories separately, but Jan and Leo Lucassen suggest that although the motivations of labour migrants and refugees differ in principle, the disparities become less obvious in practice.[5] This is especially true if we look into the economic

[1] J. Lucassen and L. Lucassen (eds), *Migration, Migration History, History: Old Paradigms, New Perspectives* (Bern, 1997).

[2] R. Reith, 'Circulation of skilled labour in late medieval and early modern central Europe', in S. R. Epstein and M. Prak (eds), *Guilds, Innovation and the European Economy 1400–1800* (Cambridge, 2009), pp. 114–42; C. Billot, 'L'Assimilation des étrangers dans le royaume de France aux XIVe et XVe siècles', *Revue Historique*, 270 (1983), 273–96. For England, see also edited volume, book and other articles arising from Mark Ormrod's Arts and Humanities Research Council (AHRC)-funded project, 'England's Immigrants 1330–1550' (University of York): N. McDonald, W. M. Ormrod and C. Tailor (eds), *Resident Aliens in Medieval England* (Turnhout, 2018); W. M. Ormrod, B. Lambert and J. Mackman, *Immigrant England 1300–1550* (Manchester, 2018); S. Cavaciocchi (ed.), *Le migrazioni in Europa, secc. XIII–XVIII. Atti della venticinquesima settimana di studi, Istituto internazionale di storia economica F. Datini, 1993* (Florence, 1994); D. Menjot and J.-L. Pinol (eds), *Les Immigrants et la ville: Insertion, intégration, discrimination (XIIe–XXe siècles)* (Paris, 1996); J. Bottin and D. Calabi (eds), *Les Étrangers dans la ville: Minorités et espace urbain du bas Moyen Âge à l'époque moderne* (Paris, 1999); M. Balard and A. Ducellier (eds), *Migrations et diasporas méditerranéennes (Xe–XVIe siècles)* (Paris, 2002).

[3] J. Lucassen and L. Lucassen (eds), *Globalising Migration History: The Eurasian Experience (16th–21st Centuries)* (Leiden, 2014), p. 3.

[4] *Ibid.*, p. 5.

[5] Lucassen and Lucassen (eds), *Migration, Migration History*, p. 14.

potential that highly skilled voluntary immigrants or exiles might have. Both groups are also likely to be attracted by the same places and settle in areas with higher economic possibilities.

As to the nature of the mechanisms under which migration operates as a phenomenon – where one country acts as the donor and the other as receiver – a variety of theoretical models for studying the causes of movement have inevitably imposed themselves as 'pull-and-push' factors. In order to determine why international migration happens, neoclassical economics has found an explanation in wage differentials and employment conditions between countries. It generally assumes that workers from a low-wage country will move to a high-wage country. On the macro level, the decline in the supply of labour in the low-wage country will lead to a decrease in the wage differential and the eventual elimination of movement. On the micro level, the individual migrant decides to move on the basis of a simple cost–benefit calculation.[6] The 'new economics of migration', in contrast, does not consider that decisions to migrate are taken by one individual, but rather collectively, most often as a household, in order to minimise risks that might occur to the existing family income from different market failures.[7] Such micro-level decision processes are generally ignored by the dual labor market theory, which links international immigration to the structural requirements of developed nations' industries.[8] Instead of focusing on the situation in the sending country, according to this approach, labour migration is completely driven by the permanent demand for workers intrinsic to the economies of advanced industrial societies. The world systems theory assumes that the movement of people is determined by the same principle, adding historical and cultural to economic factors as the main causes of migration.[9] It sees immigration as a natural consequence of economic globalisation and capitalist penetration into the developing world.[10]

[6] D. S. Massey, J. Arango, G. Hugo, A. Kouaouci, A. Pellegrino and J. E. Taylor, 'Theories of international migration: A review and appraisal', *Population and Development Review* 19:3 (1993), 431–66, at 433–6.

[7] O. Stark, 'Migration decision making: A review article', *Journal of Development Economics*, 14 (1984), 251–9.

[8] C. M. Tolbert, P. M. Horan and E. M. Beck, 'The structure of economic segmentation: A dual economy approach', *American Journal of Sociology*, 85 (1980), 1095–116; M. J. Piore, *Birds of Passage: Migrant Labor in Industrial Societies* (Cambridge, 1979).

[9] I. Wallerstein, *The Modern World System, Capitalist Agriculture and the Origins of the European World Economy in the Sixteenth Century* (New York, 1974).

[10] A. Portes and J. Walton, *Labor, Class, and the International System* (New York, 1981); E. Morawska, 'The sociology and historiography of immigration', in V. Yans McLaughlin (ed.), *Immigration Reconsidered: History, Sociology, and Politics* (New York, 1990), pp. 187–240; S. Sassen, *The Mobility of Labor and Capital: A Study in International Investment and Labor Flow* (Cambridge, 1988).

Of course, since antiquity, cities have always represented centres of economic and administrative activity, as they are characterised by more employment opportunities, the hope of greater social mobility, and more freedom of thought and actions.[11] For these reasons they continue to attract people from outside their boundaries. The social backgrounds of people migrating to cities vary, according to the geographic distance and the duration of stay. Traditionally, unskilled labour came from the surrounding rural areas and tended to be only seasonal. Conversely, skilled artisans migrated from afar and established themselves for longer periods or permanently. They were generally part of more exclusive social networks, based on trade and administrative relations that connected different cities.[12] They were also a medium for the diffusion of new skills and thus more likely to make an impact on the development of the political, spatial, economic and cultural dimensions of the cities to which they migrated. Urban migration was mostly controlled by local authorities and to a lesser extent by supra-local governing bodies. They tended to restrict immigration in order to limit potentially destabilising effects for the native population, but sometimes institutions actively tried to attract immigrants, in particular, certain kinds of skilled artisan.[13] These active immigration policies to attract skilled labour were spurred on by high mortality rates. Until the eighteenth century, urban mortality rates were so high that the only way to maintain the increase in population and economic growth of cities was through immigration.[14] Such was the case in late medieval and early modern England, where foreign merchants and skilled artisans who contributed to economic development enjoyed legal and fiscal privileges from the government.[15]

However, once the migrants had entered the new town, several other issues arose, most notably the question of integration into the new community. The study of integration or assimilation as part of migration history finds its theoretical roots in the pioneering works produced by late nineteenth- and early twentieth-century sociologists such as Tönnies, Durkheim, Weber and Simmel. Although immigrants were

[11] P. Clark, *European Cities and Towns* (Oxford, 2009), p. 10.

[12] A. Winter, 'Population and migration: European and Chinese experiences compared', in P. Clark (ed.), *The Oxford Handbook of Cities in World History* (Oxford, 2013), p. 407.

[13] *Ibid.*, p. 411.

[14] L. Lucassen and W. Willems (eds), *Living in the City: Urban Institutions in the Low Countries 1200–2010* (Routledge, 2012), p. 7; Winter, 'Population and migration', p. 403.

[15] There are numerous works that deal with the impact of alien merchants and Huguenots in England from the fourteenth to the seventeenth centuries: A. Beardwood, *Alien Merchants in England: Their Legal and Economic Position, 1350–77* (Cambridge, Mass., 1931); N. Goose and L. Luu (eds), *Immigrants in Tudor and Early Stuart England* (Brighton, 2005); L. Luu, *Immigrants and Industries of London 1500–1700* (London, 2005).

not at the core of their work, it is important to highlight several ideas that influenced later studies and that remain integral to the main themes of this book. The notion of community as a category of analysis was originally developed by Ferdinand Tönnies, in his first book in 1887, in which he made a direct contrast between the medieval and modern periods by introducing concepts of community (*Gemeinschaft*) and society (*Gesellschaft*). The former supposedly represented the structure of the past, while the latter embodied the behaviour of modernity.[16] For Tönnies, community (*Gemeinschaft*) is realised in the bonds of kinship, of neighbourhood and of friendship. It is a form of social integration where the house, the village and the city, as well as the guild, the corporation and the parish, are the basis of a community with strong shared beliefs and values. Society (*Gesellschaft*), on the contrary, is based on impersonal ties and materialised through contractual relationships, rationality, production and the exchange of goods, commerce and the market. 'Society' therefore means a higher division of labour, and a predominance of rational goals, self-interest and interdependence. In most cases, an established community opens up to new members on the basis of an agreement and contract decided upon in mutual understanding and with the acceptance of actions offered for the future.[17] It is from this point that the term 'integration' enters the vocabulary of sociologists and gets further developed as a concept to fit different geographical areas and periods.

According to Émile Durkheim, the set of people's norms, beliefs and values common to the average member of the same society makes up what he called the collective consciousness, or a shared way of understanding and behaving in the world.[18] The collective consciousness (social integration) binds individuals together across the whole society, regardless of their personal situation in time and space in a given country. These social similarities create a form of solidarity that can appear in several shapes: domestic solidarity, professional solidarity, national solidarity etc.[19] For Durkheim, thus, every society integrates its members, or should do so. Behavioural models, values and norms are transmitted through family, school and professions. Inserting newcomers into society is only one special case in an overall process of integration. Nevertheless, he considered that assimilating strangers was a long and complex procedure, which cannot be done without the assent of all members of the host community.[20] His

16 F. Tönnies, *Community and Association (Gemeinschaft und Gesellschaft)*, trans. C. P. Loomis, (London, 1955), pp. 1–116.

17 *Ibid.*, p. 56.

18 É. Durkheim, *De la Division du travail social: Livre I*, 8th edn (Paris, 1967), pp. 46, 105, 110–11.

19 *Ibid.*, pp. 30–49.

20 *Ibid.*, pp. 140–1.

contemporary, Max Weber, in his *Economy and Society* confirmed Durkheim's assumptions that the integration of people on the move was complicated, adding the idea that conflict was inevitable. He claimed that the newcomers themselves can group around the same language and form their own group solidarity, and may thus be taken as a direct threat to the shared identity of the host community.[21] Weber, however, recognised that different communities can coexist with one another.[22]

At the same time, the German philosopher and sociologist Georg Simmel was interested in the dynamics of social relations between individuals and groups in industrial societies. In 1908, he wrote a text called *The Stranger*, in which he suggested several contemporary interpretations of the stranger within the urban space. Simmel defines the stranger as an individual who decides to stay, but who is still a potential traveller with ties elsewhere. However, it is not the stranger's relationship to space that is decisive in Simmel's analysis, but rather the interactions between individuals and groups. The stranger is thus found in the paradoxical position of being both a member of the majority group and outside the group (being both 'close' and 'distant').[23] Simmel's reflections inspired the founding thinking of the Chicago School, renowned in the history of the social sciences, whose landmark work spanned 1915 to 1940. One of the school's intellectuals, Robert E. Park, posited that assimilation is the eventual outcome of 'all the incidental collision, conflict and fusions of peoples and cultures' resulting from migration.[24]

Most of these concepts are satisfactory when it comes to the study of the incorporation of migrants into the existing community. However, they do not tell us much about integration within the medieval context. In their analyses of urban society, Tönnies, Simmel and Durkheim all saw the Middle Ages as a period of a lower division of labour, where community is imposed on the individual. However, medieval society formed different groupings based on a feeling of common political, spatial, religious or professional identity, which sometimes had all the characteristics of *Gesellschaft*. Moreover, within the conceptual framework of medieval communities (urban, national or corporate), the

[21] M. Weber, *Economy and Society*, trans. G. Roth and C. Wittich (New York, 1968), p. 390.

[22] *Ibid.*

[23] G. Simmel, *Soziologie: Untersuchungen über die Formen der Vergesellschftung*, herausgegeben von Otthein Rammstedt (Frankfurt am Main, 1992), pp. 764–71.

[24] R. Park, 'Human migration and the marginal man', *American Journal of Sociology*, 33 (1928), 881–93.

inclusion or exclusion of new members remain central components of how they functioned. According to Miri Rubin,

> community is neither obvious nor natural, its boundaries are loose, and people in the present, as in the past will use the term to describe and construct worlds, to persuade and exclude. That our subject lived, worked and played in groups, that they trusted, depended on each other, mutually helped each other is beyond doubt – but they did so in a knowing and deliberating way, choosing communities when possible, or negotiating their places within groups when less freedom of choice was available.[25]

The hierarchical structure of the public sphere of the medieval town implies that various communities that controlled political and legal processes created boundaries around them in order to exclude those whom they considered not to be aligned with their values.[26] The people outside these boundaries would be marginal, whether they were elites or vagrants.[27] The creation of these communities relied heavily on the fact that their relationships were based upon trust.[28] In such a context, the case of strangers is distinctive. Their arrival is usually tolerated during the formation of urban centres, or to fulfil demographic shortages. However, this openness of urban structures in their initial period toward the influx of all kinds of new arrival becomes progressively limited, to grant access only to the rich and well-off kind of migrant.[29] This situation is one in which urban society was founded on trustworthy kin relationships between neighbours; strangers and migrants are automatically seen with suspicion and regarded as untrustworthy.[30]

The aforementioned sociological and historical works help us to delineate the key theoretical frameworks on integration to focus on in this study. However, they tend to neglect the experience of the emigrant prior to departure. The first one to highlight this lacuna in the social sciences was the Algerian sociologist, and Pierre Bourdieu's student, Abdelmalek Sayad in his pioneering work on Algerian immigrants in France in the second half of the twentieth century. For him,

> any study of migratory phenomena that neglects the conditions of origin of immigrants is condemned to give only a partial and ethnocentric view. On the

25 M. Rubin, 'Small groups: Identity and solidarity in the late Middle Ages', in J. Kermode (ed.), *Enterprise and Individuals in Fifteenth-Century England* (Gloucester, 1991), pp. 132–50, at p. 134.

26 B. Geremek, *Les Marginaux parisiens aux XIVe et XVe siècles* (Paris, 1976), p. 13.

27 B. Hanawalt, *'Of Good and Ill Repute': Gender and Social Control in Medieval England* (Oxford, 1998), p. 18.

28 G. Rosser, *The Art of Solidarity in the Middle Ages: Guilds in England 1200–1500* (Oxford, 2015), pp. 151–2.

29 Geremek, *Les Marginaux parisiens*, p. 285.

30 *Ibid.*

> one hand, such studies give consideration only to the immigrant, not to the emigrant, as if his existence began at the moment he arrived in France. On the other hand, the implicit and explicit problematic of such studies is always the immigrant's adaptation to the 'welcoming' society.[31]

This means that we are interested in the immigrant as a whole, that we are committed to defining the social group to which this individual originally belongs, with its practices and everyday behaviours, and the extent to which all of these are challenged by the fact of immigration. Sayad was able to do so through a qualitative study, by interviewing numerous Algerians resident in France and their families in the country of origin. Applying exactly the same approach in this study would of course not be possible, as we cannot speak directly to our subjects. Nor can the medieval evidence fit the modern criteria. However, the approach that follows the emigrants can still be useful, and I will make an attempt to compare the sources from the country of origin with the sources in the country of destination in order to obtain similar information.

Taken altogether, the conceptual frameworks and approaches laid down here will be useful in exploring the experiences of migrant communities in the medieval urban context. I shall argue that while there may have been conflict between immigrants and natives, which could involve explicit exclusion and physical violence, the eventual outcome was the integration of the newcomers and the adaptation of the host society to these realities. In order to achieve this outcome, the migrants had to negotiate their integration into the new community. Negotiations of social relationships after settlement are threefold: first, between the migrant and the government; then between migrant and native societies; and finally between migrants themselves. This would include the perception of integration both from a social and an administrative point of view. Administratively, the integration is straightforward, as one is considered 'assimilated' once all the technocratic procedures are fulfilled the highest form of integration being naturalisation or citizenship, as it granted certain sets of privileged political and economic rights. Socially, however, this process of 'integration' becomes more difficult as other external factors (not only the immigrants' behaviour, but also their social environments) play an important role. That is to say, if the immigrant community faces rejection from the natives, intervention from the government in support of the migrants may help, as the natives would then be more likely to adapt to these realities.

[31] A. Sayad, *L'Immigration ou les paradoxes de l'altérité* (Brussels, 1991).

Cultural interaction and change through migration have been constituent features of human history. This paradigm, throughout history, might create the construction of Others, based on ethnicity or other, larger categories. As Dirk Hoerder defines it: 'on a cognitive level this process provided simple recognizable structures for the perplexing multiplicity of peoples. On the level of social relations it provided boundaries and permitted in-group solidarity. On the level of power relationships it denigrated the Other.'[32] Migrants have not only had to adapt to their new city, speak a different language or dialect, and adopt a new religion or religious culture, but have also transformed the demographic composition, legal framework and even the architectural perspective of the host city.[33] Often these changes, combined with other factors, would trigger a reaction from local communities in various forms – seeking an intervention from political elites to exclude the outsiders, discrimination or even physical violence. Outbreaks of confrontation have been way too easily attributed by historians to the expression of national sentiment and systematic xenophobia. In times of economic growth, migrants get little attention: it is only in times of crisis that they come to be at the centre of public debate. They are no longer only invisible workers, or heirs of immigration identified by their social affiliation: they are transformed into a separate social group, whose identity, their own culture, calls into question the host culture and national cohesion.[34] However, most immigrants spend almost the entirety of their lives peacefully in the host country, and the aforementioned forms of exclusion should rather be assigned to Pierre Bourdieu's notions of symbolic violence.[35] On the rare occasions when native populations reaffirm their exclusiveness and superiority by physical force, they do so in order to reestablish their perceived social and political hierarchies.[36]

Most of these aspects related to the phenomenon of migration or the mobility of peoples have been touched upon indirectly or directly in the historiography of medieval Europe. Many works that have appeared over the past forty years and adopt the perspective of an urban history dealing with social and economic developments make room for migrants in the chapter or chapters devoted to the urban population, a place that is often reduced, mainly due to a lack of sources. In his study of the Florentine

[32] D. Hoerder, *Cultures in Contact: World Migrations in the Second Millenium* (London, 2002), p. 3.

[33] D. Menjot, 'Introduction: Les gens venus d'ailleurs dans les villes médiévales: Quelques acquis de la recherche', in C. Quertier, R. Chilà and N. Pluchot (eds), *Arriver en ville: Les migrantes en milieu urbain au Moyen Âge* (Paris, 2013), pp. 15–32.

[34] Sayad, *L'Immigration*.

[35] P. Bourdieu, *Langage et pouvoir symbolique* (Paris, 2001), pp. 79, 264–72, 307.

[36] Weber, *Economy and Society*, pp. 901–4.

textile industry in the fourteenth century, Franco Franceschi found a significant number of workers both from elsewhere in Italy and from northern Europe, including Brabantine and Flemish workers, and devotes a chapter of his book (*Migrazioni*) to their presence in the industry.[37] In Genoa in the fifteenth century, the textile industry recruited its workers in its *contado* and the villages on the coast or in the valleys of the interior.[38] This phenomenon was also a regular occurrence in late medieval Girona in Catalonia. The labour force, especially in the textile sector, came from the neighbouring countryside, but the further we go into the fifteenth century, the further the geographical distance becomes.[39] On the other hand, Catalan artisans can be found, along with mercenaries, royal ambassadors and consuls, merchants and ship-owners, living and working as far away as Dubrovnik in the fifteenth century.[40]

Venice, severely affected by epidemics and endemic wars at the end of the fourteenth century, went even further and loosened up her strict policies on unfree labour in order to attract Albanian and Dalmatian workers to fulfil the shortages.[41] Similar policies would be developed by Louis XI when he specifically gave privileges to foreign craftsmen to settle in the cities of Cherbourg, Dieppe, Toulouse and Bordeaux in order to repopulate them.[42] Although the amount of archival material would allow a more systematic study of the wider history of late medieval French immigrant communities, with the exception of a detailed study on Brittany,[43] work to date has focused more on the legal status and condition of foreigners vis-à-vis the government and on entry into

37 F. Franceschi, *'Oltre il tumulto': I lavoratori fiorentini dell'arte della lana fra Tre et Quattrocento* (Florence, 1993), pp. 119–35. He looked into the alien presence in the Florentine textile industry in another chapter in the collection of essays: F. Franceschi, 'I tedeschi e l'arte della lana in Firenze fra Tre et Quattrocento', in G. Rossetti (ed.), *Dentro la città stranieri e realtà urbane nell'Europa dei secoli XII–XVI* (Naples, 1989), pp. 278–90.

38 J. Heers, *Gênes au XVe siècle* (Paris, 1961).

39 S. Victor, *La Construction et les métiers de la construction à Gérone au XVe siècle* (Toulouse, 2008), pp. 146–9.

40 N. Fejic, 'Les Catalans à Dubrovnik et dans le Bassin adriatique à la fin du Moyen Âge', *Anuario de Estudios Medievales*, 24 (1994), 429–52. The Spanish presence in Dubrovnik has been considered in more detail in Fejic's doctorate, published in Serbo-Croat, and in several other articles in French. N. Fejic, *Španci u Dubrovniku u srednjem veku* (Belgrade, 1988); N. Fejic, 'Les Espagnols à Dubrovnik', in Menjot and Pinol (eds), *Les Immigrants et la ville*, pp. 83–90.

41 A. Ducellier, 'Les Albanais dans les Balkans et en Italie: Courants migratoires et connivences socio-culturelles', in Cavaciocchi (ed.), *Le migrazioni in Europa*, pp. 233–70; B. Doumerc, 'L'Immigration dalmate à Venise à la fin du Moyen Âge', in *ibid.*, pp. 325–34; P. Lanaro, 'Corporations et confréries: Les étrangers et le marché du travail à Venise (XVe–XVIIIe siècles)', *Histoire Urbaine*, 21 (2008), 31–48.

42 Billot, 'L'Assimilation des étrangers', 274–5.

43 L. Moal, *L'Étranger en Bretagne au Moyen Âge: Présence, attitudes, perceptions* (Rennes, 2008).

the *naturalité*.[44] More recently, collective surveys and scientific meetings have been devoted to these people 'on the move' from 'elsewhere', which have resulted in several collections of essays bringing together more localised case studies.[45] All of these works have attempted to show the great diversity of migrant experience from one city to another and from one era to another. Even though the European historiography of migration for the medieval period is still largely incomplete, the aforementioned works have several common conclusions in the broader context of migration studies. The rather vague terminology of migrant, stranger, foreigner, immigrant or mobility will vary according to historians, particularly because they deal with different realities according to time, region, distance of mobility and sources. Moreover, although experiences were very different for any given group of migrants, most of the studies confirm that the history of migration is a profoundly urban process.

When it comes to England, the historiography stands in slightly better shape in terms of late medieval migration. The pioneering study by William Cunningham (1897) gave an overview of the alien presence and their economic activities in medieval England, and presented an excellent starting point for further research.[46] Following this work and throughout the twentieth century, several studies appeared that focused on specific groups of migrants, such as Italian merchants, or on the legal status of merchants.[47] Others attempted to point the way to studies of even more specific categories, such as Gascons during the Hundred Years War.[48] More broadly, some local studies have made contributions by providing us with information about the number, origins and fortunes of more humble immigrants who settled in Southampton, Ipswich,

44 *Lettres de naturalité* were an embryonic form of naturalisation. B. d'Alteroche, *De L'étranger à la seigneurie à l'étranger au royaume (Xie–XVe siècles)* (Paris, 2000); J. Gilissen, 'Le Statut des étrangers à la lumière de l'histoire comparative', in *L'Étranger, recueils de la société Jean Bodin pour l'histoire comparative des institutions* (Brussels, 1958), vol. I, pp. 5–57; E. Soloman, 'La Condition juridique des étrangers dans les législations anciennes et le droit moderne', unpublished Ph.D. thesis, University of Paris (1844); J. Mathorez, *Histoire de la formation de la population française: Les étrangers en France sous l'ancien régime*, 2 vols. (Paris, 1919–21).

45 H. Peregrine (ed.), *Freedom of Movement in the Middle Ages: Proceedings of the Twentieth Harlaxton Symposium* (Donington, 2007); Quertier, Chilà and Pluchot (eds), *Arriver en ville*; Cavaciocchi, *Le migrazioni in Europa*; Menjot and Pinol (eds), *Les Immigrants et la ville*; Bottin and Calabi, *Les Étrangers dans la ville*; Balard and Ducellier (eds), *Migrations et diasporas méditerranéennes*.

46 W. Cunningham, *Alien Immigrants to England* (New York, 1897).

47 Beardwood, *Alien Merchants in England*; K. Kim, *Aliens in Medieval Law: The Origins of Modern Citizenship* (Cambridge, 2000); J. L. Bolton, 'Alien merchants in England in the reign of Henry VI, 1422–61', unpublished B.Litt. thesis, University of Oxford (1971); H. Bradley, 'The Italian community in London, 1350–1450', unpublished Ph.D. thesis, University of London (1992); T. H. Lloyd, *Alien Merchants in England in the High Middle Ages* (Brighton, 1982).

48 A. Peyregne, 'Les Émigrés gascons en Angleterre (1453–1485)', *Annales du Midi*, 66 (1954), 1–15.

Norfolk, Yorkshire and London throughout the fifteenth century.[49] All of these studies have raised the issues of the availability of sources and the analytical problems surrounding the study of migration, such as belonging, discrimination, persecution and the need to think carefully about immigrants' contribution to economic development, as well as their integration into the job market. More recently, a major project run by the late Mark Ormrod at the University of York and funded by the Arts and Humanities Research Council (AHRC), 'England's Immigrants 1330–1550', and its various outputs have shed new light on various aspects of the alien presence in late medieval England. Apart from the creation of a database with the names of more than 65,000 immigrants, the team managed to posit some very important conclusions about the development of England's first regulatory framework on nationality, immigration and naturalisation.[50] Overall, in comparison with current literature on the Continent, existing studies lead us to believe that England attracted a lot more immigration than its continental counterparts, due to the number of suitable sources, as well as favourable pull-and-push factors.

[49] J. L. Bolton, (ed.), *The Alien Communities of London in the Fifteenth Century: The Subsidy Rolls of 1440 and 1483–4* (Stamford, 1998); R. B. Dobson, 'Aliens in the city of York during the fifteenth century', in J. Mitchell (ed.), *England and the Continent in the Middle Ages, Studies in Memory of Andrew Martindale*, Harlaxton Medieval Studies VIII (Stamford, 2000), pp. 249–66; P. Fleming, 'Identity and belonging: Irish and Welsh in fifteenth-century Bristol', in L. Clark (ed.), *The Fifteenth Century, Vol. VII: Conflicts, Consequences and the Crown in the Middle Ages* (Woodbridge, 2007), pp. 175–93; R. A. Griffiths, 'The island of England in the fifteenth century: Perceptions of the peoples of the British Isles', *Journal of Medieval History*, 29 (2003), 177–200; N. J. M. Kerling, 'Aliens in the county of Norfolk, 1436–85', *Norfolk Archaeology*, 33 (1965), 200–15; D. Keene, 'Metropolitan values: Migration, mobility and cultural norms, London 1100–1700', in L. Wright (ed.), *The Development of Standard English, 1300–1800: Theories, Descriptions, Conflicts* (Cambridge, 2000), pp. 93–114; A. A. Ruddock, 'Alien Hosting in Southampton in the fifteenth century', *Economic History Review*, 16 (1946), 30–7; S. L. Thrupp, 'Aliens in and around London in the Fifteenth Century', in A. E. J. Hollaender and W. Kellaway (eds), *Studies in London History Presented to Philip Edmund Jones* (London, 1969), pp. 251–75; S. L. Thrupp, 'A survey of the alien population of England in 1440', *Speculum*, 32 (1957), 262–73.

[50] The database is available online at www.englandsimmigrants.com and is based on alien subsidies from the fifteenth century and on denization letters (the English embryo form of naturalisation act). It contains the immigrants' names, place of origin, gender, status, networks (family, household, community) and geographical dispersion. The project also resulted in two books, two Ph.D. theses and numerous articles: McDonald, Ormrod and Tailor (eds), *Resident Aliens*; Ormrod, Lambert and Mackman, *Immigrant England 1300–1550*; J. Bartlett, 'Looking at t'other: Robert Thornton's *Yorkshire Oryent*, c. 1400–1473', unpublished Ph.D. thesis, University of York (2015); C. Linsley, 'Nation, England and the French in Thomas Walsingham's *Chronica Maiora* 1376–1420', unpublished Ph.D. thesis, University of York (2015); B. Lambert and W. M. Ormrod, 'Friendly foreigners: International warfare, resident aliens and the early history of denization in England, c. 1250 – c. 1400', *English Historical Review*, 130 (2015), 1–24; B. Lambert and W. M. Ormrod, 'A matter of trust: The royal regulation of England's French residents during wartime, 1294–1377', *Historical Research*, 89 (2016), 208–26.

The migration of Flemish textile workers, which is at the core of this book, still remains without a comprehensive study. It has been mentioned incidentally in works dealing with other aspects of English economic and social history.[51] The main debate surrounding this migration has revolved around the question of whether such Flemish workers had any influence on the development of the English cloth industry, which grew exponentially from the mid fourteenth century onwards. From very early on, historians have tried to pinpoint one specific reason as the root cause for the success of English woollen manufacture and its eventual 'victory' over the Flemish.[52] Ultimately, the debate surrounding the explanations for the rise of the English cloth trade have shifted around four hypotheses:

1) the regional shift of cloth manufacture. Several studies have suggested that the advantages of a lack of guild regulation, the proximity of wool-growers and cheaper labour influenced cloth-makers to move from urban to rural areas, lowering production costs and thus making cloths more competitive on the export market.[53]
2) the introduction of the fulling mill. The biggest proponent of this hypothesis, Eleanora Carus-Wilson, claimed that the use of the fulling mill provided a reduction in cloth-production costs, which was overall reflected in the increased number of manufactured fabrics.[54]

[51] Cunningham, *Alien Immigrants*, pp. 100–11; M. McKisack, *The Fourteenth Century, 1307–1399* (Oxford, 1959), p. 368; F. Consitt, *The London Weavers' Company* (London, 1933), pp. 33–60; H. De Sagher, 'L'Immigration des tisserands flamands et brabançons en Angleterre sous Edouard III', in W. Ashley and P. Berghmans (eds), *Mélanges d'histoire offerts à Henri Pirenne par ces anciens élèves et ses amis à l'occasion de sa quarantième année de l'enseignement à Université de Gand* (Brussels, 1926), pp. 109–26; H. Heaton, *The Yorkshire Woollen and Worsted Industries from the Earliest Times up to the Industrial Revolution*, 2nd edn (Oxford, 1965), pp. 14–20.

[52] As we will see in Chapter 1, English textile industries faced difficulties and a severe decline in production at the end of the thirteenth and the first half of the fourteenth centuries, only to experience growth from the 1350s.

[53] E. Miller, 'The fortunes of the English textile industry during the thirteenth century', *Essays in Economic History Presented to Professor M. M. Postan, Economic History Review*, 18 (1965), 64–82.

[54] E. Carus-Wilson, 'An industrial revolution of the thirteenth century', *Economic History Review*, 11 (1941), 39–60. Her views were strenuously challenged by several scholars, Edward Milller and Anthony Bridbury being amongst the most vocal: Miller, 'The fortunes of the English textile industry', 71–2; A. Bridbury, *Medieval English Clothmaking: An Economic Survey* (London, 1982), pp. 16–26. For a summary of different debates and some constructive criticism of the Carus-Wilson thesis, see J. H. Munro, 'Symbiosis of towns and textiles: Urban institutions and the changing fortunes of cloth manufacturing in the Low Countries and England 1280–1570', *Journal of Early Modern History*, 3 (1999), 1–74, at 12–20; J. H. Munro, 'Industrial energy from water-mills in the European economy, 5th to 18th centuries: The limitations of power', in S. Cavaciocchi (ed.), *Economia e energia secc. XIII–XVIII. Atti della trentaquattresima settimana di studi a cura di Simonetta Cavaciocchi* (Florence, 2002), pp. 248–55; J. Oldland, *The English Woollen Industry, c. 1200 – c. 1560* (Abingdon, 2020), pp. 10–11, 169–70.

3) royal intervention to tax wool exports in order to foster domestic wool production.[55]
4) the immigration of Flemish textile workers and the importation of their skills.

As the thesis of the fulling mill has been convincingly refuted, the widely accepted factors responsible for the expansion of the industry after 1350 come down to a combination of government protectionist policies (fiscal measures on wool) and the rise of the guilds, while the immigration of Flemings is accepted as a factor by some historians and not favoured by others. One of the aims of this book is to provide a convincing case about the impact of Flemish immigrants on the rise of English urban cloth-making.

Already in 1655, Thomas Fuller gave a very positive account of Flemish immigration in his *Church History of Britain*. Believing that England had no cloth production of any better quality than *frieses* (or friezes – a cheap type of cloth) throughout the thirteenth century, the clergyman painted a vivid picture of the newcomers' arrival. 'Happy the yeoman's house', he said, 'into which one of these Dutchmen [sic] did enter, bringing industry and wealth along with them.'[56] Scholars of the nineteenth and the first half of the twentieth centuries followed his lead and credited the immigration of Flemings with nothing less than the birth of English cloth manufacture. While explaining that the origins of England's wealth lay in its woollen industry, the influential political economist William Ashley saw the immigration of Flemish weavers as the cause of the expansion, and the English woollen industry's consequent reorientation towards export.[57] Backing their claims with archival evidence, William Cunningham, Ephraim Lipson and Louis Salzman, too, were struck by the close coincidence of the arrival of Flemish textile workers and the boost of the new industries that followed in the mid fourteenth century.[58] They all considered Edward III's reign as a landmark for the success of the English woollen

[55] Higher customs duties and occasional bans on wool exports were occasionally imposed throughout the fourteenth century, which gave the English cloth industry a cost advantage of 25–30 per cent. Munro, 'Symbiosis of town and textiles', 37–40.

[56] T. Fuller, *The Church History of Britain: From the Birth of Jesus Christ until the Year M.DC.XLVIII*, 6 vols. (Oxford, 1845), vol. II, p. 286.

[57] W. Ashley, *An Introduction to English Economic History and Theory, Part II: The End of the Middle Ages*, 10th edn (London, 1925), p. 195.

[58] W. Cunningham, 'The commercial policy of Edward III', *Transactions of the Royal Historical Society*, New Series, 4 (1889), 202–3; W. Cunningham, *The Growth of English Industry and Commerce during the Early and Middle Ages*, 5th edn (Cambridge, 1922), pp. 308–9; E. Lipson, *The Economic History of England, Part I: The Middle Ages*, 5th edn (London, 1929), pp. 399–402; L. Salzman, *English Industries of the Middle Ages: Being an Introduction to the Industrial History of Medieval England* (London, 1913), pp. 197–205.

industry and praised his programme for developing local manufacture and fostering export, which included the invitation to Flemish weavers to set up their trade in England as one of those measures.[59] Across the Channel, historians have been equally impressed by the effectiveness of Edward III's measures. 'The English king gave them [the Flemings] asylum', the eminent Henri Pirenne wrote in his *Histoire de Belgique*, 'and the counties of Kent and Suffolk . . . became the cradle of an industry that would compete with Flanders half a century later.'[60]

The influence that the migration of workers from the Low Countries may have had on the growth of the English textile industry was viewed more sceptically by twentieth-century scholars. The first one to offer a counter-argument to the early economic historians was H. L. Gray, when he examined the location of the cloth industry in the second half of the fourteenth century. Centres with the highest proportion of cloths produced were in the south-west, which was not a region where a Flemish presence had been previously attested. This led him to conclude that 'it was difficult to believe that the foremost woollen producing district in the country in 1356 owed its prosperity to such an immigration'.[61] Henry Johnson was quick to point out that the invitation to the Flemish weavers to England by Edward III had nothing to do with the promotion of a native cloth industry, but was rather to coerce the Flemish into joining him into an alliance, and a war with France.[62] An authority on late medieval Flemish drapery, Pirenne's student Henri De Sagher devoted an article to the subject in 1926 and concluded that 'traditional historiography has attached an importance to immigration out of all proportion with its real role'. 'Nowhere in England', he continued, 'can we discern a decisive influence on the future of the trade.'[63] In her 1959 overview of the fourteenth century, May McKisack considered the arrival of foreigners as a symptom, rather than a primary cause, of expansion.[64] Eleanora Carus-Wilson adopted these views later in her career.[65]

[59] The interventionist measures taken by Edward III in order to boost the local industries are discussed in more detail in Chapter 1.

[60] H. Pirenne, *Histoire de Belgique dès origines à nos jours*, 5th edn, 4 vols. (Brussels, 1928), vol. IV, p. 325.

[61] H. L. Gray, 'The production and exportation of English woollens in the fourteenth century', *Economic History Review*, 39:153 (1924), 13–35, at 21–2.

[62] H. Johnson, *The History of the Worshipful Company of the Drapers of London*, 3vols. (Oxford, 1914), vol. I, pp. 65–8.

[63] De Sagher, 'L'Immigration des tisserands flamands', pp. 123, 125.

[64] McKisack, *The Fourteenth Century*, p. 368.

[65] E. Carus-Wilson, 'Trends in the export of English woollens in the fourteenth century', *Economic History Review*, 3:2 (1950), 165. Her assessment in 1950 was somewhat neutral, as she admitted that there was no comprehensive study of this migration, but in 1987 Carus-Wilson even used McKisack's words for her conclusion. Carus-Wilson, 'The woollen industry', in E. Miller and

Some of the local studies further amplified these views. Writing in 1965 on Yorkshire's woollen and worsted industries, Herbert Heaton stated that the Flemish presence in the county's medieval cloth manufacture was small and, its chronology not matching that of the development of textile production, that its influence was negligible.[66] Derek Keene made similar observations, claiming that Flemish influence on the revival of Winchester's cloth industry from the 1350s was minimal.[67] These interpretations found favour with several influential historians. In his *Medieval English Economy*, Jim Bolton only reflected Heaton's conclusions.[68] More importantly, even one of the greatest authorities on the medieval textile industry, John Munro, was approving of Heaton and Keene's views.[69] Looking at the matter in 2005 from the perspective of immigrants' contributions to the English economy during the sixteenth and early seventeenth centuries, Nigel Goose called the importance of foreign immigration for the establishment of the English textile industry in the fourteenth century wildly exaggerated and not to be compared with that of the low price of wool and the general availability of labour.[70] Interestingly, all of them ignored the findings of a local study on Colchester by Richard Britnell, who considered that the arrival of Flemings was critical to the growth of broadcloth production.[71]

Several historians have been a bit more cautious in their appraisal and given somewhat neutral views. Frances Consitt provided a detailed account of the Flemish presence in London, without problematizing their contribution to cloth manufacture.[72] Looking at government policies as attempts to attract foreign skills before the sixteenth century, Lien Luu devoted several pages to Edward III's invitation to Flemish weavers. She acknowledged that the pull-and-push factors were favourable, and

S. Pollard (eds), *Cambridge Economic History of Europe: Trade and Industry in the Middle Ages*, 2 vols. (Cambridge, 1987), vol. II, pp. 613–90, at pp. 676–7.

66 Heaton, *The Yorkshire Woollen and Worsted Industries*, p. 17.

67 D. Keene, *Survey of Medieval Winchester*, 2 vols. (Oxford, 1985), vol. I, pp. 299–318.

68 J. L. Bolton, *The Medieval English Economy 1100–1500* (London, 1980), p. 286.

69 J. H. Munro, 'The "industrial crisis" of the English textile towns, 1290–1330', in M. Prestwich, R. H. Britnell and R. Frame (eds), *Thirteenth-Century England* (Woodbridge, 1999), vol. VII, pp. 103–42, at pp. 122–3; Munro, 'Medieval woollens: The western European woollen industries', vol. I, pp. 240–80.

70 N. Goose, 'Immigrants and English economic development in the sixteenth and early seventeenth centuries', in Goose and Luu (eds), *Immigrants in Tudor and Early Stuart England*, pp. 136–60, at pp. 153–4.

71 Britnell, *Growth and Decline*, p. 72. The aforementioned authors were also unable to consider John Oldland's Ph.D. thesis, which was defended slightly later than the last of these works was published, but Oldland came to similar conclusions for London as Britnell for Colchester. J. R. Oldland, 'London Clothmaking, c. 1270 – c. 1550', unpublished Ph.D. thesis, Royal Holloway and Bedford New College, University of London (2003), pp. 62–4.

72 Consitt, *The London Weavers' Company*, pp. 33–60.

that there was growth in the cloth industry after the arrival of the Flemish, but that the extent of their influence was still to be investigated.[73] In an essay published in 2011, Jonathan Good was more concerned with the relationship between Flemings and Brabanters than with the existing debate.[74] While interpreting the evidence about the Yorkshire cloth industry, Edward Miller and John Hatcher attributed rather more influence to Flemish and Brabantine textile workers than Herbert Heaton did.[75]

One of the main obstacles that has stood in the way of every attempt at a critical assessment of the impact of Flemish immigration on the late medieval English cloth industry is the complete absence of numbers to fall back on. De Sagher estimated that during the entire fourteenth century no more than 200 Flemish textile workers could have settled in England.[76] May McKisack admitted that Edward III's policies undoubtedly attracted a lot of textile workers from Flanders, but concluded that their numbers or influence on the English cloth industry were impossible to assess even approximately.[77] Lawrence Poos came to the same conclusions for rural areas in Essex in 1991.[78] Convincing conclusions were never reached, as all of these works had different topics as their primary focus. Moreover, none of the aforementioned studies examined the immigration of Flemings in enough detail to make strong hypotheses and widely confirm or dispute their influence. However, some of them, aware of the situation on the other side of the English Channel, gave hints of an open mind. Eleanora Carus-Wilson noticed the contraction of the industry in Flanders in the mid fourteenth century and confirmed that some of this was probably due to the unrest in the county, which led to the emigration of numerous artisans to England. But she concluded that it was impossible to assess the pace and scale of this immigration.[79] While concluding his observations on this immigration, John Munro said that William Ashley was 'correct to

[73] Luu, *Immigrants and Industries*, pp. 53–6.

[74] J. Good, 'The alien clothworkers of London, 1337–1381', in L. E. Mitchell, K. L. French and D. L. Biggs (eds), *The Ties That Bind: Essays in Medieval British History in Honor of Barbara Hanawalt* (Farnham, 2001), pp. 7–20.

[75] J. Hatcher and E. Miller, *Medieval England: Towns, Commerce and Crafts 1086–1348* (London, 1995), pp. 122–3. For a positive view of the influence of textile workers from the Low Countries in York, see M. Sellers, 'Textile industry', in W. Page (ed.), *The Victoria History of the Counties of England: A History of the County of York* (London, 1907), vol. III, pp. 406–29, and 'Social and economic history', in *ibid.*, vol. III, pp. 435–86.

[76] De Sagher, 'L'Immigration des tisserands flamands', p. 115.

[77] McKisack, *The Fourteenth Century*, p. 367.

[78] L. R. Poos, *A Rural Society after the Black Death: Essex 1350–1525* (Cambridge, 1991), p. 70.

[79] Carus-Wilson, 'The woollen industry', p. 676.

observe that the Flemish civil wars, and their brutal terminations, of 1323–8 and 1344–9, did result in banishment, exile or flight of many artisans', and asked, 'but to what effect?'[80] This book will attempt to give an answer to this question, as the main focus will be on those who were banished and on those who left voluntarily after these revolts and settled in England. I will show that the combination of local, royal and continental records can unearth a lot more evidence of a significant presence of textile workers from the Low Countries than any of these studies has suggested.

The general economic trends in fourteenth-century England and its towns in particular were also indirectly favourable to immigrants. During the twelfth and thirteenth centuries, English society had become very market-oriented, with significant levels of market output and commercial activity.[81] By 1300, new towns had been founded and existing centres expanded to form an urban system that would remain intact up until the sixteenth century, even with the occasional outbreaks of plague from 1349 onwards. This urban network stretched from London as the capital, with around 60,000 inhabitants, through to provincial centres like Norwich, York and Bristol credited with more than 12,000 inhabitants each, down to numerous market towns like Colchester, Great Yarmouth or Lynn with 2,000–5,000 inhabitants each.[82] Although it is estimated that throughout the fourteenth century towns formed less than 20 per cent of the English population, their demand for food and raw materials represented a wide range of marketing opportunities for country-dwellers as well.[83] Most trade was local, or between an urban area and its hinterlands, but some towns were places where long-distance trade was more likely to develop. Indeed, as Bruce Campbell pointed out: 'long-distance trade may have been the smallest and riskiest branch of medieval commerce, far eclipsed in volume and value by local exchange of staple commodities: its economic multiplier effects were disproportionally great as were the profits reaped by those successful engaging in it'.[84] England's overseas trade principally consisted of exports of wool,

[80] Munro, 'The "industrial crisis"', p. 123.

[81] R. H. Britnell, *The Commercialisation of English Society 1000–1500*, 2nd edn (Cambridge, 2009), pp. 79–154.

[82] R. B. Dobson, 'The General Survey 1300–1540', in D. M. Palliser (ed.), *The Cambridge Urban History of Britain* (Cambridge, 2008), p. 275.

[83] R. H. Britnell, 'The towns of England and northern Italy in the early fourteenth century', *Economic History Review*, 44 (1991), 21–35, at 21.

[84] B. Campbell, *The Great Transition: Climate, Disease and Society in the Late Medieval World* (Cambridge, 2016), p. 30.

cloth, lead, tin and pewter, in return for imports of raw materials, foodstuffs and manufactured goods. The most important markets were Flanders and the Low Countries, but there were other major trading links with the Baltic, France, Spain, Portugal and the Mediterranean.[85] These established commercial networks only facilitated the movement of people and were the precursor for some of them to choose to stay on a more permanent basis.

Conversely, the Low Countries had become the most densely populated and one of the most urbanised societies in Europe already in the twelfth century. Because of their wealth, built on trade and cloth manufacture, the cities of Arras, Douai, Ghent, Bruges, Ypres, Lille and, increasingly important by the later fifteenth century, Brussels and Antwerp enjoyed a degree of political independence that almost matched that of Italian city-states. Also in terms of demography, the cities of the Low Countries were close to the Italian city-states. Ghent's population was estimated at 64,000, Bruges around 45,000 and Ypres around 25,000, and seven other cities had around 10,000 inhabitants.[86] Paris, for comparison, is estimated to have had between 150,000 and 200,000 inhabitants, while Florence, Venice and Milan had at least 100,000 each.[87] Also, the overall level of urbanisation was higher than in England and quite elevated for the late medieval period. It is estimated that 36 per cent of the total population of fifteenth-century Flanders lived in cities.[88] Such a degree of development was achieved to a large extent because of the concentration of wealth based on the production and exportation of textiles. However, we will see in Chapter 1 how the fortunes of the cloth industry in Flanders depended heavily on the political situation in England.

The devastating effects of the Black Death and the drop in population in the second half of the fourteenth century did not have any major consequences for established trading links with the Continent, but they did for the organisation of manufacturing industries.[89] While the size of the English population was halved, the productivity of labour and average standards of living rose. For many manufacturers, demand per

85 Bolton, *The Medieval English Economy*, pp. 287–95; R. H. Britnell, *Britain and Ireland 1050–1530: Economy and Society* (Oxford, 2004), pp. 326–33.

86 M. Boone, 'Gouverner les villes flamandes au Moyen Âge: Aspects politiques, idéologiques et financiers', in B. Arizaga Bolumburu and J. A. Solorzano Telechea (eds), *La gobernanza de la ciudad Europea en la edad media* (Logrono, 2011), pp. 267–97; A. Brown and J. Dumolyn (eds), *Medieval Bruges, c. 850–1550* (Cambridge, 2018).

87 Campbell, *The Great Transition*, pp. 122–4.

88 M. Boone and W. Prevenier, 'Les villes des Pays-Bas méridionaux au bas Moyen Âge: Identité urbaine et solidarité corporative', *Bulletin du crédit communal*, 183 (1993), 25–42, at 29.

89 Campbell, *The Great Transition*, p. 360.

head of population increased.[90] Despite attempts to hold down wages, workers themselves enjoyed high real wages, as lower food prices enhanced their purchasing power.[91] These conditions were beneficial for urban textile industries as well, and gains in living standards after the Black Death enabled more consumers to purchase more cloth of better quality.[92] Higher domestic demand enhanced the ability of urban textile manufacturers to become more competitive on international markets as well. The shortage of workers caused by the Black Death reduced any strict control of newly arrived immigrants by the civic authorities. The rise of those who obtained the status of citizen was most visible in the mid fourteenth century. For example, the registers of new freemen in the city of York show that, apart from those immigrants who came from Yorkshire and elsewhere in the British Isles, there was a steady inflow from the Continent during the years of the outbreak of plague.[93]

Resident aliens in England were nothing new in the late thirteenth and fourteenth centuries: numerous merchants, members of the clergy and craftsmen from overseas chose to settle on a permanent basis. In urban environments, therefore, cultural exchange, assimilation and identity come to mind as prominent features. Another problem that most aliens in England might face was their legal status, which in practice was never straightforward. A clear distinction between those who were subjects of the king (*indigene regni*) and those born overseas (*de natis ultra mare*) had been made by 1351. This was created for the purposes of classifying numerous children born to English parents overseas, an increasingly prominent occurrence during the Hundred Years War. Those who fulfilled the conditions were issued grants at royal discretion.[94] Similar types of protection had been granted earlier to foreign merchants or important individuals, so that they could enjoy fiscal privileges related to customs within the realm as if they were native

[90] Britnell, *The Commercialisation*, p. 168.

[91] C. Dyer, *An Age of Transition? Economy and Society in England in the Later Middle Ages* (Oxford, 2005), p. 30.

[92] J. Hatcher, *Plague, Population and the English Economy, 1348–1530* (London, 1977), pp. 68–9; D. Woodward, 'Wage rates and living standards in pre-industrial England', *Past and Present*, 91 (1981), 28–40. Recent debates are summarised in J. Hatcher, 'Unreal wages: Long run living standards and the "Golden Age" of the Fifteenth Century', in B. Dodds and C. D. Liddy (eds), *Commercial Activity, Markets and Entrepreneurs in the Middle Ages: Essays in Honour of Richard Britnell* (Woodbridge, 2011), pp. 1–24, and C. Dyer, 'A golden age rediscovered: Labourers' wages in the fifteenth century', in M. Allen and D. Coffman (eds), *Prices, Money and Wages* (London, 2014), pp. 180–95.

[93] E. Miller, 'Medieval York', in P. M. Tillott (ed.), *The Victoria History of the Counties of England: A History of the County of York: The City of York* (London, 1961), p. 108.

[94] A. Ruddick, *English Identity and Political Culture in the Fourteenth Century* (Cambridge, 2013), p. 102.

(*tamquam indigena*). They became an almost routine element of the chancery's business in the course of the fourteenth century and were offered without discrimination to a wide range of national groups, including the French, Iberians, Italians, Germans and people from the Low Countries.[95] Over time, these letters of protection, issued in the form of letters patent, would extend their competence and, by the end of the fourteenth century, become accessible to alien craftsmen resident in England as well. They would become known as letters of denization, an embryonic form of the naturalisation that we know today.

Although letters of protection gave aliens a certain status of security for continued residence, some of them were still vulnerable during wartime measures. French residents and those under the suzerainty of the French king, such as Flemings and Bretons, were first in line. In 1294, their goods were confiscated, while in 1377 the parliament of Richard II petitioned for the expulsion of all subjects of the French king from English soil.[96] In peacetime, aliens were generally acceptable, but in wartime they would soon become the subject of suspicion. As Andrea Ruddick puts it: 'Although there was no official, all-encompassing "anti-alien" policy during the reigns of Edward I, II and III, the concept of being an "alien" was nonetheless a politically significant identity.'[97] We will also see throughout this book that despite the more pragmatic crown policies towards resident aliens, local craftsmen, in particular, did their best to mobilise their guilds to limit aliens' options to expand their trade.

This book, then, is an addition to the migration, social and economic history of England and Europe, focusing on the fortunes of the community of textile workers from the Low Countries that settled in various English towns during the second half of the fourteenth century. By combining both the archival material from continental Europe and England the main purpose of this study will be to shed new light on the economic contribution of Flemish immigrants in England. It will be an attempt to answer the following research questions: What was the profile of the Flemish immigrants, and how numerous were they? How did Flemish weavers transfer their skills to the English? What was the process of that transfer? Did political, economic and social events on the local level have any influence on the diffusion of skills? Where did resistance come from among guild organisations, entrepreneurs and the like? Did the immigrants' influence transcend the economic transfer of skills, and what might have been the impact on the cultural level, such as donations to local churches, and the funding of or integration into

[95] Lambert and Ormrod, 'Friendly foreigners', 2–3.

[96] Lambert and Ormrod, 'A matter of trust', 226.

[97] Ruddick, *English Identity*, p. 116.

existing religious confraternities, hospitals and other charitable institutions? Indeed, this study will show that the number of immigrants was far higher than previously thought, and that they were better placed in terms of capital and skills than their English counterparts.

METHODOLOGY AND SOURCES

In order to fully understand the reasons behind Flemish immigration to England, we must bear in mind that before he or she becomes an immigrant, the migrant is always first an emigrant, and therefore it is imperative that our study should start not with the concerns of the receiving society, but with the sending communities.[98] Exploring the history and structure of the sending country will allow us to find out what the determinants for departure were, and thus reconstitute the whole trajectory of the individuals and groups under examination.[99] It is only then that we can pass on to different empirical and theoretical questions surrounding the political, social and economic impact on the host society of the group under examination.

This approach will be applied in order to reconstruct the conditions that first led immigrants from the Low Countries to emigrate to England and then how they settled, integrated and contributed to the English economy. Thus, a particular feature of this study is the integration of English and continental sources, and it relies heavily on prosopographical methodology. The main purpose is to identify and quantify the immigrants from the Low Countries in England, while examining qualitatively their experiences. The study focuses mostly on London, Colchester and Great Yarmouth, localities which were not chosen at random, but because of the incredibly high survival rate of their local records. More precisely, their judicial records, and borough court rolls in particular, form the cornerstone of this book. When and wherever possible, the extant relevant material from other English towns has been used, in order to reinforce the argument. Thus, a variety of the extant material allowed a more detailed analysis for the cities of Lincoln, Boston, York, Winchester, Bristol, Lynn and Norwich. The manorial courts of Clare, Hadleigh and Sudbury were included to illuminate Colchester's hinterlands. All of the findings in the English sources were constantly compared with the archival material held in Belgium and France.

98 P. Bourdieu and L. Wacquant, 'The organic ethnologist of Algerian migration', *Ethnography*, 1 (2000), 173–82, at 174.

99 Sayad, *L'Immigration*, p. 24.

One of the remarkable things about the judicial records of medieval England is that they contain not just a few surviving excerpts, but thousands of cases spread across both local and central courts. Although the procedures and aims of manorial, borough or royal courts differed widely, they all recorded the names of the people involved and the nature of the cases or fines. Both civil pleas and felonies (criminal matters) included a number of immigrants from the Low Countries, who appear alongside English-born individuals or other aliens. They feature in a variety of cases and roles: as the perpetrators or victims of crime, as the sufferers of acts of misfortune (mainly accidental deaths), as the aiders and abettors of criminals, as pledges or debtors, or as witnesses, or the finders of bodies. Such records have already been used by scholars to analyse the histories of localised patterns of crime, the level of violence, the credit relationships of various communities, and attitudes towards law enforcement.[100] However, in the context of the presence of aliens, they have received little attention.[101] The data from these sources can facilitate the collection of immigrants' names and estimates of their number, show patterns of alien residency, and provide information about their legal status and profession, as well as the presence of women.

As the most extensive and valuable sources that allow us to establish the long-term settlement of immigrants from the Low Countries and conduct an analytical study of their lives thereafter, the borough court records of Colchester and Great Yarmouth deserve to be described in more detail first. The key judicial institution of these two medium-sized towns in eastern England functioned in a very similar way in both places. To maintain law and order, the bailiffs of Colchester had two judicial bodies of the borough court at their disposal: the court of pleas, and the hundred court. The court of pleas dealt with private litigation concerning debt, detention of chattels, breach of contract and trespass, that is, cases of violation of private property and physical aggression that fell short of felony. Minor crimes, including night wandering and the carrying of weapons, and all kinds of police work, such as fines for prostitution, and making and selling ale and bread against the assize, were

100 For example, A. Musson and W. M. Ormrod, *The Evolution of English Justice* (London, 1999); P. Maddern, *Violence and Social Order: East Anglia 1422–42* (Oxford, 1992); B. Hanawalt, *Crime and Conflict in English Communities 1300–1348* (Cambridge, Mass., 1979); J. Davis, *Medieval Market Morality: Life, Law and Ethics in the English Market Place* (Cambridge 2011); C. Briggs, *Credit and Village Society in the Fourteenth Century* (Oxford, 2009).

101 A study on alien presence in late medieval Lincolnshire used gaol deliveries and coroners' rolls as the principal sources. A. Kissane and J. Mackman, 'Aliens and the law in late medieval Lincolnshire', in McDonald, Ormrod and Tailor (eds), *Resident Aliens*, pp. 105–23.

brought to the hundred court.[102] In Great Yarmouth, the borough court was organised in almost the same manner; it was just that its instances (i.e. competent judicial bodies) bore different names from those at Colchester. The exact equivalent for Great Yarmouth of the court of pleas in Colchester was the so-called court of petty and great pleas (*querele* and *placita* in Latin), while the equivalent of the hundred court was the court leet.[103] The important thing that distinguishes Great Yarmouth's borough court rolls from Colchester's is the presence of the particulars of the customs accounts. Indeed, imports and exports from this port town were kept by the local authorities, who probably copied what was enrolled for the royal administration. As the latter customs accounts do not survive at all for the period of this study, the local records in Great Yarmouth represent an invaluable source for medieval England as a whole.

In terms of timespan, the main focus of this study runs from after the exile of numerous textile workers from Flanders in 1351 until 1381, when members of the Flemish community were massacred in a number of places in England during the Peasants' Revolt. For this thirty-year period the number of surviving rolls in Colchester and Great Yarmouth is quite voluminous. As can be seen in Table 0.1, for Colchester there are thirteen surviving rolls, each containing eight to fifty-seven membranes. Great Yarmouth borough court was even more voluminous, as its survival rate amounts to twenty-three rolls containing on average twenty membranes for the thirty-year period (1351–81). Court records are extant to a similar extent for both towns for the years leading up to 1351 and following on from 1381, and were also used to examine patterns of immigrant presence. The standard membrane, be it for the court of pleas in Colchester or for the court of petty and great pleas in Great Yarmouth, contained entries with the names of the plaintiffs, the type of plea that was brought before the court, the names of the defendants and the names of those acting as pledges for the prosecution. Additional information might be included, such as the names of attorneys, the amount of debt, the damages claimed by the plaintiff and the background of the plea, as well as any legal tools to force the defendant to appear in court, such as distraint.[104] One membrane (recto–verso) typically contains at least forty cases. The membranes of the leet-court usually

[102] For more details on the work of the borough court, see R. H. Britnell, 'Colchester courts and court records, 1310–1525', *Essex Archaeology and History*, 17 (1986), 133–40.

[103] For an extensively detailed description of the borough court records of Great Yarmouth, see J. D. Rodziewicz, 'Order and society: Great Yarmouth 1366–1381', unpublished Ph.D. thesis, University of East Anglia (2008).

[104] *Ibid.*, pp. 25–6.

Table 0.1 *Number of surviving court rolls: Colchester 1351–81*

Court roll	Year/term	Number of membranes
CR 9	1351–2	8
CR 10	1353–4	14
CR 11	1356–7	14
CR 12	1559–60	19
CR 13	1360–1	5
CR 14	1364–5	14
CR 15	1366–7	18
CR 16	1372–3	17
CR 17	1374–5	18
CR 18	1376–7	20
CR 19	1378–9	28
CR 20	1379–80	31
CR 21	1381–2	57

Source: ERO, D/B 5, CR 9–21

contain the names of the capital pledges, who were actually those who pronounced the fines to the residents of Great Yarmouth. Below them are the names of those residents who were supposed to attend the leet session but had not shown up. Fines follow for misdemeanours such as breaking the assize of bread and ale, night wandering, physical aggression and forestalling.[105] The court rolls for Colchester were partially transcribed and translated by Herbert Isaac Jeayes, and later corrected and published by a former mayor of Colchester, William Gurney Benham, in four volumes.[106] However, some information from the manuscripts was omitted, and in this case they can only serve as calendars. Therefore, where Jeayes's translations correspond to the manuscript, I have referred to his editions, while in cases where I refer to the manuscript from the Essex Record Office (ERO), it means that both Jeayes and Benham omitted valuable information for this study. In the case of Great Yarmouth, there is neither a calendar with transcriptions nor translations.

In order to obtain information for London similar to that in the borough courts of Colchester and Great Yarmouth, we must turn to a

105 Physical aggression in Great Yarmouth was usually entered as 'hamsoken', which meant that the attack happened in the house of the victim. 'Forestalling' was intercepting goods on their way to market, or just trading before the market opened. See Britnell, *Growth and Decline*, pp. 131–3.

106 *The Court Rolls of the Borough of Colchester*, ed. W. G. Benham and H. I. Jeayes, 4 vols. (Colchester, 1921–41). Each edition covers different periods of the fourteenth century: vol. I (1310–52), vol. II (1353–67), vol. III (1372–9) and vol. IV (1379–83).

Table 0.2 *Number of surviving court rolls: Great Yarmouth 1351–81*

Court roll	Year/term	Number of membranes
CR 72	1351–2	11
CR 73	1352–3	14
CR 74	1353–4	19
CR 75	1354–5	15
CR 76	1358–9	15
CR 77	1359–60	14
CR 78	1360–1	15
CR 79	1361–2	24
CR 80	1363–4	24
CR 81	1366–7	26
CR 82	1367–8	26
CR 83	1369–70	18
CR 84	1370–1	17
CR 85	1371–2	18
CR 86	1373–4	18
CR 87	1374–5	21
CR 88	1376–7	13
CR 89	1377–8	14
CR 90	1378–9	17
CR 91	1379–80	16
CR 92	1380–1	14

Source: NRO Y/C4/72–92

combination of extant judicial records for the second half of the fourteenth century. Given the size of the city, London's legal institutions were divided into three courts that dealt with different problems related to property, wills, civil litigation and minor infractions: the court of husting, the mayor's court and the sheriff's court. Of these three courts, only the court of husting survives for the period of this study. However, its plea rolls mostly handled cases related to land and property, and very few of them involved immigrants from the Low Countries. The sheriff's and mayor's courts dealt with personal actions, such as debt, trespass or covenant, and are therefore very similar to the borough courts of Colchester and Great Yarmouth. Unfortunately, they only contain several rolls that cover a few years between the late thirteenth century and early fourteenth century.[107] Nevertheless, later legal proceedings

[107] Only part of a 1320 roll for the sheriff's court survives, while there are nine rolls of the mayor's court containing pleas for the period between 1298 and 1307. It should be mentioned that a

recorded in the mayor's court have been in part preserved in the so-called plea and memoranda rolls. These documents run from 1323 until 1482 and are entirely translated in six volumes.[108] Penny Tucker considered that only a small part (maybe one-third) of pleadings from the mayor's court were compiled in the plea and memoranda rolls.[109] However, despite the limited number of copied entries, numerous cases relating to the Flemish community that settled in London may be found there. Another valuable source from London that was used for this study was the so-called Letter Books of London. These run chronologically from 1275 until 1496 and are kept in seven different books named in alphabetical order from letter A to letter L.[110] More economic in character, Letter Books in a way complemented the information recorded in the plea and memoranda rolls. They contained such information as writs and returns, political occurrences, the proceedings of assemblies, the ordinances of crafts, and the assessments and appointments of civic officers. Significant quantities of material related to the guild of Flemish weavers in London and some of their economic activities during the second half of the fourteenth century are kept in Letter Books G and H.

In the absence of complete sets of local records, other judicial documents have been used to complement this study. These include those of the higher jurisdiction courts kept at the National Archives (TNA) in Kew, the King's Bench, the Court of Common Pleas, coroner's rolls and gaol deliveries.[111] The evidence from these central courts was particularly useful in the case of Lincolnshire, where no local record of the same value survives. The Court of Common Pleas includes mostly civil actions to recover property or debt, and it excludes felony. The jurisdiction of the King's Bench was divided into two parts: the 'crown' side, which served as a forum for all kinds of criminal case throughout the kingdom, and the 'plea' side, which dealt with actions of trespass and appeal for felony, or served to correct errors by other courts.[112] Both of these records run uninterrupted for the period of the study and are quite voluminous. The plea rolls of the Court of Common Pleas contain between 1,000 and 2,000 membranes a year, whereas those of the

number of original bills relating to cases from the mayor's court survives in the London Metropolitan Archives and runs from the 1320s up to 1550. LMA, CLA/024/02/001–002.

108 *Calendar of the Plea and Memoranda Rolls Preserved among the Archives of the Corporation of the City of London at the Guildhall*, A. H. Thomas and Philip E. Jones (eds), 6 vols. (Cambridge, 1926–61).

109 P. Tucker, *Law Courts and Lawyers in the City of London, 1300–1550* (Cambridge, 2007), pp. 9–10; Henry Riley Thomas considered that these cases from the mayor's court were recorded in the plea and memoranda rolls as some sort of precedent. *CPMR*, vol. I, pp. vii–vii.

110 *Calendar of Letter-Books of the City of London: A–L*, ed. R. R. Sharpe (London, 1905).

111 TNA, CP 40; KB 27; KB 29; KB 161; JUST 2; JUST 3.

112 J. H. Baker, *An Introduction to English Legal History*, 3rd edn (London, 1990), pp. 45–6.

King's Bench could fill up to several hundred. Given their size and the time constraints, I had to make some delimitations. I was able to go through the entirety of the King's Bench rolls for the years 1350–1400, while for the Court of Common Pleas, I sampled twenty terms across the period as representative material to show the patterns of immigrants' activity. Civil pleas in these records that involved Flemings were particularly useful for determining their business connections and trade patterns with both natives and other immigrants.

Information about such serious crimes as homicide, rape, grand theft, abduction or adultery can be found in the coroner's rolls and gaol deliveries. The former served as the court of first instance, where homicides and accidental deaths were recorded. Suspect felons were usually held in prison, or on bail, in their counties while waiting for officials from the central courts for trial. The justices acting as commissioners of gaol delivery were sent two or more times a year on circuit to hear and determine the cases of the accused held in county prisons.[113] Apart from the names of victims and perpetrators, the coroner and the justices of gaol deliveries often recorded their residences, occupations and origin, and details about the stolen goods, as well as the names of those who had (in cases of alleged murder) found the body, or potential witnesses. These records, together with the borough court rolls and other judicial sources of the crown, were used mostly to determine the social context of Flemish migration to England.

Although the details from the pleas in local and central courts are invaluable in reconstructing the interactions between various social groups, they inevitably contain some problems that need to be addressed. There are numerous gaps in the available records, and one must combine numerous sources in order to trace the immigrants from the Low Countries. Unfortunately, the borough court of Great Yarmouth is the only local source for which the records survive in an unbroken series. Amongst the central courts, this is the case for the Common Pleas and to some extent the King's Bench. While the unbroken series of records is helpful in rendering more convincing the immigrants' diffusion throughout different regions, as well as some details of their lives (occupations, wealth, gender and social networks), these do not outweigh other imperfections. First, the total number of immigrants is probably under-recorded, as those who appear in judicial records are usually noted because they were involved in some sort of legal infraction. The vast majority, like the native population, would never have become

[113] Maddern, *Violence and Social Order*, pp. 30–49; Hanawalt, *Crime and Conflict*, pp. 4–5.

embroiled with the law in any way. The immigrants' 'nationality' is not systematically recorded, so we have to rely on our ability to recognise them by their foreign forenames and surnames, which will be discussed in more detail below. The same goes for their occupations; that sometimes must be determined indirectly, or in combination with other sources where Flemings appeared. Moreover, the vast majority of pleas for debt, breach of covenant or detinue only very occasionally provide more details and mention the types of goods and the amounts of money concerned. As such they permit only a qualitative study of the economic context.

More direct sources for the immigrants' involvement in the English economy lie in the particulars of the customs and alnage accounts kept at the National Archives.[114] The alnager was the royal official appointed to certify the size of the cloth (for the sake of the buyer) that was to be exported. In order to put a seal on the cloth before it was shipped from England, the alnager imposed a subsidy of 4d per cloth, and wrote down how many cloths were sold, where they were made and by whom. We will see later that most Flemish immigrants were involved either in the production of or trade in cloth; the particulars of customs and alnage accounts allow us to quantify the immigrants' importance for the growth of the English economy.

All of the findings in the English sources were constantly compared with the archival material held in Belgium and France. The most important documents were those held in the State Archives of Belgium in Brussels and the ones in the archives départementales du Nord in Lille. These consisted of various charters, preserved in the comital chamber of the accounts, that recorded numerous sentences and orders pronounced by the count. They range from 801 to 1700 and are kept under the first series (1e reeks) collection in Brussels and under Série B in Lille.[115] For both collections of charters, there are fairly good inventories (i.e. finding aids or indexes).[116] From the second half of the fourteenth century, some charters were actually the sentences of the banishment of rebels outside of the county, as will be discussed in Chapter 1. These are our main interest, as most of them contained nominatim lists of people

114 They are both kept under the records of the exchequer, customs accounts under the collection E 122 – Particulars of the Customs Accounts, alnage accounts under the collection E 101 – Accounts Various.

115 RAG, Oorkonden van Vlaanderen, 1e reeks; ADN, B, Série 263, 1566, 1567, 1595, 1596.

116 For charters in the General Archives of the Realm in Brussels, see D. De Stobbeleir, *Inventaire provisoire des Chartes de Flandre 1ère série, IXe–XVIIe siècles* (Brussels, 1994); for Lille, see Alexandre Desplanque, *Inventaire sommaire des archives départementales antérieurs à 1790, Nord, Archives civiles, Série B, Chambre des Comptes de Lille n° 1561 à 1680*, vol. II (Lille, 1872).

who were supposed to leave the county of Flanders for a certain period of time. Here we should clarify that these sources contain both the names of individual felons who were sent into exile as a form of punishment and those who were banished collectively for political reasons. The focus will be on the latter, who were exiled for their involvement in different revolts throughout the fourteenth century.

Apart from the aforementioned collections, various edited cartularies from this period that contain similar information were used as well.[117] In the first instance, Flemish names from English sources after 1351 were compared with the names from the lists. Once I had found names that are a perfect match, which means only those with the same name and occupation in both the English and Flemish sources, other sources in Flanders were investigated for the period before the banishment in order to find out more about the profile of the newcomers in England. These include the city accounts of Ghent and Bruges for the period 1340–51, where information about the political and economic profile of the immigrants before banishment can indirectly be found. Those for Ghent were transcribed and edited for the period of the study, while those for Bruges were used in manuscript form.[118] More direct information about the economic activities of exiled Flemish textile workers before banishment was also found in the incredible collection of documents related to the history of Flemish drapery compiled by Espinas and Pirenne.[119] Some other sources, such as testamentary evidence in London, or local courts of Ghent (Keure and Gedele), were also used; however, their description fits better in Chapters 3 and 5. The aforementioned continental sources provided useful information for addressing and analysing the overall living conditions of immigrants before their departure, most notably in terms of craft skills, networks and wealth.

Because of the source material that allows us to examine the experiences of immigrants prior to their exile, and because they were the most numerous immigrant group in fourteenth-century England, the book will inevitably focus more on the Flemish community. However, the presence of Brabantine immigrants will also be examined. They are

[117] *Cartulaire de Louis de Male, Comte de Flandre. Decreten van den Grave Lodewyck van Vlaenderen, 1348 à 1358*, ed. T. de Limburg-Stirum, 2 vols. (Bruges, 1898); *Cartulaire historique et généalogique des Artevelde*, ed. N. De Pauw (Brussels, 1920).

[118] *De Rekeningen der Stad Gent: Tijdvak van Jacob Van Artevelde 1336–1349*, ed. N. De Pauw and J. Vuylsteke, 3 vols. (Ghent, 1874–85); *Gentsche Stads- en Baljuwsrekeningen van Gent 1351–1364*, ed. A. van Werveke and H. van Werveke (Brussels, 1970).

[119] *Recueil des documents relatifs à l'histoire de l'industrie drapière en Flandre*, ed. G. Espinas and H. Pirenne, 3 vols. (Brussels, 1909). The first three parts of volume I cover the period of the study (vols. I,i–I,iii).

frequently found grouped together with Flemish immigrants, and in this context it would be difficult to treat them completely separately. As we will see, the conditions in Brabantine textile towns were heavily influenced by the social, economic and political developments in the county of Flanders in the fourteenth century. These were also the main driving forces for the textile workers from Brussels, Louvain or Malines to emigrate to England. Moreover, once they arrived in English towns, they stuck together with their Flemish counterparts, especially in settlements outside London, where rivalry about preserving skills and know-how was less important.

The terminology of migration that will be used across the book also deserves to be explained. The term 'immigration', or 'immigrant' in its modern use, refers to someone or a group of people who have moved for a longer-term period or permanently from one place to another across political borders. In the same way, it will be applied here to the immigrants from the Low Countries, both to those who left voluntarily and to those who were exiled for political reasons. We will see over the following chapters that some of those exiled were actually allowed to return to Flanders, but then, after some time, went back again to England. Indeed, permanent migration such as exile might unintentionally end with return, when hostile and life-threatening regimes have been loosened up or terminated, or when the conditions in the host society have become unsatisfactory. Similarly, the same set of social conditions in the sending country (i.e. social upheaval, economic decline, natural disasters) that could have generated a particular form of emigration might happen in a more localised environment and push the exiles or migrants to change their location in the host country.[120] As we will see throughout this book, there are cases of both Flemish and Brabantine exiles who would return to Flanders and Brabant for several years and sometimes even emigrate back to England. Thus, they became immigrants who would leave their country on a voluntary basis. These varieties of mobility and settlement make it rather difficult to bracket all immigrants from the Low Countries under a single term.

The book will also focus more on what in modern terms would be called first-generation immigrants. This is because the source material rarely allows us to determine for sure what happened to the children who came with their parents from the Low Countries. The problems might range from the recording of their surnames – on several occasions these would change completely, or they would adopt an occupational

[120] Sayad, *L'Immigration*, p. 17.

surname – to complete integration and blending in with local population, making it impossible for them to be recognised in the sources. Continual comings and goings between the ports of England and the Low Countries might have also played a role, in that many of them would probably be tempted to move locations when presented with better opportunities.

One question still remains. How can one recognise whether a person recorded in the English sources was Flemish, in order to compare them with the lists of exiles? There are five different ways of identifying immigrants from the Low Countries in the English sources. In some cases, such as those of Walter le Baker and John Barat, the Colchester town clerks unambiguously added that the litigant was Flemish.[121] In other cases, the plaintiff or the defendant was given the family name 'Flemyng' or 'Braban(er)'. A third group consisted of those whose surnames referred to a place within the Low Countries, such as Everard van Deste, or Diest, or Heyne van Cortrike, better known as Courtrai.[122] A fourth category, including John van Loo, John van Neke and John van Wynd, had family names preceded by the typically Middle Dutch prefix 'van'.[123] Finally, some litigants, such as Clays Seger, Copin Stuk or Lieven Cornelis,[124] went by forenames characteristic of the fourteenth-century Low Countries.[125] Probably the most interesting variation of recording is the Flemish forename Copin. It is actually a Flemish diminutive of Jacob. For example, Copin Seland, a hosteller and eventually a citizen of London, appears first with the forename Copin in 1371 as the owner of a tenement in St Swithin's Lane.[126] In 1378 the scribe records that Jacob Seland alnaged sixty-eight pieces of cloths for export, but he reappears in a petition under the name of James, when he begs leave to stop paying the maintenance of some merchants who had been his former guests but were imprisoned in London by the city authorities.[127] In the latter case, the scribes probably heard the Latin version of Jacob

121 ERO, D/B 5, CR 11, m. 3 and CR 14, m. 6, calendared in Benham, *Court Rolls*, vol. II, pp. 68, 155.

122 ERO, D/B 5, CR 12, mm. 8, 18, calendared in Benham, *Court Rolls*, vol. II, pp. 78, 121.

123 ERO, D/B 5, CR 10, m. 2, calendared in Benham, *Court Rolls*, vol. II, p. 7.

124 ERO, D/B 5, CR 10, m. 10, calendared in Benham, *Court Rolls*, vol. II, p. 22.

125 F. Debrabandere, *Verklarend Woordenboek van de Familienamen in België en Noord-Frankrijk*, 2 vols. (Brussels, 1992), vol. I, pp. 274, 296, vol. II, p. 883; M. Boone and I. Schoups, 'Jan, Johan en alleman: Voornaamgeving bij de Gentse ambachtslieden (14de–15de eeuw), symptoom van een groepsbewustzijn?', in J. De Zutter, L. Charles and A. Capiteyn (eds), *Qui valet ingenio: Liber amicorum Johan Decavele* (Ghent, 1996), pp. 39–62; G. Dupont, 'Van Copkin, over Coppin naar Jacob: De relatie tussen de voornaamsvorm en de leeftijd van de naamdrager in het Middelnederlands op basis van administratieve bronnen voor het grafschap Vlaanderen, einde 14de – midden 16de eeuw', *Naamkunde*, 33 (2001), 111–218.

126 *Letter Book G*, p. 292.

127 TNA, E 101/340/22, m. 3; *CCR, 1369–74*, p. 260.

and directly transformed it to James in the source. From Richard II's reign, the word 'Dutchman' (*Ducheman*) or 'Dutchwoman' started being used interchangeably with Flemyng or Braban by English scribes. As far as women are concerned, in some cases their surnames are transformed into 'Frowe', probably from the Dutch word for woman, *Vrouw*. This is evident in fourteenth-century Southwark.[128] However, the scribes on the other side of London Bridge were not completely unfamiliar with the form. On 21 July 1365, Katherine van Ordingham was committed to prison for assaulting the constable and beadle of Dowgate Ward, and three weeks later, when it was confirmed that she would stay at Newgate Prison, her surname is entered as 'Frowe'.[129] The names of Flemish immigrants in the present work were used as I found them in the English sources and as they were recorded by the English scribes. Thus, Lambert Funderlynde has not been corrected to Lambrecht van der Lynden, for example. Surnames that suggest a place-name origin, such as Lamkyn van Durdraght, or Margaret van Outraght, which are obviously the towns of Dordrecht and Utrecht, have also not been corrected. Note also that when I have used the word 'Flemings', I see it mostly as a term for those people coming from Flanders. In parts, where appropriate and possible, the terms Zeelander, Brabanter or Hollander have been attributed accordingly. When people's origins are unknown, but their names are obviously Dutch, the term 'immigrants from the Low Countries' is used to define all of them.

In the first chapter we will deal with the economic situation in England and that in Flanders prior to the Black Death and show how their relationship created the pull-and-push factors for this migration to happen. Moreover, I will present the turbulent political and social situation in the county of Flanders from the end of the thirteenth century until the 1350s, and explain what led to the revolts and the exile of Flemish textile workers to England. The main focus will be on the legal tools used by the comital authorities for mass expulsions of people. The second chapter will present the numbers of exiled immigrants in: London and some of its suburbs; Colchester and its hinterlands in Essex and Suffolk; and Great Yarmouth, Norwich and Lynn in Norfolk; as well as in Lincolnshire, Yorkshire, the South-West and the Midlands. Apart from their numbers, this chapter examines the immigrants' occupations, gender, the places where they settled within urban areas and, to some extent, their profile before exile. Chapter 3 takes a wider look into the social relationships and business networks of the immigrant community

[128] M. Carlin, *Medieval Southwark* (London, 1996), pp. 211, 222; Fenwick, *Poll Taxes*, vol. II, p. 562.
[129] *CPMR*, vol. II, pp. 39, 41.

in urban areas. Chapter 4 examines the economic activities of Flemish immigrants and their influence on the English textile industry. In the first place, the main focus is on the economic activities of the exiles after their arrival in England from 1351 in comparison with what they had been doing in Flanders during the 1340s, a decade before banishment. Meanwhile, the remainder of the chapter looks into their involvement in the wool trade and their general wealth. Chapter 5 focuses on the presence and occupations of Flemish women in England. Completely new evidence will reveal that immigrant women, both single and married, had a very active role in the English economy during the fourteenth century. Chapter 6 looks into the involvement of the Flemish community in the events of the Peasants' Revolt of 1381. As we will see, the Flemings were ferociously massacred in a number of places between 14 and 16 June 1381, and this has been considered in several studies. However, with some new findings from various judicial documents, this chapter sheds new light on these events and clarifies what happened in the aftermath of the attack on the Flemings.

Chapter 1

ANGLO-FLEMISH ECONOMIC RELATIONS, COMPLEX URBAN REVOLTS AND THE POLITICS OF COLLECTIVE EXILE IN FLANDERS

There are several factors in the host country and the country of origin that might cause people to migrate. Pre-existing historical contacts and a favourable economic situation in the country of destination are amongst the primary elements to influence migrants' choice. In order to explain the post-1500 migratory patterns between countries with a colonial past, or where the economic influence was intense (Germany's over Eastern European countries, for example), the 'world-system' model has been used.[1] The main tenets of this approach to migration history are built on the work of Immanuel Wallerstein, whose main idea was to establish that the sixteenth century witnessed the rise of a capitalist world economy, where different forces and relations of production were created and led to an unequal division of labour between two interdependent regions. The division of labour is based on a hierarchical power structure where one country (the core) will dominate the other (the periphery).[2] In migration history, the central idea of the scheme consists of explanations whereby the same capitalist economic processes create the situation where immigrants from the periphery want to move to the core countries. While it is impossible to claim that Flanders was England's periphery, the world-system theory also sees migration as a reaction to changes in intertwined economies. Given the increase in interdependence of the two economies prior to the mid fourteenth century and the economic disruption caused by the Hundred Years War, as well as the structural changes in cloth manufacture during the same period, adopting this model to consider the causes of movement between the Low

[1] For numerous examples in the modern and early modern periods where this model has been used, see Portes and Walton, *Labor, Class, and the International System*; Morawska, 'The sociology and historiography of immigration', pp. 187–240; Sassen, *The Mobility of Labor and Capital.*

[2] Wallerstein, *The Modern World System.* In Wallerstein's own first definition, the world system is a 'multicultural territorial division of labour in which the production and exchange of basic goods and raw materials is necessary for the everyday life of its inhabitants'.

Countries and England is perfectly valid, without implying the existence of a more generalised world system. This chapter will examine the political and economic developments in England, and in Flemish and Brabantine cities before the mid fourteenth century, and how they created the conditions for the migration of textile workers. I shall argue that the migratory process was driven by the prior intensity of trade relations, the existence of communication and transportation links, and the relative frequency of travel between the countries, as well as the political situation, which led to some involuntary migration too.

ENGLAND AND THE LOW COUNTRIES – THEIR RELATIONS

Since the tenth century and our first evidence of diplomatic contact between England and Flanders, the relationship of the two regions grew ever tighter, over the following centuries, to form a political and commercial bond that was based on common interests. Throughout the whole late medieval period the established links would have an enormous impact on the industrial prosperity of both countries and eventually create economic interdependence, which would contain both benefits and inconveniences. This commercial affinity was fostered by the fact that the principal industry of the Middle Ages, the manufacture of woollen cloth, pivoted around the Low Countries. As we will see below, favoured by its location, the county of Flanders from very early on distinguished itself by higher specialisation and division of labour that would enable the development of an export-oriented cloth industry marked by the production of superior fabrics. The proximity of England and its burgeoning production of high-quality wool, woolfells and hides imposed itself as the natural partner for the growing number of urban artisans in Flanders. By the thirteenth century the county's manufacturing industries were heavily dependent on the regular supply of English wool. However, this does not mean that cloth manufacture was non-existent in England – far from it.

The two centuries preceding the Black Death in England represented a period of growth in almost all economic sectors. Pushed by the increase in population, the area under cultivation expanded as new agricultural land was developed from marshes and forests. Commercial activity in towns accelerated, and overseas trade expanded, while landlords were encouraged to found new trade fairs.[3] England sent relatively small amount of goods overseas, wool and tin being the main items, along

[3] Britnell, *The Commercialisation*, pp. 79–81; Bolton, *The Medieval English Economy*, p. 180.

with (to some extent) cheaper cloths. Although the rich represented the main customers for imported goods such as quality textiles, wine, precious metals and expensive pottery, most of the demand for consumer goods from ordinary people was satisfied through domestic production.[4] Slow but steady growth in industrial and agricultural output brought better living standards to a number of Englishmen and - women, as an increase in demand encouraged the development of new occupations. This was particularly evident in the urban cloth industry. The manufacture of textiles certainly existed in the countryside and mainly catered for the needs of neighbours. It was in towns, however, where more specialist crafts were more likely to develop.[5] A higher degree of local specialisation achieved by some towns like Lincoln, Stamford, Winchester or York, where cloth-making developed into a major industrial activity, enabled their cloth-workers to supply markets more extensive than their neighbourhoods already by the end of the twelfth century. By 1200, English cloths were well known in Genoa and sent on from there to even more distant markets.[6] Around the same time, English cloth-making was further fostered by the diffusion of the fulling mill.[7]

Although the cloth industries of Lincoln, York, Winchester, Stamford, London and Oxford flourished for most of the twelfth and thirteenth centuries, they were mostly in the hands of a mercantile elite. Indeed, fullers and weavers were reduced to the status of dependent employees and had been forbidden from engaging in the sale of cloth outside town or from being a part of exclusive organisations such as the merchant guild.[8] Members of these organisations were usually the urban elite, and they controlled the provision of raw materials (wool and dyestuffs) and the marketing of finished goods.[9] Artisans were allowed to weave or full only for the merchants of the town.[10] At the same time, in order to facilitate the representation of their own interests, fullers, weavers and other cloth-making artisans started creating formal associations. The earliest urban guilds of craftsmen in the textile industry are attested already in the twelfth century. The first extant account of the exchequer is the pipe roll of 1130–1. It lists amounts ranging from £4 to £10 paid to the crown by guilds of weavers from London, Lincoln, Winchester, Nottingham, Oxford, Huntington and York, and by the fullers of Winchester.[11] At this stage, in contrast to the later Middle Ages, fullers

4 Hatcher and Miller, *Medieval England*, pp. 51–2. 5 Britnell, *The Commercialisation*, p. 80.
6 Miller, 'The fortunes of the English textile industry', 65. 7 *Ibid.* 8 *Ibid.*, 68.
9 Carus-Wilson, 'The woollen industry', pp. 627–9.
10 Hatcher and Miller, *Medieval England*, pp. 105, 111–12.
11 Carus-Wilson, 'The woollen industry', pp. 627–9.

and the weavers had to circumvent municipal government by seeking royal privilege directly. Urban governments, still controlled by the merchants, would probably not have authorised the creation of formal craft associations, as they feared that the artisans would occupy positions of power in towns.[12] Given the annual cost of the royal charter, it seems that fullers' and weavers' earnings allowed them to acquire these privileges, giving us an indication of fairly flourishing textile industries in English towns.

The English evidence does not tell us much about the types of cloth that these cloth-workers produced. The Assize of Measures in 1196 stipulated that all cloth produced in England had to be woven to the width of 1 yard.[13] However, from the earliest records of cloth sales in the Mediterranean basin, we find that, apart from similar cloths from France and the Low Countries, the lighter textiles from England called *Stamfords* predominated in the Mediterranean market. With signs of the development of fulling mills from the 1180s, everything indicates that most of the sector was driven by the production of cheaper woollens, like worsteds and serges.[14] The former were named after the medieval Norfolk textile town of Worstead, and their main characteristic was that these cloths were not oiled or greased, thus the name *draperie sèche*, and they weighed about one-third of a true broadcloth.[15] Slightly later, English cloth-makers would focus on an intermediate woollen, the so-called serges, also known as says, a hybrid worsted woollen (something between worsted and broadcloth).[16] Even though these cloths were cheaper and lighter, they nevertheless required several specialist skills in order to be produced, and this becomes visible throughout the thirteenth century. Growing demand for such fabrics, in both domestic and foreign markets, would certainly foster a further division of labour and the development of local specialisation in know-how.

As in England, the textile industry of the Low Countries throughout the twelfth and thirteenth centuries was predominantly urban. In the main towns of the Low Countries – Ghent, Douai, Saint-Omer, Arras and Ypres in Flanders, and Artois (Artesia), Louvain, Brussels and Malines

[12] Hatcher and Miller, *Medieval England*, p. 106.

[13] Bridbury, *Medieval English Clothmaking*, pp. 106–7.

[14] J. H. Munro, 'The rise, expansion, and decline of the Italian wool-based cloth industries, 1100–1730: A study in international competition, transaction costs, and comparative advantage', *Studies in Medieval and Renaissance History*, 9 (2012), 45–207, at 59.

[15] Munro, 'Medieval woollens: The western European woollen industries', vol. I, pp. 312–16; see Tables 5.7 and 5.8.

[16] J. H. Munro, 'Textile technology', in J. R. Strayer et al. (eds), *Dictionary of the Middle Ages* (New York, 1988), pp. 693–711; Munro, 'Medieval woollens: Textiles', vol. I, pp. 200–4.

in Brabant, and Leiden in Holland, and many of the smaller towns – it was textile manufacture that provided these towns with an industrial foundation and turned them into a market-oriented society with a growing division of labour, allowing the accumulation of wealth.[17] However, it must be noted that the chronological trajectory of the industry's growth differed according to region. The Flemish towns of Ghent, Bruges, Douai, Saint-Omer, Arras and Ypres were experiencing growth throughout the twelfth and thirteenth centuries and absolutely dominated cloth manufacture in the region until the social upheavals and changes in the industry at the beginning of the fourteenth century.[18] Textile workers in the towns of the Duchy of Brabant, such as Brussels, Malines and Louvain, would profit from this turbulent period for the Flemish cloth industry and see their industries develop exponentially from 1270.[19]

With slightly richer evidence from the sources than in England, we know that before the fourteenth century Flemish urban manufacture was organised in a manner similar to that in English towns, where it was controlled by the mercantile urban elites, who were themselves organised in a guild-like structure of merchants and entrepreneurs controlled by the city authorities.[20] At this stage (the twelfth and early thirteenth centuries), there were still no formal associations run by craftsmen, and most of the cloth-making was controlled by the commercial capital.[21] Thus, the merchant-capitalists were able to establish control over the whole cycle of manufacture and trade in raw materials. They had enough capital to acquire large amounts of wool or dyestuffs, which they would distribute among local artisans, and then buy the finished cloth from them to be put into circulation on the international market. They ordered and regulated the work of producers on demand, while potentially owning workshops of their own where labourers were put to work. Before 1300, urban governments in Flanders and Brabant were controlled by these patricians, an oligarchic elite that got its wealth from the possession of urban land and commercial activities.[22]

[17] J. Dumolyn, J. Puttevils and P. Stabel, 'Production, markets and socio-economic structures, I: c. 1100 – c. 1320', in Brown and Dumolyn (eds), *Medieval Bruges*, pp. 80–2.

[18] Munro, 'Medieval woollens: The western European woollen industries', vol. I, pp. 230–48; R. Holbach, *Frühformen von Verlag und Grossbetrieb in der gewerblichen Produktion (13.–16. Jahrhundert)* (Stuttgart, 1994).

[19] J. P. Peeters, 'De produktiestructuur der Mechelse lakennijverheid en de ambachten van wevers en volders van 1270 tot 1430', *Handelingen van de Koninklijke Kring voor Oudheidskunde, Letteren en Kunst van Mechelen*, 88 (1984), 93–158.

[20] Dumolyn, Puttevils and Stabel, 'Production, markets', p. 82. [21] *Ibid.*

[22] H. van Werveke, 'De koopman-ondernemer en de ondernemer in de Vlaamsche lakennijverheid van de late middeleeuwen', *Mededeelingen van de Koninklijke Academie voor Wetenschappen, Letteren*

More generally, these towns were more and more economically dependent upon one another, and gradually became connected to inter-regional and international trade networks, which at a later stage would result in the expansion of highly skilled, luxury-oriented industries. One of the particular features of economic development in the Low Countries was the 'gateway town', which functioned on the basis whereby a bigger town would become a node for the export from its hinterlands and for the supply of products that were missing in the network itself.[23] Such hierarchical organisation led the gateway cities to grow into nodes that concentrated capital, demand, and the distribution of finished products and raw materials, and, last but not least, know-how and knowledge, all of which facilitated the development of export-oriented cloth manufacture. From very early on, Flemish cloth was well known not only in Germany but as far east as Novgorod, where each year the Fraternity of Merchants of Saint John the Baptist gave a whole cloth of Ypres to the bishop when he said mass for them on the feast of their patron saint.[24] The growth of trade fairs in Champagne and the importance of Italian merchants in the Mediterranean trade would popularise the cloth produced in the towns of the Low Countries throughout all parts of Europe and North Africa.

Similarly, the neighbouring towns of the Duchy of Brabant would start to find their place in the international market as well. It was the cloth of Malines and Louvain that appeared first in a table of the lengths of cloths sold at Champagne trade fairs which can be dated with precision from 1288.[25] Brussels cloth would appear only in 1305 in the same source.[26] By 1298, various types of cloth from these towns would penetrate the French market. Their presence would be felt mainly in Paris, where they took an important place alongside Flemish producers.[27] Over the course of the following fifteen years, these fabrics would

en Schoone Kunsten van België, Klasse der Letteren, 8 (1946), 5–26; Holbach, *Frühformen*; and J. H. Munro, 'Industrial entrepreneurship in the late medieval Low Countries: Urban draperies, fullers and the art of survival', in Paul Klep and Eddy Van Cauwenberghe (eds), *Entrepreneurship and the Transformation of the Economy (10th–20th Centuries): Essays in Honour of Herman van der Wee* (Leuven, 1994), pp. 377–88.

[23] W. Blockmans, B. De Munck and P. Stabel, 'Economic vitality: Urbanisation, regional complementarity and European interaction', in B. Blondé, M. Boone and A.-L. Van Bruaene (eds), *City and Society in the Low Countries 1100–1600* (Cambridge, 2018), p. 38.

[24] Carus-Wilson, 'The woollen industry', p. 628.

[25] R.-H. Bautier, 'La Place de la draperie brabançonne et plus particulièrement bruxelloise dans l'industrie textile du Moyen Âge', *Annales de la Société Royale d'Archéologie de Bruxelles*, 51 (1966), 31–63, at 35–6.

[26] *Ibid.*

[27] R. Van Uytven, 'De omvang van de Mechelse lakenproductie vanaf de 14de eeuw tot de 16de eeuw', *Noordgouw*, 5 (1965), 1–22; R. Van Uytven, 'La Draperie brabançonne et malinoise du

permeate markets all over Europe. In 1303, the merchants of Munich would take some of the Brabantine cloths to Tyrol and Nuremberg. A few years later, they would appear in Italy as well. They appear first in 1307 in the accounts of the Florentine company Alberti, and then, in 1310, the scarlets of Brussels would be sold in Genoa. By 1312, the scarlets of Brussels and Malines would even reach Cyprus, and in the same year the cloth of Brussels was reported in Montpellier and the Iberian peninsula.[28]

This rise in the manufacture of textiles made sure that a significant percentage of the growing population of the later twelfth and thirteenth centuries was employed in the cloth industry.[29] Other industries were sources of employment too: in Bruges, for example, production was large enough by the thirteenth century to provide work for fifty specialised crafts. These included the leather, metal and brewing industries, as well as herring fisheries, but cloth manufacture had become the most important component of the Flemish economy.[30] The proximity of the countryside, with the production of raw materials (wool from sheep in the coastal salt marshes) and a supply of cheap labour, turned the cities of Flanders into centres of industrial activity and cloth-making in northern Europe.[31] More importantly, the strategic location of the Low Countries on the main European trade routes ensured a constant supply of raw materials from abroad and facilitated the export of finished goods.[32] 'Thus, strong urban growth, the security afforded by the castles of local nobles, and flourishing local and developing long-distance markets together formed the preconditions for the first 'industrial revolution' in European history – the urban-based mass production of woollen textiles'.[33]

The twelfth and thirteenth centuries marked the growing economic interdependence of all parts of Europe upon one another, but nothing could be compared with the extent to which the advance of the cloth industry in Flanders was based upon raw materials brought in from other lands. Both Flanders and England produced wool as the raw material. However, by the thirteenth century, England became the main provider to both nations' industries. In addition to the rapid increase in industrial output, Flanders had to import wool from England, as her own

XIIe au XVIIIe siècles: Grandeur éphémère et décadence', in M. Spallanzani (ed.), *Produzione, commercio e consumo dei panni di lana* (Florence, 1976), pp. 85–97.

28 Bautier, 'La Place de la draperie brabançonne', 36–8.

29 Dumolyn, Puttevils and Stabel, 'Production, markets', p. 82, and bibliography there.

30 *Ibid.*

31 Blockmans, De Munck and Stabel, 'Economic vitality', p. 22.

32 Dumolyn, Puttevils and Stabel, 'Production, markets', p. 80.

33 Ibid., p. 100.

domestically produced wool was inadequate both in terms of quantity and quality. The period between the twelfth and thirteenth centuries has been characterised by historians as the phase of the 'active Flemish trade': Flemish merchants carried their trade to foreign markets.[34] Despite the fact that the Zwin estuary and the city of Bruges saw a lot of foreign traders, the Flemings and especially Bruges merchants were active in foreign markets, where merchants from other Flemish and Artesian cities, including Arras, Ypres, Ghent, and even Diksmuide, joined them there.[35]

Already in the early twelfth century many Flemings were visiting England to purchase wheat and English wool, and to sell wine and woollen cloth.[36] At this stage, much of England's continental trade was controlled by Flemish merchants, who had a pivotal role in transferring goods between Flanders, the English trade fairs, London and the Champagne trade fairs. These commercial ties were strengthened by the privileges granted to Flemish traders in 1213 by King John, exempting them from tolls in York and Winchester.[37] This allowed Flemish cloth manufacturers to contract large supplies of wool, either through agents or directly from the growers, throughout the thirteenth century. They also purchased from English monasteries, but considerable quantities were bought by Flemings in other parts of England, and also in Scotland, Wales and Ireland.[38] While Flemish merchants were particularly active at the St Ives trade fairs, it seems that quite a few of them also established themselves in London.[39] Furthermore, Bruges merchants took a leading role in the Flemish 'Hanse of the Seventeen Cities', the merchant guild that managed Flemish trade abroad, and by creating commercial networks in England, they ensured a supply of what over time evolved into the primary ingredient of English wool.[40] During

[34] H. Van Werveke, 'Der Flandrische Eigenhandel im Mittelalter', *Hansische Geschichtsblätter*, 61 (1936), 7–24.

[35] J. A. Van Houtte, *De geschiedenis van Brugge* (Tielt, 1982), pp. 93–4; Dumolyn, Puttevils and Stabel, 'Production, markets', pp. 106–7.

[36] Nicholas, *Medieval Flanders*, pp. 116–18; E. Wedemeyer Moore, *The Fairs of Medieval England: An Introductory Study* (Toronto, 1985), pp. 30–1.

[37] Dumolyn, Puttevils and Stabel, 'Production, markets', p. 87.

[38] S. Rose, *The Wealth of England: The Medieval Wool Trade and Its Political importance 1100–1600* (Oxbow, 2018), pp. 45–63.

[39] Nicholas, *Medieval Flanders*, pp. 164–6; E. Varenbergh, *Histoire des relations diplomatiques entre le comté de Flandre et l'Angleterre au Moyen Âge* (Ghent, 1868), pp. 153–5; Wedemeyer Moore, *The Fairs*, pp. 13–14; J. A. Van Houtte, *An Economic History of the Low Countries, 800–1800* (London, 1977), p. 35.

[40] Dumolyn, Puttevils and Stabel, 'Production, markets', pp. 106–12.

much of the thirteenth century, the Hanse practically governed northern cloth sales at the Champagne trade fairs.

From the last quarter of the thirteenth century, however, the textile industries of England and Flanders started to go through a process of significant structural change. The causes of the onset of this transformation were the same for both – warfare in the Mediterranean and the decline of the Champagne trade fairs – but the urban industries of each country coped with it in different ways. As mentioned above, the urban cloth-makers of Flanders and England focused on the production of cheaper coarse cloths called serges.[41] It was a lighter woollen, fit for mild climates, and, because of its relatively cheap price, the densely populated Mediterranean basin with its hot springs and autumns represented the most suitable market.[42] Most of these textiles were first brought to the Champagne trade fairs by Flemish merchants and then sold to Italian merchants, who eventually re-exported them to North Africa and to other Italian cities. The combination of notarial records from Genoa and Florence, as well as from Castilian port books, shows that these cheaper textiles accounted for the overwhelming majority of thirteenth-century sales throughout the Mediterranean.[43] However, this system of the exchange of northern textiles between Flemings and Italian merchants would come to an end.

The integration of the Champagne region into the French kingdom in 1284 caused a severe decline in the trade fairs. King Philip IV saw an opportunity to capitalise on the presence of merchants by increasing tolls and confiscating their goods.[44] This only forced the merchants to withdraw, leading to the final loss in importance of the Champagne trade

[41] Although luxury woollens, such as scarlets, were produced in some Flemish cities prior to the fourteenth century, the majority of those engaged in the urban cloth industry produced lighter textiles, like *saies, estanfordes, biffes, faudeits, afforchiés, rayés* and *burels*. The techniques of making, prices, weights and the place of these fabrics in the market are discussed in more detail in J. H. Munro, *Wool, Cloth and Gold: The Struggle for Bullion in Anglo-Burgundian Trade, 1340–1478* (Brussels and Toronto, 1973), pp. 1–9; J. H. Munro, 'Industrial transformations in the north-west European textile trades, c. 1290 – c. 1340: Economic progress or economic crisis?', in Bruce M. S. Campbell (ed.), *Before the Black Death: Studies in the 'Crisis' of the Early Fourteenth Century* (Manchester and New York, 1991), pp. 110–48, at pp. 110–14.

[42] Munro, 'The "industrial crisis"', pp. 103–41.

[43] P. Chorley, 'English cloth exports during the thirteenth and early fourteenth centuries: The continental evidence', *Historical Research*, 61 (1988), 1–10, at 2–4; P. Chorley, 'The cloth exports of Flanders and northern France during the thirteenth century: A luxury trade?', *The Economic History Review*, 40 (1987), 349–79; H. Hoshino, 'The rise of the Florentine woollen industry in the fourteenth century', in N. B. Harte and K. G. Ponting (eds), *Cloth and Clothing in Medieval Europe* (London, 1983), pp. 184–204; W. Childs, 'The English export trade in cloth in the fourteenth century', in R. H. Britnell and J. Hatcher (eds), *Progress and Problems in Medieval England: Essays in Honour of Edward Miller* (Cambridge, 1996), pp. 121–47.

[44] Nicholas, *Medieval Flanders*, pp. 177–8.

fairs.[45] At the same time, wars in the Mediterranean between 1290 and 1310 not only disrupted the regular trade routes but also increased transport and transaction costs. Collecting evidence from numerous notarial records and customs accounts, John Munro demonstrated that rising transport and transaction costs doubled maritime and freight rates.[46] Naturally, the most affected were the north European textile workers, who focused on the production of export-oriented serges. Under such circumstances, it became virtually impossible for these woollens to bear the freight charges in long-distance trade and compete with local producers in the Mediterranean basin.[47] As a consequence, Flemish and English urban cloth manufacturers faced large-scale unemployment and a more general crisis within the textile industries.

The fact that serges became uncompetitive in foreign markets led English urban textile centres into a severe industrial crisis.[48] The extent of this decline is supported by both internal and external evidence. Notarial documents and cloth-price tariffs, as well as port records from the Continent, suggest that by the 1310s English serges (*Stamfords*, as well as *grays* and *blacks* from York and Lincoln) were almost completely absent from Italian, Iberian and other Mediterranean markets.[49] At the same time, the traditional urban textile centres in England were affected as well. The primary evidence to back this claim comes from the complaints of textile guilds to the king about their inability to pay the annual fee that allowed them to have royal protection and to keep their independence from town governments and mercantile elites. For example, the weavers of Oxford successfully petitioned King Edward I to agree that the annual farm of £6 they had paid since the twelfth century should be reduced to 42s.[50] The guild of weavers in Lincoln stopped paying their farm in 1320, and the fullers' guild there simply ceased to exist.[51] In Winchester, where evidence for the earliest fullers' guild in England is attested in 1130, the guild seems to have been dissolved sometime in the thirteenth century and then reconstituted in 1364.[52] Signs of decline are even clearer in the

45 J. Edwards and S. Ogilvie, 'What lessons for economic development can we draw from the Champagne fairs?', *Explorations in Economic History*, 49 (2012), 131–48.

46 Munro, 'Industrial transformations', pp. 110–48; J. H. Munro, 'The origins of the English "new draperies": The resurrection of an old Flemish industry, 1270–1570', in N. B. Harte (ed.), *The New Draperies in the Low Countries and England, 1300–1800* (Oxford, 1997), pp. 35–127.

47 Munro, 'Medieval woollens: The western European woollen industries', vol. I, pp. 228–324.

48 Miller, 'The fortunes of English textile industry', 64–82.

49 Munro, 'The "industrial crisis"', pp. 107–9; Chorley, 'English cloth exports', 6.

50 E. Carus-Wilson, *Medieval Merchant Venturers: Collected Studies* (London, 1954), p. 205.

51 Miller, 'The fortunes of English textile industry', 70.

52 Keene, *Survey of Medieval Winchester*, vol. I, p. 305; Carus-Wilson, *Medieval Merchant Venturers*, p. 226.

evidence of the dwindling number of cloth artisans. The city of Leicester, once an important textile centre, was completely deserted by its fullers at the beginning of the fourteenth century.[53] In their complaint in 1321, the London burellers stated that the number of looms had dropped from 380, thirty years earlier, to only 80 at the time when they wrote the complaint.[54] In 1334, the authorities of Northampton similarly complained that whereas there had been 300 weavers during the reign of Henry III, only abandoned houses were to be found now.[55] The drop in commercial revenue in Winchester led its authorities to petition Edward III to reduce their annual fee. The main reason for this demand was the collapse in the number of weavers, which confirms the hypothesis that the textile industry had left the town even earlier than the fourteenth century.[56]

While serges were disappearing from international trade and urban manufacture, cheaper coarse textiles from villages were gaining momentum. John Oldland has recently argued that the competition from rural cloth had only accelerated the elimination of serges. These low-priced fabrics produced in the countryside took over the domestic market very rapidly for low- and medium-quality cloths.[57] The demand for middling- and high-quality broadcloths, the production of which was also in decline in the urban cloth-making centres of England in the first half of the fourteenth century, was satisfied by imports. The export of wool as a raw material and the importation of luxury cloths mainly from the Low Countries remained the principal activity of the urban mercantile elite until the 1340s. At the same time, urban weavers initially turned to the production of coarse woollens, but they would soon be able to work on some of the higher-quality cloth in order to fill the gap created by the diminishing demand for imported cloth.[58]

In the same period, from the 1290s to 1320s, the urban textile centres of Flanders and Brabant abandoned the manufacture of lighter, cheaper serges (which relocated to the smaller towns) and turned mostly to the production of high-quality luxury cloth, which was heavily dependent on imports of English wool.[59] Compared with England, Flemish and Brabantine towns enjoyed a long established pre-eminence and reputation in the production of luxury broadcloths, and were able to sustain this

53 Miller, 'The fortunes of English textile industry', 70.
54 Riley, *Liber Custumarum*, vol. II, pp. lxvi–lxviii, 416–25.
55 *Rotuli Parliamentorum 1278–1503*, 6 vols. (London, 1832), vol. II, pp. 85–6.
56 Miller, 'The fortunes of English textile industry', 70; Carus-Wilson, *Medieval Merchant Venturers*, pp. 204–5.
57 Oldland, *The English Woollen Industry*, pp. 98–112. 58 *Ibid.*, p. 108.
59 Munro, *Wool, Cloth and Gold*, pp. 1–6.

transition a lot easier.[60] Under market pressure, urban textile industries changed from being manufacturers of all kinds of cloth to being more selective producers of highly expensive greased and striped woollens, demand for which did not diminish after the price increased. The skills of cloth-workers in the finishing stages of manufacture, as well as the use of pricey raw materials (high-quality English wool and dyestuffs), were much more important in determining the value of these luxury woollens. In order to keep the higher level of skill, these textiles had to be manufactured with strict quality standards.[61] What also differed from England during this process of industrial conversion was the development of the internal structure of the industry, which would remain typical of Flemish and Brabantine cloth manufacture for the remainder of the late medieval period. 'The cloth guilds, which could guarantee more efficiently the required standard of quality for more expensive fabrics, had acquired a pivotal role in this new industrial constellation, and slowly the wealthier guild masters, mostly weavers, replaced the capitalist merchant-entrepreneurs as the key organisers of the production chain'.[62]

Although these circumstances deepened the interdependence of the two regions, this economic situation was not sustainable on a longer-term basis. On the one hand, the county of Flanders became a political hostage to England, as its urban industries were vulnerable to the crown's occasional embargoes on wool.[63] On the other hand, very lucrative though it was, the English wool trade was mostly in the hands of foreign merchants, and this situation whereby England held an abundance of high-quality raw material but no established production of quality finished products was no bargain either.[64] Edward III, thus, embarked on a set of policies that aimed to promote the development of a native cloth industry. A statute from 1337 prohibited the export of wool and the import of foreign cloths. Every man or woman was allowed to produce cloth, and alien cloth-workers were invited to settle wherever they wanted within the realm.[65] From that moment onwards, textile workers

60 Munro, 'The "industrial crisis"', p. 139.
61 J. L. Murray, *Bruges, Cradle of Capitalism, 1280–1390* (Cambridge, 2005), p. 279.
62 Dumolyn, Puttevils and Stabel, 'Production, markets', pp. 106–22.
63 G.-G. Dept, *Les Influences anglaise et française dans le comté de Flandre au début du XIIIe siècle* (Ghent and Paris, 1928); C. Wyffels, 'De Vlaamse handel op Engeland voor het Engels-Vlaams konflikt van 1270–1274', *Bijdragen voor de geschiedenis der Nederlanden*, 17 (1963), 205–13; and H. Berben, 'Une Guerre économique au Moyen Âge: L'embargo sur l'exportation des laines anglaises, 1270–1274', in *Études d'histoire dédiées à la mémoire de Henri Pirenne* (Brussels, 1937), pp. 1–17.
64 T. H. Lloyd, *The English Wool Trade in the Middle Ages* (Cambridge, 1977), pp. 144–56.
65 *The Statutes of the Realm: Printed by Command of His Majesty King George the Third: In Pursuance of an Address of the House of Commons of Great Britain; from Original Records and Authentic Manuscripts*, ed.

from the Low Countries started to make their mark in the English records. Most notable were those who were granted individual letters of protection to ply their trade throughout the realm, as we will see in more detail below. In two recent contributions, these letters of protection to Flemings were linked to Edward III's general immigration policy, in which the government started to look at foreign residents' economic potential rather than see them as as a security threat.[66] Although immigration policies were already in place during the 1340s, and Flemish weavers granted sufficient franchises, the expected wave of immigration would appear a little later, provoked by developments on the other side of the English Channel.

At the end of the thirteenth century, there had already been some unsuccessful attempts at encouraging foreign weavers to establish their manufacture in England.[67] However, it was the political situation that led to the development of these specific immigration policies. The relationship between the houses of Plantagenet and Capet, which had been shaky since the Treaty of Paris in 1259, evolved into open Anglo-French warfare due to disagreements about the feudal status of Aquitaine in 1294.[68] As a result, the government confiscated the property of all foreigners resident in England that the crown deemed to be related to the French king. Such radical measures not only proved ineffective and caused economic problems, they also revealed that not all foreigners within the realm represented a national threat: the majority of them actually contributed more positively to their local communities. Indeed, the issues arising from this campaign inspired the crown to be more considerate when dealing with aliens in the future. When the death of Charles IV in 1328 left the French throne without a direct male heir, and the question of the succession was at stake, the English government still took actions against French interests in England, but also issued so-called letters of protection to ameliorate the harshness of the measures for as many people as possible. Even though the war that broke out with France from 1337 presented the crown with much more serious concerns than the campaigns of 1294 and 1328 had done, the consequences in

A Luders et al., 11 vols. in 12, Record Commission (London, 1810–28, reprint London, 1963), vol. I, pp. 280–1.

66 Lambert and Ormrod, 'A matter of trust', 208–26; Lambert and Ormrod, 'Friendly foreigners', 1–24.

67 E. Lipson, *The History of the Woollen and Worsted Industries* (London, 1921), p. 10. Henry III's government in 1271 was the first to come up with the policy that would encourage male and female textile workers from abroad to come to England to work for five years.

68 For the wars between England and France during this period, see M. G. A. Vale, *The Origins of the Hundred Years War: The Angevin Legacy, 1250–1340* (Oxford, 1996).

England for the French, and for other immigrants, were minimal. They would continue to be so for the remainder of the Hundred Years War.[69]

From the 1330s onwards, individual textile workers or groups of weavers who immigrated from the Low Countries were now eligible to get the same letters of protection that had previously been used to exempt foreign residents from the impact of the wartime measures if they wanted to set up their business in England. The first letter of protection with the terms of the craftsman's stay was granted in 1331 to John Kempe.[70] In 1333, the commons in parliament petitioned Edward to protect foreign cloth-workers from arrest and prosecution, so that they could 'teach the people of this land to work the cloth'.[71] With this in mind and in order to preserve and safeguard the immigrant contribution to the English economy, the government seemed to have embarked on a genuinely active immigration policy. Individual letters similar to the one granted to John Kempe were issued to other workers from the Low Countries over the following years, first to weavers William and Hanekin de Brabant in York in 1336,[72] and a year later to fifteen Zeelanders with no specified place of residence,[73] as well as to a dyer, Nicholas Appelman, and his men in Winchester in 1337.[74] Three weavers from Diest in Brabant, exercising their trade in St Ives (Huntingdonshire), in 1338 also received letters.[75] As we have seen, in 1337 a statute was passed that invited textile workers from all 'strange lands' and promised them all the legal franchises they would need.[76] Still, it seems that the settlement of newcomers immediately faced some resistance from local communities. The same year as the statute of invitation was issued, the king had to order the citizens of London to stop injuring foreign cloth-workers.[77] In 1339, a similar proclamation was repeated, while in 1344 the crown even threatened to send those Londoners who were still attacking Flemish weavers to Newgate prison.[78] Without a doubt, native artisans did not have the same vision of the foreign guests as did the crown.[79] Despite this opposition, Edward III would not change his course of action. Protections

[69] Lambert and Ormrod, 'A matter of trust', 208–26. Apart from the French, the goods of Flemings and Bretons resident in England were confiscated as well.

[70] *CPR, 1330–4*, p. 161. [71] *PROME*, vol. IV, p. 191. [72] *CPR, 1334–8*, p. 341.

[73] *Ibid.*, p. 431. [74] *Ibid.*, p. 500.

[75] *CPR, 1338–40*, p. 13. As the cloth fair was still held in St Ives, this place had probably attracted more textile workers from the Low Countries than only these three weavers.

[76] *Statutes of the Realm*, vol. I, p. 281. [77] *Letter Book F*, p. 190.

[78] *CCR, 1339–41*, p. 103; *CCR, 1343–6*, p. 486.

[79] Outside London, only the weavers of York are known to have protested against the immigration of cloth-workers from the Low Countries, in 1342. TNA, SC 8/238/11890A.

for Flemish and Brabantine artisans continued throughout the 1340s.[80] In 1351, the government would broaden its immigration policies due to developments on the other side of the English Channel when thousands of textile workers were banished from Flanders because of their involvement in the revolt against the count. Overall, economic, social and political circumstances in Flanders and England played an important role as pull-and-push factors. But we will see in what follows that fourteenth-century Flanders was marked by constant troubles: overpopulation, high taxation, hunger, warfare, and political and social conflicts, as well as plague, and many Flemings were therefore glad to leave or be forced to do so.

FLEMISH REVOLTS AND THE POLITICS OF COLLECTIVE EXILE THROUGHOUT THE FOURTEENTH CENTURY

While both England and the Low Countries were experiencing industrial conversion, vast unemployment, crop failure and famine throughout the late thirteenth and early fourteenth centuries, the county of Flanders was also marked by higher social tensions which led to outright urban rebellions in the 1280s and 1300s. Although the county of Flanders was one of the wealthiest regions in north-western Europe, its social structure represented the perfect ground for these developments. Indeed, as we have already mentioned, during the thirteenth century Flemish (and Brabantine) urban society became increasingly complex as a result of economic growth and a higher division of labour. It had also become a more stratified society, where one could distinguish between the rich and the poor, or between on the one hand the *ghemeen*, or *le commun* – mostly urban craftsmen, petty retailers and unskilled workers (the commoners) – and on the other *de goede lieden*, or *les bonnes gens* – the merchant elites (the patricians) who regulated the production and labour of the commoners, including wages, working hours and product standards. The oppositions between the two were not only social and economic, but also political. Very often the mercantile elite, who monopolised urban political power, did not represent the opinions and needs of the manufacturers. Naturally, these social contrasts led to a wave of dissatisfaction that would be reflected in violent clashes in the form of urban revolts from the 1280s onwards. The initial revolts, which culminated in the triumph of the artisans at the battle of Courtrai in 1302, prompted the inclusion of new groups into political power alongside the patricians.

[80] See, for example, the grant to John de Bruyn from Ghent, making woollen cloth in Abingdon (Berkshire), in 1343. *CPR, 1343–5*, p. 115.

Cloth manufacture, still by far the main employer in the county, had also passed from being controlled by a rich mercantile elite to guild-organised master craftsmen. The latter would form a new urban class, and gradually become a larger and politically more influential group. But this process of industrial and political change throughout the fourteenth century was disastrous for most textile workers, skilled and unskilled, men and women alike, whose job opportunities must have declined considerably. Many of them left Flanders and Brabant in search of employment, including those workers who were also forced to leave the county as political exiles after their involvement in the revolts.

Already in the 1240s several towns experienced discontent in the form of strikes.[81] However, the first signs of a generalised wave of social and political unrest appeared around 1280, when movements of collective action caused by economic crisis and the systematic exclusion from power of the mass of the urban population touched Flanders as well as other parts of the Low Countries and northern France. Revolts spread to Tournai, Ghent, Douai, Bruges, Ypres, Saint-Omer and Arras in 1280, as well as Brussels in 1282. In these disturbances textile workers played a key role.[82] These circumstances forced the French king, Philip IV 'the Fair', to start getting more directly involved in the internal political situation of Flanders. He found support among the urban oligarchies, who saw him as an instrument for getting rid of comital authority. This political constellation gradually led Flanders to become divided into two opposing camps: one side that would support the count, and the other the French king. The pro-French faction, which consisted mainly of urban oligarchs, became known as the 'Leliaerts' ('Lilies'), after the 'fleur de lys' of the French crown, while the other faction, which consisted mainly of commoners, was referred to as the 'Clauwaerts' ('Claws'), after the lion's claws on the Flemish coat of arms.[83]

81 W. Prevenier, 'La Bourgeoisie en Flandre au XIIIe siècle', *Revue de l'Université de Bruxelles*, 4 (1978), 407–28; J. Dumolyn, 'Economic development, social space and political power in Bruges, c. 1127–1302', in H. Skoda, P. Lantschner and R. L. J. Shaw (eds), *Contact and Exchange in Later Medieval Europe: Essays in Honour of Malcolm Vale* (Woodbridge 2012), pp. 33–58.

82 C. Wyffels, 'Nieuwe gegevens betreffende een XIIIde eeuwse "democratische" stedelijke opstand: De Brugse "Moerlemaye" (1280–81)', *Bulletin de la Commission Royale d'Histoire*, 132 (1966), 37–142; M. Boone, 'Social conflicts in the cloth industry of Ypres (late 13th–early 14th centuries): The Cockerulle Reconsidered', in M. Dewilde, A. Ervynck and A. Wielemans (eds), *Ypres and the Medieval Cloth Industry in Flanders: Archaeological and Historical Contributions* (Zellik, 1998), pp. 147–55.

83 J. Braekevelt, F. Buylaert, J. Dumolyn and J. Haemers, 'The politics of factional conflict in late medieval Flanders', *Historical Research*, 85 (2012), 13–31; M. Boone, 'Une Société urbanisée sous tension: Le comté de Flandre vers 1302', in R. C. Van Caenegem (ed.), *Le Désastre de Courtrai: Mythe et réalité de la bataille des éperons d'or* (Antwerp 2002), pp. 27–77.

Given the importance of English wool for the economic prosperity of Flemish towns in the second half of the thirteenth century, counts were reluctant to support the pro-French party and thereby put urban manufactures at risk from the potential imposition of higher tariffs or an embargo by the English crown. Thus, in 1297 Count Guy de Dampierre decided to renounce his feudal allegiance to King Philip, side with the English king, Edward I, and become an ally of the commoners. French troops invaded Flanders, and by 1300 the county was almost completely under French control. The property of supporters of the count was confiscated, and Bruges guildsmen who rebelled against the Lily regime were collectively banished in 1301.[84] Popular resistance grew in Ghent and especially in Bruges, where, during the early morning of 18 May 1302, French occupying troops were killed or chased away during the Good Friday revolt. Subsequently, a Flemish army mostly consisting of urban militiamen defeated the French chivalric army near Kortrijk (Courtrai) on 11 July of the same year.

The popular victory of the battle of the Golden Spurs in 1302 generally led to more socio-economic emancipation of the craftsmen and to the textile guilds' participation in the government of the large towns of Flanders.[85] In this new composition of urban governments, the normative framework that concerned the quality of manufacture and labour relations was now co-determined by the representatives of guilds. Amongst other important changes in social relations in the county's important cities that took place after this revolt was above all the organisation of cloth manufacture. The traditional structure, where a rich mercantile elite would control all stages of manufacture and marketing, which characterised a large part of the thirteenth century, became history. This role shifted instead to the richer guild masters of weavers, who were now able to hire labourers to work at their shops, or subcontract other artisans who worked from their homes, while marketing the finished cloth themselves.[86] Merchants still remained in charge of exports and focused on controlling regional supply networks, but the organisation of labour and local trade was now in the hands of these artisan–entrepreneurs.[87] The success of these weaver–drapers lay in

[84] J. F. Verbruggen, *The Battle of the Golden Spurs: Courtrai, 11 July 1302* (Woodbridge, 2002), pp. 19, 22; J. F. Verbruggen, *1302: Opstand in Vlaanderen: De Guldensporenslag* (Brussels 1977), pp. 9, 72. The city also had to send 466 hostages to Tournai: L. Verriest, 'Le Registre de la 'Loi' de Tournai, de 1302 et les listes des otages de Bruges (1301) et de Courtrai', *Bulletin de la Commission Royale d'Histoire*, 80 (1911), 369–527.

[85] Boone, *Une Société urbanisée*, p. 27–77.

[86] Van Werveke, 'De koopman-ondernemer', 5–26.

[87] Munro, 'Industrial transformations', pp. 110–48. Similar developments were observed in Normandy in the second half of the fourteenth and throughout the fifteenth centuries: J.-L.

the fact that they were able to control manufacturing processes, organise manufacturing networks, and monopolise skill and expertise through guild supervision.[88] The development of this new urban class was a process in the making throughout the second half of the thirteenth century, but after the revolt in 1302, its members were able to become involved in urban office-holding.[89]

The achievement of the textile guilds in Flemish towns hastened a political evolution in other towns in the Low Countries with somewhat related cloth industries and similar social structures. Shortly after 1302, the craftsmen and their guilds in Brabant succeeded in contesting the monopoly in urban office of the mercantile elite; however, this was only temporary. Urban uprisings broke out in Malines and Brussels in 1303.[90] In Brussels, the commoners were granted access to the urban government for three years, but in 1306 the patrician families regained absolute control.[91] The situation was slightly better for craft guilds in Malines. Even though the revolt was suppressed, the guilds were still allowed to appoint their representatives to the city's council, along with the patricians. In Louvain, the power of the patricians was likewise contested between 1303 and 1306, but here as well they remained in power. Although this political change was short-lived in the towns of Brussels and Louvain, it would not stop the ambition of textile guilds and would only pave the way for it to re-emerge later.

After the rush of victory had passed and the city-dwellers lost their military superiority, the French king was able to impose the Treaty of Athis-sur-Orge on the county on 16 January 1305. One of its main clauses included the return of all the Lily exiles and the restitution of their confiscated property.[92] Moreover, the Flemings were obliged to pay an enormous indemnity to the king.[93] Those who had gained most

Roch, *Un Autre Monde du travail: La draperie en Normandie au Moyen Âge* (Mont Saint-Aignan, 2013), pp. 87–9.

88 P. Stabel, 'Labour time, guild time? Working hours in the cloth industry of medieval Flanders and Artois (thirteenth and fourteenth centuries)', *The Low Countries Journal of Social and Economic History*, 11:4 (2014), 27–9.

89 H. Soly, 'The political economy of European craft guilds: Power relations and economic strategies of merchants and master artisans in the medieval and early modern textile industries', *International Review of Social History*, 53 (2008), 45–71.

90 H. Vandecandelaere, 'Een opstand in "zeven aktes": Brussel 1303–1306', *Cahiers Bruxellois*, 40 (2008–9), 4–67.

91 F. Favresse, *L'Avènement du régime démocratique à Bruxelles pendant le Moyen Âge (1306–1423)* (Bruxelles, 1932), p. 98.

92 *Codex diplomaticus Flandriae inde ab anno 1296 ad usque 1325*, ed. Th. De Limburg-Stirum (Bruges, 1879), vol. I, pp. 336–7, 358, 364–5.

93 J. Van Herwaarden, *Opgelegde bedevaarten: Een studie over de praktijk van opleggen van bedevaarten (met name in de stedelijke rechtspraak) in de Nederlanden gedurende de late middeleeuwen (ca. 1300–ca. 1500)*

from the victory in 1302, the textile workers, gradually felt more betrayed by their formal allies within the comital family. One of the biggest burdens on the population was now the fiscal policy of Count Robert of Béthune, who had succeeded his deceased father, Guy. In most cities of Flanders, members of the Lily party, now again with the full support of the count they had previously detested, assumed or consolidated power and introduced measures against the guildsmen.[94] In this climate of popular disappointment, the return of the previously exiled and fugitive Lilies after the Treaty of Athis seems to have been the primary cause for a new series of risings. Revolts broke out in 1309–10 in Bruges, in 1309 in the rural district of the castellany of Waas, in 1309–11 in Aardenburg and in 1311 in Ghent, provoked by discontent with the terms of the treaty.[95]

Continuing sentiments of discontent among the popular classes were further fuelled by the inexperience of the new pro-French Count Louis of Nevers, who took up office in 1322.[96] A new, massive rebellion would finally break out in Flanders in 1323–8. It started among the peasants of the coastal plain of Flanders, and soon Bruges, Ypres, Kortrijk, Geraardsbergen and other towns joined in, though in Ghent the elites held on to power, and rebellious textile workers once again fled the city.[97] Facing the massive revolt of 1323–8, for instance, Louis of Nevers had sought help in Paris, and in 1328 the rebels were crushed at Cassel by the French army, joined by the count and troops from Ghent. The punishment for the insurgents would be an exemplary one. In Bruges itself the rebel leaders were executed. Willem de Deken, burgomaster of Bruges and the main leader of the revolt, was taken to Paris for torture and execution.[98] All the goods of the culprits were confiscated or burned, and all privileges enjoyed by the rebel castellanies were revoked or revised.[99] The cities of Bruges and Ypres were condemned to have

(Assen-Amsterdam, 1978), p. 56; D. van den Auweele, 'De Brugse gijzelaarslijsten, 1301, 1305 en 1328: Een komparatieve analyse', *Handelingen van het Genootschap voor Geschiedenis*, 100 (1973), p. 120.

94 W. Te Brake, *A Plague of Insurrection: Popular Politics and Peasant Revolt in Flanders, 1323–1328* (Philadelphia, 1993), p. 51.

95 *Annals of Ghent*, ed. H. Johnstone (London, 1951), p. 99.

96 TeBrake, *A Plague of Insurrection*, pp. 46–7; J. Sabbe, *Vlaanderen in opstand 1323–1328: Nikolaas Zannekin, Zeger Janszone en Willem de Deken* (Bruges, 1992).

97 See for this period J. F. Verbruggen, *Vlaanderen na de Guldensporenslag: De vrijheidsstrijd van het graafschap Vlaanderen, 1303–1305* (Bruges, 1991) and Sabbe, *Vlaanderen in opstand*.

98 R. C. Van Caenegem, 'Nota over de terechtstelling van Willem de Deken te Parijs in 1328', *Handelingen van het Genootschap voor Geschiedenis*, 90 (1953), 140–2.

99 H. Pirenne, *Le Soulèvement de la Flandre maritime de 1323–1328: Documents inédits* (Brussels, 1900), p. xxxi; J. Van Rompaey, 'De Brugse keure van 1329 en de aanvullende privileges', *Bulletin de la Commission Royale des Anciennes Lois et Ordonnances de Belgique*, 21 (1965), 35–99.

their fortifications destroyed, and hundreds of people were sent into exile and also had to pay enormous fines.[100]

Among the various sanctions imposed upon the rebellious cities of Bruges and Ypres, the townsmen also had to provide hostages to the king. From Bruges, 500 rebels were requested to temporarily serve as hostages, while another 500 weavers and 500 fullers were ordered to leave the city of Ypres immediately and settle 'beyond the River Somme'.[101] Skilled artisans who had been exiled often opted either to settle in a foreign city in order to find work, without any hope of going back home, or wait patiently until the political tide had turned. These artisans (mostly textile workers), who were sent as a punishment to France, seem to have chosen to live in Paris, Troyes and Provins for the duration of their 'fine'. However, some of these weavers might have left for England for some time and then returned. The period coincides with Edward III's policy of encouraging Flemish weavers to settle in England and import their skills, which started almost exactly around this period. Indeed, Jan Ackerman, Henri Meyer and some other exiles from Bruges named in the 1328 charter appear in the records of the English chancery.[102] The political situation in Flanders, and the high mobility and possible adaptability of skilled artisans, might have inspired the English authorities at this point to develop a more targeted immigration policy towards textile workers. And still in 1330, Count Louis of Nevers and the aldermen of Ghent sent a list with the names of 626 weavers from the latter city to the count of Hainaut asking that they be arrested and returned to Flanders in order to be punished for all their 'evildoings against the count and against the city of Ghent'.[103] The Flemish weaver John Kemp, the first to be granted a letter patent from Edward III in 1331, inviting him to come with his men and ply his trade in England as part of Edward's policy to develop a native textile industry, may have been one of these exiles, as the name of one weaver who figures on the list of 626 names is Jehan le Kempe.[104]

The end of the revolt of 1323–8 marked an era of deep and often insurmountable class and factional divisions that characterised Flemish

[100] *Inventaire analytique des chartes et documents appartenants aux archives de la ville d'Ypres*, ed. I. Diegerick, 6 vols. (Bruges, 1853), vol. II, p. 51; *Inventaire des archives de la ville de Bruges*, ed. L. Gilliodts-Van Severen, 9 vols. (Bruges, 1871–85), vol. I, p. 401.

[101] Sabbe, *Vlaanderen in opstand*, p. 78; Brussels, *General Archives of the Realm*, Oorkonden van Vlaanderen, 1e reeks, nos 2158, 2159.

[102] *CPR, 1327–30*, p. 573.

[103] P. Van Duyse and E. De Buscher, *Inventaire analytique des chartes et documents appartenant aux archives de la ville de Gand* (Ghent, 1867), p. 118.

[104] *CPR, 1330–4*, p. 161.

urban society during this period.[105] The immediate consequence of the disturbances and the departure of so many weavers and fullers was a sharp decline in cloth production. For example, in the city of Ypres, the contraction of production after 1328 and throughout the 1330s was about 50 per cent in comparison with figures from the 1310s.[106] The textile industries of Ghent and Bruges were hit as hard as manufacture in Ypres.[107] On the other hand, the urban industry of the Duchy of Brabant would benefit from this disruption of the Flemish cloth industries and reach the highest point of its output in the 1330s.[108] However, as we will see later, even with the growth of the industry, Brabantine cloth-workers would not be without difficulties, and some of them still preferred to emigrate. The general crisis in the Flemish cloth industry meant a further loss of textile workers' political influence within urban governments. Pushed by deteriorating working conditions, a lack of opportunities for social mobility and isolation from political decision-making, cloth manufacturers, especially weavers, would become more and more radical. Thus, not long after the defeat at Cassel, disturbances returned to the county.

As relations between England and France worsened, in Flanders, highly dependent on English wool, a strong pro-English party started to develop. This broad faction considered that the count, who was now an ally of the patricians, represented the interests of the king of France more than those of the Flemish towns. In an attempt to force the count of Flanders into an alliance with England, in 1336 Edward III imposed upon the county an embargo on the exportation of English wool there. However, Count Louis of Nevers decided to align with King Philip IV of France. This decision, combined with the shortage of wool, eventually led to a generalised revolt across several towns. In 1337, both the guilds and many richer burghers (*poorters*) united against the count during a revolt in Ghent and forced him to flee to France. The city would now be

[105] J. Dumolyn and M. Lenoir, 'De sociaal-politieke verhoudingen binnen het Brugse stadsbestuur tidens het midden van de 14de eeuw (1326–1361)', *Handelingen van het Genootschap voor Geschiedenis te Brugge*, 151 (2014), 323–76.

[106] P. Chorley, 'The Ypres cloth industry 1200–1350: The pattern of change in output and demand', in M. De Wilde, A. Ervynck and A. Wielmans (eds), *Ypres and the Medieval Cloth Industry in Flanders: Archaeological and Historical Contributions* (Zellik, 1998), pp. 111–21, at p. 118; H. Van Werveke, 'De omvang van de Ieperse lakenproductie in de veertiende eeuw', *Mededelingen van de Koninklijke Vlaamse academie voor wetenschappen, letteren en schone kunsten van België*, 9 (1947), 1–32.

[107] D. Nicholas, *The Metamorphosis of a Medieval City: Ghent in the Age of Van Arteveldes, 1302–1390* (Lincoln, 1987), pp. 136–8; J. Dumolyn, F. Buylaert, G. Dupont, J. Haemers and A. Ramandt, 'Political power and social groups 1300–1500', in Brown and Dumolyn, *Medieval Bruges*, pp. 268–328, at pp. 287–9.

[108] Van Uytven, 'De omvang', 1–22 and 'La Draperie brabançonne', pp. 85–97.

ruled by five captains (*hooftmannen*) and by the deans of weavers, fullers and small guilds. Eventually it was James of Artevelde, a citizen of Ghent, who in 1338 became the chief of the five captains, which gave him considerable power over the aldermen. After he managed to seize power in Ghent, one of the first things he did was to re-establish representatives of the weavers to the city's government, from which they had been excluded since 1320 at the expense of the fullers. Many of those exiled during the 1323–8 revolt could now return. By 1340, Artevelde had established his regime all over the county. While the rebels claimed to rule in the name of the count, in practice Flanders was divided into quarters, which would be ruled by the 'Three Cities': Ghent, Bruges and Ypres, the first dominating the latter two. Flanders also turned completely from fealty to the French to an alliance with England, and in 1340 Edward III was recognised as king of France at the Friday market in Ghent.[109] Even if the legal fiction of princely rule over Flanders was maintained, in practice, however, for some years, the 'Three Cities' had ruled as virtual city-states over their rural hinterlands, acting as *de facto* administrators of princely justice as well.[110]

The 'Three Cities' wanted to establish complete control over heavy cloth production and eliminate competition from rural areas. Small towns as well as the surrounding countryside occasionally faced legal prosecution because their cloth manufacturers imitated the woollens of the established cloth centres.[111] In the early 1340s, Ypres accused Poperinge, a town in its immediate vicinity and for a long time a rival in the textile industry, of repeatedly violating its privileges dealing with the production of cloth. In 1344 the long quarrel resulted in a judicial inquiry.[112] Poperinge was found guilty and according to the sentence it had to find twenty of the main culprits. They were to be banished to England for three years, and after that period they were supposed to bring letters confirming their stay there.[113] Indeed, as the city of Ghent

[109] See, on this period: H. S. Lucas, *The Low Countries and the Hundred Years' War, 1326–1347* (Ann Arbor, 1929); D. Nicholas, *The Van Arteveldes of Ghent: The Varieties of Vendetta and the Hero in History* (Ithaca, 1988).

[110] M. Boone and W. Prevenier, 'Le Rêve d'un état urbain (quatorzième et quinzième siècles)', in J. Decavele (ed.), *Apologie d'une ville rebelle: Histoire, art, culture* (Antwerp, 1989), pp. 81–105; D. Nicholas, *Town and Countryside: Social, Economic and Political Tensions in 14th-Century Flanders* (Bruges, 1971).

[111] Murray, *Bruges*, p. 281.

[112] Espinas and Pirenne, *Recueil*, vol. I, pp. 120–53.

[113] *Ypre jeghen Poperinghe angaende den verboden: Gedinkstukken der XIVe eeuw nopens het laken*, ed. N. De Pauw (Ghent, 1899), pp. 15, 231, 'ende, die claerlike gheweiten dat menre tote twinteghen sal senden drie jaer te woene in Inghelant, dewelke tenden jare goeden lettren sullen bringhen, dat zire hare residentie wel ghehouden hebben'; *Inventaire*, Diegerick, vol. II, p. 134; Espinas and Pirenne, *Recueil*, vol. I, p. 147.

was arbitrating the dispute, the Artevelde regime seems to have wanted to demonstrate that they took the alliance seriously by sending skilled workers to England at the same time as dealing with internal affairs. This seems plausible, considering that this period coincides with Edward III's policy of further developing cloth production within his realm.[114]

Artevelde's rule was weakened by economic decline in the mid 1340s, and in 1345 he was eventually murdered by his former followers. However, the political constellation that had governed the county during the previous seven years remained intact. In 1346, Louis of Nevers died at the battle of Crécy and was succeeded by his son, Louis of Male. Determined to establish his rule over the county, in 1348 he started an invasion of Flanders with support from his French overlord. Bruges, Ypres and other castellanies gave up resistance very quickly. Ghent, led by its weavers, persevered in rebellion against the count until 13 January 1349, an event known as 'Good Tuesday', when Louis of Male, with his troops, together with a coalition of fullers, the *poorters* and the smaller crafts, stormed the city and bloodily crushed the last rebellious strongholds.[115]

On 5 August 1349, Count Louis of Male ordered an inquiry in all the towns of Flanders to punish the rebel leaders who had withstood his and his father's authority.[116] In England, Edward III anticipated the potential persecution of hundreds of skilled artisans who had been involved in the revolt. Already in May 1350, he issued letters of protection to those Flemings who, following the failure of the rebellion, had emigrated to London, Canterbury, Norwich, Salisbury, Lynn and other English cities and towns. Very similar to those granted to a number of French residents in England during the same years,[117] the documents qualified the Flemings as *incolae*, a term derived from Roman law to denote permanent residents born outside the kingdom. As a reward for their loyalty during the Flemish conflict, they were allowed to live in the realm, to leave, enter and move around freely, and to trade their goods. Officers

114 *The Parliamentary Rolls of Medieval England*, ed. C. Given-Wilson et al. (Woodbridge, 2005), vol. IV, p. 191; *Statutes of the Realm*, ed. Luders et al., vol. I, pp. 280–1.

115 M. Boone and W. Prevenier, 'La Construction d'un républicanisme urbain: Enjeux de la politique municipale dans les villes flamandes au bas Moyen Âge', in D. Menjot and J.-L. Pinol (eds), *Enjeux et expressions de la politique municipale (XIIe–XXe siècles)* (Paris, 1997), pp. 41–60; M. Boone and H. Brand, 'Vollersoproeren en collectieve actie in Gent en Leiden in de 14e en 15e eeuw', *Tijdschrift voor Sociale Geschiedenis*, 19 (1993), 168–93; J. Vuylsteke, 'Goede Disendach, 13 januari 1349', *Handelingen van de Maatschappij voor Geschiedenis en Oudheidkunde te Gent*, 1 (1894), 9–47.

116 *Cartulaire de Louis de Male*, ed. De Limburg-Stirum, vol. I, pp. 78–9; *Inventaire Bruges*, ed. Gilliodts-Van Severen, vol. II, pp. 8–9.

117 Lambert and Ormrod, 'Friendly foreigners', 8–14.

were instructed to protect them against physical aggression and their property against confiscation.[118] The investigation finished two years later, and on 5 October 1351 many of the participants in the revolt were sent into exile and took refuge in England, as we shall see later.

The official sentence after the inquiry listed the names of the main culprits who had initiated the rebellion. These survive only for the city of Bruges and for the liberty of Bruges, and they contain, respectively, the names of 464 and 128 banished rebels.[119] For Ghent, Ypres and other towns in Flanders we have to rely on the lists drawn up in 1359 of 1,460 exiles who were eligible for pardon under certain conditions.[120] Fifteenth-century copies of the city of Bruges chartulary called Groenenboek inform us that waves of revolts and other mass expulsions of craftsmen followed in 1361, 1362, 1366 and 1369.[121] These provide another 579 names for the city of Bruges and allow us to engage in an extensive prosopographical analysis of the rebels throughout the period of this study. We can easily establish that some of those who accepted pardon and returned to Flanders in 1359 would have been involved in the rebellion, and exiled again, in 1361.[122] On 25 September 1351, ten days before the sentence of banishment was pronounced by the chancery of Louis of Male, Edward III, perhaps with foreknowledge of this verdict, issued a letter patent of protection allowing all people banished from Flanders and willing to work to settle in England.[123] Shortly afterwards, artisans mentioned on the lists appear in various sources from English towns, and they remain visible for another thirty years (Map 1).

Yet the arrival of the exiles was not without problems. There was an ambiguity in their legal status and especially concerning the conditions under which they were supposed to exercise their trade. While the statute of 1337 allowed all cloth-workers from 'strange lands' to settle

118 The letters were not entered on the chancery patent rolls but were recorded in an inspeximus confirmation by London's court of husting in 1364. LMA, CLA/023/DW/93, n. 19. For the context of the confirmation, see in Chapter 2, and B. Lambert and M. Pajic, 'Immigration and the common profit: Native cloth-workers, Flemish exiles and royal policy in fourteenth-century London', *Journal of British Studies*, 55:4 (2016), 633–57, at 638.

119 SAB, Oud Archief, Groenenboek C, fos 127–35; SAB, Politieke charters 1e reeks, no. 197.

120 ADN Série B, 1596, fos. 30 r.–35 v., published in *Cartulaire Historique et Généalogique des Artevelde*, ed. De Pauw, pp. 711–32.

121 SAB, Oud Archief, Groenenboek C, fos 127–35.

122 Pardoned exiles would usually plot and organise various collective actions against the political conditions of fourteenth-century Flanders and be banished again. For a detailed analysis of the procedure, consequences and orgins of political exile in fourteenth-century Flanders, see J. Dumolyn and M. Pajic, 'Enemies of the count and of the city: The collective exile of rebels in fourteenth-century Flanders', *The Legal History Review*, 84:3–4 (2016), 461–501.

123 *CPR, 1350–4*, p. 147; *Foedera, conventiones, literae et cujuscunque generis acta publica*, ed. T. Rymer, 4 vols. (London, 1816–69), vol. III, p. 232.

wherever they wished within the realm and under the king's protection, the arrival of exiles required further precision about their legal status. Forced migration to England meant that the number of Flemish immigrants was now sufficiently high to appear significantly in English sources. It should be noted that in the local sources of towns like Colchester or Great Yarmouth, the first Flemings do not appear until 1352. The arrival of large numbers of exiled textile workers in England after the revolt against Louis of Male made them more visible to the English population than in previous years. This led to discontent among the members of the guild of weavers of London. Already in 1352, they were complaining about the presence of alien weavers in the city. After several disputes between the representatives of the London Weavers' Guild and the newcomers, which will be discussed more in detail in Chapter 6, the king was forced to clarify the exiles' legal status with a letter patent in 1352:[124]

> Whereas by statute of 11 Edward III (1337), it is ordained that foreign workers of cloth may come to England and stay there and the king will grant them so many and such liberties as shall be sufficient for them, by a petition of such workers exhibited before him and his council in the present Parliament it has been shewn that they are hindered in the exercise of their mistery as well in London as in other cities and places of the realm, wherefore he, with the assent of the prelates, earls, barons and other magnates in the present Parliament has granted to all workers of such cloths from foreign parts of whatsoever land they be, who are now in England, Ireland or Wales, or who shall come there from now, and will stay and exercise their mistery therein and bear themselves well and faithfully towards him, that they may do so safely and securely under his protection, without that that they be compelled to be of the gild of the weavers of London or other weavers or be held to pay any sums by reason of such gild, and that in any city, borough or town where they shall stay and exercise their mistery they may elect two men of their mistery to survey the work of the same foreign workers that it be duly made, and punish all insufficient or fraudulent workers by view and testimony of these two, saving pleas whereof cognisance pertains to the king. Grant also that they shall not be compelled to deliver work, when done, before they be satisfied for the same according to the covenant made with them, that in any damages, injuries or trespasses done to them, justice shall be done for them without delay by mayors, sheriffs or bailiffs in whose bailiwicks the wrong has been done, and that if any of them be taken for trespass, debt or account or other cause where bail is allowed, he shall be

[124] For more details on disputes between Flemish and native weavers in London throughout the second half of the fourteenth century, see Lambert and Pajic, 'Immigration and the common profit', 633–57. The key sections of the letter patent from 1352 are calendared in *CPR, 1350–4*, p. 232, but a complete translation can be found in *The Records of the City of Norwich*, ed. W. Hudson and J. C. Tingey, 2 vols. (Norwich, 1906 and 1910), vol. II, pp. 330–2.

released on sufficient mainprise according to the law and custom of our Realm of England.

As can be seen, the letter patent not only confirmed the existing statute of 1337, but it also extended it with additional franchises. Flemish textile workers were allowed to settle where they wanted and organise themselves in any way they preferred, without being compelled to be part of existing guilds in towns where they plied their trade. They were instead granted the right to choose two masters of their own who would supervise their trade. We will see later in Chapters 2, 3 and 6 that in London this led to the creation of a guild of alien weavers separate from the natives'. More importantly, royal and municipal officers were instructed to provide speedy justice if any damages were incurred by the Flemings, or vice versa, which basically means that they were granted the right to plead in courts of law. On top of that, if new artisans from overseas were to join them, they would enjoy the same rights. We do not know whether this last provision encouraged other immigrants from the Low Countries to come to England, but we do know that exiles from Flanders were followed by their wives and children, and by other artisans from the Low Countries (notably those from neighbouring Zeeland and Brabant).

At the same time, throughout the 1350s and the 1360s, the Duchy of Brabant was going through a turbulent period and had also seen a number of similar disturbances. While the Brabantine woollen industries benefited from the decline of Flemish urban production in the first half of the fourteenth century (and especially after the defeat at Cassel), the position of weavers and fullers did not improve much. The whole production and marketing process was in the hands of merchant-drapers, who were part of the patrician elites. Grouped around the solid guild structure and supported by the dukes, they were able to put down workers' rebellions and thus prevent any rise in wages. Most of the output was exported to France, where Brabantine cloth virtually eclipsed Flemish woollens, as Philip le Bel and subsequent monarchs clearly favoured merchants from Malines, Brussels, Antwerp and Louvain.[125] Indeed, because of frozen wages, the price of cloth was lower in Brabant than in Flanders and was thus more attractive. On top of the matter of low wages, weavers and fullers, even though they had their own guilds, had no political representation in the municipal governments, unlike

[125] Various princely accounts are a testament to this: *Inventaires mobiliers et extraits des comptes des ducs de Bourgogne de la maison de Valois (1363–1477)*, ed. B. Prost and H. Prost, vol. II (1902–13); *Nouveaux Comptes de l'argenterie des rois de France au XIVe siècle*, ed. L. Douët d'Arcq (Paris, 1851), pp. 84–9.

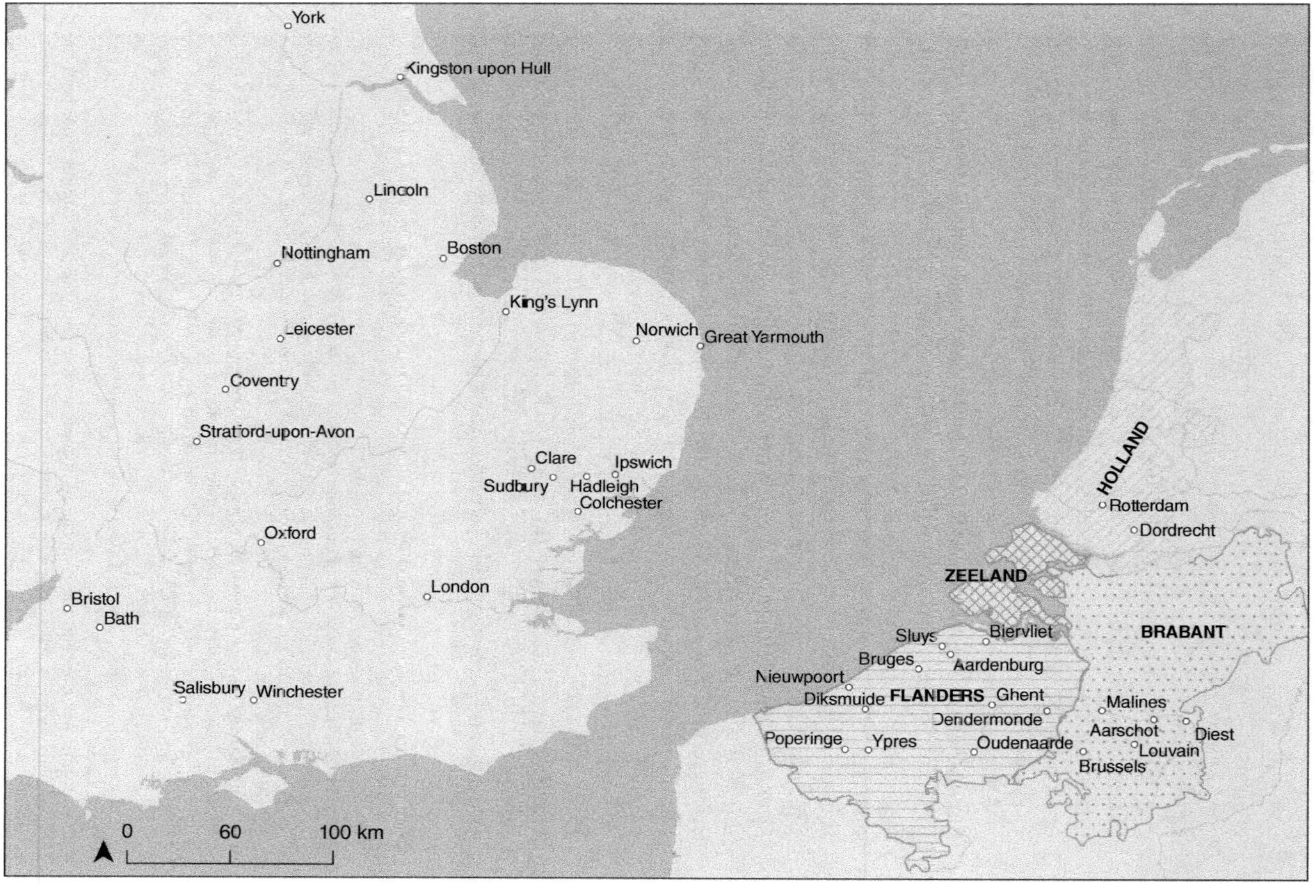

Map 1 England and the Low Countries c. 1350 – Towns of immigrants' origin and settlement (map made by Davor Salihovic)

their Flemish counterparts.[126] Moreover, the situation on the international stage would affect Brabantine textile industries. In 1334, an economic blockade was imposed on the duchy by neighbouring counties, which, together with Edward III's ban on the exportation of wool in 1336, caused a sharp drop in the number of fabrics produced.[127] More generally, the Anglo-French war further hampered Brabantine trade. When the English king moved the staple to Bruges in 1340, the Flemish towns tried to secure English wool for themselves at the expense of all other buyers.[128] On top of that, the war of succession that started in 1347 once again brought the economy of Brabant to a standstill.[129]

All these events would lead the textile workers to express their discontent through riots in Brussels and Louvain in 1340, and then again in 1350. Social tension was further increased by the devaluation of the Brabantine currency, which reduced purchasing power from 1347 onwards. The fixing of nominal wages in devalued currency fomented the social discontent that broke out in 1360 in rebellions of weavers in Brussels, Malines, Antwerp and Louvain.[130] As a result of the revolts, the artisans of the Brabantine cities were subjected to punishments similar to those of the Flemish cities. Many leaders of the revolt and their supporters were killed or banished on the orders of the aldermen. Unfortunately, the normative sources covering the aftermath of these events are not as detailed as those from Flanders and do not allow us to trace the individuals who were banished from Brabantine cities in English sources.[131] Even though the artisans were defeated on this occasion and faced reprisals thereafter, they would not back down in their quest for political representation. In 1364, another wave of disturbances would break out in Brussels and Louvain. The sources do not provide many details about

[126] Favresse, *L'Avènement Bruxelles*, pp. 98–106.

[127] Van Uytven, 'La Draperie brabançonne', p. 88.

[128] J. de Sturler, *Les Relations politiques et les échanges commerciaux entre le duché de Brabant et l'Angleterre au Moyen Âge: L'Étape des laines anglaises en Brabant et les origines du développement du port d'Anvers* (Paris, 1936), pp. 392–4.

[129] Lucas, *The Low Countries and the Hundred Years' War*, pp. 198, 256–7, 528–72.

[130] R. Van Uytven, 'Peter Couthereel en de troebelen te Leuven van 1350 tot 1363: Kritische nota over de persoon van een hertogelijk ambtenaar en zijn rol in de politieke geschiedenis van Brabant en Leuven', *Mededelingen van de Geschied- en Oudheidkundige Kring voor Leuven en Omgeving*, 3 (1963), 63–97; H. Vander Linden, *Histoire de la constitution de la ville de Louvain au Moyen Âge* (Ghent, 1892); J. Cuvelier, *Les Institutions de la ville de Louvain au Moyen Âge* (Leuven, 1935).

[131] Most of our evidence about revolts and banishments in the cities of Brabant comes from the narrative sources: E. De Dynter, *Chronicon ducum Brabantiae*, ed. P. F. X. de Ram, 3 vols. (Brussels, 1854–60), vol. III, pp. 51–3; J. De Klerk et An., *De Brabantsche Yeesten ofrymkronyk van Braband*, ed. J. F. Willems and J. H. Bormans, 3 vols. (Brussels, 1839–69), vol. II, pp. 166–71.

these revolts, but two sentences pronounced in June 1364 indicate that at least 100 weavers and fullers were banished from Brussels and another 40 from Louvain who were designated as the instigators of the revolt alongside the main ringleaders Jean de Meyere, a butcher from Brussels, and Peter Coutereel, from Louvain.[132]

In both Flanders and Brabant, besides the exiles, many others probably voluntarily left to avoid physical danger or dire economic conditions after the revolts. As we will see in Chapter 2, numerous individuals with Flemish names recorded in England are not on the lists of exiles, presumably because they emigrated of their own volition. In order to prevent any further insurgency, the urban authorities introduced measures that would be likely to push the remaining artisans to consider emigrating to England. For example, the weavers of Ghent had to deal with the humiliating conditions imposed by the fuller-dominated aldermen after the revolt. By the statute of 29 November 1349, weavers were forbidden to carry weapons or change occupations. They could no longer assemble in groups of more than three, and whoever saw them gathered had the right to take off and keep their upper clothes. If any of the remaining weavers breached the law, they still risked banishment of three to fifty years. Weavers were ousted from political office again and were made to pay an indemnity until 1375.[133] Similar measures were introduced in Brussels after the rebellion of 1360.[134] The revolts contributed further to the disorganisation of industry that already reigned over urban cloth-making in both Flanders and Brabant. Moreover, an acute scarcity of skilled textile workers was rapidly felt as a result of forced and voluntary departure of thousands of weavers and fullers.[135] Political instability and economic stagnation left the cities with numerous idle and underpaid textile workers. All of these conditions reinforced the emigration of a lot more people (other than just the exiles) who would be pushed to seek safety in England and who were not willing to return any time soon.

Nevertheless, the count's policies seem to have softened after Edward III's request, and some exiles did return. In 1359, Count Louis of Male offered a general pardon to numerous rebels from the major cities of Flanders. The artisans who returned to Bruges, such as Jan de Weerd (John Were in English sources) or Jacop de Deken, apparently had to buy

[132] Favresse, *L'Avènement Bruxelles*, pp. 118–19.

[133] *Voorgeboden der stad Gent in der XIVe eeuw (1337–1382)*, ed. N. De Pauw (Ghent, 1885), pp. 41, 51, 52, 53, 65.

[134] Favresse, *L'Avènement Bruxelles*, p. 118.

[135] Nicholas, *The Metamorphosis*, p. 155.

their status of citizen again.[136] Sometimes, only wives were allowed to return, as in the case of Lievin Fisker: he was banished after the revolt in Ghent and found refuge in London, but only his wife, Merrin, was allowed to return.[137] We will see cases in Chapter 3 where some exiles returned either to their city of origin or elsewhere in Flanders and subsequently, after several years, came back to England. In these cases, it is then difficult to consider them 'exiles', as their legal status would have changed. Also, it was common for some Flemings to change their place of residence in England while still in exile. All of these points, along with the fact that the exiles were followed by people who left voluntarily, together make it very challenging to define immigrants from the Low Countries under one single term.

The experiences of exiles from the Low Countries should also be regarded differently from those of felons, banished individually for various crimes they committed. Individual exiles were for the most part left all alone, with only the necessary goods and guidance to survive until they reached their destination.[138] Flemish exiles, although they were considered felons by the count for being 'his enemies and of his cities', were banished for political reasons principally. And although they might have been humiliated publicly before they left their towns of origin, they travelled as a collective, which would have made it a lot easier to decide how to act upon settling in a new area, compared with the cases of individual exiles. They also enjoyed an invitation and protection from the king, which would distinguish them from other immigrant groups; thus their administrative integration was held to the same standard as that of any other immigrant. For example, when John Kempe, an exile from Ghent, became a citizen of London in 1356, he was still obliged to find four pledges to guarantee his good behaviour.[139] The exiles were privileged in having collective protection from the king, but in practice, for many things, they were seen as just like any other aliens who resided in England throughout the late Middle Ages.

136 SAB, Oud Archief, Groenenboek C fo. 111r; *Cartulaire historique et généalogique des Artevelde*, ed. De Pauw, p. 719; *CPMR*, vol. II, p. 116; A. Jamees, *Brugse poorters opgetekend uit de stadsrekeningen, Deel 1: 1281–1421* (Handzame, 1974), pp. 112–13.

137 *Cartulaire historique et généalogique des Artevelde*, ed. De Pauw, p. 715.

138 W. C. Jordan, *From England to France: Felony and Exile in the High Middle Ages* (New Jersey, 2015), pp. 63–4. The authorities made sure that they were left with some money to purchase food when travelling. They were also given instructions on how to get to a intended destination, as well as being subject to surveillance, to ensure they were not left entirely unattended until they reached the port of departure.

139 LMA, CLA/023/CP/01/80, 4d.

CONCLUSION

Taken together, the situation from the thirteenth century onwards in both England and the Low Countries was such as to stimulate immigration. This chapter has shown that a combination of economic conditions, the proximity of the two countries and political developments was probably the determining factor for this migration. Political relations also ensured directly and indirectly that the textile industries of the two regions evolved together and became interdependent. This development of events was accelerated at the start of the Hundred Years War when Edward III placed an embargo on the export of English wool to Flanders in order to force an alliance with the Flemish count against the French. It did not really work, as the only ones to support the alliance were the textile workers, who were highly dependent upon imports of English wool. Gradually, the county would be deluged by a wave of urban revolts, which would finally see the victory of the count's pro-French party and the expulsion of numerous cloth-workers from their towns. In order to avoid legal and political repercussions or death, these rebels, followed by other economic migrants, would quickly move to a number of English towns, both in the old and newly established textile centres. Moreover, the medieval Low Countries had some very 'progressive' characteristics which made them the forerunner in many societal developments: a low level of feudalism, early forms of proletarianisation and wage-labour, the relatively autonomous role of women in the labour market and the reasonably independent position of children, who were more or less able to choose their own marriage partner.[140] This disconnection from family and institutions, to which one must add greater skills in the weaving industry, made it easier for Flemings to emigrate to and integrate within England. These two questions of the arrival and integration of immigrants from the Low Countries will be explored in Chapters 2 and 3.

[140] Lucassen and Willems, *Living in the City*, p. 3.

Chapter 2

FLEMISH AND BRABANTINE IMMIGRANTS AS PERMANENT RESIDENTS IN ENGLAND 1351–1400

INTRODUCTION

We have seen so far that the economic and political environment on both sides of the English Channel in the first half of the fourteenth century provided the conditions that allowed textile workers from the Low Countries to move to England after 1351. Some of them were exiled rebels but others left voluntarily. Once the English Channel had been crossed, however, new challenges appeared for all of them, whether they were economic migrants or exiles. These issues ranged from the legal situation and the choice of town for permanent settlement, to finding a residence and employment opportunities, which all represent the basis for a healthy start to life in a new place. The purpose of this chapter will therefore be to present the profile, the numbers and the occupations of the immigrants, and to identify those parts of the towns in which they took up residence. The main focus will be on those who were exiled from Flanders after the rebellion (1345–9), and on Flemish textile workers as identified from the sources on the other side of the English Channel. I will start with the fortunes of Flemish immigrants in the English capital, then continue with the market town of Colchester, situated on the east coast in the county of Essex, before finally turning my attention to Great Yarmouth, the port town of the county of Norfolk. In order to reinforce my overall argument, the Flemish and Brabantine presence will be discussed in other towns throughout England. We will see that they settled in numerous places all over the country, some of which traditional scholarship has never linked with immigrants from the Low Countries, and that their numbers were much higher than those estimated by previous scholarship.

FLEMINGS IN LONDON

The first place in England where Edward III's letters of protection are known to have had a considerable effect is London. From 1351 onwards, numerous immigrants from the Low Countries (both men and women) began to appear in the city's Letter Books, memoranda and fine rolls, and alnage accounts, as well as in a variety of other sources.[1] Most of them were textile workers originating from the county of Flanders and the neighbouring Duchy of Brabant. The latter were almost as numerous in London as their Flemish colleagues. Overall, there are at least 309 immigrants from the Low Countries (both men and women) appearing in London sources over the forty-year period 1351–91. The occupations of those 309 individuals are chiefly related to the production or sale of cloth. Most of them, 171, were weavers, followed by 16 drapers or merchant-drapers, while there were also 5 fullers, 5 dyers, 5 tailors and 2 shearers. Some of them were employed in the leather industry, such as Albright Dommel, a patin-maker, his brother, Arnold, who was a cordwainer, and Segelinus van Male, a tawyer (a leather-worker involved in the preparation of hides).[2] There were also two goldsmiths and one carpenter who can be identified as immigrants from the Low Countries. Twenty-one women who crop up either as the wives of other Flemings or on their own were employed as petty traders or workers in the first stages of the production of cloth. For example, Katherine van Ordingham was referred to as a huckster, and Margaret Kemestere, *Flemyng*, as a comber.[3] The occupations were not stated for the remaining seventy-eight immigrants, but the context in which they appear in English sources suggests their involvement in the production or sale of cloth.

The immigrant textile workers from Brabant or Flanders probably left their countries because of the economic disruption caused by urban revolts and warfare throughout the mid fourteenth century.[4] As discussed in Chapter 1, some of the immigrants were even forced to leave. The

[1] TNA, E 101/340/22, m. 3; E 101/340/23, mm. 5, 5d; TNA, KB 27/386, m. 75; LMA, CLA/023/CP 76, m. 15; *Letter Book G*, pp. 48, 104, 130, 115–19, 237, 250; *Letter Book H*, p. 77, *CPMR*, vol. I, pp. 248; II, pp. 65–6, 67, 70, 195; Consitt, *The London Weavers' Company*, pp. 188–91; *Memorials of London and London life, in the 13th, 14th, and the 15th Centuries, Being a Series of Extracts, Local, Social and Political from the Early Archives of the City of London AD 1276–1419* , ed. H. T. Riley (Longmans, 1868), p. 332; *Calendar of Letters from the Mayor and Corporation of the City of London, circa A.D. 1350–1370, Enrolled and Preserved among the Archives of the Corporation at the Guildhall*, ed. R. R. Sharpe (London, 1885), pp. 19, 75; *CFR, 1356–68*, p. 193.

[2] TNA, CP 40/397, m. 155; *CPMR*, vol. II, pp. 28, 31.

[3] *CPMR*, vol. II, pp. 39, 69.

[4] S. Boffa, *Warfare in Medieval Brabant* (Woodbridge, 2004), pp. 3–10; F. Quicke, *Les Pays-Bas à la veille de la période bourguignonne, 1356–1384: Contribution à l'histoire et diplomatique de l'Europe occidentale dans la seconde moitié du XIVe siècle* (Brussels, 1947), pp. 41–54.

names of fifty-eight immigrants who were dwelling in the capital during the twenty-five years following Edward III's decree of protection match almost exactly those of Flemish artisans who were included in the 1351 lists of banishments (see Table 2.1). We will see later that some of the exiles in other English towns came from smaller Flemish towns and villages, yet all but two of those found in London originated in the large cities of Ghent, Bruges and Ypres. In all fifty-eight cases, the lists of Flemish exiles, in combination with the London sources, provide us with an occupation. Only one of them, carpenter John de Gaunt from Bruges, had no connection to the textile sector. John de Langford, John Gallyn and John Baker worked as fullers; Lamsin Iperling was a shearer. The remaining fifty-three immigrants consisted of forty-four banished weavers and nine drapers or merchant-drapers.

As for the immigrants from Brabant, we do not have lists of exiles to systematically compare with the names from English sources and so establish their towns of origin. When their towns of origin are stated, we notice that they were also from the duchy's urban textile centres. For example, Jacob van Melstede appeared on several occasions in the memoranda rolls, but it is mentioned only in his will that he was originally from Diest in Brabant.[5] Other Brabantines might have immigrated from textile towns like Brussels, Malines or Louvain, as was the case in York, as we will see below.

While the lists of exiles very rarely allow us to establish whether they were followed by their children, wives and relatives, the situation is different with testamentary evidence and other sources in London. Only one exile, John Marchaunt of Ypres, figures on the 1359 lists with his wife. It does not necessarily follow that the others immigrated alone, as the case of Henry Clofhamer shows. Clofhamer, banished from Ghent, appears repeatedly in London sources throughout the 1350s and 1360s.[6] In 1359, his anonymous wife, who had never been mentioned before, was pardoned and recalled to Flanders,[7] which implies she had been in England during the previous years. The same goes for Lievin Fisker, a prominent weaver from Ghent, who operated his business in London in 1365, but only his wife, Merrin, is offered a pardon in 1359.[8] All thirty of the immigrants from the Low Countries who left wills were married. It is inferred from his will that William van Carlewyk, a former

[5] *CPMR*, vol. II, p. 181; M. Fitch, *Index to Testamentary Records in the Archdeaconry Court of London, Vol. I: 1363–1649*, Guildhall Library (London, 1979), p. 386.

[6] TNA, E 13/76, mm. 97–8d; *CPMR*, vol. II, pp. 65–6.

[7] *Cartulaire historique et généalogique des Artevelde*, ed. De Pauw, p. 715.

[8] TNA, E 122/70/18, mm. 1, 9. For the involvement of exiles in wool exports, see Chapter 4; *Cartulaire historique et généalogique des Artevelde*, ed. De Pauw, p. 715.

Table 2.1 *Names of Flemings appearing both in London sources between 1351 and 1375 and on the lists of exiles of 1351 and those pardoned in 1359*[i]

London sources, 1351–75	Flemish lists of exiles in 1351 and pardons in 1359
Maas van Brugge	Maes van der Brughen, weaver, from Ghent
John Brunhals	Jan Bruunhals, weaver, from Ghent
William Brunhals	Willem Bruunhals, weaver, from Ghent
Ras Bruwer	Rase de Bruwere, from Ghent
John Capelle	Jan van der Capelle, weaver, from Ghent
Henry Clofhamer	Wife of Heinric Clofhamers, from Ghent
Peter Crayman	Pieter Crayman, weaver, from Ghent
Levin van Dyke	Lievin van Dike, weaver, from Ghent
Levin Fisker	Merrin, Lievin Vischers wife, from Ghent
John Gaunsterman	Jan Gansterman, weaver, from Ghent
Levin Godhalse	Lievin Goethals, weaver, from Ghent
John le Groterre	Jan de Grutere, weaver, from Ghent
John Kempe, weaver, *Fleming*, citizen of London	Jan de Kempe, weaver, from Ghent
Laurence de Magh, merchant-draper from Ghent	Lauwerin de Maech, from Ghent
John Maaz	Jan Maes, weaver, from Ghent
Gilles Meyfrot	Gillis Meinfrot, from Ghent
William the Meyr	Willem de Meyer, weaver, from Ghent
Henry Navegher	Hanin Navegheer, weaver, from Ghent
Levin Olivier	Lievin Oliviers, weaver, from Ghent
John Pape	Jan de Pape, weaver, from Ghent
John Poules	Jan van den Poule, from Ghent
Giles Ripegast	Gilis Ripegheerste, from Ghent
Arnold Skapkynkyl, merchant and draper	Arnald Scaepscinkel, from Ghent
John van Stene, merchant-draper of Ghent	Jan van den Steene, from Ghent
John Tybes	Jan Tybus , weaver, from Ghent
Nijs van den Vyure, merchant-draper	Nijs van den Vivere, from Ghent
James Westland	Jacop Westland, from Ghent
John van Wetere	Jan van Wetere, from Ghent
William van Aughten	Willem van Auchten, from Bruges
Peter de Bakere	Pieter Bakere, weaver, from Bruges
John Cockelar	Jan van Coukelare, weaver, from Bruges
John de Cranburgh, citizen of London	Jan de Cranenburg, weaver, from Bruges
John Gallyn	Jan Gallin, fuller, from Bruges
John de Gaunt, carpenter	Jan van Ghend, carpenter, from Bruges
John de Gaunt, weaver, *Fleming*	Jan van Ghent, weaver, from Bruges
Joceus Amelryk, merchant	Joos Hemelric, from Bruges
Francis Fan Yabek, merchant and weaver	Franse van Jabbeke, weaver, from Bruges

Table 2.1 (*cont.*)

London sources, 1351–75	Flemish lists of exiles in 1351 and pardons in 1359
John de Langford, fuller	Jan van Langhevorde, fuller, from Bruges
Jacob van Loo	Jacob van Loo, weaver, from Bruges
John van Loo	Jan van Loo, weaver, from Bruges
Peter Medinhoe	Pieter Medinoghe the Younger, weaver, from Bruges
Peter More	Pieter vanden Moere, weaver, from Bruges
Giles Onyng, merchant	Gillis Conyng, weaver, from Bruges
Peter de Pape	Pieter le Pape, weaver, from Bruges
John Rossart, merchant-draper	Jan Roetsard, weaver, from Bruges
John ate Ryk	Jan Rijx, weaver, from Bruges
Paul Stolpart	Pauwels Stalpaert, weaver, from Bruges
Lamsin de Vos	Lamsin de Vos, weaver, from Bruges
Johan atte Werre	Jan de Weerd the Elder, weaver, from Bruges
Lamsin Iperling	Lamsin Yperlinc, shearer, from Bruges
John van Somerkyn/Somergham	Jan van Zomergheem, weaver, from Bruges
Jacob van Ackere, citizen of London, weaver	Jacop van Ackere, from Ypres
John van Dorme	Jan van Doorne, from Ypres
John Marchaunt, weaver	Jan Marchant, from Ypres, and his wife Griele
John Velleyn	Jan de Villain, from Ypres
Baldwin Giles	Boudin Gillis, from Poperinge
Lambert Funderlynde, weaver	Lambrecht van der Linde, from Poperinge

[i] Maas van Brugge: *CPMR*, vol. I, p. 248; Consitt, *The London Weavers' Company*, pp. 188–91 and *Cartulaire des Artevelde*, p. 714; John Brunhals: Consitt, *The London Weavers' Company*, pp. 188–91 and *Cartulaire des Artevelde*, p. 712; William Brunhals: Consitt, *The London Weavers' Company*, pp. 188–91 and *Cartulaire des Artevelde*, p. 714; Ras Bruwer: TNA, E 101/340/23, m. 5 and *Cartulaire des Artevelde*, p. 716; John Capelle: TNA, E 101/340/22, m. 3; TNA, E 122/70/18, m. 1d and *Cartulaire des Artevelde*, p. 717; Henry Clofhamer: *CPMR*, vol. II, pp. 65–6; Consitt, *The London Weavers' Company*, pp. 188–91; *Memorials of London*, ed. Riley, p. 332 and *Cartulaire des Artevelde*, p. 712; Peter Crayman: *Letter Book G*, p. 250 and *Cartulaire des Artevelde*, p. 712; Levin van Dyke: *CPMR*, vol. II, pp. 65–6 and *Cartulaire des Artevelde*, p. 716; Levin Fisker: TNA, E 122/70/18, m. 1 and *Cartulaire des Artevelde*, p. 715; John Gaunsterman: *CPMR*, vol. II, pp. 65–6; *Memorials of London*, ed. Riley, p. 332 and *Cartulaire des Artevelde*, p. 714; Levin Godhalse: Consitt, *The London Weavers' Company*, pp. 188–91 and *Cartulaire des Artevelde*, p. 715; John le Groterre: TNA, E 101/340/22, m. 3; *Letter Book G*, p. 131 and ADN, Série B, 1596, fo. 22r; John Kempe: Consitt, *The London Weavers' Company*, pp. 188–91; *CPMR*, vol. II, p. 116; *Letter Book G*, 182, 250; LMA, CLA/023/DW, roll 93, n. 19 and *Cartulaire des Artevelde*, p. 713; Laurence de Magh: *CPMR*, vol. II, p. 67 and *Cartulaire des Artevelde*, p. 716; John Maaz: *CPMR*, vol. II, pp. 65–6 and *Cartulaire des Artevelde*, p. 712;

Table 2.1 (*cont.*)

Gilles Meyfrot: TNA, E 101/340/23, m. 5d and *Cartulaire des Artevelde*, p. 711; William the Meyr: *CPMR*, vol. I, p. 248; *Letter Book G*, p. 250; *Memorials of London*, ed. Riley, p. 332 and *Cartulaire des Artevelde*, p. 716; Henry Navegher: *CPMR*, vol. II, pp. 65–6 and *Cartulaire des Artevelde*, p. 713; Levin Olivier: Consitt, *The London Weavers' Company*, pp. 188–91; *Letter Book G*, p. 48; *Cartulaire des Artevelde*, p. 716; John Pape: *CPMR*, vol. I, p. 248 and *Cartulaire des Artevelde*, p. 714; John Poules: *CPMR*, vol. II, p. 8 and *Cartulaire des Artevelde*, p. 713; Giles Ripegast: *CPMR*, vol. I, p. 248 and *Cartulaire des Artevelde*, p. 715; Arnold Skapkynkyl: *CPMR*, vol. II, p. 70 and *Cartulaire des Artevelde*, p. 712; John van Stene: *CPMR*, vol. II, p. 9 and *Cartulaire des Artevelde*, p. 711; John Tybes: *CPMR*, vol. I, p. 248 and *Cartulaire des Artevelde*, p. 711; Nijs van den Vyure: TNA, E 101/340/23, m. 5; *CPMR*, vol. II, p. 70 and *Cartulaire des Artevelde*, p. 712; James Westland: LMA, CLA/023/DW, roll 93, n. 19 and *Cartulaire des Artevelde*, p. 711; John van Wetere: *CPMR*, vol. II, p. 84; *Memorials of London*, ed. Riley, p. 332 and *Cartulaire des Artevelde*, p. 715; William van Aughten: *Memorials of London*, ed. Riley, p. 332 and *Cartulaire des Artevelde*, p. 709; Peter de Bakere: *CPMR*, vol. II, p. 6 and *Cartulaire des Artevelde*, p. 720; John Cockelar: LMA, CLA/023/DW, roll 93, n. 19 and SAB, Cartulary Groenenboek C, fo. 111r; SAB, Politieke charters 1e reeks, no. 495; John de Cranburgh: *Calendar of Letters from the Mayor and Corporation of the City of London*, p. 75 and SAB, Cartulary Groenenboek C, fo. 111r; SAB, Politieke charters 1e reeks, no. 495; John Gallyn: TNA, E 101/340/23, m. 1d and SAB, Cartulary Groenenboek C, fo. 111r; SAB, Politieke charters 1e reeks, no. 495; John de Gaunt, carpenter: *Letter Book G*, p. 117 and *Cartulaire des Artevelde*, p. 721; John de Gaunt, weaver: TNA, KB 27/386, m. 75 and SAB, Cartulary Groenenboek C, fo. 111r; SAB, Politieke charters 1e reeks, no. 495; Joceus Amelryk: *CPMR*, vol. II, p. 198 and SAB, Cartulary Groenenboek C, fo. 111r; SAB, Politieke charters 1e reeks, no. 495; Francis Fan Yabek: *CFR, 1356–68*, p. 193 and *Cartulaire des Artevelde*, p. 719; SAB, Cartulary Groenenboek C, fo. 112r; SAB, Politieke charters 1e reeks, no. 495; John de Langford: *Letter Book G*, p. 117; LMA, CLA/023/DW, roll 93, n. 19 and *Cartulaire des Artevelde*, p. 720; Jacob van Loo: TNA, E 101/340/23, m. 5d and *Cartulaire des Artevelde*, p. 720; SAB, Cartulary Groenenboek C, fo. 111r; SAB, Politieke charters 1e reeks, no. 495; John van Loo: *CPMR*, vol. II, pp. 65–6; Consitt, *The London Weavers' Company*, pp. 188–91 and *Cartulaire des Artevelde*, p. 720; SAB, Cartulary Groenenboek C, fo. 111r; SAB, Politieke charters 1e reeks, no. 495; Peter Medinhoe: *Calendar of Letters from the Mayor and Corporation of the City of London*, p. 19 and SAB, Politieke charters 1e reeks, no. 495; Peter More: *CPMR*, vol. II, p. 251 and *Inventaire Bruges*, vol. II, p. 114; Giles Onyng: *CPMR*, vol. II, p. 195 and SAB, Cartulary Groenenboek C, fo. 110 v; Politieke charters 1e reeks, no. 495; Peter de Pape: *CPMR*, vol. I, p. 248 and SAB, Politieke charters 1e reeks, no. 495; John Rossart: *CPMR*, vol. II, p. 67 and SAB, Cartulary Groenenboek C, fo. 111r; Politieke charters 1e reeks, no. 495; John ate Ryk: *CPMR*, vol. I, p. 248 and SAB, Cartulary Groenenboek C, fo. 113v; Paul Stolpart: *CPMR*, vol. II, p. 84 and SAB, Cartulary Groenenboek C, fo. 116r; Lamsin de Vos: LMA, CLA/023/DW, roll 93, n. 19 and *Cartulaire des Artevelde*, p. 720; SAB, Cartulary Groenenboek C, fo. 111r; SAB, Politieke charters 1e reeks, no. 495; Johan atte Werre: Consitt, *The London Weavers' Company*, pp. 188–91 and *Cartulaire des Artevelde*, p. 719; Lamsin Iperling: LMA, CLA/023/CP 76, m. 15 and SAB, Politieke charters 1e reeks, no. 495; John van Somerkyn: *CPMR*, vol. I, p. 248; Consitt,

Table 2.1 (*cont.*)

The London Weavers' Company, pp. 188–91 and *Cartulaire des Artevelde*, p. 719; SAB, Politieke charters 1e reeks, no. 495; Jacob van Ackere: *CPMR*, vol. II, p. 116; *Letter Book G*, p. 250 and *Cartulaire des Artevelde*, p. 732; John van Dorme: TNA, E 101/340/23, m. 5d; TNA, E 122/70/18, m. 1d and *Cartulaire des Artevelde*, p. 733; John Marchaunt: *Letter Book G*, pp. 48, 204 and *Cartulaire des Artevelde*, p. 734; John Velleyn: *Letter Book H*, p. 77 and *Cartulaire des Artevelde*, p. 733; Baldwin Giles: *CPMR*, vol. II, pp. 65–6 and *Cartulaire des Artevelde*, p. 731; Lambert Funderlynde: *Letter Book G*, p. 104 and *Cartulaire des Artevelde*, p. 730.

bailiff of Brabantine weavers, emigrated with his wife, Elizabeth, alias Lucebet.[9] Some of them, such as Nicholas van den Achere, in addition to his wife and two children, had a sister, whose child, John, was born in London.[10] Such evidence implies that the immigrants in London were followed not only by their close family, but by their relatives, too, as we will see in Chapter 3.

Upon their arrival, there are indications that they settled around the wards of Candlewick and Cheap, and areas around the River Thames, primarily inhabited by London drapers and weavers (Map 2).[11] John Eversword of Zealand owned a house at Candlewick Street. St Swithin's church, which was still in the same street up until it burned down in the Great Fire of London (1666), was the place where six Flemings chose in their wills to be buried, implying that they also lived in the vicinity.[12] Katherine the Dutchwoman lived in a house in Finch Lane, Cheap, while some Flemish women and men rented tenements in Thomas Gissors' properties in *Grenewiche* and Grantham Lanes, two streets near the River Thames separating Dowgate and Vintry Wards.[13] A dyer, Francis van Braban, leased a tenement in Thames Street for 100s a year.[14] Along the same street, Lamsin Iperling and his wife, Agnes, were

9 LMA, GLMS 9171/1, fo. 132.

10 LMA, GLMS 9171/1, fo. 97d.

11 For the parishes of settlement of London drapers in the fourteenth century, see E. Quinton, 'The drapers and the drapery trade of late medieval London, c. 1300–c. 1500', unpublished Ph.D. thesis, University of London (2001), pp. 25–6.

12 M. Fitch, *Index to Testamentary Records in the Commissary Court of London, Vol. I: 1374–1488* (London, 1969), p. 189: Herman van den Lynden, tailor in 1390, LMA, GLMS 9171/1, fo. 201, Roger van der Ofstede in 1375, *ibid.*, fo. 26v, Walter Paridane, in 1390, *ibid.*, fo. 218d and William van Reven in 1376, *ibid.*, fo. 26v; *CPMR*, vol. II, p. 209.

13 Misc roll DD n. 413, *London Assize of Nuisance 1301–1431: A Calendar*, ed. Helena M. Chew and William Kellaway (London, 1973), p. 413; *CPMR*, vol. III, pp. 31–5, amongst the tenants in Grantham Lane and Grenewhich Lane were: William van Hulst, Lucebet Frowe, Lawrence van Hulst and Giles van the Broke.

14 TNA, E 40/2547.

accused by Mathilda Baudry of intrusion into a house near All Hallows-by-the-Tower before the Court of Common Pleas of London in 1353.[15]

Even when we do not have any specific mention of the immigrants' place of residence, the information from some sources suggests that they were indeed clustered in the aforementioned areas. In 1362, Laurence Shearman, *Fleming*, accused two compatriots, John Mone and Peter Mone, of mayhem that happened in the Candlewick Ward of London. One evening, just before curfew, Laurence was ambushed by Peter and John near the parish of St Martin Orgar in Candlewick Street. John attacked him with a sword and cut off a finger from Laurence's right hand. He managed to escape, but the wounds were so bad that his hand stayed immobilised (which was probably fatal for his trade as well, since, given his anglicised surname, he might have been a shearer).[16] More generally, when immigrant weavers were granted the right to form two separate guilds, it was decided that the Flemings hold their meetings at St Lawrence Pounteney (Candlewick Street, modern-day Canon Street) and the Brabanters at St Mary Somerset (Thames Street).[17] Both examples imply that the majority of immigrant textile workers lived around these areas.

The evidence suggests that the immigrants from the Low Countries settled on the south side of London Bridge. Martha Carlin argued that Flemish immigration to Southwark was visible in both the fourteenth and fifteenth centuries.[18] Indeed, the surviving poll-tax returns show that there were at least thirty-three people with Flemish names there in 1381. They were mostly women with suggestive names such as Trude Frowe, or Bette Frowe, and were employed as spinsters or servants with hostelers and stewmongers, implying that some of them were active as prostitutes.[19] As we will see in Chapter 5, most immigrants from the Low Countries who appeared in the available sources were associated with stew-keeping. However, some leather and textile workers also seem to have found their way across London Bridge. A cordwainer, John Burgeys, had a servant called Gerkine, whose name suggests that he was from the Low Countries, while a dyer, Torinus Fleming, had all his cloths and other goods confiscated from his house in Southwark, where he was dwelling in 1375.[20]

Although evidence of admissions to the freedom of the city of London does not survive for this period, we know from other sources that at least

15 LMA, CLA/023/CP 76, m. 15.
16 TNA, KB 27/405, m. 17.
17 *Memorials of London*, ed. Riley, pp. 345–6.
18 Carlin, *Medieval Southwark*, pp. 157, 211, 222.
19 Fenwick, *Poll Taxes*, vol. II, p. 564. For more about prostitution in Southwark and elsewhere, see Chapter 5.
20 Fenwick, *Poll Taxes*, vol. II, p. 559; *CPR, 1374–7*, p. 150.

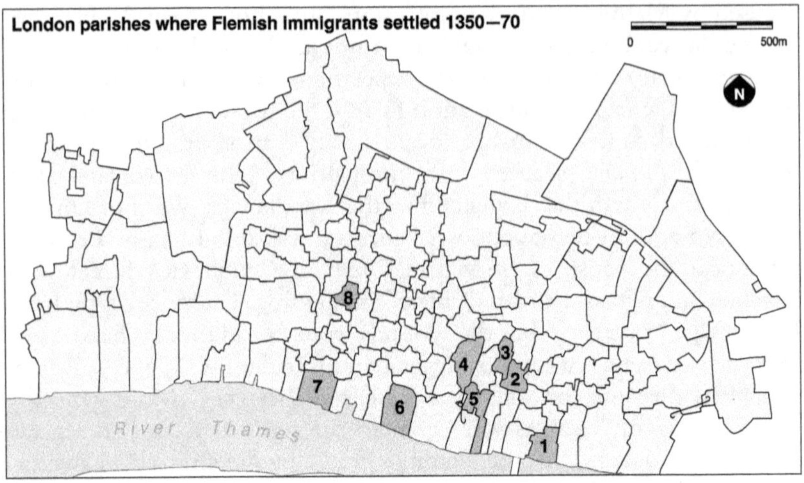

1 St Botolph's Billingsgate
2 St Clement Eastcheap
3 St Nicholas Acon
4 St Swithin, Candlewich Street
5 St Lawrence Pounteney, church where Flemish weavers held their meetings and employed journeymen.
6 St Martin Vintry, where Flemings were massacred during the Peasants' Revolt.
7 St Mary Somersete, church where Brabantine weavers held their meetings and employed journeymen.
8 St Matthew, Friday Street

Map 2 London parishes c. 1350–1400 (map made by Sarah Wroot)

five Flemings became citizens. For instance, John Kempe, from Ghent, Jacob van den Ackere, from Ypres, and John de Cranburg, from Bruges, all three of them banished in 1351, are recorded as citizens of London.[21] There is also evidence that a second generation of exiles stayed in London. Ralph Cloffhamer, the son of an exile, Henry Cloffhamer, from Ghent became a bailiff of Flemish weavers in 1375.[22] Even though there are some successful stories of integration, the reaction of London cloth-workers to the arrival of numerous artisans from overseas, as we will see later, was anything but welcoming. This sort of reception was probably due to the fact that the immigrants from the Low Countries were suddenly quite visible to the natives. While no textile worker from the Low Countries appears in the city's Letter Books and

[21] *CPMR*, vol. II, p. 116; *Calendar of Letters from the Mayor and Corporation of the City of London*, p. 75. Along with them, Copin Seland and John Ewersword were also mentioned as citizens of London.
[22] *Letter Book G*, p. 329.

memoranda rolls in the first half of the fourteenth century, the number of Flemish names in English sources grew drastically after the sentence of banishment was pronounced in 1351. That they were probably numerous enough is exemplified by the creation of their own guild separately from that of the weavers of London.[23] Even though Edward III's letter patent of 1352 gave Flemings the right to organise themselves into guilds and elect their bailiffs in any town in England where they settled, there is no evidence of them doing so elsewhere than in London. Nevertheless, having their own guild would be a major point of dispute with native weavers throughout the second half of the fourteenth century.

Many of the exiles in London had occupied key positions in Flanders during the years of the revolt. It is interesting that both fullers and weavers held important positions either within the guilds or in the city government prior to their exile. Levin Godhalse had served as an alderman of Ghent in 1348.[24] Giles Ripegast had been one of the city captains in Ghent,[25] John de Cranburgh held the same position in Bruges, while John van Langford was the *vinder* ('the man who finds a judgment') of the fullers' guild.[26] Lamsin de Vos was one of Bruges' most important weaver–drapers and had acted as dean of its weavers' guild in 1347.[27] Guild wardens, usually called the dean (*deken*) and the 'finders' (*vinders*), were responsible for punishing violations of their rules and privileges (*keuren*).[28] Exiles John Cockelar and Lamsin Iperling had sold large quantities of cloth and fabric for linings to the Bruges city government throughout the 1340s.[29] Unlike Colchester and Great Yarmouth, London attracted the top layer of Flanders' highly regarded textile industry. (See Table 2.2.)

[23] *CPR, 1350–4*, p. 232. A letter patent in 1352 effectively defined their legal position within the realm

[24] *De Rekeningen der stad Gent*, ed. De Pauw and Vuylsteke, vol. III, p. 273.

[25] Ripegast was one of the few who returned to Flanders after being pardoned in 1359. P. Rogghé, 'Gemeente ende Vrient: Nationale omwentelingen in de XIVde eeuw', *Annales de la Société d'Emulation de Bruges*, 89:3–4 (1952), 101–35, at 125.

[26] SAB, Stadsrekeningen 1343–4, fo. 56r.

[27] Like Ripegast, de Vos returned after 1359. Espinas and Pirenne, *Recueil*, vol. I:2, p. 576; Murray, *Bruges*, pp. 287, 292.

[28] P. Stabel, J. Puttevils, J. Dumolyn, B. Lambert, J. M. Murray and G. Dupont, 'Production, markets and socio-economic structures II: c. 1320–c. 1500', in Brown and Dumolyn, *Medieval Bruges*, p. 173.

[29] SAB, Stadsrekeningen, 1343–4, fos 56v, 58v, 61v; 1344–5, fos 58r, 63r; see also Chapter 4.

Table 2.2 *Positions in civic office and guilds held by the exiles before their arrival in England*[i]

Year	Exile (occupation)	Position held
1343	John de Cranburgh (weaver)	City captain Bruges
1343	Lievin Fisker (weaver)	Alderman Ghent
1345	Giles Ripegarst (weaver)[ii]	City captain Ghent
1347	Baldwyn Wymes (fuller)	*Vinder* guild of fullers Bruges
1347	John van Langheford (fuller)	*Vinder* guild of fullers Bruges
1347	John Balling (fuller)	*Vinder* guild of fullers Bruges
1347	Lamsin de Vos (weaver)	Dean of the weavers Bruges
1348	Lievin Godhalse (weaver)	Alderman Ghent

[i] John de Cranburgh: SAB, Stadsrekeningen 1343–4, fo. 56r; Lievin Fisker, Lievin Godhalse, Giles Ripegarst: *De Rekeningen der Stad Gent*, ed. De Pauw and Vuylsteke, vol. III, pp. 213–14, 273; Baldwyn Wymes, John van Langheford, John Balling: SAB, Charters ambachten, no. 1240; Lamsin de Vos: Espinas, Pirenne, *Recueil*, vol. I:2, p. 576.
[ii] Giles Ripegarst was also a bailiff of the guild of Flemish weavers in London in 1352, *Letter Book G*, p. 16.

Apart from the lists of banished people, the source material from Flanders before and after the rebellion (1341–61) can be used to trace the names of those who left voluntarily for London. Most weavers who do not figure on the lists of exiles, but who do appear in London, must have left Flanders because of the deteriorating conditions in the cloth industry caused by the revolt and the measures against the weavers introduced by the count in order to prevent further revolts, which have been discussed in Chapter 1.[30] In Ghent, the records covering these actions taken by comital and municipal authorities are detailed enough to allow us to engage in such an analysis. These include various measures imposed on weavers from 1349, such as heavy taxation, being held as hostages, or an obligation to take an oath never to rebel against the count. They all contain the names that we can compare with the records in London and establish the background for some of the Flemings who were economic migrants.

After the city of Ghent fell under comital control in December 1348, new aldermen were installed, and it seems that those aldermen who had served in the period of the Artevelde regime were immediately

[30] These included forbidding weavers from carrying weapons, assembling in groups publicly or changing occupation.

imprisoned or exiled.[31] In order to ensure the surrender of Ghent, Louis of Male demanded 150 ringleaders of the rebellion as hostages. They were to be sent to Oudenaarde to await the sentence of the count.[32] Some of them escaped to England even before they had been taken as hostages.[33] A contemporary, Giles Li Muisis, relates that these rebels saw no point in turning up before the authorities, as they were sure that they would be executed.[34] Most of the 150 hostages belonged to the elite of the weavers' guild, and some of them were hit with a heavy fine called a 'tax levied from the hostages'.[35] Among them figured Giles Ripegarst and John Bastard, as well as Lievin Godhalse, who all settled in England after 1351 and were involved in setting up the guild of Flemish weavers in London.[36]

We can assume that most of those who were taken as hostages fled to England. About two-thirds of the names that were listed as hostages of the count after the surrender of Ghent in 1349 were also offered a pardon in 1359. This implies that these 100 individuals were probably exiled in 1351. There is no evidence that the remaining fifty hostages were forced to leave Ghent, but some of their names match those that can be seen immediately afterwards in London amongst the Flemish exiles. For example, William Lanote and John Yonkere were taken as hostages, but do not appear amongst those who were pardoned in 1359.[37] Nevertheless, they acted as bailiffs of Flemish weavers in London throughout the 1360s and 1370s. Both individuals also brokered the ordinances of the Flemish weavers in London in 1366, together with William Le Maire, John Van Wettere and Henry Clofhamer, all three of whom both were hostages and received pardon.[38] Given the chronology, the general context of the revolt and the fact that all these people were weavers, we can conclude that it is highly likely that these were the same individuals in both the Flemish and English sources.

31 Rogghé, 'Gemeente ende Vrient', 123–4.

32 *Cartulaire historique et généalogique des Artevelde*, ed. De Pauw, pp. 133–7; *De Rekeningen der Stad Gent*, ed. De Pauw and Vuylsteke, vol. III, pp. 409–10.

33 *Ibid.*, pp. 134, 137. The count ordered that those who escaped should be replaced with other rebels.

34 *Recueil des chroniques de Flandre*, ed. J. J. De Smet (Brussels, 1837–65), vol. II, p. 287.

35 *De Rekeningen der Stad Gent*, ed. De Pauw and Vuylsteke, vol. III, pp. 349, 467–78: 'dit es ontfaen van den giselen'. See also *Cartulaire historique et généalogique des Artevelde*, ed. De Pauw, pp. 133–7.

36 *Letter Book G*, p. 16; Consitt, *The London Weavers' Company*, p. 188. They were involved as brokers of the approval of the ordinances in 1352. Giles Ripegarst was elected bailiff of the Flemish weavers' guild the same year.

37 *De Rekeningen der Stad Gent*, ed. De Pauw and Vuylsteke, pp. 472–8.

38 *Memorials of London*, ed. Riley, pp. 331–3; *Letter Book H*, p. 50.

Another measure imposed on the main culprits of the revolt was a 'loan' to the city of Ghent in 1349.[39] This loan, even if so named, seems to have been an involuntary one, and each rebel paid a different amount, ranging from 1s, paid by John Oudenard, up to £80 groot imposed on John Van Artevelde's wife. Contributions were taken from 278 people, and most of them were either amongst the hostages in 1349 or amongst the exiles in 1359. For example, the weavers John Pape and John Maas, who both appear as contributors to this loan in the city accounts, resided in London during the 1350s and 1360s, and they were also on the list of pardoned exiles in 1359.[40] On the other hand, Lievin van Ordyngham appears only in this list and twice in the English sources.[41] He paid the tallage for the export of wool in 1360 and also sold 74 ells of cloth of Paris and 3 ells of cloth of Hainaut to the Great Wardrobe in London.[42] The only time he appears in Ghent sources after the revolt of 1345–9 was in 1357, and it is specifically mentioned that he resides in England.[43]

At the same time, 290 weavers took an oath never to take up weapons against the count and the city authorities, a legal measure reflecting the same communal and corporatist logic as a collective banishment. If we compare their names with the 278 rebels who paid the loan to the city, almost all of them are a match. However, it is not clear when exactly the list of individuals who took oaths was compiled. There is no date on the original document; only on the dorse has someone added in a contemporary hand '1349' and also '1362'.[44] Both dates might be correct, but there is no way to determine the exact date. For his prosopographic study of Ghent weavers in the fourteenth century, Wout Saelens went with the assumption that these weavers took an oath after the return of the exiles in 1359 and new disturbances in Ghent at the beginning of the 1360s.[45] However, whether the document was made in 1349 or in 1362, both dates can fit the purpose of this study, as the names of those who took the

39 *De Rekeningen der Stad Gent*, ed. De Pauw and Vuylsteke, vol. III, pp. 335–44.

40 *Ibid.*, pp. 341, 344; *CPMR*, vol. I, p. 249; *CPMR*, vol. II, pp. 65–6; *Cartulaire historique et généalogique des Artevelde*, ed. De Pauw, p. 712.

41 *De Rekeningen der Stad Gent*, ed. De Pauw and Vuylsteke, p. 342.

42 TNA, E 122/70/14 and E 101/394/12. 43 SAG, 301/1, fo. 187.

44 RAG, Oorkonden van Vlaanderen, chronologisch supplement, no. 643; Espinas and Pirenne, *Recueil*, vol. I:2, pp. 505–10.

45 Wout Saelens, 'TQuadie van Gent', unpublished MA thesis (Ghent University, 2015): see especially his database for the weavers who figure in the list of hostages and in the list of oaths in the appendix. Even though we do not have direct evidence for any revolt in Ghent between 1359 and 1362, Saelens was probably more inclined to date this document to 1362, because the evidence suggests that some form of revolt happened in the city of Bruges during the same period. As discussed in Chapter 1, according to Groenenboek in Bruges, 218 individuals were banished from the city because they had participated in a revolt against the count and the city. It follows from this that if the disturbances happened in Bruges, probably the same happened in Ghent.

oaths match the names of Flemish weavers in London sources between the 1350s and 1370s. For example, a weaver, Lievin van Cockelar, took an oath never to rebel against the count, but from the beginning of the 1370s he alnaged vast amounts of rayed cloth in London.[46] The same can be said for John van Everyngham, who was even a bailiff of Flemish weavers in London.[47] It is perfectly possible that these two weavers took an oath either in 1349 or in 1362 and then moved to London for economic reasons. (See Table 2.3.)

Straightaway after the victory and the constitution of the new city government in Ghent, direct taxes on the weavers called *weversgeld* and *weversleercnapgeld* were reintroduced. A weekly tax of 12 mites, or half a penny on the groot, and £12 *Parisis* yearly for each apprentice was first imposed on the weavers between 1326 and 1333 by the *poorters*-led regime. It was reintroduced in 1349 and levied until the return of weavers into the city government in 1359. Unfortunately, the names of those who paid the *weversgeld* do not survive, but the city accounts of Ghent do provide particulars for the *weversleercnapgeld* for the years 1351–4 and 1357. The latter contains the names of masters and apprentices, as well as the parishes where the tax was levied. The continuity from 1351 until 1354 allows us to compare the names with the list of oaths and the list of pardons in 1359, and with the names of Flemings traced in English sources, and establish their status prior to their arrival in England. Giles van Molle was one of the masters who paid the *weversleercnapgeld* for his apprentice, Clais van over de Beke, in 1351 but operated his business in Colchester at least from 1360, when he appears for the first time in the borough court with his wife, Marieta.[48]

As can be seen from Table 2.3 there are thirty-one weavers in English sources who do not appear on the list of exiles, but whose names match the weavers in Flemish sources related to the events of the rebellion years 1345–9. What is more, these individuals do not appear in the sources for Ghent during the 1350s and 60s.[49] This implies that the conditions

[46] TNA, E 101/340/22, m. 3, E 101/340/23, m. 5; Espinas and Pirenne, *Recueil*, vol. I:2, p. 507.

[47] Espinas and Pirenne, *Recueil*, vol. I:2, p. 507; *Letter Book G*, p. 250; TNA E 101/340/23, m. 5d.

[48] Espinas and Pirenne, *Recueil*, vol. I:2, p. 454; Benham, *Court Rolls*, vol. II, pp. 121, 224, and *Court Rolls*, vol. IV, p. 176.

[49] SAG, 301 and 330. In order to reinforce my argument, I went through the annual registers of the aldermen and the Ghent city accounts for the twenty-year period, and those that appear in London are missing from these sources in Ghent. Apart from the case of Lievin van Ordyngham, only in one other case are the exiles from London mentioned. This was the case of John van Wettre in 1361, but, as in the case of Lievin van Ordyngham, it is specifically mentioned that he is in London: SAG, 301/1, fo. 64r. For the context of the case, see this chapter and the part on exiles in London.

Table 2.3 *Flemings who left voluntarily traced from the sources linked with the rebellion*[i]

London sources	Bruges and Ghent sources
Peter Basseveld	Pieter van Bassevelde, from Bruges
Peter Boye	Pieter Boye, from Ghent
Giles van Brele	Gillis van Briele, from Ghent
John Brest	Jan Brest, from Ghent
John Canyngham	Jan van Caeneghem, from Ghent
Lewyn Cokelar	Lievin, Kokelere, from Ghent
William Dotter	Willem Dotter, from Ghent
Giles van Eke	Gillis van Eke, from Ghent
John van Everyngham	Jan van Evergheem, from Ghent
Henry Halling	Heine Hallinc, from Ghent
John Jaghere	Jan de Jaghere, from Ghent
William Jaghere	Willem de Jaghere, from Ghent
William Lanote	Willem Lenoetz, from Ghent
John van Lethe	Jan van Lede, from Bruges
John Marlebeke	Jan van Marlebeke, from Ghent
John Meinfrot	Jan Meinfrot, from Ghent
Giles van Molle	Gillis van Molle, from Ghent
Giles Motard	Gillis Muetard, from Bruges
Levyn van Ordingham	Lievin van Oerdegheem, from Ghent
John Oudenard	Jan Oudenard, from Ghent
William Paw	William de Paeu, from Ghent
John Rasyngham	Jan de Raseghem, from Ghent
Giles Robyn	Gillis Ruebin, from Bruges
John atte Ryk	Jan Rijx, from Bruges
Lewyn Singheem	Lievin van Sigheem, from Ghent
Clais Scotelare	Clais Scotelare, from Bruges
Matthew Stulpard	Mathijs Stulpaert, from Ghent
Peter Walraven	Pieter Walraven, from Ghent
Peter Wattre	Pieter Watere, from Ghent
William Wettre	Willem van Wettre, from Ghent
John Yonkere	Jan die Jonghere, from Ghent

[i] Peter Basseveld: LMA, CLA/023/CP 76, m. 15 and SAB, Stadsrekeningen 1343–4, fols 56v, 58v, 61v; 1344–5, fols 58r, 63r; Peter Boye: TNA, E 101/340/23, m. 5 and Espinas, Pirenne, *Recueil*, vol. I:2, p. 458, Giles van Brele: TNA, E 101/340/23, m. 5d and Espinas, Pirenne, *Recueil*, vol. I:2, p. 507; John Brest: TNA, E 122/70/18, m. 5 and Espinas, Pirenne, *Recueil*, vol. I:2, p. 468; Lewyn Cokelar: TNA, E 101/340/22, m. 3, E 101/340/23, m. 5 and Espinas, Pirenne, *Recueil*, vol. I:2, p. 507; William Dotter: TNA, E 122/70/18, m. 1d and Espinas, Pirenne, *Recueil*, vol. I:2, p. 460; Giles van Eke: TNA, E 101/340/23, m. 5 and Espinas, Pirenne, *Recueil*, vol. I:2, p. 507; John van Everyngham: *Letter Book G*, p. 250 and Espinas, Pirenne, *Recueil*, vol. I:2, p. 508; TNA, E 101/340/23, m. 5d and Espinas, Pirenne, *Recueil*, vol. I:2, p. 507; Henry Halling: TNA, E 122/70/18, m. 9 and *Cartulaire des Artevelde*, p. 135; John Jaghere: TNA, E 122/70/18, m. 1 and

Table 2.3 (*cont.*)

Espinas, Pirenne, *Recueil*, vol. I:2, p. 507; William Jaghere: TNA, E 101/340/23, m. 5 and Espinas, Pirenne, *Recueil*, vol. I:2, p. 507; William Lanote: *Memorials of London*, ed. Riley, p. 332 and Espinas, Pirenne, *Recueil*, vol. I:2, p. 507; John van Lethe: *CPMR*, vol. I, p. 248 and Espinas, Pirenne, *Recueil*, vol. I:2, p. 507; John Marlebeke: TNA, E 101/340/23, m. 5 and Espinas, Pirenne, *Recueil*, vol. I:2, p. 507; John Meinfrot: TNA E 101/340/23, m. 5d and Espinas, Pirenne, *Recueil*, vol. I:2, p. 507; Giles van Molle: Benham, *Court Rolls*, vol. II, pp. 121, 224; Benham, *Court Rolls*, vol. IV, p. 176 and Espinas, Pirenne, *Recueil*, vol. I:2, p. 456; Giles Motard: *CPMR*, vol. II, p. 248 and J. F. Verbruggen, *Het gemeenteleger*, p. 112; Levyn van Ordingham: TNA, E 101/394/12, E 101/392/3, m. 2 and *De Rekeningen der Stad Gent*, ed. De Pauw and Vuylsteke, p. 342; SAG, 301/1, fo. 187; John Oudenard: Benham, *Court Rolls*, vol. III, p. 132 and Espinas, Pirenne, *Recueil*, vol. I:2, p. 470; William Paw: Benham, *Court Rolls*, vol. II, pp. 200–1 and Espinas, Pirenne, *Recueil*, vol. I:2, pp. 457, 466; John Rasyngham: TNA, E 101/340/23, m. 5 and Espinas, Pirenne, *Recueil*, vol. I:2, p. 505; Giles Robyn: *CPMR*, vol. I, p. 248 and J. F. Verbruggen, *Het gemeenteleger*, p. 115; John atte Ryk: *CPMR*, vol. I, p. 248 and J. F. Verbruggen, *Het gemeenteleger*, p. 115; Lewyn Singheem: TNA, E 101/340/23, m. 5 and Espinas, Pirenne, *Recueil*, vol. I:2, p. 509; Clais Scotelare: LMA, CLA/023/CP 76, m. 15 and SAB, Stadsrekeningen 1343–4, fols 56v, 58v, 61v; 1344–5, fols 58r, 63r; Matthew Stulpard: TNA, E 122/70/18, m. 2d and *Gentsche Stads- en Baljuwsrekeningen 1351–1364*, ed. A. van Werveke and H. van Werveke (Brussels, 1970), p. 20; Peter Walraven: TNA, E 122/70/18, m. 2d and Espinas, Pirenne, *Recueil*, vol. I:2, p. 469; William Wettre: TNA, E 122/70/18, m. 9 and *Cartulaire des Artevelde*, p. 135; John Yonkere: *Memorials of London*, ed. Riley, p. 332 and Espinas, Pirenne, *Recueil*, vol. I:2, p. 507.

imposed on weavers after the revolt outlined above were certainly the push factor. Moreover, a deep decline in the cloth industry's output, especially after 1360,[50] and of the number of weavers in Ghent,[51] suggests that the exiles were not the only textile workers who emigrated to England. Everything indicates that these weavers from Ghent are quite likely to have left for both political and economic reasons and permanently settled in London without having any possible return in mind. As we will see later, even the surviving wills of the immigrants from the Low Countries in London show that they wanted to be buried in the city and only made bequests to its parishes, suggesting that no return was worth considering. Moreover, the demand for the types of cloth they produced was high in the English capital, and in addition the franchises and protection from Edward III they enjoyed gave them much better conditions in which to exercise their trade than in Ghent during the second half of the fourteenth century.

[50] Nicholas, *The Metamorphosis*, pp. 24–40. [51] *Ibid.*, pp. 135–77.

FLEMINGS IN COLCHESTER AND ITS HINTERLANDS IN ESSEX AND SUFFOLK

Shortly after the Flemish sentence of 1351 was issued, the rolls of the lawhundred court and the court of pleas of the Essex town of Colchester reveal a significant increase in the number of people from the Low Countries who entered into private litigation. Over the next thirty-two years, 298 litigants with Dutch names were recorded, whereas, in the preceding forty years, not a single one had been. All of them were resident in the town, and most were active in the textile sector, either as artisans or as small entrepreneurs. Borough court records preserved for only fifteen of the forty-one years between 1345–6 and 1384–5 still allow one to discern an obvious trend.[52] In August and September 1352, the first three visitors from across the North Sea since the start of the rolls' survival in 1310 made their appearance (3.2 per cent of the total cases that year in both the lawhundred court and the court of pleas). During the year 1353–4, already 24 out of a total of 127 cases (18.9 per cent) involved litigants from the Low Countries. In 1356–7, the number drops to 12 out of 129 (9.3 per cent). In 1359–60 the court dealt with them in 36 of 286 cases (12.6 per cent). The roll for 1360–1 has only been preserved fragmentarily but still contains 131 cases, 21 of which refer to people from the Low Countries (16 per cent). In 1366–7, they appear in 36 of 387 cases (or 7.5 per cent) (see Figure 2.1). Their number of appearances reached a peak, 20 per cent of all pleas, in 1371–2, only to see a sharp drop to 8 per cent a year later. In 1376–7 the appearance of individuals with Dutch names in Colchester borough court began to recover and then levelled off throughout the 1380s. These trends indicate that there was a steady inflow of new immigrants and that their numbers probably remained the same throughout the whole of the second half of the fourteenth century. This can also be confirmed by the number of people from the Low Countries who took up residence in Colchester over the course of the second half of the fourteenth century. Between 1352 and 1367, there were 126 individuals with Dutch names who pleaded in the borough court, while 172 new arrivals did so over the next seventeen years.

The immigrants from the Low Countries opposed each other in court just as much as they did Englishmen during the first years after their arrival, most frequently in disputes concerning assault or trespass. An exile from Ghent, Clais Segher, along with Simon de Vos from Bruges led an investigation whereby they found John Camber, an exile from

[52] ERO, D/B 5, CR9, mm. 7, 8, 8d, calendared in Benham, *Court Rolls*, vol. I, pp. 230–7. For the preservation of the borough court rolls, see Britnell, 'Colchester courts and court records', 133–40.

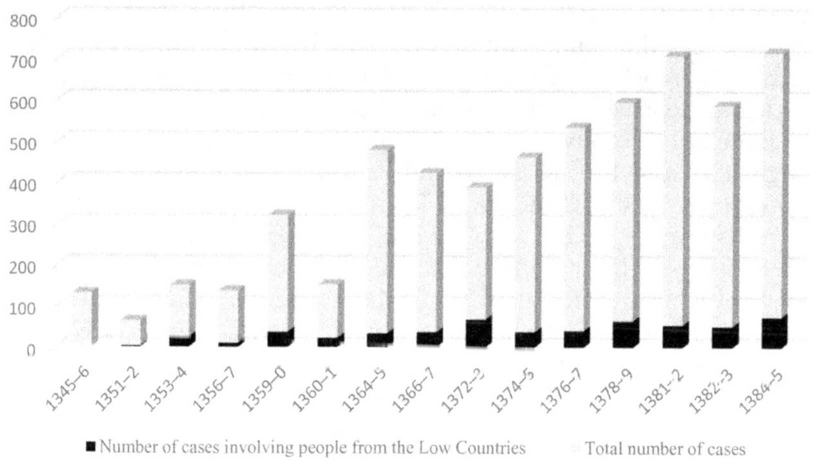

Figure 2.1 Number of cases involving people from the Low Countries compared with the total number of cases before the Colchester borough courts between 1345 and 1385.

Diksmuide, guilty of owing 60s to John van Neke.[53] During the same session of the court, Clais acted as a plaintiff against another exile from Ghent, Lievin Cornelis, but also found himself accused of assaulting Clais Bever and Tyryn Brewer.[54] In 1361, John Camber appears again, when he was summoned by Walter Baker, a weaver from Ghent, for unspecified debts.[55] A series of the aforementioned pleas suggest that at their arrival Flemish exiles manifested themselves as a group with strong prior relationships and, occasionally, animosities. As the town's economy grew towards the end of the 1350s, pleas of an economic nature overtook those for physical aggression, and the Flemings became slightly more involved in litigation with the English than with other immigrants. Hanin Heyne, for example, appeared in court after a dispute had arisen over the sale of wool and a washing bowl with native Colcestrian Richard Bysouthen in 1360.[56] We do not know the outcome of this specific plea, but cases like this, involving Flemings and natives, become more prevalent from the 1360s, as the immigrant community became more integrated into the economic life of the town.

Of the 298 persons from the Low Countries, 35 can be identified with absolute certainty as Flemings exiled in 1351 or pardoned in 1359 and

[53] ERO, D/B 5, CR 10, m. 1, calendared in Benham, *Court Rolls*, vol. II, p. 27. [54] *Ibid.*
[55] ERO, D/B 5, CR 13, m. 14, calendared in Benham, *Court Rolls*, vol. II, p. 132.
[56] ERO, D/B 5, CR 12, m. 18, calendared in Benham, *Court Rolls*, vol. II, p. 121.

again banished in 1361 (see Table 2.4). Most of them, thirteen, came from Ghent, the county's most populous city, which played a leading part in the rebellion of the 1330s and 1340s and was most severely hit during the repression in its aftermath. The abbey village of Saint Bavo, in its immediate vicinity, furnished another three litigants. Eleven exiles originated from Bruges, the second largest city of Flanders, while the secondary towns of Oudenaarde, Diksmuide, Nieuwpoort and Bailleul were responsible for the remaining eleven.[57] Bearing in mind this only refers to those who appeared before the town's borough court during the years for which records survive and who were recorded under the same name as they were on the lists of banishment, the real number of Flemish exiles in 1350s Colchester must have been higher.

The same goes for a rough estimate of their total number. We have seen that 126 immigrants appeared in court during 1351–67 and another 172 over the next 16 years. As some of the immigrants might have returned or passed away at some point during this thirty-two-year span of survival of the court rolls, using only the initial period (1351–67) in order to provide a rough estimate of their total number might be more cautious. Some of the 126 Flemings appeared with their wives and children on the lists of exiles, suggesting that they were followed by their families.[58] In Colchester, the cases of Gerard, Lievin and John van der Heide show that this trend was reflected in the court rolls as well.[59] On numerous occasions too, Flemish immigrants like Giles Berempoot from Bruges or Walter Baker, *Flemyng*, from Ghent appeared in borough courts together with their wives.[60] Knowing that an average Flemish household in this period consisted of four to five people, and taking into account that the 126 identified were only those who pleaded in the borough courts, the total number of immigrants from the Low Countries could have been as high as 300.[61] They might not have matched the Dutch refugees of the 1580s, who were responsible for more than 20 per cent of the inhabitants of the Essex town, but Flemish and Brabantine textile workers and their families might have made up up to 10 per cent of the population of 1350s Colchester, which never exceeded 3,000 people.[62]

57 For these towns' position in the Flemish urban network, see P. Stabel, *Dwarfs among Giants: The Flemish Urban Network in the Late Middle Ages* (Louvain, 1997), passim.

58 See Chapter 1. 59 *Cartulaire historique et généalogique des Artevelde*, ed. De Pauw, pp. 718, 725.

60 TNA, JUST 2/33A, m. 7; ERO, D/B 5, CR 11, m. 1, calendared in Benham, *Court Rolls*, vol. II, p. 68.

61 W. Prevenier, 'La Démographie des villes du comté de Flandres', *Revue du Nord*, 45 (1983), 255–76, at 256; R. Mols, *Introduction à la démographie historique des villes d'Europe du XIVe au XVIIe siècles*, 3 vols. (Louvain, 1954–6), vol. II, pp. 100–30.

62 Britnell, *Growth and Decline*, p. 49; N. Goose, 'The Dutch in Colchester in the 16th and 17th centuries: Opposition and integration', in R. Vigne and C. Littleton (eds), *From Strangers to Citizens: The Integration of Immigrant Communities in Britain, Ireland and Colonial America, 1550–1750* (Brighton, 2001), pp. 88–9.

Table 2.4 *Names of Flemings appearing both in the Colchester borough court rolls between 1351 and 1367 and on the lists of exiles of 1351 and those pardoned in 1359*[i]

Court rolls	Lists of exiles and pardons
Leuin Backener	Lievin Backere, from Ghent
Walter le Baker, 'outre Flemyng'	Wouter le Backere, from Ghent
William de Breggis, 'Flemyng'	Willem de Brugghe, from Ghent
Lievin Cornelis	Lievin Cornelis, from Ghent
Hanyn Derex	Hannin Diederix, from Ghent
John van Neke	Jan van Eke, weaver, from Ghent
Henry Everard	Heinric Everard's wife, from Ghent
Lewyn Hadican	Lievin Haenkin, from Ghent
Lievin Hortowe	Lievin Hertoghe, from Ghent
John Raven	Jan de Raven, from Ghent
Simon Sporeman	Moenin Sporeman, from Ghent
John Synay	Jan van Synay, from Ghent
John fan loo	Jan van Loo, weaver, from Ghent
Boudin Adam	Boudin Adaem, from Bruges
John Ballyng	Jan Balling, fuller, from Bruges
Giles Berempoot	Gillis Berempoet, weaver, from Bruges
Heyne van Cortrik	Hanin van Courtrike, weaver, from Bruges
John Goodenote	Jan Goedghenoot, weaver, from Bruges
Cent Kempe	Cent Kempe, from Bruges
James Pappe	Coppin Pappe, weaver, from Bruges
John Passelyn	Jan Pacelin, weaver, from Bruges
Peter van Tyelt	Pierres de Tielte, weaver, from Bruges
Simon de Vos	Moenin de Vos, from Bruges[ii]
John van Wynd	Jan van Vinct, *poorter*, from Bruges
John Barat, *Flemyng*	Jan Baraet, from Oudenaarde
John Hodmaker	Jan Hoedmakere, from Oudenaarde
Arnald Roufot	Arnout Roevoet, from Oudenaarde
Jacob Marcolf	Jacop Marcolf, from Oudenaarde
Lievin van the Hede	Wouter van der Heide, from Saint Bavo Lievin, his son
John van the Hede	Jan, his son
Gerard van the Hede	Gherard, his son
John Cambere	Jan de Cammere, from Diksmuide
Copin Stuk	Copin Stucke, from Diksmuide
William Bollard	Willem Bollaert, from Bailleul
John Clerc, *Fleming*	Jan de Clerc, from Nieuwpoort

[i] Leuin Backener: ERO, D/B 5, CR 13, m. 3, calendared in Benham, *Court Rolls*, vol. II, p. 132 and *Cartulaire des Artevelde*, p. 714; Walter le Backer: ERO, D/B 5, CR 13, m. 3, calendared in Benham, *Court Rolls*, vol. II, p. 132 and *Cartulaire des Artevelde*, p. 714; John Ballyng: ERO, D/B 5, CR 15, m. 2, calendared in Benham, *Court Rolls*, vol. II, pp. 186–7 and *Cartulaire des Artevelde*, p. 720; John Barat, *Flemyng*: ERO, D/B 5, CR 14,

Table 2.4 (*cont.*)

m. 5d, calendared in Benham, *Court Rolls*, vol. II, p. 155 and *Cartulaire des Artevelde*, p. 726; Giles Berempoot: TNA, JUST 2/33A, m. 7 and SAB, Cartulary Groenenboek C, fo. 114r; William Bollard: ERO, D/B 5, CR 15, m. 5d, calendared in Benham, *Court Rolls*, vol. II, p. 226 and *Cartulaire des Artevelde*, p. 731; William de Breggis, *Flemyng*: ERO, D/B 5, CR 13, m. 5, calendared in Benham, *Court Rolls*, vol. II, p. 138 and *Cartulaire des Artevelde*, p. 716: John Camber: ERO, D/B 5, CR 13, m. 3, calendared in Benham, *Court Rolls*, vol. II, p. 132 and *Cartulaire des Artevelde*, p. 729; Levin Cornelis: ERO, D/B 5, CR 10, m. 11d, calendared in Benham, *Court Rolls*, vol. II, p. 26 and *Cartulaire des Artevelde*, p. 714; Heyne Cortrik: ERO, D/B 5, CR 12, m. 17d, calendared in Benham, *Court Rolls*, vol. II, p. 121 and *Cartulaire des Artevelde*, p. 719; Hanyn Derex: ERO, D/B 5, CR 14, m. 3d, calendared in Benham, *Court Rolls*, vol. II, p. 152 and *Cartulaire des Artevelde*, p. 714; John Goodnote: calendared in Benham, *Court Rolls*, vol. II, pp. 85–6 and SAB, Cartulary Groenenboek C, fo. 115r; Levyn Hadican: ERO, D/B 5, CR 12, m. 11d, calendared in Benham, *Court Rolls*, vol. II, p. 101 and *Cartulaire des Artevelde*, p. 715; Wouter van der Heide, Lievin, Gerard and Jan his sons: ERO, D/B 5, CR 12, m. 13d, calendared in Benham, *Court Rolls*, vol. II, p. 115 and *Cartulaire des Artevelde*, p. 718; Lievin Hortowe: ERO, D/B 5, CR 10, m. 11, calendared in Benham, *Court Rolls*, vol. II, p. 25 and *Cartulaire des Artevelde*, p. 713 John Hodmaker: ERO, D/B 5, CR 13, m. 4, calendared in Benham, *Court Rolls*, vol. II, p. 138 and *Cartulaire des Artevelde*, p. 725; Cent Kempe: ERO, D/B 5, CR 16, m. 14d, calendared in Benham, *Court Rolls*, III, p. 140 and SAB, Cartulary Groenenboek C, fo. 115r; John van Loo: ERO, D/B 5, CR 10, m. 2d, calendared in Benham, *Court Rolls*, vol. II, p. 7 and *Cartulaire des Artevelde*, p. 712; Jacob Marcolf: ERO, D/B 5, CR 16, m. 14d, calendared in Benham, *Court Rolls*, III, p. 140 and *Cartulaire des Artevelde*, p. 718; John van Neke: ERO, D/B 5, CR 10, m. 2d, and *Cartulaire des Artevelde*, p. 716; James Pappe: ERO, D/B 5, CR 19, m. 8, calendared in Benham, *Court Rolls*, vol. III, p. 176 and SAB, Cartulary Groenenboek C, fo. 115r; John Passelyn: ERO, D/B 5, CR 14, m. 10d, calendared in Benham, *Court Rolls*, vol. II, p. 164 and SAB, Cartulary Groenenboek C, fo. 115r; Arnold Roufot: ERO, D/B 5, CR 13, m. 4, calendared in Benham, *Court Rolls*, vol. II, p. 138 and *Cartulaire des Artevelde*, p. 725; Simon Sporeman: ERO, D/B 5, CR 11, m. 1, calendared in Benham, *Court Rolls*, vol. II, p. 68 and *Cartulaire des Artevelde*, p. 713; Copin Stuk: ERO, D/B 5, CR 10, m. 10, and *Cartulaire des Artevelde*, p. 729; John Synay: ERO, D/B 5, CR 10, m. 2d, calendared in Benham, *Court Rolls*, vol. II, p. 7 and *Cartulaire des Artevelde*, p. 716; Peter Thylte: TNA, JUST 2/33A m. 7 and SAB, Cartulary Groenenboek C, fo. 114v; Simon de Vos: ERO, D/B 5, CR 10, m. 11d, calendared in Benham, *Court Rolls*, vol. II, p. 26 and SAB, Politieke charters 1e reeks, no. 495; John van Wynd: ERO, D/B 5, CR 10, m. 8, calendared in Benham, *Court Rolls*, vol. II, p. 18 and *Cartulaire des Artevelde*, p. 719.

[ii] In Middle Dutch, Moenin is a diminutive for Simon. Debrabandere, *Verklarend Woordenboek van de Familienamen in België en Noord-Frankrijk*, 2 vols. (Brussels, 1992), vol. II, p. 992.

With a lack of testamentary evidence for Colchester, it is more difficult to reconstruct in which part of town the Flemish newcomers settled. None of them figures in the very few surviving leases and deeds of the town.[63] Only very occasionally are names of streets mentioned in pleadings – for instance, Copin Christian was charged for breaking into the house of James (alias Copin) van Mershe in Lodderslane (modern-day Abbeygate Street) and carrying away 6s.[64] In 1380, Copin van Brugges accused John Porter of withdrawal from service and breaking the covenant to work for him in the art of winding (transferring yarn onto bobbins, ready for weaving) for one year in East Street.[65] On six other occasions textile workers from the Low Countries were associated with East Street. This location is mentioned by the scribes either as a place in cases for debt where the litigants made transactions or where they were involved in violence.[66] This might have been the neighbourhood in which the highest concentration of both native and immigrant textile workers lived and worked. Some immigrants seem to have rented houses to other newcomers. In 1374, a Flemish weaver, John Barremakere, sued John de Ipre for debt regarding the unpaid rent.[67] Unfortunately, the location of this residence is not mentioned. Most of the Flemish exiles acted no differently from the other townsmen and shared premises with both natives and foreigners.[68] Other Flemings lodged with natives; for instance, when John Quarham was fined for being a 'Flemish malefactor', he was said to be living with John Busch. Another mention to this effect is an unnamed Flemish woman living with Alice Hall.[69] In several cases, the Flemings in Colchester were involved in affrays that occurred in somebody's house, but it is not clear whether they lived there, or

[63] ERO, D/B 5 R1, fos 42–56, edited in *The Oath Book or Red Parchment Book of Colchester*, ed. W. G. Benham (Colchester, 1907), pp. 59–74.

[64] Benham, *Court Rolls*, vol. III, p. 84.

[65] ERO, D/B 5, CR 20, m. 5.

[66] ERO, D/B 5, CR 21, mm. 9, 48; ERO, D/B 5, CR 22, mm. 5, 5d, 7d, 8; ERO, D/B 5, CR 25, m. 28. On one occasion Copin van Mersh accused Margaret Mons of owing him 3s 4d, for which she became his debtor in the house of John Cok in East Street, but a few years later, together with his wife, Copin was accused of owing 18d to Thomas Kentish for wool bought in East Street. James Pappe was also accused of owing 40d to John Rodebright junior, which he lent in East Street in order to pay this amount to John Note. Finally, several other Flemings were involved in violence around the same areas. Katherine Schefford was charged with violent assault on John Nel, *Braban*, in Stephen Baron's house located in the same street. The same year, John Nel, *Braban*, Isabelle Van Tene and Margaret Comberton were fined for assaults on Nigel Braban, two unnamed Flemings and Alice Mountfort.

[67] ERO, D/B 5, CR 17, m. 14, calendared in Benham, *Court Rolls*, vol. III, p. 67.

[68] Britnell, *Growth and Decline*, pp. 10–11.

[69] ERO, D/B 5, CR 12, m. 7d; CR 13, m. 14, calendared in Benham, *Court Rolls*, vol. II, pp. 76, 136.

whether it was where they held informal gatherings.[70] The little evidence there is suggests a concentration of Flemish presence near Hythe, also a centre of the textile trade since the 1330s (see Map 3).[71] Over a hundred years later, in the 1450s, it was still the main port of call for immigrants from the Low Countries, now engaged in beer-brewing.[72]

The extant poll-tax return does not help either in determining whether the immigrants clustered around one particular area of the town or not. This is because of the way in which the subsidy was compiled. Although the 1377 assessment was probably made by individuals appointed to go from parish to parish, it was unfortunately not recorded in that manner. More generally, we are unable to use this source to expand on the immigrants' profile, as the return does not add much to the information about their experiences that can be observed in a variety of other sources. The return for Colchester is basically a list with the names of 2,955 individuals who paid the tax. It contains no details about the rate according to which they were assessed, or about the taxpayers' occupations. In some instances, it also fails to name spouses and servants, these being listed simply as wives or servants. The assessment of 1377 allows us only to show that some Flemings who lived in Colchester had not managed to evade payment. Moreover, we can recognise only 89 immigrants who had paid the tax out of 298 who appear in the borough court. Anglicisation or omission of names, as well as evasion, might be just some of the reasons for this. For example, Reginald van Trude, Hanyn van Myre and Cent Kampe can be identified in both the poll-tax list and the court rolls.[73] Some other immigrants from the Low Countries, like James Pappe, Paul Barremaker or Copin van Mersh, pleaded regularly in the borough court (i.e. they appear in all the surviving rolls between 1360 and 1385), but were not included in the poll-tax assessment.

What could have driven at least 298 immigrants from the Low Countries to Colchester, an English provincial town with fewer than 3,000 inhabitants? There is no direct proof that the government took a role in directing the new arrivals from the Low Countries to specific locations, as it did in the case of protestant refugees in the sixteenth century, despite the fact that the crown's invitation to Flemish exiles may have attracted a lot more individuals than previously

[70] Peter Vanholt was accused of violent assault on Gilbert Clogmaker in William Strenger's house, while Outre Camber and Arnold Fleming caused an affray by drawing knives in Richard Baker's house. Benham, *Court Rolls*, vol. IV, pp. 40, 152.

[71] Britnell, *Growth and Decline*, pp. 72–3. [72] *Ibid.*, pp. 196–7.

[73] Fenwick, *Poll Taxes*, vol. I, pp. 197, 201.

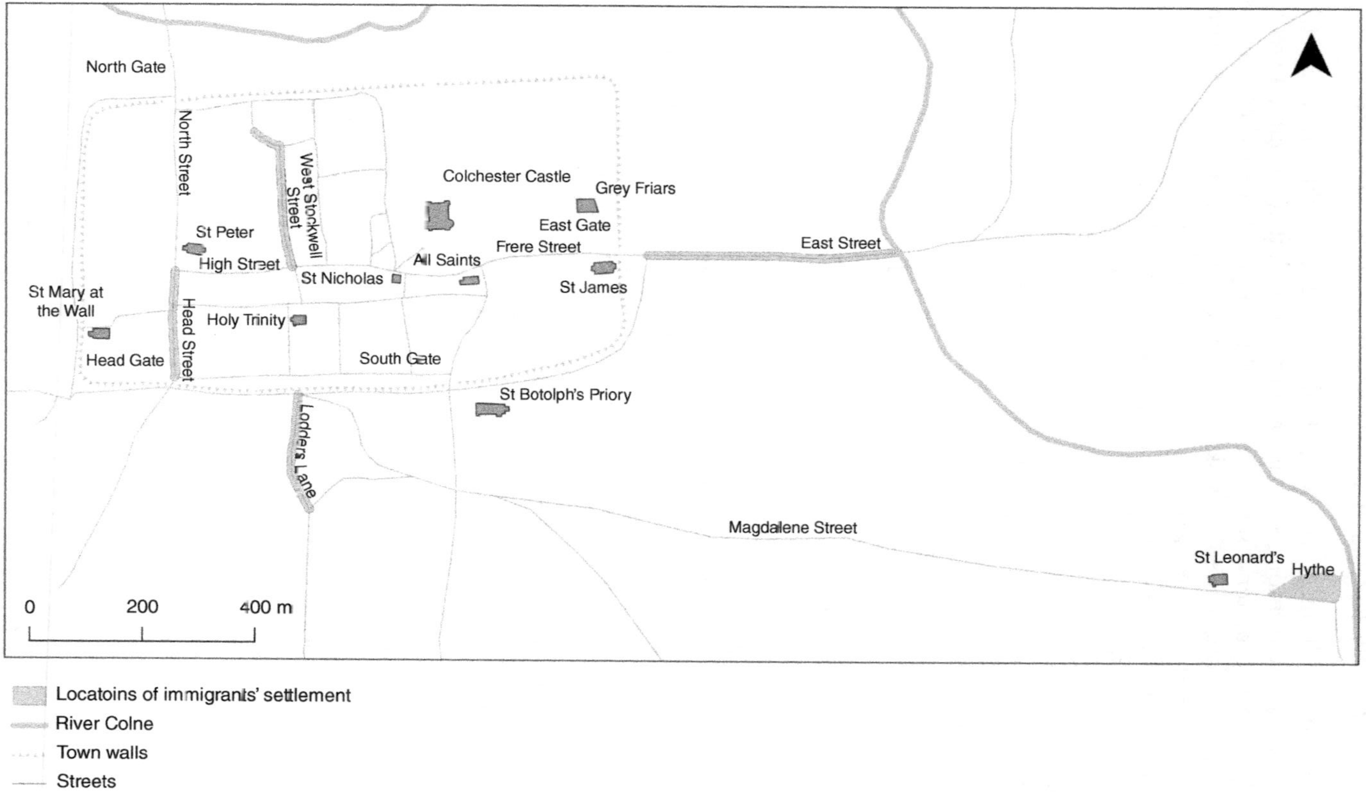

Map 3 Colchester c. 1300–1400 (map made by Davor Salihovic)

believed.[74] Nothing confirms Fuller's assertion that Edward III 'bestowed them through all the parts of the land, that clothing thereby might be the better dispersed'.[75] Neither do we have indications of attempts to attract the highly skilled visitors on a local level. The main reason for Flemish artisans to settle in Colchester would have been its position on the east coast, close to Ipswich, a major sea port with strong trade links with Flanders,[76] as well as the proximity of London.

Although Colchester fulfilled most of the basic needs for the development of cloth manufacture (supply of wool, proximity of London and other ports, fulling mills), the town seems to have followed the national trend at the dawn of the fourteenth century and seen its industry decline. The nature and quantity of litigation in its court rolls over the period 1310–45 suggest that the number of textile workers in the town was negligible. This situation appears to have been the case even during the 1330s and 1340s, as Colchester had no textile industry of its own worthy of the name before the Black Death.[77] For newly arrived skilled clothworkers, this lack of competition must have been most welcome. In contrast to Flanders or even London in the 1350s, where local manufactures were zealously protected by the weavers' guild, Colchester had no occupational institutions that could bar outsiders from participation.[78] Characterised by small units of production and independence of action, the town's cloth industry only took its first steps towards more formal organisation in 1407. Men could change occupations and pick up new skills from anyone who was willing to teach them because there were no clearly defined apprenticeship rules in place.[79] With such conditions, Colchester presented a perfect working environment for immigrant clothworkers with different traditions in weaving and fulling.[80]

74 Luu, *Immigrants and Industries*, pp. 53–87, in particular pp. 70–6.

75 Fuller, *Church History*, vol. II, pp. 286–7.

76 N. R. Amor, *Late Medieval Ipswich: Trade and Industry* (Woodbridge, 2011), pp. 47–8. Both Flemish and English merchants had called at Colchester ever since the twelfth century, but in much smaller numbers than in the 1350s. J. Cooper (ed.), *The Victoria History of the Counties of England: A History of the County of Essex: The Borough of Colchester* (London, 1994), vol. IX, p. 61.

77 Britnell, *Growth and Decline*, pp. 12, 18–21, 57–63, 67, 76.

78 For London, see Lambert and Pajic, 'Immigration and the common profit', pp. 633–57. See also Chapters 3 and 4. For Flanders, see P. Stabel, 'Guilds in late medieval Flanders: Myths and realities of guild life in an export-oriented environment', *Journal of Medieval History*, 30 (2004), 187–212.

79 Britnell, *Growth and Decline*, pp. 77–8, 139.

80 Still offering a wide variety of cloth in the thirteenth century, the larger Flemish cities, the main suppliers of exiles in 1351, avoided competition from the smaller communities by concentrating on heavy luxury woollens during the fourteenth century. Munro, 'Industrial transformations', pp. 111–14. Fulling mills had been introduced in several towns in Flanders and Brabant during the twelfth and thirteenth centuries but were no longer used in the fourteenth, on the grounds that they produced an inferior textile. R. Van Uytven, 'The fulling mill: Dynamic of the revolution of industrial attitudes', *Acta Historiae Neerlandica*, 5 (1971), 1–14.

The first outburst of the Black Death also occurred around the time the Flemings arrived. The shortage of labour was immediately felt in Colchester, after a brutal arrival of the plague and mortality rates exceeding 40 per cent.[81] In this context the Flemish newcomers were more likely to be accepted by town officials, which was reflected in the admissions into the franchise. Whereas only Arnold Fleming is known to have become a freeman of the town during the 1350s, six others, including an exile from Bruges, Cent Kampe, seem to have done so during the 1360s, possibly after the conditions set in 1359 had shattered all hopes of an easy return.[82]

The 298 people from the Low Countries who appeared before the borough court between 1351 and 1385 must have included Flemings who had left voluntarily as well. Colchester became a desirable location for them because it offered a cheap and reliable source of wool, free from the frequent embargoes and high export taxes that hampered trade with Flanders.[83] While the Black Death-related labour scarcity in England, and most definitely in Essex, led to an increase in real wages and the overall improvement in standards of living for both urban and rural employees, it had the opposite effect in Flanders.[84] From the 1360s onward, Ghent's export-oriented textile industries saw a period of rapid decline that resulted in high unemployment. The artisans who were lucky to remain employed did see higher wages, but these were unable to keep up with the high inflation brought on by the Flemish count's continuous devaluations of the currency between 1348 and 1360. Unsurprisingly, poverty in Flanders became a serious problem throughout the second half of the fourteenth century.[85]

All of these conditions paved the way for both exiles and voluntary economic migrants to be joined by an increasing number of people whose surname referred to the Duchy of Brabant or to one of its towns and cities. From 1359 onwards, textile workers like Hannekin Claisson

[81] Britnell, *Growth and Decline*, pp. 22, 72, 96; Cooper (ed.), *The Victoria History*, vol. IX, p. 24; Poos, *Rural Society*, p. 90.

[82] William de Gaunt, John Ducheman and John Danel, Hanyn Heine, Paul Barremakere, and John Lindholt (referred to in other cases as a Fleming), in 1360, 1366, 1371, 1376, 1377. ERO, D/B 5 R1, fo. 47d.

[83] For an overview of stand-offs in the Anglo-Flemish wool trade during the first half of the fourteenth century, see Lloyd, *The English Wool Trade*, pp. 7–37, 75, 107–8, 112–14.

[84] C. M. Barron, 'Introduction: England and the Low Countries, 1327–1477', in C. M. Barron and N. Saul (eds), *England and the Low Countries in the Late Middle Ages* (Stroud, 1995), p. 11.

[85] M. Boone, 'L'industrie textile à Gand au bas Moyen Âge ou les resurrections successives d'une activité réputée moribonde', in M. Boone and W. Prevenier, *La Draperie ancienne des Pays-Bas: Débouchés et stratégies de survie XIVe–XVIe siècles*, Actes du colloque tenu à Gand le 28 avril 1992 (Louvain, 1993), p. 17; Nicholas, *The Metamorphosis*, pp. 120, 176; J. H. Munro, 'Bullion flows and monetary contraction in late medieval England and the Low Countries', in J. F. Richards (ed.), *Precious Metals in the Later Medieval and Early Modern Worlds* (Durham, NC, 1983), p. 113.

from Malines in Brabant, Everard van Deste, John Braban, or Hannekin de Louvayn began to appear in pleas in the borough court of Colchester.[86] As in London, they must have left because of the economic stranglehold caused by revolts, warfare and the political situation throughout the 1350s and 1360s.[87] Throughout the second half of the fourteenth century, there is nothing to suggest that there were official divisions and frictions between the two groups as there were in London. It appears that Flemish and Brabantine textile workers looked to cooperate and organise the manufacturing process together rather than to make life harder for everyone.

Both Flemings and Brabanters would continue to plead their causes in the Colchester borough courts for the rest of the fourteenth century. The outbursts of revolt between 1359 and 1361 induced a new wave of banishments in 1361 and 1366, which was one of the reasons the steady inflow of Flemish immigrants remained at the same level as during the 1350s.[88] During the same years, there are reasons to assume that a second generation of those banished in 1351 was brought up in England too. Some of them found their way to Colchester's tribunals. In 1375 and 1377, John Backere, 'Flemyng', and Walter Camber appeared in court, potential relatives of exiles Walter le Backere and John Camber recorded in the borough court in 1361.[89] Other examples include the sons of Hanyn Johnsone and William Vande Strat, who were both involved as defendants in pleas for breach of contract regarding the apprenticeships of their sons in the trade of weaving.[90] We cannot know whether their children were born in England or whether they all came together from Flanders, but from the little direct evidence at our disposal, it can be observed that the second generation of immigrants tended to engage in the same trades as their parents.

Apart from Colchester, some smaller villages in Essex saw an influx of Flemish weavers as well. It is in the coastal town of Maldon that they have left most traces. An exile from Ghent, Jacop Marcolf, settled in this town with his wife, Margaret. In 1370, he was murdered by Gerard van Dendermonde,[91] who, after inquiry, was found guilty and subsequently

[86] Benham, *Court Rolls*, vol. II, pp. 77–8.

[87] Boffa, *Warfare in Medieval Brabant*, pp. 3–10; Quicke, *Les Pays-Bas à la veille de la période bourguignonne*, pp. 41–54.

[88] SAB, Groenenboek C, fos 111–18.

[89] For John Backer, see ERO, D/B 5, CR 17, m. 10d, calendared in Benham, *Court Rolls*, vol. III, p. 81. For Walter Camber, see ERO, D/B 5, CR 18, m. 19, calendared in Benham, *Court Rolls*, vol. III, p. 144.

[90] Benham, *Court Rolls*, vol. III, p. 40; ERO D/B 5 CR 24, m. 59.

[91] TNA, JUST 2/33A, m. 6.

hanged.[92] Another exile, John Preme, *webbe*, seem to have lived here until 1381.[93] Apart from the exiles, weavers from other parts of the Low Countries followed as well. In 1364, John Webbe and Giles Braban, *webbe*, were supposed to appear at the court of the King's Bench court in order to reply to an accusation by Roger and John Hammond from Wodham (modern-day Woodham Ferrers).[94] Ten years later, the witnesses found that a certain Giles Braban, who might have been the same person, was murdered by Torinus Fleming and Henry van Drene, *Flemyng*, and further investigation was ordered.[95] Unfortunately, we cannot know what happened subsequently, as the rest of the case does not survive. Around the same period, in 1377, following the coroner's investigation in the Essex settlement of Ging-Joyberd-Laundry (Buttsbury), it was found that a certain Claykyn Seland was murdered by William Wombekin, *Flemyng*, with a dagger.[96] Also, in Castle Hedingham, Peter le Walssche, *Flemyng*, *webbe*, was accused of manslaughter in 1374, suggesting that even the Flemish weavers might have followed the trend of moving to the countryside at the end of the fourteenth century.[97]

IPSWICH, CLARE, SUDBURY AND HADLEIGH

Due to the lack of sources, the question of the Flemish presence in fourteenth-century Suffolk has inevitably involved a good deal of speculation. Some of the earlier commentators attributed a great deal of importance to the legend of Flemish influence on the cloth industry in the area, while some others disputed this.[98] Recently, the most balanced views have been those provided by Nicholas Amor, who concluded that when it comes to the influence of Flemish immigration on the cloth industry of Suffolk it depends when and where one looks, while stressing the lack of sources for the period when Edward III's policies probably had the most impact.[99] Royal records do attest to a Flemish presence in the second half of the fourteenth century. On a roll of the poll tax for an

92 TNA, JUST 3/168, m. 6.
93 TNA, KB 145/3/6/1; see Chapter 6 on the revolt of 1381 for more context.
94 TNA, KB 27/416, m. 30d REX.
95 TNA, JUST 2/35/5, m. 3.
96 TNA, JUST 2/33A, m. 1.
97 TNA, JUST 2/35/5, m. 3.
98 Pirenne attributed a great deal of importance to the Flemish presence in Suffolk, while Bailey, Dymond and Betterton did the same in order to dispute it: Pirenne, *Histoire de Belgique*, vol. IV, p. 325; M. Bailey, *Medieval Suffolk: An Economic and Social History 1200–1500* (Woodbridge, 2007), p. 158; M. Bailey, 'Technology and growth of textile manufacture in medieval Suffolk', *Proceedings of the Suffolk Institute Archaeology and History*, 42 (2009), 13–20; A. Betterton and D. Dymond, *Lavenham: An Industrial Town* (Lavenham, 1982), p. 1.
99 N. Amor, *From Wool to Cloth: The Triumph of the Suffolk Clothier* (Bungay, 2016).

unidentified hundred, two weavers, Lucas Braban and Giles Braban, paid the subsidy in 1381.[100] Two major towns of this area, Bury St Edmunds and Lowestoft, are unfortunately completely lacking in suitable sources for the period of this study.[101] We do know, however, that some alien weavers took residence in Lowestoft, as Henry Flemmyng, *webber*, and John Flandrensis, *webber*, were accused of the murder there of Matthew Webbester in 1364.[102]

The port town of Ipswich has several extant rolls of the borough court from the 1370s, which can be used in order to establish the extent of the Flemish presence. Although there are only membranes for three years of the so-called petty court, the nature of the cases and the frequency with which Flemish immigrants appear suggest similar patterns to those in Colchester or Great Yarmouth. For example, Nicholas van Relengast was involved in a case of trespass against Christian Bake, and Thomas Webber from Norwich accused Arnold Webber, *Flemyng*, of debt.[103] Some of them, like Augustine Flemmyng or Boudin Meyhewsonne, settled in Ipswich with their wives, while some other women, like Beatrice van Zaren, or a female tailor, Agnes Duchewoman, acted in their own right in the borough court.[104] It is clear that textile workers from the Low Countries were present in Ipswich and might have formed as important a community as in Colchester. The established commercial networks between the port towns of the Low Countries and Ipswich from before the 1350s, together with the massive banishment of textile workers, certainly provided the conditions for a high number of immigrants to choose this town as a place of settlement.

However, some smaller towns, such as Clare, Hadleigh and Sudbury, which became developing centres of the cloth-making industry from the mid fourteenth century on, do allow us to investigate whether there was any Flemish presence in the area after the banishment of 1351. Their manorial court records survive for several years in the second half of the fourteenth century and do give us a glimpse of the presence of the Flemish and their activities. The manorial court had three main functions: the control of seigneurial rights and revenue; handling interpersonal relationships and disputes; and maintaining peace and order.[105] The extant manorial court records for Clare, Hadleigh and Sudbury contain leet-courts and sections that record tenant pleas for debt, breach of covenant and trespass, which makes their formats very similar to those

[100] Fenwick, *Poll Taxes*, vol. II, p. 535.
[101] Amor, *Late Medieval Ipswich*, pp. 47–50.
[102] TNA, KB 9/115 9d, KB 27/416, m. 6 REX.
[103] SRO, C/2/3/1/28, m. 4, C/2/3/1/29, m. 2.
[104] SRO, C/2/3/1/29, mm. 2d, 3d.
[105] Davis, *Medieval Market Morality*, p. 289.

of the borough courts of Great Yarmouth and Colchester.[106] The main difference is of course in the relative size and the fact that the borough courts of Colchester and Great Yarmouth seem to provide a few more details in some pleadings.

Although it was severely touched by the Black Death, Clare is estimated to have had around 700–800 inhabitants in the second half of the fourteenth century.[107] Traces of a developing cloth industry are visible in the occupational structure of its tenants from this period onwards, and there is evidence as well that wool was brought in from the surrounding countryside.[108] In its leet-court, there seems to have been a specific section for dyers, as they were the ony ones who were fined regularly for throwing dye waste into the streets.[109] For the period 1351–81, there are six extant rolls of the manor court for the borough of Clare. Some rolls group several years together, and, as for Colchester, Flemish names become visible from 1352. Even though their names were usually entered with a suggestion of their origin, there are twenty-nine of them who we can claim with certainty were Flemish immigrants.[110] These were nineteen men and ten women, of whom there were five married couples, and there are no exiles that can be recognised. They appeared in a variety of pleadings; however, they mostly appeared (twenty times) in the leet-court in order to pay fines for violent behaviour. In 1353, for example, Sarra, the wife of Gerard Braban, struck Sarra, the wife of Leuing (Lievin) Braban, who raised the hue justly.[111] Regular litigation was also part of the new arrivals' lives, and they used the court of Clare to bring eighteen pleas for trespass, sixteen for debt, and two for breach of covenant. The person to appear most frequently in litigation over the twenty-year period was the immigrant Lybekin Braban. He pleaded in seventeen different cases; eight of them concerned pleadings for debt and six others for trespass, while he was also brought to the leet-court three times.

[106] On manorial courts, see Briggs, *Credit and Village Society*; C. Briggs, 'Manor court procedures, debt litigation levels, and rural credit provision in England, c. 1290–1380', *Law & History Review*, 24:3 (2006), 519–58; J. Davis, 'Market courts and lex mercatoria in late medieval England', in M. Allen and M. Davies (eds), *Medieval Merchants and Money: Essays in Honour of James L. Bolton* (London, 2016), pp. 271–90.

[107] Davis, *Medieval Market Morality*, p. 285; Davis based his estimates on 1377 poll tax records for Clare with Rigby's multiplier of 1.9.

[108] *Ibid.*

[109] TNA SC 2/203/55–61. It is not clear if this was a sort of licensing fee, or if they were in fact throwing dirt in the streets.

[110] Some of their forenames, such as Lybekin, Clays and Hannekin, suggest that the immigrants in Clare with the surname Braban, Flemmyng or Selander are indeed from the Low Countries

[111] TNA, SC 2/203/53.

The occupations of immigrants from the Low Countries are entered very occasionally, and these can only be determined indirectly. This pattern was observed by James Davis for other litigants in the manorial court of Clare.[112] There is at least one weaver and one cordwainer bearing the same forename – Nicholas (Clays) Braban, *tixtor*, and Clays Selander, cordwainer.[113] In two cases for debt, Lybekin Braban was involved against John Chaundeler, who was presumably providing him with wax to grease the weaving loom, and another against the servant of Peter le Webbe, who was distrained by two pieces of cloth.[114] Also, given the occupational structure of the exiles and of those who settled in London, Colchester and Great Yarmouth, we can assume that most of the immigrants in Clare were involved in the textile sector as well.

The situation was similar in the neighbouring town of Hadleigh. This developing cloth-making town had twice as many inhabitants as Clare who paid the poll tax in 1381. On the basis of some rather patchy surviving particulars of this subsidy, it is estimated that about 20 per cent of Hadleigh's population was involved in the cloth industry.[115] However, none of the individuals who paid the subsidy in this return can be said with certainty to have been of Flemish origin. Also, the number of surviving court rolls here was rather lower than for Clare. There are only four surviving rolls for the thirty-year period that succeeded the arrival of the exiles. Only those for 1359–60, 1361–2, 1366–7 and 1373–4 survive. Nevertheless, the extant rolls do allow us to establish that there was some Flemish presence.

With this fragmentary evidence we can determine that there were at least ten Flemings who settled in Hadleigh during the 1360s and 1370s. As for Clare, all of them appear with suggestive surnames, and they were involved in similar types of cases. Thus in 1366, Nicholas Pyry struck Copin Flemyng and drew his blood.[116] On the same roll, John Cok, a cobbler, accused Beatrix Flemmyng of breach of covenant. To make sure she appeared in court, her combs were distrained, suggesting her involvement in the cloth industry.[117] The same year, when Athelard Selander was accused of trespass by Bartholomew Longe, he was distrained by four pockets of madder, suggesting that some of the dyestuffs in this textile town were provided by immigrants.[118] Textile workers from the Low Countries probably distributed madder and other dyestuffs both to

[112] Davis, *Medieval Market Morality*, p. 287. [113] TNA, SC 2/203/54, SC 2/203/56.

[114] TNA SC 2/203/55. Distraining refers to confiscating something from a person in order to compel them (e.g.) to appear in court.

[115] R. H. Britnell, 'The woollen textile industry of Suffolk in the later Middle Ages', *The Ricardian*, 13 (2003), 86–99, at 86.

[116] CCA-U15/16/35. [117] *Ibid.* [118] *Ibid.*

immigrants and to English cloth-workers. Apart from the manorial court, some immigrants from the Low Countries, like John Durdraught and William Swyndraught, were also indicted for murders that they committed in this town.[119]

The surviving leet rolls of the manor court of Sudbury show that Flemings settled there as well. Thus in 1356, John Flemyng did hamsoken on Galfride Pynel, who raised the hue justly, while two brothers, Robert and John Quyk, drew blood from a certain Fleming.[120] It seems that some of them were of various professions in the textile sector, as a fuller named John Braban appeared in 1389.[121] A little earlier, in 1368, Franciscus van Sint Tryde was indicted for the murder of John Braban, who had recently taken up residence in Sudbury. At the same time, Henry Heyne, *Braban*, and Isabel Flemyng were accused of aiding and abetting the aforementioned Franciscus.[122] Given the proximity of Colchester, this might have been the same Henry Heyne who had obtained the status of freeman in 1361.[123] Nevertheless, all this evidence from the Stour Valley suggests that immigrants from the Low Countries not only chose to live and work in urban areas, but also settled in smaller locations where the potential for cloth production was expanding. Eighty years later, most immigrants from the Low Countries were still living in East Anglia.[124]

FLEMISH IMMIGRANTS AND EXILES IN GREAT YARMOUTH

Situated on the east coast in the cloth-making region of Norfolk, Great Yarmouth was another place that attracted the immigration of Flemish exiles. With its population estimated at around 3,500 based on 1377's poll tax, collected from 1,941 people over 14 years old, the town was the second largest in the region after Norwich.[125] The town's main industries included fishing and shipping; however, the cloth, leather and beer trades flourished too, because of the large presence of transient merchants.[126] Even though this town was basically Norwich's outport, its abundant borough court records reveal some distinctive features of Flemish immigration which make it important for inclusion in the present study. The

119 TNA, JUST 2/178, m. 1.
120 TNA, SC 2/204/4, m. 5.
121 TNA, JUST 2/33A, m. 15d.
122 TNA, JUST 3/216/3, m. 100.
123 *The Oath Book*, ed. Benham, p. 68.
124 Thrupp, 'A survey of the alien population in England in 1440', 266; Kerling, 'Aliens in the county of Norfolk, 1436–85', 209.
125 Rodziewicz, 'Great Yarmouth', pp. 19–20; Fenwick, *Poll Taxes*, vol. II, p. 75.
126 A. Saul, 'English towns in the late Middle Ages: The case of Great Yarmouth', *Journal of Medieval History*, 8 (1982), 75–88.

town's location and its proximity to the coastal towns of Flanders, as well as to English inland wool and cloth centres, ensured it was a natural destination for Flemings banished after 1351.

Compared with London and other localities in this study, Great Yarmouth has the advantage of very well-preserved local judicial records. This is especially true for the period after the revolt in Flanders and the exile of rebels to England, since its borough court rolls run almost uninterrupted from 1351 until 1400. However, they can raise a few methodological problems. Because of its mercantile activity, in litigation of various kinds in the town's borough court one can find thousands of individuals with names originating from the Low Countries. Therefore, the following questions arise: among these litigants, who was just a transient merchant and who was a permanently settled immigrant? Even in the case of the exiles, known to have been banished and unable to return to Flanders, one may wonder how many of them actually settled in Great Yarmouth, and how many were based in the surrounding towns in England and just used its port for the import and export of goods?

The arrival of Dutch-speaking immigrants after the exile was not anything new for the residents of Great Yarmouth. Already before 1351 and the massive arrival of banished rebels in England, Great Yarmouth, in contrast to Colchester, had very strong mercantile links with Bruges and the coastal towns of Flanders, as well as with Holland and Zeeland. In the fourteenth century, during the six weeks of the herring fair in February and March, Great Yarmouth would host on average 360 ships a year, and their crews would increase the population by at least 2,000 inhabitants during this period.[127] Most of these ships originated from the fishing towns of the Zwin estuary, Diksmuide, Blankenberghe and Sluys, but also from Holland and Zeeland. Other Flemish transient merchants were drapers from Bruges and Ypres who would go to inland towns such as Norwich and Lincoln to acquire wool and woolfells from wool-growers or brokers, and then load it onto ships in Yarmouth and so back to Flanders. Even on the other side of the Channel, it seems that Great Yarmouth men were regular visitors. For example, Thomas of Beverley, a member of a prominent Yarmouth family, acquired citizenship in Bruges.[128] Thomas de Drayton from Great Yarmouth was a business partner of the Bruges money-changer Pieter Daudenarde.[129] These links with Bruges prior to the exile of 1351,

[127] Rodziewicz, 'Great Yarmouth', pp. 18–19, and the references she provides.

[128] Jamees, *Poorters*, p. 55. [129] Murray, *Bruges*, p. 271n.

and later, justify the highest presence of banished Flemings in that town in Norfolk.

As explained earlier, the Great Yarmouth borough court records consist of petty pleas, great pleas, the leet-court, recognizances and the particulars of the customs accounts. We can determine indirectly from all of them whether the immigrants settled permanently, but the best section of the court rolls for this purpose is that concerning the leet-court. These were held in June, when the herring season would still not have started, and the fairs would be over. During this quietest month for trade, the presence of transient merchants and fishermen would be at its lowest level, and people with Dutch names who appear in the leet-court would more probably be permanent residents.[130] The leet rolls unfortunately survive only from 1367, so we do not have such information for the first fifteen years of the present study. However, they then run uninterrupted until 1400 and contain the fines for various cases brought to the court following police work, such as trading as a citizen while not being one, throwing garbage improperly, forestalling and regrating (buying goods at market in order to resell them for profit near the same market), hosting prostitutes, night wandering, exercising two occupations and unacceptable violent behaviour. These fines were imposed on the inhabitants by the bailiffs and capital pledges, who would first summon all the people who lived at any given leet (to check that everybody was in the tithing) and hear the criminal presentments that had happened over the course of the year. Some Flemings, such as the weavers from Bruges Lippin Sceepstale and William Cappelle, or the fuller John Witbrood, would repeatedly be fined for various offences over the twenty-four-year period for which the leet rolls survive. Interestingly, whenever these three and other immigrants from the Low Countries were summoned to the leet court in Great Yarmouth to pay various fines, such as for trading as a citizen when they were not, or for regrating various products, they were usually recorded in the same line by the scribe. It looks as if they had come collectively to the court, or were associated together in the mind of the town clerk. For example, on the Southmiddle leet roll in 1378, four Flemings were fined for being regrators of ale and beer. Just below them, John Tailor, a Dutchman, was fined as a common forestaller (a person who bought goods before the market starts in order to sell them at an enhanced price).[131] Further on, in

[130] Rodziewicz, 'Great Yarmouth', pp. 141–2.

[131] NRO, Y/C4/90, m. 12. Written on the membrane in the following order: 'Katerina Boudyn, Beatrix Cappelle, Aughte Legate, Thomas Seyntjones, Henry Hasard, tailor et *Ducheman* sunt comunes regratores de cervisia et ber idem ipsi in mercia.' Just below them on the same

the same year and on the same membrane, on the South leet roll, William Tailor, *Ducheman*, John Elys, *webster*, Paul Souter, Paul Dumburgh, Gerard Souter, Henry van Campe and Jacob Tailor, all of them immigrants from the Low Countries, were fined for cutting and selling woollen and linen cloths in contravention of the statute and trading as citizens while they were not.[132]

The tithing system would be an even more important factor in establishing whether the immigrants settled on a permanent basis in Great Yarmouth. 'Tithing' referred to a group of men who played a role in policing medieval society, and enrolment in a tithing was expected of all secular men over the age of 12 who had been in the borough for over a year and a day.[133] Great Yarmouth was divided into four leets, and each one of them had its tithingmen. The lists of those who joined the tithing do not survive, and we cannot know with certainty how many people were in any of the Great Yarmouth tithings. The only information we have are the names of those who paid fines for failing to join the tithing, which would appear at the beginning of every leet roll, straight after the names of capital pledges. Some immigrants from the Low Countries who kept appearing for over twenty years in the Great Yarmouth borough court would occasionally be fined for failing to join the tithing.[134] This automatically means that they were considered a part of the community rather than transient merchants. Be they foreign or denizen, women never appeared in the leet-court for this offence. However, on one occasion, William, the servant of a presumably single Flemish woman, Katerina Bowdyn, was fined for failing to join the tithing.[135]

When it comes to the petty and great pleas, on several occasions the information from the pleadings leads us to conclude that the exiles settled permanently in Great Yarmouth. In 1355, Gertruda fan Outraght accused an exile from the liberty of Bruges, Mace fan Rotterdam, of detention of chattels. In the pleadings, it is stated that one Robert Houdestok left six barrels of beer in the house of Mace van Rotterdam for the aforementioned Gertruda, which Mace had not transferred to her.[136] From this case we get the information that an exile, Mace van

membrane: 'Johannes Tailor, *Ducheman* est comunis forstallator diversis mercandis ad grande nocumento civitatis.'

132 *Ibid.*, William Tailor, Ducheman, John Elys, Webster, Paul Souter, Paul Dumburgh, Gerard Souter, Henry van Campe, Jacob Tailor, Ducheman scindunt et vendent panni di linen et lanna contra statute et mercandirant tam quam burgenses et non sunt.'

133 Rodziewicz, 'Great Yarmouth', pp. 1, 89.

134 NRO, Y/C4/95, mm. 8, 9, Y/C4/96, mm. 9, 10.

135 NRO, Y/C4/94, m. 4.

136 NRO, Y/C4/76, m. 4d.

Rotterdam, owned a house, which is direct evidence of longer-term settlement abroad. Another example is the cases for withdrawal from service. This type of litigation would also fall under the jurisdiction of the borough court, and there were ten cases that involved Flemings entered into petty pleas over the period 1351–81. For instance, an exile from Bruges, Christian fan the Scelle, weaver, sued John van Gaunt for withdrawal from service.[137] If some of the exiles had been transient merchants, it would have been quite unlikely that they would have settled disputes of withdrawal from service in Great Yarmouth borough court rather than in their hometown. In Bruges, for example, such disputes as withdrawal from service would have been settled within the guild.[138] The presence of Flemish wives and of Flemish brothel-keepers, as we will see later, also suggests that most of the immigrants settled permanently in Great Yarmouth and reflects their importance in that town. Nevertheless, some of the Flemings who appear in the sources for Great Yarmouth did settle in other places in Norfolk. For example, Copin Ysaak, an exile from Dixmuide, appears on several occasions as a wool exporter in the customs accounts for Great Yarmouth.[139] However, he was actually a resident of Lynn, as he took up citizenship of that town in 1351.[140] Michael Baleward and Colin Edelman, respectively a weaver and a fuller exiled from Bruges, paid tolls for the import of herring, madder and skins from the port of Great Yarmouth to Norwich in 1353, suggesting that some of the exiles took up residence in the latter town.[141]

With all this in mind, how many immigrants from the Low Countries can be counted as longer-term residents of Great Yarmouth? The number of those for whom we can determine that they settled permanently is 192. To make this number and analysis more pertinent, on top of the methodological problems suggested above, only men and women who had appeared in Great Yarmouth borough court at least twice in the course of 1351–81 have been included. In this sense, the permanent settlement of Flemish immigrants is so obvious that some of them repeatedly kept appearing for various reasons in the borough court, be

[137] NRO, Y/C4/91, m. 5.

[138] These disputes were settled by the deans of guilds and are preserved in the judgments of the guild Deans Wijsdomen van dekenen, which survive only for Ghent in the fourteenth century, SAG series 156. These were transcribed by Marc Boone.

[139] NRO, Y/C4/74, m. 17; *Bronnen tot de geschiedenis van den handel met Engeland, Schotland, en Ireland*, ed. H. J. Smit, 2 vols. (The Hague, 1942), vol. I:1, p. 283, doc. no. 518.

[140] *A Calendar of the Freemen of Lynn, 1292–1836, Compiled from the Records of the Corporation of the Borough by Permission of the Town Clerk* (Norwich, 1913), p. 12.

[141] NRO, Y/C4/74, m. 19.

it as a pledge, defendant or plaintiff, or to pay a fine. For example, Lippin Sceepstale, a weaver from Bruges, appeared an incredible 104 times, John Witbrood, a fuller, 46 times, and William Cappelle, a weaver, 26 times. Nevertheless, out of these 192 immigrants, 158 are men and 34 are women. Most of the immigrants were employed in the textile sector, and there were fifty weavers, thirteen fullers, and seventeen tailors; the second-largest group were the leather-workers, while for twenty-nine the occupation is unknown (Table 2.5). However, given the occupational structure of the population in Flanders in the same period, those immigrants whose occupation is unknown were probably involved in the textile sector.[142] For an exile from Nieuwpoort, John Dickbuch, the occupation was never mentioned in the list of exiles, or in the Great Yarmouth court; however, he appears in the particulars of customs accounts as a wool exporter in 1353 and in a case for debt against a fuller exiled from Bruges, Bernard Gallin, suggesting that John Dickbuch was involved one way or another in the textile industry.[143] Also, the occupational names given to the exiles, such as Jacob Webster, de *Rotherdam extra maris*, and Everard Tailor, *Flemyng*, who appear in the coroner's rolls as a victim and a witness respectively, strongly suggest both the origin and occupation of these people.[144] The same Everard Tailor, *Flemyng*, was involved in two cases in the borough court of Great Yarmouth around the same period: he sued for detinue Edmund and Katerina Paston, for whom he had produced a chalon.[145] Also, in a trespass case, where he is involved with his wife against John Peytevin, Everard was distrained by a tunic, which confirms that he was indeed a tailor.[146]

Cordwainers and craftsmen from the leather trade were particularly numerous amongst the immigrants from the Low Countries and accounted for 16 of the 192 people. In 1340 in the military musters, after weavers and fullers of Bruges, cordwainers provided the highest number of its members for the expeditions.[147] Flemish artisans were all part of the urban militia which, together with the cavalry army and the troops provided by the rural communities, were at the disposal of the Flemish

[142] W. Prevenier, 'Bevolkingscijfers en professionele structuren der bevolking van Gent en Brugge in de XIVe eeuw', in *Album Charles Verlinden* (Ghent, 1975), pp. 269–303; W. Prevenier, 'La Démographie des villes du comté de Flandre', 255–75; J. Dumolyn, 'Population et structures professionnelles à Bruges aux XIVe et XVe siècles', *Revue du Nord*, 81 (1999), 43–64.

[143] NRO, Y/C4/74, m. 18; NRO, Y/C4/79, m. 23.

[144] TNA, JUST/2/102, mm. 2, 3. The same patterns were suggested for women in medieval Exeter and Colchester by M. Kowaleski, *Local Markets and Regional Trade in Medieval Exeter* (Cambridge, 1995), p. 153; Britnell, *Growth and Decline*, p. 75, n. 2.

[145] A chalon was usually a blanket.

[146] NRO, Y/C4/79, m. 22; NRO, Y/C4/80, m. 12d.

[147] J. F. Verbruggen, *Het gemeenteleger van Brugge van 1338 tot 1340 en de namen van de weerbare mannen* (Brussels, 1962), pp. 172–7.

Table 2.5 *Occupations of male immigrants from the Low Countries in Great Yarmouth*

Weavers	Fullers	Tailors	Shearers	Cordwainers	Dyers	Porters	Merchants	Unknown
50	13	17	4	16	1	4	4	29

Dataset based on: NRO, Y/C4/72–95

count in case of civil war, an offensive campaign or the defence of a town. The cavalry army was made up of professional soldiers such as knights and nobles who fought on horseback, while infantrymen came from the urban militia and troops from the countryside.[148] Also, after 1361 one can notice the increased presence of cordwainers amongst the exiles.[149] Gervase Rosser and Derek Keene have argued, for medieval Westminster and Winchester, that the Dutch-speaking community that settled in these places had a strong influence on this trade; however, there is still no detailed study on cordwainers in medieval England or the Low Countries.[150]

Out of these 192 Flemings, there are at least 62 whose names match the lists of people banished from Flanders. Most of them came from the coastal towns located in the western part of the county. The most numerous were those from Bruges, followed by the exiles from Dixmuide, Nieuwpoort and Ypres (Table 2.6). What is striking and very different from London and Colchester is that only one exile from Ghent took up longer-term residence in Great Yarmouth. Given their specialisation in rayed cloths, which were never associated with the Norfolk area, Ghent weavers probably saw no reason to migrate to Great Yarmouth.[151] On the other hand, those from Bruges were associated with types of cloth similar to those that were produced in Norfolk before the exile to England.

We know that fourteen Flemish immigrants came with their wives. Some of them remained as widows and did not return to Flanders. For

[148] J. F. Verbruggen, *The Art of Warfare in Western Europe during the Middle Ages: From the Eighth Century to 1340* (Amsterdam, 1977); J. F. Verbruggen, 'Vlaamse gemeentelegers tegen Franse ridderlegers in de 14de en 15de eeuw', *Revue Belge d'histoire militaire*, 24 (1981), 359–82, at 359.

[149] SAB, Groenenboek C, fos 110r–118r.

[150] G. Rosser, *Medieval Westminster 1200–1540* (Oxford, 1989), p. 178; Keene, *Medieval Winchester*, p. 289.

[151] See Chapter 4 for discussion about the types of cloth that the Flemish textile workers specialised in.

Table 2.6 *Names of Flemings appearing both in the Great Yarmouth borough court rolls between 1351 and 1381 and on the lists of exiles of 1351 and those pardoned in 1359*[i]

Court rolls	Lists of exiles and those pardoned
Michael Baleward	Michael Balewaerd, from Bruges
Nicholas Bastard	Claykin Bastard, from Nieuwpoort
John Barekyn	Jan Barekin, from Diksmuide
William Cappel	William van der Cappelle, weaver from Bruges
John Casseler, weaver	Jan van Catselare, weaver from Bruges
Walter Colsad	Wouter Collessad, fuller from Bruges
John Crooc	Jan de Crooc, from Ypres
John Dickbush	John Dickbusche, from Nieuwpoort
Egidius Flec	Gillis Vlec, from Veurne
Arnold van der Doorne	Arnout van der Doorne, from Ghent
John Cuper from Flanders	Jan de Cupre, weaver from Diksmuide
Copyn Frothe	Coppin de Vroede, from Ypres
John Riqward	Jan Riquaert, from Veurne
Mace de Rotherdam	Maes van Rotterdamme, from the Liberty of Bruges
John Layfot	Jan Lichtvoet, from Veurne
Bernard Gallin	Bernaerd Gallin, fuller from Bruges
Peter of ye Skelle	Peter van der Scelle, weaver from Bruges
Peter Stullard	Peter Stullaert, shearer from Bruges
Clays de Walker	Clays de Waukere, weaver from Bruges
Lamsin Weyns	Lamsin Feyns, fuller from Bruges
Simon de Wyde, fuller	Simoen de Wijde, fuller from Bruges
John Cappel de Flandre	Jan van der Cappelle, weaver from Bruges
Lippin Sceepstale, Webister	Lippin Sceepstale, weaver from Bruges
John Losekyn	Jan Losekin, weaver from Bruges
John Man, de Flandre	Jan de Man, fuller from Bruges
Copkyn Keyser	Jacop Keyser, from Nieuwpoort
Nicholas Slepestaf	Clays Slepstaf, from Bruges
John Cranehaus	Jan Cranhals, from Oudenaarde
John de Houten	Jan Houtin, from Dendermonde
John fan Ypre	Jan van Ypre, weaver from Bruges
John Sarazyn	Jan Sarazen, weaver from Bruges
Nicholas Makeler	Clais Machelere, weaver from Bruges
Christian van the Scelle	Christian van der Scelle, weaver from Bruges
Jacob de Ipre	Jacob van Ypre, weaver from Bruges
William Brokere	Jan de Broukere, filius Willems, from Ardembourgh
Baldwin Broukere	Boudin Broukere, from Ardembourgh
Walter Bastard	Wouterkin de Bastard, from Nieuwpoort
John Timerman	Hannekin de Temmerman, from Oudenaarde
Lambert Veys	Lamsin Veys, shearer from Bruges
Walter Ingilbrigth	Wouter Ingelbrechts, from Dendermonde
John Gys, weaver	Jan Ghijs, weaver from Bruges

Table 2.6 (*cont.*)

Court rolls	Lists of exiles and those pardoned
John de Gistele	Jehan Ghistele, weaver from Bruges 1361
Baldwyn Wymes	Boudin Wemins, fuller from Bruges
Lambert Yonge, fuller	Lamsin Jonghe, fuller from Bruges
Baldwin Feldacker, fuller	Boudin Veldacker, fuller from Bruges
Nicholas Edelman, fuller	Collin Edelman, fuller from Bruges
Peter Thoroud	Pieter van Thouroud, wever from Bruges
John Boidin	Hannekin Boidin, from Nieuwpoort
John Gerolf, fuller	Jan Gherolf, fuller from Bruges
Peter Arnold	Peter Arnout, from Bruges
Nicholas Houweghe	Clais Houweghe, carpenter from Bruges
John Colkirke	Jan de Colkirke, saddler from Bruges
Nicholas Palding	Clais Paelding, fuller from Bruges
Giles Hortere	Gillis Hoertere, from Biervliet
Peter Welmakere	Peter de Vielmakere, from Ghent
Peter Sand	Peter Zande, weaver from Ghent
John Meleward, weaver	Jan Melgeward, weaver from Bruges
Peter Sceepstale	Peter Sceepstale, weaver from Bruges
John fan Fourne	Jan van Vurne, fuller from Bruges Groenenboek 1361
Clays Boulyn	Clais Boelin, from Ardenbourg
Hanekyn Franke	Hannekin Vranke, weaver from Bruges
John Wevere	Hannekin de Wevere, from Oudenaarde

[i] Michael Baleward: NRO, Y/C4/74, m. 17d and *Cartulaire des Artevelde*, p. 719; John Barekin: NRO, Y/C4/73, m. 2 and *Cartulaire des Artevelde*, p. 729; Clays Bastard: NRO, Y/C4/76, m. 3 and *Cartulaire des Artevelde*, p. 730; Walter Bastard: NRO, Y/C4/74, m. 18d and *Cartulaire des Artevelde*, p. 730; John Boidin: NRO, Y/C4/74, m. 17d and *Cartulaire des Artevelde*, p. 730; Baldwyn and William Broukere: NRO, Y/C4/74, m. 18d and *Cartulaire des Artevelde*, p. 729; John Cappel: NRO, Y/C4/79, m. 23d and *Cartulaire des Artevelde*, p. 719; William Cappel: NRO, Y/C4/73, m. 2 and *Cartulaire des Artevelde*, p. 719; John Casseler: NRO, Y/C4/79, m. 22 and SAB, Politieke charters 1e reeks, no. 495; John Cranehaus: NRO, Y/C4/82, m. 17d and *Cartulaire des Artevelde*, p. 725; John Crooc: NRO, Y/C4/75, m. 2d and *Cartulaire des Artevelde*, p. 732; John Cupere: NRO, Y/C4/76, m. 4 and ADN B 1566, fo. 21; Walter Collesad: NRO, Y/C4/76, m. 4 and *Cartulaire des Artevelde*, p. 720; John Dickbush: NRO, Y/C4/79, m. 22 and *Cartulaire des Artevelde*, p. 730; Arnold van Der Dorne: NRO, Y/C4/75, m. 2d and *Cartulaire des Artevelde*, p. 715; Colin Edelman: NRO, Y/C4/74, m. 17d and *Cartulaire des Artevelde*, p. 721; Baldwyn Feldaker: NRO, Y/C4/74, m. 17d and *Cartulaire des Artevelde*, p. 720; Giles Flec: NRO, Y/C4/72, m. 4 and *Cartulaire des Artevelde*, p. 730; Hannekyn Franke: NRO, Y/C4/82, m. 1 and SAB, Cartulary Groenenboek C, fo. 115r; Copin Frothe: NRO, Y/C4/76, m. 4 and *Cartulaire des Artevelde*, p. 733; Bernard Gallyn: NRO, Y/C4/79, m. 14 and *Cartulaire des Artevelde*, p. 720; John Gerolf: NRO Y/C4/74, m. 17d and *Cartulaire des Artevelde*, p. 720; John Gistele: NRO, Y/C4/74, m. 18d and Cartulary Groenenboek C, fo. 115v; Giles Hortere: NRO, Y/C4/74, m. 17d and *Cartulaire des Artevelde*, p. 725; John de Houten : NRO, Y/C4/86, m. 14 and *Cartulaire des Artevelde*,

Table 2.6 (*cont.*)

p. 727; Nicholas Houweghe: NRO, Y/C4/74, m. 17d and *Cartulaire des Artevelde*, p. 721; Walter Inghilbright: NRO, Y/C4/74, m. 18d and *Cartulaire des Artevelde*, p. 727; Jacob de Ipre: NRO, Y/C4/74, m. 17d and *Cartulaire des Artevelde*, p. 719; Copyn Keyser: NRO, Y/C4/80, m. 20d and *Cartulaire des Artevelde*, p. 729; John Layfoot: NRO, Y/C4/75, m. 4 and *Cartulaire des Artevelde*, p. 730; John Losekin: NRO, Y/C4/79, m. 23d and SAB, Cartulary Groenenboek C, fo. 114r; Clais Makeler: NRO, Y/C4/95, m. 7d and SAB, Cartulary Groenenboek C, fo. 114v; John Man: NRO, Y/C4/80, m. 20 and *Cartulaire des Artevelde*, p. 720; John Meleward: NRO, Y/C4/87, m. 1d and SAB, Cartulary Groenenboek C, fo. 115v; Clays de Palding: NRO, Y/C4/74, m. 17d and *Cartulaire des Artevelde*, p. 720; John Riquart: NRO, Y/C4/76, m. 4 and *Cartulaire des Artevelde*, p. 730; Mace de Rotherdame: NRO, Y/C4/76, m. 3 and *Cartulaire des Artevelde*, p. 728; Peter Sand: NRO, Y/C4/74, m. 17d and *Cartulaire des Artevelde*, p. 712; Lippin Sceepstale: NRO, Y/C4/79–96 passim and SAB, Cartulary Groenenboek C, fo. 114v; Peter Sceepstale: NRO, Y/C4/83, m. 11 and SAB, Cartulary Groenenboek C, fo. 118v; Christian van Skelle: NRO, Y/C4/96, m. 4d and *Cartulaire des Artevelde*, p. 719; Peter van Skelle: NRO, Y/C4/76, m. 4 and *Cartulaire des Artevelde*, p. 719; Clays Slepestaf: NRO, Y/C4/81, m. 16 and SAB, Cartulary Groenenboek C, fo. 113v; Peter Stullard: NRO, Y/C4/75, m. 1 and SAB, Cartulary Groenenboek C, fo. 115v; John Timerman: NRO, Y/C4/74, m. 17d and *Cartulaire des Artevelde*, p. 726; Lambert Veys: NRO, Y/C4/74, m. 17d and *Cartulaire des Artevelde*, p. 721; Clays de Walker: NRO, Y/C4/78, m. 8 and *Cartulaire des Artevelde*, p. 719; John Wevere: NRO, Y/C4/74, m. 1 and *Cartulaire des Artevelde*, p. 726; Lamsin Weyns: NRO, Y/C4/78, m. 5 and *Cartulaire des Artevelde*, p. 721; Peter Welmaker: NRO, Y/C4/74, m. 18d and *Cartulaire des Artevelde*, p. 716; Simon de Wyde: NRO, Y/C4/79, m. 22 and *Cartulaire des Artevelde*, p. 720; Baldwyn Wymes: NRO, Y/C4/82, m. 1d and *Cartulaire des Artevelde*, p. 720; Lamsin Yonge: NRO, Y/C4/74, m. 17d and *Cartulaire des Artevelde*, p. 720; John fan Ypre: NRO, Y/C4/86, m. 12 and SAB, Politieke charters 1e reeks, no. 495.

example, Bernard Gallyn, a fuller exiled from Bruges, sued John, the son and executor of the goods of an exile, John Dickbush, for unspecified debts.[152] He was a pledge in a case where Catherine, the widow of an exile from Dixmuide, John Banekyn, was accused of owing a debt to John Countyng from Brabant.[153] Similarly, Leticia, the widow of one of the leading Yarmouth men, John Corpisti, a hosteler, sued a weaver from Bruges, John Cappel de Flandre, for an unspecified debt.[154] The evidence suggests that women either supplemented the household income by trading in victuals, producing and selling ale and beer, or by working

[152] NRO, Y/C4/79, m. 23. [153] *Ibid.*

[154] *Ibid.*, m. 23d. On the same membrane John Fastre, an executor of the will of Galfride Webster, sued Lippin Webster (Sceepstale) and John Losekin for a debt.

in the first stages of cloth production. For example, an exile from Bruges, Baldwin Wymes, and his wife, Katerina, sued one Beatrix fan Oudewater for detention of chattels, which concerned the sale of a tunic.[155] The case might have been only between Katerina and Beatrix, Baldwin probably acting as a legal guardian, while Beatrix acted as *femme sole*, which was common practice in late medieval England, even for married women.[156] Some women also seem to have migrated alone and found jobs as servants in a wide range of activities and even fallen into prostitution, as we will see in Chapter 5. Other family members or relatives might have followed. For example, two weavers from Bruges, Peter and Christian van der Scelle, appear on numerous occasions in Great Yarmouth court rolls, as well as on the list of banished rebels, which may indicate that they were related.

The evidence for second-generation immigrants is a little bit more explicit for Great Yarmouth than for other towns. For example, a tailor, Deryk fan Delft, and Paul Souter paid fines for not joining the tithing with their sons, Walter and Mews, at a leet-court session held in 1385.[157] A year later, another tailor, William Taylor, *Ducheman*, who appeared in the borough court for different matters between 1360 and 1390, was also fined for not joining the tithing with his son, John.[158] Sometimes the evidence is not that explicit, and any relation has to be deduced from the surname. In 1384, a Flemish immigrant, William Blondekin, fuller, paid a fine for failing to join the tithing at his subleet in Great Yarmouth.[159] William might have been the son or a relative of Andries Blondekin, one of the fullers banished from Bruges thirty years earlier.[160] Unfortunately, the descendants of the first newcomers appear on only a few occasions in the borough court, making it impossible to allow detailed analysis of second-generation immigrants' experiences. It is possible, however, to establish that these specific individuals did not improve their administrative status in comparison with their parents. For example, Paul Souter's son, Mews, was fined on four occasions for acting under the guise of being a citizen, suggesting that being born in the town did not improve one's chances of becoming enfranchised.[161] More generally, there is no evidence that any of the Flemings resident in Great Yarmouth were able to become freemen. The analysis of the twenty-seven extant leet-court sessions over the period of the study suggests that

155 NRO, Y/C4/82, m. 1.

156 M. McIntosh, 'The benefits and drawbacks of "femme sole" status in England 1300–1630', *Journal of British Studies*, 44 (2005), 410–38.

157 NRO, Y/C4/97, m. 14d.

158 NRO, Y/C4/98, m. 12.

159 NRO, Y/C4/96, m. 9.

160 *Cartulaire historique et généalogique des Artevelde*, ed. De Pauw, p. 720.

161 NRO, Y/C4/98, m. 12d; Y/C4/99, m. 12d; Y/C4/108, m. 18d.

the pathway to freedom for outsiders was probably very difficult in Great Yarmouth.[162] The fact that immigrants from the Low Countries would repeatedly pay fines to the city authorities for trading as citizens while they were not would support this argument. However, as we will see in Chapter 4, in terms of cloth production and the retail trade, not entering the franchise did not represent a major setback for most of the immigrants from the Low Countries.

The locations where Flemings settled in Great Yarmouth are more difficult to determine than in London or Colchester. Even though the petty pleas and the leet rolls mention their houses, the street name is never clearly mentioned in the records. John Witbrood was, for example, fined for throwing garbage in front of his house in Otlysrowe and blocking the watercourse.[163] He was a fuller, and therefore it is not surprising that he settled somewhere near a watercourse; however, the street under this name is very hard to find. He was fined twice for failing to join the tithing in the North leet, together with his colleague, Herman Fuller, and their apprentices, John and William. Heyne van Hoghes, fuller, was fined on the same occasion.[164] It seems that the North leet was the part of town where most of the Flemish fullers settled. Five of them, including John Wythbrood, his servant, John Hermanesson, Lambekyn Cobeler, Herman Fuller and William Blondekyn, were fined for failing to join the tithing of this subleet in 1384.[165] Flemings with other occupations, like Lippin Sceepstale, weaver, Jacob Tailor, *Flemyng*, Henry van Campe, Paul Souter, and Giles Souter, cordwainers, were fined for failing to join the tithing in the South leet.[166] Moreover, immigrants from the Low Countries were fined for offences in all four leets, which does not narrow down the places in the town. Whether it was for trading under the guise of being a citizen, forestalling or physical aggression, they appear in any administrative section. Some of them – usually fullers and those from the leather trades – were accused of throwing garbage into the harbour.[167] However, this does not necessarily mean that they settled near the port. (See Map 4.) Flemings seem to have been spread all over Great Yarmouth and settled wherever they could find a place. There is no evidence to suggest that they formed a ghetto; however, as we will see later, they tended to keep tight connections within their own community.

[162] For more on the difficulties of becoming enfranchised in Great Yarmouth, see Chapter 4.

[163] NRO, Y/C4/85, m. 1. [164] NRO, Y/C4/95, m. 8. [165] NRO, Y/C4/96, m. 9.

[166] NRO, Y/C4/96, m. 10d.

[167] Paul Souter, Walter Pouchmaker, Peter fan Reylond and others were fined on numerous occasions for throwing garbage in the port over 1367–85 (see leet rolls for these years).

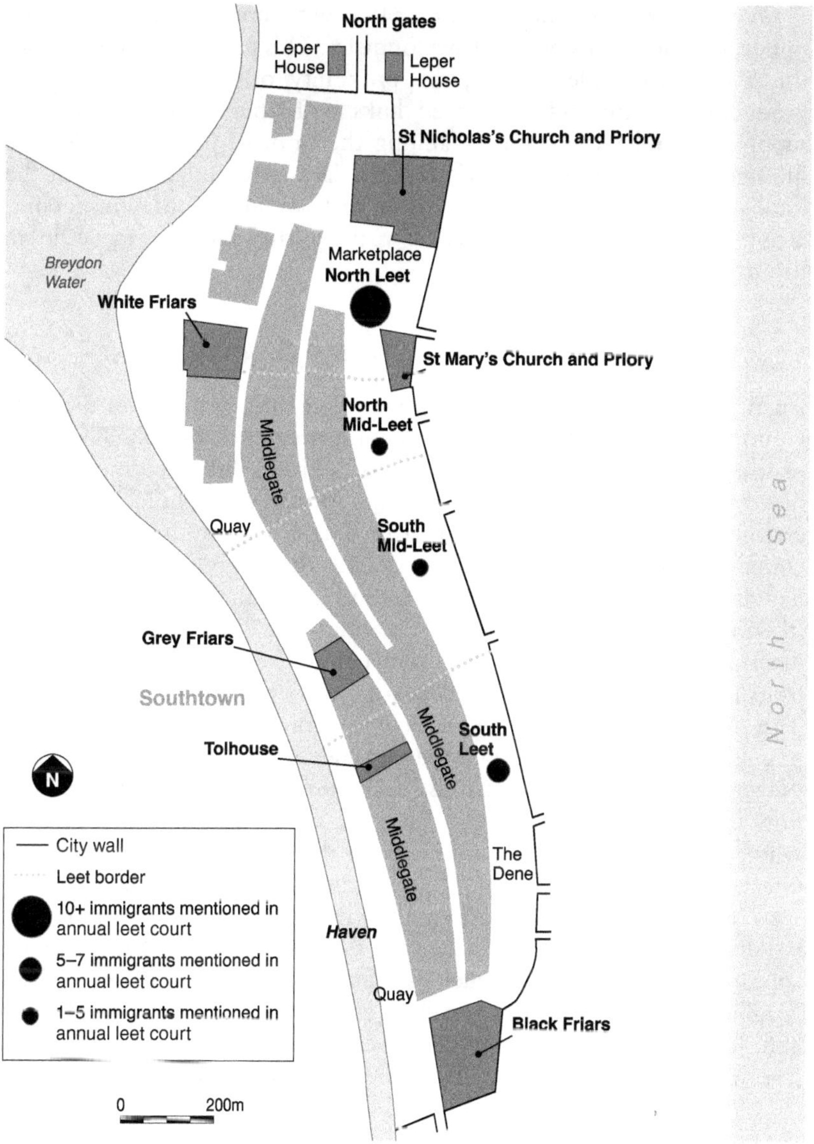

Map 4 Great Yarmouth c. 1300–1400 (map made by Sarah Wroot)

Overall, Great Yarmouth was a place with preexisting links to the important port towns of the Low Countries. This prior knowledge about the lively mercantile activity, the proximity of Norwich as a cloth production centre and established links with the countryside for the supply of wool were certainly among the primary pull factors for the immigrant textile workers. Additionally, lack of competition from the local workers and no formal association that would limit the immigrants' activity were also instrumental in making the decision to settle in this town.

TH IMMIGRANT PRESENCE IN NORWICH AND LYNN

Apart from Great Yarmouth, the presence of immigrants from the Low Countries is noticeable in other major towns of Norfolk. There are reasons to believe that the urban area of Norwich attracted most of the newcomers. Unfortunately, the available sources that would allow us to engage in an analysis similar to that for Great Yarmouth are much less complete. The so-called Old Free Book, which served as a register of new freemen, contains gaps for the second half of the fourteenth century (the folios for the years 1350 to 1364 are missing), and it is very hard to determine whether any of the exiles entered into the franchise, apart from John Fonteigne from Oudenaarde, who was admitted in 1368.[168] The rolls of the leet-court, which contain information for the study of population structure, are extant only for the sessions of 1374 and 1390.[169] Nevertheless, these two leet rolls make clear that immigrants from the Low Countries were present in this town on a permanent basis. Those who appeared in the leet-court did so for the same type of offences as in Great Yarmouth. For example, Florencius Taylor, alien, and his wife were fined as forestallers, and Henry Sawer, a Fleming, for trading in woolfells while not being a citizen.[170] Some of the Flemings who appeared in this leet-court, such as Henry Buk, John Prikker, William Maghler and Simon Fisher, as well as exiles Clays Makeler from Bruges and John Bemond from Poperinghe, made several visits to Great Yarmouth during the 1370s. In the borough court of Great Yarmouth

168 J. L'Estrange, *Calendar of the Freemen of Norwich, from 1317 to 1603*, ed. W. Rye (London, 1888), p. 54; P. Dunn, 'After the Black Death: Society and economy in late fourteenth-century Norwich', unpublished Ph.D. thesis, University of East Anglia (2003), p. 11.

169 NRO, NCR 5b/10, 11. For an analysis of immigration earlier in the century through similar sources, see E. Rutledge, 'Immigration and population growth in early fourteenth-century Norwich: Evidence from the tithing roll', *Urban History Yearbook*, 15 (1988), 15–30.

170 NRO, NCR 5b/10, mm. 3, 3d.

these individuals were involved in cases concerning the trade in wool, which would suggest that they had actually lived in Norwich and only used the port for commercial purposes.[171]

In order to further examine the experiences of immigrants from the Low Countries in Norwich, we must rely on the royal judicial records, such as the coroner's rolls, gaol deliveries or pleas from the King's Bench. The county of Norfolk has a relatively high number of extant coroner's inquests and gaol deliveries during the period of study, some of which covered incidents that took place at Norwich.[172] While the information from these records is concerned with violent offences and limits our scope for quantitative investigation of the immigrants' economic activities, it still allows us to show their presence in this town. As in the borough courts of Great Yarmouth and Colchester, the scribes were not required to record the origin of the victims or perpetrators, but in many instances they took care to do so. Such was the case with John Van Ostborch de Flandre, who was indicted for killing Richard Foyt de Brabancia in 1354, or with John Blad de Flandre and John Wolf de Flandre, accused of the murder of one Richard filius Hisbradissone from Holland, making it clear that the victims originated from Brabant and Holland and the perpetrators from Flanders.[173] Similar patterns may be observed in all other recorded cases with fatal outcomes that involved immigrants from the Low Countries, which suggests that they settled disputes among themselves. For example, in 1355 Florence de la Brele, John de Braban and Jacob Snidewinde were indicted for the death of Andrew Fuller de Flandre, while Peter de la Beke de Flandre, John van Casselle, Nicholas Dansbeke and John Borse were accused of killing Walter, son of John van Fourne de Flandre.[174] As with trespass cases in the borough courts of Great Yarmouth and Colchester, the cases of physical violence remained mostly within the immigrant community.

Overall, the documentary evidence shows that there were at least 102 Flemings who settled in Norwich. However, only six of them can be recognised on the lists of rebels banished from Flanders (Table 2.7). The occupations of the immigrants from the Low Countries in Norwich follow the pattern of those in other English towns. It is the records from the leet-court that provide us with such information. When Simon

[171] NRO, NCR 5b/10, m. 3d. As wool exporters and traders in Great Yarmouth: NRO, Y/C4/88, mm. 11d, 12d; and as those who paid the cocket seal (a certificate that the duty for wool destined for export had been paid): TNA, E 122/149/12; NRO, Y/C4/89, m. 4; NRO, Y/C4/91, m. 1.

[172] TNA, JUST 3/134; JUST 3/223/1; JUST 3/139; JUST 3/158.

[173] TNA/JUST/3/139, m. 26; *CPR, 1354–8*, p. 284; TNA, JUST 3/223/1, m. 15.

[174] TNA, JUST 2/102, m. 25.

Table 2.7 *Names of Flemings appearing both in Norwich and Lynn sources between 1351 and 1381 and on the lists of exiles of 1351 and those pardoned in 1359*[i]

Norfolk sources	Lists of exiles and pardons
Nicholas Ansbeke, Norwich	Clais van Ansbeke, weaver from Bruges
John Bemond, Norwich	Jan Bemond, from Poperinghe
John Borse, Norwich	Jan Borse, weaver from Ghent
John van Cassele de Flandre, Norwich	Jan van Cassele, exile from Dam
John van Ostburgh, de Flandre, Norwich	Jan van Oostborgh, weaver from Bruges
Boudin Spileman, Norwich	Boudin Speilman, fuller from Ypres
Levekyn Burnebrot, Lynn	Lievin Bornebrot, weaver from Ghent
Peter Croc, Lynn	Pieter de Crooc, fuller from Ghent
Peter fan Harsille, Lynn	Pieter van Harselle, weaver from Ghent
Coppin (Jacob) Ishaak, de Dixmuth, Lynn	Jacop Isaac, weaver from Dixmuide
John Meysmaker, Lynn	Jan de Mesemakere, weaver from Ghent
Sigardus de Wulf, Lynn	Seger de Wulf, weaver from Ghent
John Spinrocke, Thetford (Norfolk)	Hannin Spinrocke, weaver from Bruges

[i] Nicholas Ansbeke, Norwich: TNA, JUST 2/102, m.25 and SAB, Politieke charters 1e reeks, no. 497; John Bemond, Norwich: NRO, NCR 5b/10, m. 1 and *Cartulaire des Artevelde*, p. 731; John Borse, Norwich: TNA, JUST 2/102, m. 25 and *Cartulaire des Artevelde*, p. 715; John van Cassele de Flandre, Norwich: TNA, JUST 2/102, m. 25 and *Cartulaire des Artevelde*, p. 727; John van Ostburgh, de Flandre, Norwich: TNA, JUST 3/139, m. 26; *CPR, 1354–8*, p. 284 and *Cartulaire des Artevelde*, p. 719; SAB, Politieke charters 1e reeks, no. 497; Boudin Spileman, Norwich: NRO, NCR 5b/10, m. 1d and *Cartulaire des Artevelde*, p. 735; Levekyn Burnebrot: TNA, C 255/4/13 and Espinas, Pirenne, *Recueil*, vol. I:2, p. 454; Peter Croc, Lynn: TNA, C 255/4/13 and *Cartulaire des Artevelde*, p. 717; Peter fan Harsille, Lynn: TNA, C 255/4/13 and *Cartulaire des Artevelde*, p. 712; Coppin (Jacob) Ishaak, de Dixmuth, Lynn: *A Calendar of the Freemen of Lynn, 1292–1836*, p. 12 and *Cartulaire des Artevelde*, p. 729; John Meysmaker, Lynn: NRO, KL/C 17/9 and *Cartulaire des Artevelde*, p. 711; Sigardus de Wulf, Lynn: TNA, C 255/4/13 and *Cartulaire des Artevelde*, p. 711; John Spinrocke, Thetford (Norfolk): TNA, JUST 2/102, m. 4a and SAB, Politieke charters 1e reeks, no. 497.

Fisher was fined for trading retail while not being a citizen in 1374, he was described as tailor.[175] The same goes for Clays Macheler, Arnald Webster, alien, and John Puttok, *webster*, who were all weavers.[176] John Founteigne, a Fleming from Dendermonde, who became a freeman of Norwich, brought a plea of trespass to the Court of Common Pleas against a weaver, John Flemmyng, and his wife, Margaret.[177] For an exile

[175] NRO, NCR 5b/10 mm. 1, 1d.
[176] NRO, NCR 5b/10, m. 3d; NCR 5b/11, m. 2d.
[177] TNA, CP 40/430, m. 407d.

from Ypres, Boudin Spilman, it is already noted on the list of exiles that he was a fuller, but this is also confirmed in the leet-court in 1374, as he was caught throwing fuller's earth on the road, outside the city wall.[178] Leather-related crafts were represented by Reginald Tawyer, alien, Rysberg Patynmaker, alien, and John Souter, Flemmyng, who all settled in Norwich at some point in the second half of the fourteenth century.[179]

From the mid fourteenth century, immigrants from the Low Countries also start to appear in the available sources for Lynn. One exile, Coppin Ishak from Diksmuide, was admitted to the freedom of Lynn in 1351.[180] As we will see later, he operated from Great Yarmouth and was involved in the wool trade. There are four surviving leet rolls that can be used for this study: those for 1352, 1359, 1375 and 1379 are extant. We cannot engage in an extensive study as in London, Colchester and Great Yarmouth; however, these records do allow us to shed some light on the Flemish presence and their activities in this town. In 1359, John Smyth, *Flemyng*, and five other immigrants from the Low Countries were fined for defaulting or forestalling.[181] One year later, Herman Tailor, who was admitted to the freedom in 1359, drew blood from Henry van Delft.[182] An exile from Ghent, John Meysemaker, drew blood from Christina Flemmyng.[183] Obviously, Coppin Isaac was not the only Fleming to settle permanently in Lynn after the exile. Indeed, the particulars of the poll-tax records, as well as judicial proceedings after the Peasants' Revolt of 1381, show that the Flemish community was still present in the 1370s.[184] We can say with some certainty that there were at least forty-eight Flemings that settled in Lynn: forty-six men and two women. We can determine their occupations, as they were sometimes stated when Flemings were fined for various offences in the surviving leet rolls: for example, Reynekin Braban, *webster*, was fined for drawing blood from Clays Webster; or Godfride Duchman, tailor, and Hannekyn Lister, who were fined on two occasions for throwing dirt around their houses.[185] The same pattern is also noticeable from the

178 NRO, NCR 5b/10, m. 1d; *Cartulaire historique et généalogique des Artevelde*, ed. De Pauw, p. 735.
179 NRO, NCR 5b/10, 11. 180 *A Calendar of the Freemen of Lynn, 1292–1836*, p. 12.
181 NRO, KL/C17/6. Next to the aforementioned John Smyth, there were also Hannekyn Flemmyng, Henry Braban, John Rylond, Robert Conyng and Henry de Delft on this leet roll.
182 NRO, KL/C17/7. *A Calendar of the Freemen of Lynn, 1292–1836*, p. 13.
183 NRO, KL/C17/9. *Cartulaire historique et généalogique des Artevelde*, ed. De Pauw, p. 711.
184 Fenwick, *Poll Taxes*, vol. II, pp. 156–62; A. Réville, *Le Soulèvement des travailleurs d'Angleterre en 1381* (Paris, 1898), pp. 96–7.
185 NRO, KL/C17/8. Other Flemings whose occupations can be determined based on their forenames were: NRO, KL/C17/6, Hankyn Flemmyng, porter, and Hannekyn Lister; NRO,

coroner's rolls when William Dendermond, a fuller, was accused of the murder of Beatrix Conyng de Flandre in the house of an exile from Courtrai, Seger de Gaunt.[186] However, the occupational structure of those who had taken residence in Lynn becomes clearer in 1371.

When new hostilities between England and France broke out in 1369, Anglo-Flemish diplomatic relationships were gradually put in difficulty as well. In these circumstances, Flemish merchants who had partnerships with both the French and the English were granted the right on 24 July 1370 to trade peacefully with France unless the goods were weapons or foodstuffs.[187] Apart from the disruption of maritime commercial routes, mercantile ships suffered from the widespread piracy in the waters of the English Channel.[188] Nevertheless, the English did suspect the violation of this agreement, as several complaints from Flemish masters to Edward III who saw their ships and goods seized suggest.[189] The Flemings retaliated, and English goods were seized on 27 August 1371.[190] A series of diplomatic documents shows that at the core of this dispute were merchants and ship-owners; however, Flemish exiles managed somehow to find themselves caught in the middle of this dispute as well.

On 25 August 1371, Edward III ordered the bailiffs and mayors of Hull, Boston, Great Yarmouth, Norwich, Ipswich, London, Lynn, Lincoln, York and Bristol to arrest all banished Flemings resident in England and seize their goods as retaliation for the treatment of English merchants in Flanders.[191] The officers were instructed to record the names of the men under arrest and the value of the goods in their possession, and return the writ to the chancery.[192] The only returned writ with the names of Flemings under arrest and the value of their goods survives for Great Yarmouth, and it is held in its borough court.[193] For other towns, there are only subsidiary documents which confirm that these arrests indeed happened. For example, a month after the arrests, Edward III learned that the bailiffs of Norwich kept in prison a great number of Flemish craftsmen. Even though the Flemings offered sufficient mainpernors to mainpern for

KL/C17/9, Allard Cordwainer; NRO, KL/C17/11, Lievin Webster, KL/C17/13, Godfride Duchman. Clearly, their forenames suggest Flemish origin, and the surname was probably their actual occupation.

186 TNA, JUST 3/152, m. 9. 187 Lloyd, *The English Wool Trade*, p. 218.

188 D. Nicholas, 'The English trade in Bruges in the last years of Edward III', *Journal of Medieval History*, 5 (1979), 23–61, at 34–5.

189 *CCR, 1369–74*, pp. 225–6. 190 Nicholas, 'The English trade in Bruges', 35.

191 *CCR, 1369–74*, p. 329. The order in London was even more specific and mentions 'all banished workers of Flanders'; see the original *Letter Book G*, fo. 228v.

192 *Ibid.*, *ibid.* 193 NRO, Y/C4/84, m. 1d.

them, the bailiffs were still refusing to set them free.[194] The sheriffs of London were ordered to relieve Copyn Seland, a Fleming and citizen of London, from the payment of expenses for thirty Flemings who were apparently his workers living with him prior to the arrest and who stayed in prison at his cost for seven weeks.[195] Amongst the returned writs in the chancery, one document concerning Lynn, although subsidiary, provides us with several interesting details. On 20 November 1371 (three months after the arrests), the mayor of Lynn requested the release of eleven Flemings under arrest, as they were unable to sustain themselves any more. The mayor relates that the aforementioned prisoners had only some goods, the instruments to work their craft and no animals, and that they sold all of it in order to sustain the cost of imprisonment.[196] Moreover, it was added that one of them, Hannekyn Conyng, *webster*, had died because of lack of food.[197]

The names and occupations of eleven Flemings were listed in the document. There were seven weavers, two fullers, one tailor and one cordwainer. Amongst these Flemings were exiles from Ghent: Peter the Croc, fuller, Levyn Burnebrot, *webster*, Peter fan Harsille, *webster*, and Segard Wulf, *webster*.[198] The latter appeared in Boston as an accomplice of John and Peter Stokyng, Flemings who murdered John de Brabant in 1356. It was said that Segard Wulf and seven other accomplices escaped from Boston after the crime was committed, but it appears that this exile from Ghent took up new residence in Lynn.[199] The evidence concerning the Flemings under arrest, together with that of the leet and coroner's rolls, suggests that the number and occupational profile of exiles in Lynn was probably the same as in Great Yarmouth. The main difference between the three major towns in Norfolk is that Great Yarmouth somehow had not attracted exiles from Ghent, or weavers from the Duchy of Brabant. They seem to have been more likely to choose to settle in Norwich and Lynn, where the possibility of finding work in cloth-making was a lot higher than in Great Yarmouth. Indeed, this pattern seems to be logical, as textile workers from both Brabant or

194 *CCR, 1369–74*, p. 326. A mainpern is a surety, and a mainpernor a guarantor of a prisoner's attendance in court.

195 *Ibid.*, p. 260.

196 TNA, C 255/4/13.

197 *Ibid.*, 'Hannekyn Conyng webistre qui mortus est in prisona defectu alimenti.'

198 *Ibid.* See Table 2.7 for references in Flemish sources. Other Flemings named in this returned writ were Levyn Skoemakere, soutere, John de Gant, fuller, Levyn Milnere, *webster*, Levekyn Bot, *webster*, Levekyn Spoliard, *webster*, Arnold Taylor and Hannekyn Conyng, *webster*.

199 TNA, JUST 2/67, m. 17. See also the sections on Boston and Lincoln below.

Ghent possessed better skills in weaving than those from Bruges, or Diksmuide, who were the most numerous in Great Yarmouth.

As far as smaller towns in Norfolk are concerned, John Spinrocke, an exile from Bruges, was murdered by a certain immigrant from the Low Countries, Henry from Brabant, in 1363 in the town of Thetford.[200] Also, in Swaffham, near Lynn, Adam Polain, *Flemyng*, was accused of entering Walter Flemmyng's house and the theft of various goods, including 4 ells of linen cloth worth 12d.[201]

FLEMINGS IN YORK, LINCOLN AND BOSTON

Even though Herbert Heaton attempted to downplay the importance of Flemish immigration in the northern county of Yorkshire,[202] he did acknowledge that immigration from the Low Countries to the city of York, during the reign of Edward III, was considerable. Indeed, in concert with Edward III's policy of attracting foreign skill, two weavers from Brabant, William and Hanekin, were granted letters of protection to settle in York and continue their trade as early as 1336.[203] Moreover, to judge by the evidence from admissions into the franchise, the city of York seems to have had a steady inflow of textile workers from all over the Low Countries from the 1340s up until the end of the fourteenth century. From 1339 to 1349, nine immigrants from the Low Countries involved in the textile sector were admitted to the freedom of the city.[204] The immigration might have also been higher than previously thought, since outside the English capital, only the weavers of York are known to have contested the immigration of textile workers from the Low Countries, in 1342.[205] The evidence from the admissions to the freedom of the city shows that York had not remained virgin territory for Flemish exiles. Lawrence Conync, a weaver from Deinze, and Georgius Fote, a fuller from Poperinge, became freemen in 1354, while an exile from Bruges, John van Sint-Truden, a weaver, did so later in 1389.[206] Overall, there were forty-two immigrants from the Low Countries involved in

200 TNA, JUST 2/102, m. 4a; SAB, Politieke charters 1e reeks, no. 497.

201 TNA, KB 27/415, m. 5 REX.

202 Heaton, *The Yorkshire Woollen and Worsted Industries*, pp. 8–21.

203 *CPR, 1334–8*, p. 341.

204 Thomas de Ipre (1339), Johannes Spoland de Dist, *textor* (1344), Nicholas Admare de Braban, *webster* (1345), Johannes de Colonia, *webster* (1345), Hankynus de Durdraught, *toundour* (1345), Henricus Morell de Flandre (1347), Arnaldus de Diste (1348), Petrus de Poperinghe (1349) and Johannes de Diste (1349), *Register of the Freemen of the City of York, Vol. I: 1272–1558*, ed. F. Collins (Durham, 1897), pp. 37, 40.

205 TNA, SC 8/238/11890. Petition, Weavers of York, 1342.

206 *Register of the Freemen of York*, ed. Collins, vol. I, p. 48.

the textile sector who entered the franchise from 1339 to 1377. One of them was Godfrey van Upstall, a weaver from Brabant, who was granted a denization letter, which in return for an oath of allegiance to the crown granted the same rights to the foreigner as enjoyed by the English.[207] Although Godfrey was a weaver, he was involved in the international trade and exported goods through Hull.[208] Some others, like Thomas Braban, a weaver from Malines, who came with his wife, Mary, and got his freedom in York in 1354, chose to set up a shop and engage only in the production of cloth. Thomas employed Robert Burwell as an apprentice in 1367.[209] Three years later, he was murdered by his compatriot, Godfrey de Burcell, *Braban*.[210]

Apart from the admissions to the franchise, surviving coroner's rolls show that numerous other textile workers from the Low Countries settled in the city of York. In 1355, a weaver, Rumkin Braban, allegedly murdered a tailor, John Bowland, near Castlegate.[211] In 1361, another weaver from the Low Countries, Lamkin Braban, was murdered near Staingate, and three of his compatriots, Giles van Glassynbek, William Potter and Walter Potter, were the main suspects.[212] Three other Flemish weavers, Tidkinus fan Aken, John fan Aken and John Bussche, were accused of the murder of cordwainer Simon de Ledes in 1367.[213] The same year, John Berd, a Brabantine, allegedly murdered a weaver from Brabant, Hayne Wascher, who had settled in York with his wife, Isolda.[214] Sometimes, deceased Flemings were not victims of violence but died instead from natural causes, as in the case of William Fox, *Braban*, in 1361, who was found dead in Northstreet, near Mickelgate; after the coroner's inquest, it was established that the cause of his death was the pestilence.[215] As with the admissions to the freedom, the predominance of weavers from Brabant can be observed, though fullers were not absent either. In 1367, John Clerk, a fuller and Fleming, along with another Fleming, William Devenryk, were summoned to appear before the justices of peace.[216] A few years later, Jacob Fleming, *walker*, was accused of the murder of a fuller from Brabant, John fan Gysle.[217] Although these examples from the coroner's rolls highlight the

[207] He became a freeman in 1375 but got the denization letter in 1393; on van Upstall and his activities, see M. Twycross, 'Some aliens in York and their overseas connections', *Leeds Studies in English*, 29 (1998), 359–80, at 367–8. On denization letters, see Lambert and Ormrod, 'Friendly Foreigners'.

[208] *Bronnen*, ed. Smit, pp. 359–60, 367, 422–3.

[209] *CPR, 1364–7*, p. 325.

[210] TNA, JUST 2/219, rot. 5.

[211] TNA, JUST 2/215, rot. 4.

[212] TNA, JUST 2/215, rot. 10.

[213] TNA, JUST 2/218, m. 4, KB 27/425, m. 22 REX.

[214] TNA, JUST 2/219, rot. 1.

[215] TNA, JUST 2/218, m. 4.

[216] TNA, JUST 2/217, rot. 5.

[217] TNA, JUST 2/219, rot. 2.

immigrants' involvement in anti-social behaviour, they still provide evidence that the presence of textile workers from the Low Countries in York went beyond those who were admitted to the franchise.

Coroner's rolls, admissions to the freedom, testamentary evidence, poll-tax returns and a variety of other sources for the city of York show that, overall, there were 105 immigrants from the Low Countries involved in the textile sector who settled there permanently between 1350 and 1370. Of these immigrants, ninety-five were men and ten were women, who appear as the wives of other immigrants. As in other towns in England, most of them, fifty-seven, were weavers. There were also five fullers, five tailors, four dyers and one shearer, but for the remaining thirty-three immigrants the occupation is unknown. Nevertheless, these numbers of immigrants would certainly have made a large contribution to the production of an average 390 cloths sealed yearly by the alnager in the city of York during the 1350s.[218]

The poll-tax returns for the city of York do not add any new names to the immigrant community of York, only a confirmation that some of those who appeared in other sources had paid the tax. However, the surviving returns for other parts of Yorkshire provide evidence that the countryside had also seen textile workers from the Low Countries, something already pointed out by Herbert Heaton. He found six Brabantine weavers who paid the subsidy in Bawtry, Spofforth, Ripon, Skipton, Whetherby and Ripley.[219] Twenty years later, weavers from Brabant were still present in the Yorkshire countryside. In 1399, the weavers of York complained that the weavers from the countryside had repeatedly violated their privileges for more than twenty years by producing dyed and rayed cloths. This was a privilege granted exclusively to the weavers of York, Beverley, Kirkeby, Malton, Scarborough and Tresch (Thirsk). Amongst the accused weavers, we find John Brabaner and Henry Brabaner in Helmesley, John Mons, *Brabaner*, at Whitby, John Brabaner in Lethum and Henry Brabaner in Ripon.[220] While the evidence from the countryside focuses mostly on weavers, immigrant fullers also seem to have found their way outside of York and into the county. During the sessions of the peace in 1361, the justices issued an order for the capture of six fullers for various felonies they were accused of. Amongst them was Gocelin Braban, a fuller, who was later captured and indicted for the murder of another fuller from the Low Countries,

218 Gray, 'The production and exportation of English woollens', 34.

219 Heaton, *The Yorkshire Woollen and Worstee Industries*, p. 17.

220 *Calendar of Inquisitions Miscellaneous, Vol. VI: Chancery, 1392–99*, pp. 242–8.

Richard Fote, who had recently taken up residence in England in the city of Beverley.[221]

Adjacent to Yorkshire, in Lincolnshire, the Flemish presence is detected as well.[222] For this area, local records are missing for the period of this study, and most of the evidence here is based on the extant judicial records, such as coroner's and gaol delivery rolls.[223] This source material is rather limited, as it focuses on felony cases and presents only the immigrants' violent behaviour. Nevertheless, some conclusions as to the permanent settlement of immigrants from the Low Countries might be observed when combined with certain other extant sources from the city of Lincoln or the Court of Common Pleas. Criminal records from Lincolnshire show that immigrants from the Low Countries were spread all over the county. Out of seventy people with Flemish names that appeared in the coroner's rolls, most of them appeared in Boston (forty-six) and Lincoln (fourteen). However, some of them, like Lambert Braban de Loveyn, who was accused of the theft of cloth in 1354, took up residence in Sleaford, while the remaining nine immigrants from the Low Countries settled in Pinchebeck, Holbeach, Limber and Whaplode. It is not surprising that higher numbers of Flemings appear in the rolls for Boston and Lincoln. Apart from the fact that these were the two biggest towns of the county and probably attracted most of its trade, they have the highest survival rate of records concerning felony cases as well.[224]

Given the mercantile nature of Boston as a port town, and of Lincoln as a staple town, one might wonder whether the Flemings who appear in the coroner's rolls were permanent residents or just transient merchants whose violent disputes ended up with fatal consequences. The first hint to suggest permanent residence is the presence of exiles in this town. Thus, when two Flemings, John and Peter Stokyng, presumably brothers, were accused of killing John, a son of Michael de Brabant, it is added that they had eight other Flemings as accomplices, and one of these was an exile from Ghent, Segher de Wulf.[225] Apart from the latter, five other exiles can be identified in Boston and Lincoln (see Table 2.8). Another sign of permanent settlement was the high presence of craftsmen, most notably weavers, fullers and cordwainers. For example, two brothers

221 *Yorkshire Sessions of the Peace 1361–1364*, ed. B. Putnam (Cambridge, 1939), pp. 20, 22, 27, 37.

222 On aliens in late medieval Lincolnshire, see Kissane and Mackman, 'Aliens and the law in late medieval Lincolnshire', pp. 105–23.

223 TNA, JUST 3/142, m. 48.

224 Kissane and Mackman, 'Aliens and the law in late medieval Lincolnshire'.

225 TNA, JUST 2/67, m. 17. Others were Lewin de Clerk, Mathias de Cortrik, Rase van Hulst, John van de Troye, William de Gaunt, Flemmyng, and Henry Sutor de Oldenard.

Table 2.8 *Names of Flemings appearing in Lincolnshire and Yorkshire sources between 1351 and 1381 and on the lists of exiles of 1351 and those pardoned in 1359*[i]

Yorkshire and Lincolnshire sources	Lists of exiles and pardons
Laurencius de Coninc, de Flandre, *webster*, York	Lauwerens Coning, weaver from Deinze
Georgius Fote, de Flandre, *walker*, York	Joris Voet, fuller from Poperinghe
John de Seint-Trude, weaver, York	Jan van Sinte Truiden, weaver from Bruges
Bartholomew Friend, de Flandre, Boston	Meeus Vriend, fuller from Bruges
John van Gerdesbergh, Boston	Jan van Gerardsberghe, from Ghent
John Goderman, de Gaunt, Lincoln	Jan Goedername, weaver from Ghent
John Fan Lynde, Lincoln	Jan van den Lynde, weaver from Ypres
Sigradus de Wulf, Boston	Segher de Wulf, weaver from Ghent

[i] Laurencius de Coninc, de Flandre, *webster*, York: *Register of the Freemen of the City of York, Vol. I: 1272–1558*, ed. F. Collins, Surtees Society no. 96 (Durham, 1897), p. 48 and *Cartulaire des Artevelde*, p. 725; Georgius Fote, de Flandre, *walker*, York: *Register of the Freemen of York*, ed. Collins, vol. I, p. 48 and *Cartulaire des Artevelde*, p. 730; John de Seint-Trude, weaver, York: TNA, E 122/7/10, m. 10 and SAB, Groenenboek C, fo. 118r; Bartholomew Friend: TNA, JUST 2/67 m. 27; TNA, JUST 3/32/2, m. 157d and *Cartulaire des Artevelde*, p. 720; John van Gerdesbergh, Boston: TNA, JUST 2/67, m. 17d and *Cartulaire des Artevelde*, p. 711; John Goderman, de Gaunt, Lincoln: *CPR, 1364–7*, p. 88 and *Cartulaire des Artevelde*, p. 711; John fan Lynde: TNA, E 372/221, m. 16d and *Cartulaire des Artevelde*, p. 732; Sigardus de Wulf: TNA, JUST 2/67, m. 17 and *Cartulaire des Artevelde*, p. 711.

from Brabant, Walter and Adam Appel, were accused to have murdered a fuller exiled from Bruges, Bartholomew Friend, in 1364. Similarly, when John Clerk, a cordwainer from Sluys, and John Adam, a *webster* from Brabant, were pronounced to have died under suspicious circumstances by the coroner, other immigrants from the Low Countries were the main suspects.[226] Moreover, John Goderman, an exile from Ghent, was allegedly murdered by a weaver, John Burnet, from Diest in Brabant, in 1365,[227] while in 1375, a certain Galfride Webster, *Braban*, was held responsible for the murder of Reginald Webster, *Braban*, who had both taken up residence in Lincoln.[228] Moreover, if we look into towns like

[226] TNA, JUST 2/67, mm. 27, 29, 29d.

[227] TNA JUST 3/149, m. 8; JUST 3/32/2, m. 103; *CPR, 1364–7*, p. 88.

[228] TNA, KB 27/459, m. 34 (REX).

Colchester or Great Yarmouth, where both coroner's rolls and local records survive, we can confirm that those involved in royal judicial records are also found in their borough courts as permanent residents, suggesting that a similar trend was happening in other English towns without detailed local records. Three immigrants from the Low Countries, Herman de Coloyne, Adam Queldyk and an exile from Ypres, John van Lynde, were among thirteen men responsible for the payment of the fee farm by the guild of weavers of Lincoln to the crown for three years in a row from 1376 until 1379.[229] This suggests that by this time the Flemings tended to join the local guild of weavers and avoid creating their own, like those in London, as we saw earlier.

In the surviving records of poll taxes from 1381 for Boston, few immigrants from the Low Countries are noticeable. William Flemmyng and Alice, his wife, paid the subsidy, while a certain John Sleght had Lamkin from Flanders for a servant.[230] Apart from Alice, there were three other Flemish women who appeared in the coroner's rolls, two in Lincoln and one in Boston. All of them were married and seem to have been involved in cloth production. Katerina, wife of William Seland, tailor, and Alice, wife of William de Coloyne, *Braban*, were accused of the theft of diverse cloths. However, they were both subsequently acquitted.[231] William de Coloyne, *Braban*, might have been related to a weaver called Herman de Coloyne, *Braban*, who also settled in Lincoln and was a member of the local guild.[232]

We have seen that London attracted the most prominent Flemish and Brabantine textile workers. However, it seems that the case of Lincolnshire was a little bit different, or this might be a reflection of the limits of the available sources. In 90 per cent of Lincolnshire cases in the coroner's rolls, felons from the Low Countries, when accused, were said to have no chattels or goods to be distrained by. In cases where they had some possessions, the amounts were low. When an exile from Ghent, John van Gerdesbergh, was accused of the murder of John van Dorne, he was distrained by 6d found on him.[233] It looks as if Lincolnshire attracted poorer ranks of textile workers from the Low Countries. In comparison, when members of the mercantile community of Easterlings, more commonly known as Hanseatic merchants, appear in the coroner's rolls as defendants, their goods are usually estimated at 40s at least.[234]

[229] TNA, E 372/221, m. 16d. See also A. Kissane, *Civic Community in Late Medieval Lincoln: Urban Society and Economy in the Age of the Black Death, 1289–1409* (Rochester, 2017), pp. 25–6, 93–123.

[230] Fenwick, *Poll Taxes*, vol. II, pp. 22, 23.

[231] TNA, JUST 3/142, mm. 47, 51d.

[232] See n. 229.

[233] TNA, JUST 2/67, m. 17.

[234] TNA, JUST 2/67, m. 26.

FLEMINGS IN THE SOUTH AND SOUTH-WEST

We saw above that in May 1350 Edward III issued letters of protection to those Flemings who, following the failure of the rebellion, had emigrated to England. He specifically stated that they settled in London, Canterbury, Norwich, Salisbury, Lynn, and other English cities and towns.[235] The fact that Salisbury was specifically mentioned makes us believe that some number of exiles certainly settled there during the 1350s.[236] Unfortunately, the records of Salisbury for the 1350s are completely missing, thus making an extensive quantitative analysis impossible. However, the extant coroner's rolls from the 1360s and 1370s suggest that exiles did settle in this town. A weaver from Salisbury, William ate Forde, was murdered by one John Penchener, a Fleming, while a weaver exiled from Ghent, Luppin Lyghtfoot, was allegedly murdered by John Andreu, a bellows-maker from Northwich in Cheshire, in 1377.[237] Salisbury was known for producing rays, a striped fabric manufactured to narrower specifications than standard broadcloth, very similar to those from Ghent. Given the type of cloth the Ghent exiles were producing in London during the 1370s, as we will see in Chapter 4, it is not surprising that some of them actually found their way to Salisbury after the banishment in 1351, as the coroner's rolls suggest. Moreover, the poll taxes reveal that even in the 1370s, some Flemings involved in the textile industry still lived there. For example, Walter Flemyng, Lodewyk Combere and Hugo Braban with their servants and some other immigrants from the Low Countries paid the subsidy in 1379.[238]

Not far from Salisbury, the city of Winchester had also seen the presence of Flemings from the 1340s.[239] A dyer from Flanders, Nicholas Appelman, with other fullers and dyers in his company settled in Winchester during the second half of the 1330s.[240] Their numbers increased from the 1350s, and this is attested in the city's borough court. In 1361, Clays Flemyng and Giles Flemyng drew blood from a weaver, John Plom, and got licence to agree, which was brokered by another

[235] The letters were not entered on the chancery patent rolls but were recorded in an inspeximus confirmation by London's court of husting in 1364. LMA, CLA/023/DW/93/19.

[236] For example, Colchester and Great Yarmouth were not specifically mentioned, and we have seen in previous pages that considerable numbers of Flemings found their place in these towns.

[237] TNA, JUST 2/199, mm. 2d, 8.

[238] Fenwick, *Poll Taxes*, vol. III, pp. 112, 113, 114, 115, 116, 117. Apart from Walter and Hugo and their servants, there are Edward Braban, Johannes Gyngyvere, Richard ate Brugge, William Gys, Giles Flemyng and Johannes Fogheler with obviously Flemish names.

[239] Keene, *Survey of Medieval Winchester*, p. 380.

[240] *CPR, 1334–8*, p. 500.

Fleming, Simon Monyn.[241] Several other affrays between Flemings occurred the same year, and it was said that all of them were carrying knives with sharpened points, contrary to a recent proclamation.[242] Lippin Flemyng was fined for forestalling and appeared on several other occasions both alone and with his servants in debt and trespass cases.[243] As can be seen, their forenames confirm their origin from the Low Countries, but apart from them, immigrant women were present too. For example, in 1364, Isabel Shepster raised the hue against Margaret Braban.[244]

In his extensive work on medieval Winchester, Derek Keene also noticed a Flemish presence in the borough court records, but he concluded that 'there was nothing to suggest that any of the weavers of the fourteenth and early fifteenth centuries were alien in origin'.[245] Indeed, in most of the cases recorded in the borough court of Winchester, the occupations of Flemings were not stated. This information was provided in only three cases: those of John Flemyng, glover, Nicholas Armourer, *Flemyng*, and Lambert Appelman, dyer.[246] This led Keene to the conclusion that some Flemish immigrants may have worked for Winchester weavers, but that it was perhaps in finishing and in organisational skills, rather than in weaving, that the aliens made their contribution.[247] However, in 1367 William Taye, *Fleming*, and his wife, Margaret, brought a trespass case against a local weaver, John Plom.[248] The latter appears to have abducted their servant, who was of Flemish origin as well.[249] At the same time, John Plom was involved in a brawl with Copin Flemyng, Oliver Flemyng and John Flemyng.[250] It is very interesting that these two cases shifted to the court of the exchequer, as John Plom brought a case against the mayor and bailiffs for false imprisonment. He pleaded that William Taye, *Fleming*, entered his (John's) house and carried away cloth to the value of 20 marks. However, the bailiffs responded that John Plom was arrested because he had summoned Francis Flemyng, *webbe* (another term to denote a weaver), John Flemyng, *webbe*, and Peter Flemyng, *webbe*, as well as a second John Flemyng, *webbe*, and at the point of a sword extracted oaths that they

241 HRO, W/D1/8, m. 10. Licence to agree means the court allowed them to resolve the issue.

242 HRO, W/D1/8, m. 10d.

243 HRO, W/D1/11, m. 1, W/D1/11, m. 8d.

244 HRO, W/D1/11, m. 8. Apart from Margaret Braban, it is attested that Simon Monyn came with his wife, Beatrix, and William Taye with his wife, Margaret. See W/D1/8, m. 10 and W/D1/13, m. 5.

245 Keene, *Survey of Medieval Winchester*, p. 301.

246 HRO, W/D1/16, m. 19d, W/D1/16, m. 18d; TNA, CP 40/402, m. 131d.

247 Keene, *Survey of Medieval Winchester*, p. 301.

248 HRO, W/D1/13, m. 5.

249 *Ibid.*

250 *Ibid.*

would never exercise their craft in the city of Winchester.[251] This information leads us to the conclusion that most of the immigrants from the Low Countries in Winchester were indeed weavers, as in other towns in England. The immigrants would appear to have suffered strong opposition from the local textile workers, as another case like this one from the court of the exchequer appeared five years later in the borough court. In this case, it was claimed that Richard Frost and William, a servant of Robert Douning, attacked Matthew Flemyng and John Flemyng, and made them swear at knife-point that they would never enter, or stay in, the city of Winchester.[252]

In order to downplay the importance of Flemish textile workers to the English industry, as we saw in the Introduction, H. L. Gray used the argument that there was no evidence of their presence in Bristol and the West Country during the reign of Edward III. The counties of Gloucestershire and Hampshire, together with Bristol, were responsible for the manufacture of a quarter of the total cloth production in England in the mid fourteenth century, and therefore this conclusion would seem logical.[253] However, as there are no extant local sources for the period of this study, we have to rely on the royal records. The poll-tax records confirm that there were eleven weavers who paid the subsidy in the city of Bath in 1381. At least two of them were from the Low Countries.[254] Also, in nearby Worcester, amongst three weavers who were listed was one William Braban.[255] Moreover, John Braban, with his servant Godfride, resided in Stow-on-the-Wold in Gloucestershire.[256] A little earlier, in 1360, Henry Braban was robbed and killed at Kingswode, near Bristol.[257] All of these cases would indicate the presence in the West Country of textile workers from the Low Countries.

This is further confirmed by the King's Bench indictments file for Bristol from 1363, produced in connection with the Statute of Labourers. This informs us that Gray's hypothesis about the absence of Flemish weavers in the region was wrong. Out of twenty-four weavers who were fined for taking excessive wages in Bristol, nineteen of them were of Flemish origin.[258] One of them, John Langhe, *Flemyng*, *webbe*, was an

[251] TNA, E 13/88, m. 20. [252] HRO, W/D1/18, m. 4d.

[253] Gray, 'The production and exportation of English woollens', 21–2.

[254] Fenwick, *Poll Taxes*, vol. II, pp. 453–4. [255] *Ibid.*, vol. III, pp. 130–1.

[256] *Ibid.*, vol. I, pp. 264, 284. A certain Margaret Braban appeared as well in Kifsgate Hundred.

[257] *CPR, 1358–61*, p. 387.

[258] TNA, KB 9/29 mm. 12, 15, 16.

> Per magna inquisitione ville Bristoll. Textores qui perciperunt excessivi salarii: Lyvyn Flemmyng serviens Thomas Caprenter, Georgius Flemmyng, serviens eiusdem Thomasi,

exile from Ghent.[259] That the textile workers were well settled in Bristol is further attested by another case, from 1372, when the bailiffs of Bristol brought a trespass case to the court of the King's Bench against Katerina Frank, Flemmyng, and Gerard Goldsmith.[260] Indeed, a mixed jury that was composed only of weavers, amongst whom were the exiles from Ghent, and Ypres Peter uten Berghe and John Feld, inquired into the claim that Katerina Frank had stolen several pieces of white and mixed cloth from a weaver, John Hanam.[261] It seems that Gerard Goldsmith and his wife, Johanna, helped Katerina escape the authorities and leave for London. We do not know what happened subsequently, as the proceedings for when the verdict was pronounced do not survive. We do know that there were continual contacts between Flemish residents in London and Bristol. In 1370, a Fleming, John Fynger, ran off with the goods of another Fleming, John Clerk, as well as the latter's wife, Katerine. As John Fynger had not appeared in connection with the pleadings, an inquiry was ordered, after which it was established that he had escaped together with Katerine to the western parts of the kingdom, to Gloucestershire.[262]

We may note that weavers from the Low Countries worked both for native and Flemish masters. The presence of exiles and Brabantines suggests that they had probably arrived at the same time as they did in the English towns on the east coast. In the market town of Exeter, for example, a certain weaver, Wilkyn Webster, *Flemyng*, was a householder in 1372.[263] Furthermore, Kowaleski gives a few more references to permanent Flemish settlements in Exeter during the second half of the fourteenth century, with an argument that amongst the numerous foreign merchants that passed through Exeter, some probably remained there for a longer term.[264] However, the abundant surviving court

Wilkyn Braban, serviens Roberti Spenser, William Abbot, Thomas Abbot, filius dicti William, Johanes Langhe, Flemmyng, webbe, Lyvinus, serviens Johanni Hanam, Gerardus Flemyng, webbe, Christianus Flemyng, webbe, Johannes Boner, serviens dicti Christianus, John Braban, serviens Richardi Sampson, Annok Braban, serviens dicti Richardus, Fienn Flemyng, webbe serviens Roberti Foweshule, John wan Strewe, webbe, serviens Willelmi Lavenok, webbe, Janyn Flemyng serviens Walteri Riedmaker, Robert Copin serviens dicti Walterus, John Braban, webbe serviens Richardi Clerk, Hannekyn serviens Roberti Voxhule, Hannekyn Flemmyng, serviens Willelmi Bokemille.

259 *Ibid.* 260 TNA, KB 27/447, m. 24d REX, KB 29/26, m. 27d.

261 *Ibid. Cartulaire historique et généalogique des Artevelde*, ed. De Pauw, p. 733: all members of the jury appear in the indictment file as weavers who received fines for taking excessive wages. Most of them, including the victim, John Hanam, had Flemish apprentices worlking for them. See note 258.

262 TNA, KB 27/439, m. 66. 263 Kowaleski, *Local Markets Exeter*, p. 39 and Appendix 3, p. 394.

264 *Ibid.*, p. 77.

records at the Devon Record Office do not show a large influx of Flemings during the 1350s into this town.

FLEMINGS IN THE MIDLANDS (COVENTRY, NOTTINGHAM AND OXFORD)

Writing about the important industrial centre of the city of Coventry, a prominent economic historian, Eleanora Carus-Wilson, noticed the presence of immigrants in its textile trade. Apart from those from the Low Countries, she considered that the immigration of textile workers from Ireland to Coventry was even higher, but that both of groups contributed to the industrial development of the city.[265] Although the source material is rather fragmentary, there is ample evidence that from the 1350s textile workers from the Low Countries settled in Coventry, and that their numbers were similar to those in other English cities. The surviving assize roll of 1358 makes it clear that those Flemings who found their way to Coventry were involved in the textile industry. Thus, Arnald le Braban, *webbe*, Michael le Braban, *webbe*, Reginald le Webbe, called Braban, were fined 3s each for taking excessive wages, while Margaret Braban, *kempster*, paid a fine for charging 2d for combing 1lb of wool in a manner that fell foul of the Statute of Labourers.[266] In 1359, Andrew Braban, a fuller, with his servant, Henry Braban, struck one John Walkere near Stoneleigh.[267] Indeed, this village on the Avon near Coventry had at least two fulling mills, suggesting that fullers from the Low Countries in Coventry actively used them to full their cloth.[268] A similar picture of the Flemish presence prevails also when we look at the surviving coroner's rolls. As in other towns where the coroner's rolls survive, in Coventry too, Flemish immigrants committed most of the felonies against their compatriots. In 1362, when Margaret la Longe, *Braban*, was murdered by Robert Senlere, *Braban*, the first witness on the scene (or the so-called finder) was another Brabanter, Henry de Tene, while one member of the jury was Gerkine Braban.[269] Also in the 1360s, when

[265] E. Carus-Wilson, 'The overseas trade of late medieval Coventry', in E. Perroy (ed.), *Economies et sociétés au Moyen Âge: Mélanges offerts à Edouard Perroy* (Paris, 1973), pp. 371–81; Carus-Wilson, 'Trends in the export of English woollens', 162–79.

[266] TNA, JUST 1/971, m. 1d. [267] TNA, CP 40/396, m. 198d, CP 40/397, m. 94d.

[268] L. F. Salzman (ed.), *The Victoria History of the Counties of England: A History of the County of Warwick: Knightlow Hundred* (London, 1951), vol. VI, pp. 229–30.

[269] TNA, JUST 2/182, m. 1.

Matthew Bursel killed James Braban in self-defence, the first witness on the scene was Katarina Braban.[270]

The drapers of Coventry seem to have had business connections with Flemish exiles from London as well. Indeed, John Donty, a draper from Coventry, owed 6s for a red cloak to James van den Ackere, who was a weaver exiled from Ypres living in London.[271] In the particulars of the poll-tax records of 1379, there are nine married couples, one single man (Henry Braban) and one single woman (Margareta Braban) with the surname 'Braban'.[272] For some of them the occupation is specified as *webbe*, and all twenty of these immigrants paid 4d towards the poll tax. What is striking is that both in the 1350s and in the poll-tax records of the late 1370s, the term used for Flemings in Coventry is always *Braban*. Whether they were all from Brabant or not still remains to be investigated. However, Coventry made its name on the international market through the 'Coventry blues' (a woollen cloth dyed blue), and the expertise of Brabantine weavers, coming from the duchy whose textile industry was greatly expanding by the 1350s, had certainly helped this development.[273] Apart from Coventry in Warwickshire, the presence of immigrants from the Low Countries was attested in Stratford-upon-Avon and Henley on Arderne (modern-day Henley-in-Arden).[274]

From the 1360s, the medium-sized provincial town of Nottingham became the residence of some immigrants from the Low Countries. In its voluminous extant borough court rolls we find evidence of litigation that can provide us with some aspects of immigrants' life experiences in this town in the second half of the fourteenth century. For example, in 1362, William Strelley brought a plea of covenant against Albright Walker, *Braban*, who agreed to repair a piece of cloth made by William, but allegedly wasted and crushed it by his *walking* (fulling)

[270] TNA, JUST 2/182, m. 2. Matthew Bursel was assisted by a certain John Mensill, but was subsequently pardoned; see *CPR, 1364–7*, p. 376.

[271] TNA, CP 40/440, mm. 19, 577. For more on James van den Ackere, see the section on Flemings in London in this chapter.

[272] Fenwick, *Poll Taxes*, vol. II, pp. 679, 680, 683, 687, 688.

[273] For a description of 'Coventry blues', see Carus-Wilson, 'The overseas trade of late medieval Coventry', p. 372; Bautier, 'La Place de la draperie brabançonne', 40.

[274] TNA, CP 40/405, m. 133, Reginald Braban was accused of withdrawal from the service of John Norton in Henley on Arderne; TNA, JUST 2/186, m. 2, Henry Braban, who settled in Stratford-upon-Avon, killed Thomas Mandyt. John Braban and his wife were members of the Holy Cross guild in Stratford and paid 22d for the building of a wall. Shakespeare Birthplace Archives, BRT1/3/2.

craft.[275] Three years later, John Swynard accused of breach of covenant another immigrant, Giles Braban, who allegedly failed to weave a linen cloth within an agreed term.[276] In the remaining ten borough court rolls covering the period between 1362 and 1378, we find another fifty-two cases that involved litigants from the Low Countries. As in Colchester and Great Yarmouth, these complaints heard by the court mainly concerned issues of debt and the detention of goods (detinue), but a good proportion of the litigation also fell under the broad category of trespass. Overall, in these fifty-two cases, twenty-four individuals from the Low Countries can be identified, as some of them appeared in the borough court of Nottingham on several occasions opposing natives, or other immigrants from the Low Countries, either to respond to accusations of wrongdoing or to claim damages as compensation. All twenty-four immigrants were characterised as *Braban*, implying that they came from the Duchy of Brabant and were engaged in cloth production. Henry Drope, *Braban*, was a weaver and Nicholas Cole, *Braban*, worked as a fuller, while Margaret Kembester, *Braban*, was engaged as a comber.[277] Although the cases from the borough court of Nottingham provide some interesting details about the involvement of immigrants from the Low Countries in its cloth production, the sample of individuals is too low to permit any broader analysis and conclusions.

Some other places that had seen a degree of permanent settlement by Flemings deserve to be mentioned here as well. Probably one of the most unexpected places to find any Flemish presence was the city of Oxford. Its poll taxes show that there were at least two weavers from the Low Countries who had settled there with their wives. Arthebuk Flemyng, *webbe*, and Goldhende, his wife, paid 18d, while John Moke, *Flemyng*, *webbe*, paid 8d with his wife, Isabella.[278] The guild of weavers in Oxford was granted a charter already in 1130; however, by 1323 the craftsmen petitioned the king to abolish its existence, as they were so poor that they could not pay the annual fee farm to the crown. In 1352, the charter was confirmed, and the weavers of Oxford were discharged from the arrears arising from previous years.[279] How much of this was due to the possible arrival of Flemish exiles in 1351 is difficult to investigate further, due to

[275] Nottinghamshire Archives (hereafter NA) CA 1272, m. 3. [276] NA, CA 1275, m. 13d.

[277] NA, CA 1280a, m. 2; NA, CA 1289, m. 1; NA, CA 1277a, m. 22.

[278] Fenwick, *Poll Taxes*, vol. II, pp. 343, 345.

[279] A. Crossley (ed.), *A History of the County of Oxford, Vol. IV: The City of Oxford* (London, 1979), pp. 35–48.

the lack of sources. Like Oxford, it seems that Cambridge had seen the occasional immigrant from the Low Countries, as Henry van Dale and John Flemyng were captured and accused of the murder there of Henry Fleghe from Louvain in Brabant in 1363.[280] Another inland town where some Flemish-related disturbances took place was Northampton. John Beket, *Fleming*, was murdered by a certain John Roderham in 1357, and John Fyndegold (Vinderhoude), a twisterer, *Flemyng*, by William Brakele, *Fleming*, in 1359.[281]

CONCLUSION

We have seen that various pull-and-push factors played a role in stimulating the settlement of Flemish immigrants all over England. Edward III's favourable immigration policies from 1337 on encouraged the first weavers to cross the Channel and settle in established textile centres during the 1330s and 1340s. Later on, it was events on the other side of the Channel that pushed thousands of skilled workers to emigrate to England. Indeed, after the revolt in 1351 almost 2,000 rebels were banished from the county of Flanders. We cannot know whether all of them went to England. However, the evidence presented suggests that a very large majority amongst them found refuge in England, as Edward III granted them protection, and indeed they become very visible in English sources from the 1350s on. Most of them were followed by other family members or rebels who do not figure on the lists of banished people, as the number of Flemings who do not match the lists is a lot higher than those who do. Some of those who do not figure on the lists might have settled in England for economic reasons as well, as the textile industry in Flanders was already in decline, due to several embargos on the export there of English wool and endemic warfare. The influx of numerous Flemish immigrants was matched by that of textile workers from the Duchy of Brabant, who certainly possessed similar skills and arrived in England at the same time. Thus, it leaves us overall with some 1,100 people who figure in the sources of London, Great Yarmouth and Colchester, and in other towns in England during the thirty-year period 1351–81. At least 200 of them can be traced to Flanders, as they match perfectly the lists of people banished after the rebellion of 1351. This is striking, given the very pessimistic estimates of previous studies about the

[280] TNA, JUST 3/223/1, m. 330.
[281] *CPR, 1358–61*, p. 260; TNA, JUST 3/140; *CPR, 1354–8*, p. 528.

number of Flemings who migrated, and especially about the localities of their settlement and of the cloth industry. De Sagher suggested that no more than 200 textile workers from the Low Countries settled across the whole of England.[282] The numbers and findings presented above suggest strongly that the accepted views and hypotheses must be reconsidered.

[282] Gray, 'The production and exportation of English woollens', 13–35; De Sagher, 'L'Immigration des tisserands flamands', pp. 109–26; Bolton, *The Medieval English Economy*, p. 268; Heaton, *The Yorkshire Woollen and Worsted Industries*, pp. 8–21.

Chapter 3

SOCIAL RELATIONSHIPS AND BUSINESS NETWORKS OF THE FLEMISH COMMUNITY IN ENGLAND

INTRODUCTION

We have seen in previous chapters that the immigrants did not really create a ghetto in any of the three main towns chosen for the purpose of this study, but preferred rather to settle in areas where their trades were already established among the natives.[1] The number of Flemish immigrants arriving in England during the 1350s was high enough to become visible to their English neighbours. They were probably obliged to act quickly in order to integrate within all spheres of urban English life, as, for a large share of the immigrant population, there was no hope of return, having been banished for eternity. One of the ways to speed up the process of integration was by expanding their social and business networks. As we will see, some of the immigrants already possessed substantial social capital, through political connections in Ghent and Bruges. Moreover, the fact that they arrived as a large group of migrants with similar backgrounds (e.g. textile workers, exiles with families) provided them with the basis for forming a network of family and friends that would reduce the economic and psychological risk of migration. The evidence confirms this pattern, as the immigrants from the Low Countries held closer relationships with their compatriots. Inevitably, they mixed with the native population; however, as we will see later, their relationships with the English were largely based around business matters. But what were the strategies used by the new arrivals to strengthen their position in the new environment? How did Flemings create and expand their social and business networks? The present chapter is concerned with exploring the integration process of the immigrant community, and with how that reflected on both their daily life and the organisation of trade. It will examine the social and business

[1] See Chapter 2 and the sections on London, Colchester and Great Yarmouth, and Maps 2, 3 and 4.

networks of the Flemish immigrants as evidenced in the surviving testamentary records and through the judicial documents.

INTEGRATION INTO THE HOST SOCIETY AND DEVELOPING A NETWORK

Enjoying a wide network of reliable contacts is a good indicator of success in business and of one's standing in a society, and may help getting through significant changes in life in general. The size of a person's network connections and the resources that the same person can mobilise through such networks represent his or her (symbolic, economic and cultural) social capital.[2] The medieval city, with its marketplace and formal institutions that performed legal, religious and political functions, provided a space where people could interact in many ways and develop friendly or business networks, generating various forms of social capital. The available formal institutions in English towns such as borough and royal courts and parish churches provided activity that allowed individuals to create and expand networks, whether their participation in these institutions was voluntary or involuntary.[3] This was one of the ways for the participants to create personal networks based upon respect, trust, and shared experience that comprised people beyond their own families, immediate neighbours, and personal friends.

For the immigrants from the Low Countries in England, the existence of borough and royal courts, the marketplace and the church in towns where they settled, provided them with a setting where they could develop both informal and formal networks. Their participation in formal institutions was facilitated by Edward III shortly after the banishment. Indeed, soon after the immigrants' arrival, the king issued a letter patent in 1352, which in a way defined their legal position within the realm and granted them the right to plead in English courts of law.[4] The available judicial institutions in English towns provided the Flemish community with legal framework around which they were able to organise their economic activities. Moreover, the immigrants' participation in local and royal courts would put them in contact not only with other residents engaged in similar occupations, but also with the dominant members of the community who held urban office, defined the rules

[2] P. Bourdieu, 'Le Capital social: Notes provisoires', *Actes de la Recherche en Science Sociale*, 31:1 (1979), 2–3.

[3] M. K. McIntosh, 'The diversity of social capital in English communities 1300–1640 (with a glance at modern Nigeria)', *Journal of Interdisciplinary History*, 29:3 (1999), 459–90, at 459.

[4] *CPR, 1350–4*, p. 147. For this letter, see Chapter 6 and the context of the following conflicts between native and Flemish weavers.

in the market and maintained connections with native and foreign merchants.[5] Mixing with the natives in local institutions would provide the newcomers with information about the area and the community that could assist them economically. These interactions would allow the immigrant artisans to establish long-lasting relationships that would go beyond just economic interests, helping them to learn whom to turn to for advice or assistance.

We established in Chapter 2 that about 1,200 immigrants from the Low Countries settled in England. The extant borough and royal court rolls, in combination with poll-tax and testamentary records, provide evidence for the contexts in which these immigrants interacted and created ties with other individuals: in the marketplace, in political and guild structures, in business and in social settings, as well as in the family. The poll-tax records and the lists of exiles provide us with basic information about their family structures. In addition to the immediate family members and relatives, in the wills we may observe the loosely defined informal ties of friendship with neighbours and closer business partners. Meanwhile, the broader social networks with or without economic ties can be reconstructed through the court records. The focus here will be on the study of the number of connections in the network of textile workers from the Low Countries. We will also examine how far these connections extended beyond the family to incorporate occupational ties, and links within and without the immigrant population, as well as any ties they formed outside their town of settlement.

Although the combination of sources available to us contains valuable information for reconstructing the immigrants' social and business networks, they each contain some limits to this endeavour. Apart from information on wealth and the parish of burial (the place where a person had lived), wills provide a wide range of facts that can help us reconstruct the relationships between family members, business partners or neighbours. However, no testamentary evidence concerning Flemish immigrants is extant for Colchester and Great Yarmouth for the period of the study, and only those from London could be used. Given the size of its territory, the legal development of the city and the size of the population, the city of London enjoyed several jurisdictions of probate, which was determined by a Londoner's wealth and whether he or she owned London burgage land or land outside the city.[6] Enrolled wills are

[5] McIntosh, 'The diversity of social capital', 463.

[6] J. Colson, 'Local communities in fifteenth-century London: Craft, parish and neighborhood', unpublished Ph.D. thesis, Royal Holloway London (2011), p. 51.

preserved at various city courts from the thirteenth century.[7] In the fourteenth century, those who were wealthy and owned property within the London burgage tended to have their wills enrolled in the court of husting,[8] while those who were even wealthier and owned property in more than one diocese had their wills enrolled in the prerogative court of Canterbury.[9] However, as the immigrants do not appear in the former, and the amount of extant wills in the latter is disappointingly low for the fourteenth century, these records were not used here. The testamentary evidence that I have focused on are the wills enrolled with the courts of the bishop of London: in the archdeaconry and commissary courts of London.[10] This means that, as far as textile workers are concerned, the evidence is quite fragmentary and leaves us with only twenty-nine wills overall enrolled by the Flemish community of London in the period 1374–1405.

Justin Colson has suggested that among the problems encountered when using wills in London for the purpose of prosopographical study are the limited number of individuals who made the wills and testaments, their strong adherence to convention, which possibly limited the scope for individual expression, and their limited intended purpose.[11] The wills of Flemings are no exception to this rule, but still provide a glimpse of the types of relationship and interaction the immigrants had throughout their stay in London. Indeed, the formal bequests to various people can be an indicator of personal relationships between the testator and other individuals. The most popular candidates for receiving bequests include employees, servants and apprentices. Other types of bequest that regularly appear in wills are those to charitable institutions, and in the immigrants' case this occurrence might be a good indicator of their level of integration. Another way to evaluate the immigrants' relationships was their choice of executors, whose role was to fulfil the final wishes of the testator concerning the distribution of goods. The importance of this role implies that it involved a significant amount of trust and suggests that the chosen person was someone who had a close relationship with the testator.

7 On the availability of wills in London during the Middle Ages, see *ibid.*, pp. 51–5.

8 *Calendar of Wills Proved and Enrolled in the Court of Husting London AD 1258–1688*, ed. R. R. Sharpe, 2 vols. (London, 1890).

9 *Index of Wills to the Prerogative Court of Canterbury and now Preserved in the Principal Probate Registry, Somerset House, London*, 12 vols. (Canterbury, 1893).

10 LMA, MS 9171/1; LMA, MS 9051/1; Fitch, *Index Commissary Court*; Fitch, *Index Archdeaconry Court*.

11 Colson, 'Local communities', p. 55.

The court records, and the borough court rolls in particular, make it possible to observe interactions between members of the whole community, rather than from just the personal perspective of one individual, as is the case with the wills. The court rolls can indicate who the major actors were in the town's business and politics, as well as who traded with whom and to what extent, evidencing connections and hierarchies within the urban community. The pleas of debt, detinue, breach of covenant and the broad category of trespass in the borough courts of Great Yarmouth and Colchester as well as the Court of Common Pleas expose the types of commercial interaction among the immigrants from the Low Countries in English towns. Cases for debt encompassed loans, default in rent payments, money owed for wages and goods sold on credit. Pleas involving breach of contract were cases in which an individual failed to uphold an employment agreement, which was usually concluded orally. Detinue cases were those involving goods left in the care of one individual for either work or storage purposes and which were not returned to their owner. The final type of civil litigation comprised cases related to private property or physical aggression, both falling under the broad notion of trespass.[12]

In the second half of the fourteenth century, the authorities in Colchester and Great Yarmouth met several times a week to hear individual pleas brought by the town dwellers and helped them resolve disputes. The total number of suits a year heard at the court of pleas in Colchester rose steadily from sixty-two in 1351–2 to reach a peak of 878 pleas in 1387–8. Richard Britnell showed that this growth of activity in the court was linked with the overall economic expansion of the town, and more specifically of its cloth industry, that took place between 1353 and 1380.[13] This is further confirmed if we look more closely at the types of plea. As can be seen in Table 3.1, the proportion of debt litigation went from about 20 per cent of all cases in 1351–2 to about 65 per cent of all pleas in 1384–5. At the same time the proportion of cases for trespass went through the reverse process. While the rise in the total number of cases for trespass presumably followed the increase in population, its proportion relative to the overall number of pleas brought to the court fell from more than 50 per cent of cases in 1351–2 to only 20 per cent of cases in 1387–8. The growth of business was reflected in

[12] For more about the types of plea and the functioning of the borough court, see: M. Kowaleski, 'Town courts in medieval England: An introduction', in R. Goddard and T. Phipps (eds), *Town Courts and Urban Society in Late Medieval England, 1250–1550* (Woodbridge 2019), pp. 17–42, and the bibliography there; Baker, *An Introduction to English Legal History*, pp. 60–4.

[13] Britnell, *Growth and Decline*, pp. 98–104.

Table 3.1 *Pleas brought to Colchester borough court 1351–85*

Year	Debt	Breach of contract	Detinue	Account	Trespass	Unknown	Other	Total
1351/2	12	5	1	0	42	1	1	62
1353/4	32	9	8	0	72	4	2	127
1356/7	61	5	9	0	51	2	1	129
1359/60	125	37	14	1	106	2	1	286
1360/1	52	9	21	0	47	0	0	131
1364/5	224	29	18	0	175	0	0	446
1366/7	243	35	25	0	81	0	3	387
1372/3	173	36	12	0	100	0	1	322
1374/5	205	45	21	0	154	2	0	425
1378/9	395	44	6	0	83	4	0	532
1381/2	467	49	19	2	113	1	3	654
1382/3	402	23	25	1	84	2	0	537
1384/5	481	41	23	0	92	0	6	643

Dataset based on: ERO, D/B 5, CR 9–22

the fact that there was a rise in the total number of court cases as a result of a considerable increase in debt litigation.

The immigrants from the Low Countries made use of the available courts as soon as they arrived. Of the 3,036 cases treated in the town's court of pleas between 1351 and 1383, 327, slightly more than 10 per cent, involved newcomers from the Low Countries. Their activity in the court corresponded roughly to the proportion of immigrants in the overall population of Colchester, which also stood at around 10 per cent, as we saw in the previous chapter. Considered over the whole period between 1351 and 1383, Flemings most frequently appeared in court for trespass, accounting for 165 cases, or 50.4 per cent overall, slightly higher than those for debt, which added up for 134 cases, or 41 per cent. Cases for breach of contract and detention of chattels involving immigrants from the Low Countries were below 10 per cent, which constitutes the same proportion as the overall average for this type of litigation heard before the courts in Colchester. Except during the first years after their arrival, when the involvement of Flemings in cases for trespass was much more pronounced, the patterns of their litigation tended to follow the general activities of the court from 1360 onwards (Table 3.2). As economic activity in the town increased towards the end of the 1350s, pleas for debt or breach of contract involving Flemings (twenty-one of the fifty-eight cases, or 36.2 per cent between 1361 and 1367) caught up with those for trespass and assault (which dropped to thirty-three cases, or 56.9 per cent), bringing the immigrants' averages closer to the overall ones.

As far as the number and types of plea are concerned, a slightly different trend might be observed in Great Yarmouth during the same period in comparison with Colchester. Given Great Yarmouth's character as a port town heavily engaged in trade, the activity in the borough court was proportionally higher, relative to the town's population. Yarmouth's total number of pleas stood almost at the same level as in Colchester, 3,454 as against 3,036, while its population was around half. Although the borough court of Great Yarmouth heard more cases on average a year than Colchester borough court, it followed a similar pattern in terms of the types of plea. The majority of proceedings between 1351 and 1384 consisted of pleas for debt, constituting 1,683 cases, followed by 1,112 cases for trespass, while the cases for broken contract and detention of chattels accounted for 422 and 237 cases respectively. Over the same period (1351–84), the proportion of pleas in the borough court of Great Yarmouth involving immigrants from the Low Countries was slightly more than 10 per cent, or 359 cases. In 170 cases they were in litigation for debt, followed by 142 cases for

Table 3.2 *Pleas brought by immigrants to Colchester borough court 1351–85*

Year	Debt	Breach of contract	Detinue	Account	Trespass	Unknown	Other	Total
1351/2	0	0	0	0	2	0	0	2
1353/4	7	0	0	0	14	3	0	24
1356/7	1	0	0	0	7	1	0	9
1359/60	8	1	0	0	22	6	0	36
1360/1	7	0	0	0	15	0	0	22
1364/5	11	2	1	0	18	1	0	33
1366/7	17	0	2	0	17	0	0	36
1372/3	28	5	2	0	32	0	0	67
1374/5	11	9	0	0	17	0	0	37
1376/7	17	4	0	0	19	0	0	40
1378/9	29	2	0	0	33	0	0	64
1381/2	15	3	1	0	16	0	0	35
1382/3	30	2	3	0	16	0	0	51
1384/5	40	7	2	0	25	0	0	74

Dataset based on: ERO, D/B 5, CR 9–22

Table 3.3 *Types of plea brought to Great Yarmouth borough court 1351–84*

Type of plea	Number of entries	Percentage
Debt	1687	48.8
Trespass	1112	32.2
Breach of covenant	442	12.8
Detinue	240	6.9

Dataset based on: NRO, Y/C4/72–95

Table 3.4 *Types of plea brought by immigrants to Great Yarmouth borough court 1351–84*

Type of plea	Number of entries	Percentage
Debt	170	47.5
Trespass	142	39.7
Breach of covenant	32	8.9
Detinue	15	4.2

Dataset based on: NRO, Y/C4/72–95

trespass, while the pleas for broken contract and detinue accounted for 47 cases altogether (see Table 3.3).

By appearing most commonly in pleas of debt, immigrants from the Low Countries followed the general trends of the court. However, they brought pleas for trespass to a slightly higher degree than the natives, or 39.7 per cent as against 32.2 per cent (see Table 3.4). We must bear in mind that some of the pleadings that fell under trespass might have been of an economic nature as well. It has been shown that cases for trespass do not necessarily imply that there was physical violence involved. Trespass was used in some cases when cloth had been given for fulling or weaving and was torn or destroyed in the process.[14] For example, in 1366 in Colchester, Katherine, the wife of Clais Segher, was accused of trespass by John Webbe. Later in the pleadings the plaintiff noted that Katherine was supposed to break the wool for him, but stole dyed cloth worth 30s, so no physical violence happened, but the case was still entered as trespass.[15] In any case, the higher level of economic activity among the

[14] Baker, *An Introduction to English Legal History*, pp. 60–4.
[15] ERO, D/B 5, CR 15, m. 5, calendared in Benham, *Court Rolls*, vol. II, p. 193.

Flemings in Great Yarmouth than among those in Colchester may be explained by several factors. In addition to its proximity to an established textile production centre like Norwich, as a port town Great Yarmouth was characterised by a higher presence of merchants relative to its size, all of which fostered a lively exchange of capital and goods.

It is also important to mention that immigrants from the Low Countries made use of such royal courts as the King's Bench and the Court of Common Pleas, which can also be useful in the assessment of their social and business networks. Because of the sheer volume of actions heard before the Court of Common Pleas, I was obliged to sample the material, to get an impression of the types of plea immigrants from the Low Countries brought to this court. Out of a total of 120 rolls extant from the period 1352–82, I randomly chose twenty for examination, each one containing pleas for one term of a year. A representative sample of 100 cases that involved textile workers from the Low Countries was extracted in order to demonstrate some patterns of their connection to other actors of commercial activity. As we will see, the cases in the royal courts involving immigrants from the Low Countries paint a slightly different picture in comparison with those from the borough courts. More than three-fourths of all cases dealt with debt, detinue and withdrawal from service, and only seventeen cases were concerned with trespass. We can observe that the immigrants' business networks went far beyond their own community. In 89 out of 100 cases they were in litigation with English people and 7 times with their compatriots, and 4 times the Flemings opposed other aliens. In these cases, the amounts of debt ranged from 40s to £40, suggesting that immigrant artisans were operating within serious business networks. As far as other royal judicial documents are concerned, such as the King's Bench, gaol deliveries or the coroner's rolls, I was able to go through all available material in those geographical areas where the Flemish presence was detected over the period of study. However, only thirty-nine cases involved immigrants from the Low Countries. Even though these documents mostly contain information about individuals involved in felonies, they can still shed some light on the types of contact that existed between the immigrants' community and the natives'.

THE IMMIGRANTS' SOCIAL NETWORKS

Minor problems notwithstanding, the wills in London are valuable for the present study, as they contain prosopographical information that allows us to identify personal relationships. The twenty-nine extant wills from the Flemish community in London are illustrative enough to permit the reconstruction of networks and demonstrate that the immigrants from the Low Countries represented a closely connected community. Two wills left by two sisters-in-law, Lelia Blawer and Mabila (Belia) Petersone, provide an especially good example of how immigrants in London were connected to one another. In this case, the wills show that each woman had a small network of her own, but they were both related through family and occupational ties. The individual acting as a 'bridge' between two network clusters was John Peterson, called Ewersward, a haberdasher, who was Lelia's brother and Mabila's first husband.[16]

Lelia Blawer wanted to be buried in the churchyard of St James Garlickhythe next to her husband, a dyer, Peter Blawer, and Belia Petersone wished to be buried at St Martin Orgar in Candlewick Street.[17] We notice that both of them had ties through their husbands, who were both in the textile sector and also lived in the same locations as other artisans from the clothing industry.[18] John Ewersward and Peter Blawer even did business together over the years they were alive.[19] Both Lelia and Belia bequeathed various amounts to their respective churches and the clerics in them, a very common practice for testators in the Middle Ages. However, it is through the bequests to friends and family that we are able to reconstruct the relationships amongst Flemings in London.

The first noticeable thing about their wills is that they only bequeathed money, goods and real estate to other immigrants from the Low Countries. For example, Lelia left 2s 6d to John de Pape, who was her tailor, and 2s to a certain Gys Deigher.[20] She bequeathed 40s to John Dankart, her relative, while he lived with her brother, John Ewersward.[21] It seems that Dankart was Lelia's brother's servant or apprentice, who both tended to be employed through family connections, or simply amongst Flemings, as will be seen in the following sections in this chapter.[22] The remainder of all her goods, chattels, and

16 For a translation of the wills in their entirety, see Appendices 3 and 4.

17 Obviously, Peter was a Fleming, as his name suggests, the Dutch version of this surname being Blauwere (*blauw* – blue, *were* – dye, Peter the blue-dyer). Peter had died one year earlier, in 1384, and enrolled his will at the archdeaconry court, which, unfortunately, does not survive in its entirety: see Fitch, *Index Archdeaconry Court*, vol. I, p. 40.

18 Candlewick Street was traditionally known as a place where drapers and weavers lived, while the parish of St James Garlickhythe near the Thames was a place where dyers operated their business.

19 *CPMR*, vol. II, p. 284.

20 Probably just an occupational name, 'Dyer'; to judge by his forename, Gys is obviously an immigrant from the Low Countries.

21 It is written in Latin 'cognato meo', which could also mean her brother-in-law, or just a relative.

22 A similar pattern of kin relationships between masters and servants was observed in Yorkshire by Jeremy Goldberg in: P. J. P. Goldberg, *Women, Work, and Life Cycle in a Medieval Economy: Women in York and Yorkshire c. 1300–1520* (Oxford, 1992), p. 177.

debts she left wholly to Mathilde, her daughter. However, as Mathilde was a minor at the time, Lelia left her guardianship to the aforementioned John Dankart, her relative, and her brother, John Ewersward. She named John and his wife, Belia, her executors, and left all her ventures in her house, together with the stew-house (brothel)in Medelane Street, to her brother, John Ewersward. An interesting bequest is that of the stew-house, which is the first direct evidence of Flemish women being brothel-keepers, as will be discussed in Chapter 5.

On the other hand, Belia's will reveals some other interesting relationships when combined with other London sources. She bequeathed to her relative, William Mommart, and his wife, Katharine, 60s, one *kertel* (kirtle, a tunic worn by men or women) of red colour and one *courtepi* (a short cloak) also of red (*sangueyn*), and to each of their children the sum of 6s 8d.[23] William Mommart might have been related to a Flemish weaver, Michael Mommart, who appeared in London sources on a few occasions.[24] She bequeathed a veil to Margaret, wife of John van Saverne, and 6s 8d to her son, John van Saverne (who was apparently a godson of Belia's). John van Saverne was a weaver who had emigrated from Ghent to England and even became a bailiff of Flemish weavers in London in 1375.[25] Through the networks of her relatives engaged in the weaving trade, Belia might have met her second husband, John Otemele, who was a Flemish weaver residing in London from at least 1366.[26] We do not know exactly when John Petersone passed away, or when she remarried, but in her will Belia makes bequests to her two husbands' relatives separately: 40s sterling to be divided among the relatives of John Otemele and 4 marks sterling among those of John Petersone.

Although the extent of intermarriage between aliens and the English is difficult to detect, such marriages were not uncommon in late medieval England.[27] However, in case of Belia, she chose to stay among Dutch speakers for both of her marriages. It seems that other immigrants from the Low Countries in the second half of the fourteenth century followed a similar pattern. Some of them, like Lamsin Yperling, a shearer from

23 For a detailed discussion about various items of clothing present in late medieval London, see K. L. French, *Household Goods and Good Households: Consumption and Domesticity after the Plague* (Philadelphia, 2021).

24 *Letter Book G*, p. 182; Fitch, *Index Archdeaconry Court*, vol. I, p. 260. Michael Mommart was not officially banished from the city, but the Mommarts appear as more or less prominent weavers in fourteenth-century Bruges. See J. F. Verbruggen, *Het gemeenteleger*, p. 112, or Jamees, *Poorters*, p. 66, and see also SAB, Wetsvernieuwingen, reeks 114, fols 3v, 12r, 35, 42v, 51r, where deans of weavers appear to have been linked with the Mommart family.

25 *Letter Book H*, p. 17.

26 *CPMR*, vol. II, pp. 65–6.

27 A. Ruddick, 'Immigrants and intermarriage in late medieval England', in McDonald, Ormrod and Taylor (eds), *Resident Aliens*, pp. 181–200.

Bruges, or Lievin Vischer, a weaver from Ghent, were followed by their wives, Agnes and Merrin, to London, after their exile in 1351.[28] For those who were not exiles, the evidence suggests that they were also mostly married to immigrants from the Low Countries. Typical Dutch names like Aughte or Lucebet, who were the wives of William van Karlewyk and John Legat, suggest this pattern.[29] Still, there is one case where the intermarriage between Dutch speakers and English speakers is explicitly mentioned. It is the case of Walter Bukke, a cordwainer from the Low Countries, whose daughters married skinners Robert Faun and John Frenshe.[30]

The wills of Lelia and Belia reveal that at least five immigrant families living in London and engaged in the textile sector were related through kinship ties. This strongly suggests that there was some sort of an established network of chain migration. These families probably did not all arrive at the same time. Those who arrived first retained ties on both sides of the English Channel, and were presumably a source of information that work prospects might be better in London than in the Low Countries. They would also represent trustworthy individuals for newly arrived kin members or friends from back home, which in all likelihood facilitated the operation of business in a new environment. These tight-knit relations doubtless made it easier for immigrants to adapt, especially after banishments throughout the 1350s.

Although other wills left by the Flemish community contain less detail than those of Belia and Lelia, they exhibit similar features. For twenty testators, we know the location of their parish of burial. Eight of them were buried at St Swithin's Church, four at St Laurence Pountney, three at St Martin Vintry and two at St James Garlickhythe, and All Hallows the Great and St Martin Orgar each had one testator. Practically all these parishes were associated with the textile trades, either by their proximity to the locations where clusters of textile workers lived, or by the fact that these churches were known as hosts to fraternities of various textile trades. We notice that, apart from living in the same parishes, immigrants from the Low Countries also tended to bequeath their goods to other Flemings and have their compatriots as executors. For example, a weaver, Walter Paridane, appointed two compatriots, John Kneghtkyn and Martin van Barse, as his administrators.[31] Similarly, another weaver, William van Reven, had Peter Abraham, a Fleming, and John Giers as both executors and administrators.[32] Others, like William van Karlewyk,

[28] LMA, CLA/023/CP/76, m. 15; Jamees, *Poorters*, p. 74.

[29] LMA, MS 9171/1, fo. 132; NRO, Y/C4/91, m. 10d.

[30] *Letter Book H*, p. 353.

[31] LMA, MS 9171/1, fo. 218d.

[32] LMA, MS 9171/1, fo. 33d.

a weaver, or Herman van der Lynden, a tailor, bequeathed all their movables and immovables to their wives and nominated them as executors at the same time.[33] Generally, the executors handled the day-to-day business of distributing an estate, selling goods and commissioning acts of charity, which are quite important tasks demanding a certain amount of trust. The nomination of family members and their compatriots for this role implies that the immigrants from the Low Countries held strong personal ties amongst themselves.

In terms of connection between the testators, one person, Dom Lambert, acted as a bridge for four of them. He was a confessor for John Maynard (St Laurence Pountney), John Mitten (St Martin Vintry), Peter Smyth (St Martin Vintry) and John Obrant (St Swithin), who left their wills between 1380 and 1382.[34] Although it is not specifically mentioned in their wills, Dom Lambert might have been a Fleming himself, suggesting that foreign testators resorted to their compatriots for spiritual guidance as well. The wills, nevertheless, still reveal that there was some level of integration into the native society. Charitable and confraternal affiliations were quite common. For example, Nicholas van den Achere left 40d to be distributed to the poor, as well as another 2 florins to the hospital of St Katharine by the Tower.[35] Belia Petersone, too, left £4 to be distributed amongst the poor.[36] We have seen that the Flemish weavers formed their own guild shortly after their arrival in the 1350s, but the wills also mention that they were members of the parish fraternities, which focused more on sociability than on issues arising from a particular craft. It seems that they were associated with fraternities where the majority of members were natives, as was Belia Petersone, who bequeathed 2s to the fraternity of Carmelites in Fleet Street. But an exile from Bruges, Peter Smyth de Flandre, left a bequest of 2s to the fraternity of *Cortrike* (Courtrai), which was held at the church of St Martin Vintry, suggesting that there were also fraternities that probably restricted membership to immigrants from the Low Countries.[37] This church is known to be the place from which the Flemings were dragged off and killed during the Peasants' Revolt of 1381, and for the first time there is direct evidence that the Flemings actually congregated there.

Another example of exclusive association, where the members consisted only of immigrants from the Low Countries, was the guild of Flemish weavers in London. As mentioned in the previous chapter, already in 1352 Flemish weavers managed to organise themselves into a

[33] LMA, MS 9171/1, fos 132, 201. [34] LMA, MS 9171/1, fos 73, 74, 89, 89d.
[35] LMA, DL/C/B/004/MS09171/1, fo. 97d. [36] LMA, MS 9171/1, fo. 235.
[37] LMA, MS 9171/1, fos 89, 89d.

separate guild from the London weavers.[38] This decision was probably made not just on the basis of the different organisational and production methods that existed between Flemish and English textile workers. Creating a formal group with compatriots might have given them a feeling of security, as they could turn to it for advice or help. Their guild was most probably a place for socialising with other Flemings, which also kept them informed about the conditions and circumstances in cloth manufacture. In the wake of the Statute of Labourers, formal association also gave them a sense of collective action, and the Flemish weavers of London did not hesitate to organise a strike in 1355 in order to demand higher daily wages.[39]

The Flemish weavers were to elect two of their fellow countrymen to survey the work and good behaviour of other craftsmen from Flanders. Thus, the names of their bailiffs, among whom were exiles such as Lambert Funderlynde, John le Gurterre and Henry Navegher, were recorded regularly in the city's Letter Books from the end of 1352 onwards (Table 3.5). The weavers, as the most numerous occupational group among the immigrants, were probably the only ones who had the capacity to get their ordinances approved. We saw in Chapter 2 that many of the exiles in London had occupied key positions in Flanders within the textile guilds or in the city government during the years of the revolt.

Although there seems to have been cohesion between the groups of Flemish and Brabantine weavers during the 1350s, this situation had changed by the end of the decade. The evidence suggests that Brabantine weavers were under the dominance of Flemish exiles. For example, in 1352 the first agreement was made between alien and English weavers in order to acknowledge the aliens' right to work in London without being under the rule of the native weavers' guild. Although the indenture described aliens as Flemings and Brabanters, the delegation who brokered the deal was composed only of Flemish

[38] *CPR, 1350–4*, p. 232. For the context of this grant, see Lambert and Pajic, 'Immigration and the Common Profit', p. 644.

[39] *CPMR*, vol. I, p. 249. This strike was probably a response to the measures taken by the government to prevent the economic situation that arose after the arrival of bubonic plague of 1349. The government issued the Statute of Labourers in 1351 with the primary goal of keeping wages at the 1346 level. It seems that Flemish exiles were demonstrating their discontent with these measures. For more information on the Statute of Labourers, see: C. Given-Wilson, 'The problem of labour in the context of English government, c. 1350–1450', in J. Bothwell, P. J. P. Goldberg and W. M. Ormrod (eds), *The Problem of Labour in Fourteenth-Century England* (York, 2000), pp. 85–100; L. R. Poos, 'The social context of the Statute of Labourers enforcement', *Law and History Review*, 1 (1983), 27–52, at 43–5, 48.

Table 3.5 *Bailiffs of the Flemish weavers in London 1352–77*[i]

Year	Bailiffs
1352	Henry Worre
1353	Henry Were and John de Someryngham
1354	Giles Ripegarst and Peter atte Broke
1355	John Marchaunt de Ipre and Leuyn Oliver
1358	John Vanevergam and Lambert Funderlynde
1361	John le Gruttere and Peter Vanthebrok
1363	John Jonkere and William atte Brugges
1364	John Vunkyn and Giles van Belle
1365	Gerard Vanderheth and Baldewyn Gylot
1366	Gerard van Brugge and William van Brugge
1367	John van Wettre and Paul Stolpard
1368	Peter atte Broke and Henry van the Necke
1369	John Van Everyngham and Henry Naverger
1370	Gerard van Brugge and William van Dayser
1371	John van Everyngham and Dederic Jorys
1372	Henry van Necke and Peter atte More
1373	John Everyngham and Peter Van Broke
1375	Peter atte Broke and John Fanasseverne
1376	William Lanotes and William Vandaye
1377	John Veleyn and Ralph Clofham

[i] *Letter Book G*, pp. 2, 16, 48, 104, 131, 237; *CPMR*, vol. II, p. 84.

exiles.[40] Also, if we look at the names of those who were elected as bailiffs of the aliens' weavers' guild throughout the 1350s, they were always Flemish exiles (Table 3.5). In the first decade of their arrival, Flemings possessed the skills, capital and political leverage to bring about the establishment of the guild. However, after the war in Brabant in 1356, the number of skilled craftsmen from this duchy increased, and they became powerful enough to extricate themselves from the dominance of the guild of Flemish weavers. The Brabantine weavers managed to obtain their own ordinances and to form their own guild. From 1362 onwards, the city's Letter Books show that they elected two of their own masters in the same way as the masters of the guild of

[40] LMA, CLA/023/DW/01/80/184. For a full transcription, see Consitt, *The London Weavers' Company*, pp. 188–91. Those who brokered the deal were the exiles John and William Brunhals, Henry Clofhamer, Levin Godhalse, John Kempe, John van Loo, Levin Olivier, Giles Ripegast, John van Somergham and John atte Were, some of whom became bailiffs later. See Tables 2.1 and 3.5.

English weavers and the guild of Flemish weavers.[41] The discord escalated further when, in 1370, the Flemish weavers petitioned the mayor and aldermen of London to order that the Flemings hold meetings at St Laurence Pounteney and the Brabanters at St Mary Somerset, 'because that the Flemings and the Brabanters were wont to fight and make very great affray in the City'.[42] However, a few years later, the two groups united again and appear to have been without quarrels well into the fifteenth century.

Those from other trades, such as fullers or dyers, seem to have had no problems integrating with the native guilds. When ordinances of fullers were approved in 1376, amongst the fifty-five of those who attached their names to observe that the ordinances were enforced, John Flemmyng and Loy de Dole appeared, who were probably of Flemish origin.[43] A dyer, Peter Blawere, wanted to be buried in the parish church where he lived, at St James Garlickhythe, which was associated with the fraternity of dyers.[44]

In other towns where some sort of guild structure existed for the textile trades, the evidence suggests that Flemings were not excluded and chose not to create a separate guild, as they did in London. In order to safeguard their ordinances, the guild of weavers in Lincoln was obliged to pay a yearly fee farm of £6 to the king.[45] We saw in Chapter 2 that among thirteen weavers who guaranteed the payment, for several years in a row three Flemings appeared, together with ten other native weavers.[46] Although the evidence is fragmentary, it seems that the weavers of York managed somewhat successfully to integrate Flemish and Brabantine weavers into their guild. In 1342, the weavers of York complained against the privileges that were issued to Brabantine and other foreign weavers to settle in that city, because they were producing coloured and rayed cloths.[47] The native weavers specified that by the charter granted to them by Henry II, the weavers of York were the only ones allowed to make such types of cloth, in return for an annual tallage towards which the aliens avoided contributing. When the same

41 *Letter Book G*, pp. 157, 175, 204, 235.
42 *Memorials of London*, ed. Riley, pp. 345–6.
43 *Letter Book H*, p. 37.
44 For more information, see the will of his wife later in this chapter. For his business involvement around St James Garlickhythe, see TNA, CP 40/444, m. 130 and CP 40/448, m. 50.
45 Kissane, *Civic Community Lincoln*, pp. 25–6, 93–123.
46 TNA, E 372/221, m. 16d. These payments were recorded yearly on the pipe rolls. For some years, the names of those who were responsible for the collection of money and payment appear. The fact that Flemish weavers appear along with native weavers for the years where names are available is confirmation that they were effectively members of the local guild.
47 TNA, SC 8/238/11890.

charter was confirmed in 1376, amongst the weavers who attached their names as observers there were no Flemings, suggesting that at that time the aliens might have not been a part of the guild.[48] However, there are signs of cooperation between the two groups prior to this. In 1362, Thomas de Brandesby, a crier of the Court of Common Pleas, accused thirty weavers of York of owing him £7 3s. Two weavers from the Low Countries, Thomas Braban and Levin Geffard, who both became freemen of York in the 1350s, were also part of this group. We do not have further details about the case, but presumably the group of weavers either brought a case together and then made an error in procedure that caused the crier to launch his own lawsuit, or they failed to provide cloth for Thomas.[49] Whatever the case, this evidence suggests that in York textile workers from the Low Countries worked with natives. This is further confirmed in 1358 when the alderman of the weavers' guild in York brought a case to the court of the exchequer against Rumkinus Webster, *Braban*, for escaping from his custody, presumably on the way to respond to someone else's accusation.[50] This suggests that the alien weavers were part of the York weavers' guild, otherwise it would have not been the responsibility of the guild officers to capture them and bring them to justice.

Similarly to those of London, Flemish fullers in York seem to have been a part of the guild together with the natives. In 1364, the fullers of York got their ordinances approved by the local authorities, and amongst thirty masters who swore to observe them was one Lamkin Spalding, whose forename suggests Flemish origin.[51] It seems that outside London, where there was a lot more at stake in terms of quality cloth and contacts with the mercantile community, the Flemings saw no need to organise in a separate guild. Nevertheless, the advantage of sharing a guild with the natives certainly helped their integration into the local community and the faster development of business networks within their own craft.

THE IMMIGRANTS' BUSINESS NETWORKS

As can be seen above, although we have wills and incidental evidence from the Flemish weavers' guild in London, the scope of the information about the immigrants' business networks remains rather limited. Because

[48] *York Memorandum Book*, ed. M. Sellers, 2 vols. (1912–14), vol. I, pp. 238–9.

[49] TNA, CP 40/411, mm. 16d and 334.

[50] TNA, E 13/81, m. 71d.

[51] *York Memorandum Book*, vol. I, pp. 71–7. For evidence of numerous fullers from the Low Countries settled in York, see TNA, JUST 2/217, m. 39, JUST 2/219, m. 2.

of the formulaic nature of wills, we get only a glimpse of their personal ties, while the evidence from the Letter Books provides us with the names of bailiffs of the Flemish weavers elected annually to supervise the statutes and other members of the guild. This only tells us that the immigrants created a network with a vertical structure, which, like any other craft guild, certainly enabled and fostered the formation of business relationships, but it does not tell us more about the interactions between its members. The judicial records, however, allow us not only to identify the immigrant business networks, but also to determine the extent of their interactions within the network of immigrants, as well as with other actors in the marketplace. We will observe how these interactions evolved and evaluate whether the immigrants' connections expanded over time, along with the integration process. We will also try to determine who the main actors were within the network of immigrants from the Low Countries – that is, who the well-established immigrants were with a good reputation and knowledge of local trading conditions, who would facilitate connections between new arrivals and natives. The immigrants' business networks can thus be divided into four categories: those that arose from contacts with Flemish merchants and craftsmen; those produced by contacts with English merchants and artisans within their town of residence; those arising from connections in other towns in England; and those generated by contacts with people from overseas (both their compatriots and other alien merchants).

The first category consisted of the immigrants' relationships stemming from contacts with individuals from the Low Countries residing in their town of settlement. The analysis of these connections comes from the borough courts of Colchester and Great Yarmouth, where Flemish and Brabantine litigants opposed members of their own community 302 times between 1351 and 1384. These include interactions evidenced by 178 cases for trespass, 102 cases for debt and 22 cases for breach of covenant or detention of chattels, all providing us with an insight into the nature of their business relationships with their compatriots.

During the first years after their arrival, Flemish exiles seem to have grouped around existing contacts with their fellow weavers and fullers from the Continent in order to set up their trade and enter the English structures of cloth production. This is best exemplified through the interactions made in the borough court of Great Yarmouth between various litigants and two immigrants from Bruges: Walter Collesad, a fuller, and Peter van Skelle, a weaver. Between 1352 and 1358, Walter Collesad appeared six times in the borough court of Great Yarmouth, while Peter van Skelle did so five times. In these cases, they opposed only banished Flemings involved in cloth manufacture. The disputes had arisen five times from trespass, four times from debts and twice from breach of covenant, and all indicate the cooperation between the exiled weavers and fullers.[52] In 1353, Walter Collessad was first accused in the borough court for an unspecified debt by Peter van Skelle from Bruges, and then, a few months later, Walter acted as plaintiff against John Lythkyrke, a weaver banished from Aalst.[53] A year later, Walter was again sued for debt by John Cuper, another weaver, who was exiled from Dixmuide.[54] Although these cases do not contain more details about amounts of credit, or for what goods or services the money was owed, they still reflected some sort of business relationship. Numerous works on the credit networks of urban communities in medieval England have shown that debt litigation automatically created either temporary or long-lasting professional ties.[55] In the same manner, the litigation in court involving Peter van Skelle exhibited similar connections. In 1354, Peter and his associate, Clays Bastard, a weaver from Nieuwpoort, pledged to ensure the appearance in court of Maas de Roterdame in order to reply to Johanna Marche's accusation of debt.[56] During the same year, Peter and Clays separately appeared in court opposing Bernard Gallin, a fuller exiled from Bruges. Both were accused of debt which seemed to be owed for services provided, so presumably they had not paid Bernard for fulling tasks he had performed.[57] These associations between immigrant weavers and fullers reinforced the solidarity of a group, where their preexisting contacts made the organisation of the production process a lot easier in the first years after their arrival.

The Flemings' contacts with other immigrants from the Low Countries in borough courts are also characterised by the circulation of credit. Copin Amelry, for example, was summoned twice in the borough court of Colchester in 1379, because he failed to repay the 15d he borrowed from Hanyn Blankard and another 13d from Hanyn Chambre.[58] In the same session of the court of pleas, Hanyn Blankard acknowledged that he owed 16d to John Hyd, a Flemish weaver residing in Colchester.[59] The latter seem to have been one of the central figures in the immigrants' network of cloth-workers. Indeed, John Hyd extended credit to other weavers from the Low Countries on five other occasions. Between 1375 and 1380, he pursued cases for debt against Arthur Braban, John Oudenard, John van Hust, James Pappe and Hanyn van Tene,

[52] NRO, Y/C4/75, mm. 2, 3, 4, 6d. [53] *Ibid.*, mm. 2, 2d. [54] NRO, Y/C4/76, m. 4.

[55] Kowaleski, *Local Markets*, p. 280; Davis, *Medieval Market Morality*, p. 349.

[56] NRO, Y/C4/76, m. 3.

[57] NRO, Y/C4/76, m. 6. A kyte was apparently a sort of gown or a dress, see *CPMR*, vol. II, p. 69.

[58] ERO, D/B 5 CR 19, mm. 23, 23d, calendared in Benham, *Court Rolls*, vol. III, p. 197.

[59] *Ibid.*

which all seemed to be loans given in advance on the understanding that these individuals would work for him for a given sum. In the second half of the fourteenth century, it was common for weavers in Colchester either to work for others or be independent from wage-earning, like John Hyd, who was able to contract out some of his weaving to others. For weavers to accept work at piece-rates, they presumably expected the wage to be paid in advance. The credit relationships between Flemish immigrants do not show a pattern, where one individual would repeatedly extend credit to others, as very few Flemings borrowed from the same person. They had what Chris Briggs has described as horizontal credit relationships, that is, between social equals, where instead of one group acting as lenders and another as borrowers, individuals most frequently involved in credit tended to act both as creditors and as debtors. Such credit relationships were not a way for the wealthy members of the group to consolidate power by exploiting poorer immigrants.[60]

The second category of business network arose from the professional contacts of artisans from the Low Countries with the English. The general growth in economic activity in English towns after 1355 and the increase in the immigrants' level of integration also reinforced the relationship with the local population. This was reflected in the borough courts of Great Yarmouth and Colchester, as disputes with the English, responsible for 358 pleas, outstripped those between fellow Flemings (302 pleas). Among the Anglo-Flemish cases, the number of proceedings for assault and minor theft (122 pleas) was lower than the litigation for trespass between exclusively Flemish parties (178 pleas), while the proceedings for debt stood at 197 pleas, surpassing those involving only the members of immigrant community, which stood at 102 cases. In proceedings for breach of contract and detention of chattels, the immigrants from the Low Countries opposed the members of their own community (twenty-two pleas), just as much as they did the English (twenty-nine pleas). The fact that the number of pleas for debt, broken contract and detention of chattels between the English and the immigrants from the Low Countries far exceeded those for trespass is suggestive of a pattern of economic collaboration rather than violent confrontation between the native population and the alien newcomers.

The immigrants' business relationships with the English reveal more about their involvement in various stages of cloth production. On a regular basis, Flemish cloth-workers bought wool from English suppliers

60 Briggs, *Credit and Village*, pp. 131–50, 172.

and were contracted to work the cloth of local drapers.[61] In 1385, Thomas Kentish brought a plea of debt against Copin atte Mersh, in which he claimed that the latter owed him 18d for a portion of wool that Copin's wife, Sybilla, had picked up at Thomas' house some time before, but never paid.[62] The immigrants from the Low Countries also maintained contacts with London drapers. In 1364, a Flemish weaver, Lambekyn Ruyt, was commissioned by a prominent London draper, James Andrew, to produce a piece of cloth.[63] Some business contacts with the English would transcend the mere transactional nature of the relationship and grow into a more informal type of connection based on trust. When a Flemish weaver of London, John Kempe, became a citizen, one of his sureties was a woolman, John Bennet, who also acted as his attorney while he was absent from London in 1370.[64] Business relationships that could grow into friendships were certainly helpful to some of the immigrants when they were entering the franchise, as they needed to acquire a sufficient number of sureties who would guarantee their trustworthiness.

Of course, the immigrants' relationships with the English included the extension of credit. In 1382, William Fairere came to the borough court of Colchester and acknowledged a debt of 22s to a Flemish fuller, Copin atte Mersh.[65] Another Flemish fuller, John Lyndholte, on two occasions came before the bailiffs of Colchester to acknowledge that he had borrowed larger sums, of 22s 4d, from William Mate and 63s 8d from William Wynde.[66] One interesting case of a credit relationship includes a deal between a weaver exiled from Bruges, James Pappe, and an English weaver, John Note. James Pappe was accused of owing 7s 10d to John Note, of which 7s was for cloth and the remaining 10d was the sum he had borrowed. In answer to the accusation, James acknowledged the debt, and proposed a settlement where he would have to weave for John Note until he had worked off his debt. The bailiffs accepted this type of settlement and gave the parties license to agree.[67] It seems that the settlement never fully materialised, as James Pappe borrowed 40d from another weaver, John Rodebright, to pay off this debt.[68]

The immigrants' business relationships were not reserved to artisans and merchants dwelling in their town of residence, as can be demonstrated by the third category of their contacts. The cases recorded in royal courts inform us that their products were sold through business

[61] *CPMR*, vol. II, p. 24. See Chapter 4 as well. [62] ERO, D/B 5, CR 25, m. 28.
[63] *CPMR*, vol. II, p. 24. [64] *Ibid.*, p. 116. [65] Benham, *Court Rolls*, vol. IV, p. 79.
[66] ERO, D/B 5 CR 19, m. 9, calendared in Benham, *Court Rolls*, vol. III, pp. 173, 178.
[67] Benham, *Court Rolls*, vol. IV, pp. 66–7. [68] *Ibid.*, p. 111.

contacts that stretched beyond the local merchants or middlemen. There are cases that included business agreements with drapers and merchants from relatively close by or towns from within the same county, such as the case of William Braban, a weaver from Horncastle in Lincolnshire, who was accused by William Chamberlain from Bilsby of detaining some (unspecified) goods.[69] These contacts went even further than the interactions with individuals from the same county. For example, a Flemish weaver residing in London, James van den Ackere, agreed to produce goods (presumably cloth) valued at 60s, which John Donty, a draper from Coventry, failed to pay.[70] Similarly, John atte Wyre, who was a bailiff of weavers from Brabant in London, complained that Johanna Braban from Northampton had stolen woollen cloth and other goods from him to the value of 40s.[71] Some weavers from London, like Matthew Pepir, *Braban*, *webbe*, went on their own to villages in the city's proximity (Woburn, Bedfordshire) in order to sell their products and got into affrays.[72]

Finally, some business relationships of immigrants from the Low Countries had also arisen from contacts with merchants and artisans from overseas. Some of them, like Matthew van Hale, *Braban*, marketed cloth through Italian merchants operating their businesses in London.[73] A weaver exiled from Bruges, John van Sint Trude, who had settled in York, exported cloth from the port of Boston.[74] John's contacts were also merchants and captains of ships from abroad. Nevertheless, as we will see below, they maintained contact with their relatives and business contacts back home in the Low Countries. Banished Flemings in London still maintained contact with friends and relatives on the other side of the Channel as well. The latter seem to have benefited from the permanent residence in England of exiles, who were able to host them and offer guidance about the main actors in the market.

MIGRANT NETWORKS

Migrant networks are sets of interpersonal ties that connect migrants, former migrants and non-migrants in origin and destination areas through ties of kinship, friendship and shared community origin.[75] The

[69] TNA, CP 40/483, m. 265d. [70] TNA, CP 40/440, mm. 19, 577.
[71] TNA, KB 27/396, m. 26d. [72] TNA, KB 27/447, m. 107d. [73] TNA, CP 40/386, m. 5d.
[74] TNA, E 122/7/14, m. 10; *Register of the Freemen of York*, ed. Collins, vol. I, p. 87; SAB, Groenenboek C, fo. 118r.
[75] D. S. Massey et al., 'Theories of international migration: A review and appraisal', *Population and Development Review*, 19 (1993), 431–66, at 448.

existence of such networks is relevant, as they enhance migration flows by reducing the risk and cost of movement. The personal networks of migrants act also as channels of information about the employment opportunities, structures and attitudes of the host society, which increases the probability of migration to be successful and safer.[76]

The evidence suggests that there were continual comings and goings between England and the Low Countries, for both mercantile and artisanal activities, and that this factor did the most to maintain the ties between the host country and the country of origin. Banished Flemings in London still maintained contact with friends and relatives on the other side of the Channel. According to a verdict by the Ghent bench of aldermen, for example, John van Wetere, a bailiff of the Flemish weavers' guild in 1367, received annual visits from Ghent money changer Feyns de Backer in his house in the English capital at the end of the 1350s.[77] Another Flemish weaver, John Kempe, who became a citizen of London, exported white cloths to Flanders through another weaver–draper, Francis van Yabek.[78] They were both banished from Flanders and settled in London in 1351, but the latter probably returned to Bruges after the general pardon was granted in 1359 and used contacts remaining in London for the trade of wool and cloth.[79] It is known that several other Flemings had returned after 1359. Amongst them were weavers Giles Ripegast and Lamsin de Vos, as well as a fuller, Baldwin Veltaker.[80] All three of them seem to have settled back in very well: Lamsin de Vos became the dean of weavers in 1363 and stayed in office until 1369; Giles Ripegast also became an alderman of Ghent in 1376; while Baldwin Veltaker was *vinder* of the fullers' guild on two occasions, in 1370 and 1373.[81] Animosity and mistrust towards those who had returned can be detected as well. In 1366, for example, a weaver of Ghent, Godfrey Clofhamer, attached his name as one of the masters to the newly approved ordinances of Flemish weavers in London.[82] A year later, he moved to Ypres, but in order to be able to enter into the franchise there he needed a special supplication from the aldermen of Ghent, suggesting that some of the municipal authorities were not too keen to accept

[76] M. Boyd, 'Family and personal networks in international migration: Recent developments and new agendas', *The International Migration Review*, 23 (1989), 638–70.

[77] SAG, Series 301: Registers of the Keure, vol. I, 1360–1, fo. 64r. Verdict Aldermen of the Keure, 18 January 1360.

[78] *CFR, 1356–69*, p. 193.

[79] SAB, Groenenboek C, fo. 112r; *Cartulaire historique et généalogique des Artevelde*, ed. De Pauw, p. 719.

[80] *Cartulaire historique et généalogique des Artevelde*, ed. De Pauw, pp. 715, 720, 721.

[81] SAB, Wetsvernieuwingen, reeks 114, fos 3v, 12r, 35, 42v, 51r; NRO, Y/C4/82, m. 1v.

[82] *Memorials of London*, ed. Riley, p. 332.

banished rebels.[83] Five years later, he returned to London, and it seems that stays on both sides of the Channel were beneficial to the development of his mercantile network, which probably even allowed him to become the bailiff of the Flemish weavers' guild in 1384.[84] Some immigrants were even forced to leave England and, presumably, return to Flanders. This was the case of those who had in effect committed felonies, like John Symmond, who had to 'abjure England' through the port of Harwich after he was found guilty of killing another Fleming, John Spynk, in Colchester.[85]

Continual comings and goings of exiles between England and the Low Countries allowed the establishment of migrant networks that facilitated chain migration. There is ample evidence that exiles and other immigrants from the Low Countries were followed both by their wives and children, as well as relatives and friends. About 80 per cent of the immigrants and exiles were married, and the evidence suggests that they were followed by their wives. Most of the female names appearing as the wives of textile workers from the Low Countries in the poll tax, judicial records and wills seem to have been Dutch. The aforementioned Godfrey Clofhamer was followed by his brothers John and Ralph, who were also weavers.[86] Some Flemish craftsmen like Lippin Sceepstale and John Gerard had their nephews join them in Great Yarmouth to learn their craft.[87] The economic instability in Flanders, or dreams of better opportunities in England, led some younger Flemings to join their uncles established there. It might have been the case that it was more valorised to do an apprenticeship in England and return to the Low Countries as master with a wider range of business contacts.

If we look more generally at servants and apprentices from the Low Countries, there are indications that they were appointed by their compatriots through similar migrant networks. In 1385, John van Rouns, a Flemish weaver living in Colchester, was accused by William and Margaret van de Strat of breaking the apprenticeship agreement with

[83] Espinas and Pirenne, *Recueil*, vol. I:3, p. 804. 'Godevard Clofhamer, tisseran de Gand à la grande prière et instance des eschevins de Gand, fut fait Bourgeois payant £5.'

[84] *Letter Book H*, p. 250; *CPMR*, vol. II, p. 205.

[85] TNA, JUST 2/33A, m. 10d.

[86] *CPMR*, vol. II, pp. 205, 251; *Letter Book H*, p. 77.

[87] NRO, Y/C4/95, m. 9v; NRO, Y/C4/98, m. 12v. 'Lippin Slepstale, Heryan, nepos eius et Martyn, serviens eius excedunt etatem xii anorum et non sunt in decena.' The forename of John Gerard's nephew was Gosekine, suggesting an obviously Flemish origin: 'Gosekine nepos Johanni Gerardi traxit sanguine felonice de Dirico serviens Johanni Yepeswich.' The interesting characteristic here is that their relatives are mentioned only after fifteen years of their continual residence in Great Yarmouth. Moreover, the town clerks used the forenames and the Latin word *nepos* when the cases were entered into the borough, another suggestion that some of the Flemings were quite well known to the authorities, and probably to the wider population.

their son, Clays, who was supposed to be in John's service for the term of one year.[88] John and William had been involved in several other cases in the borough court with other immigrants from the Low Countries prior to this litigation, and it is probable that the apprenticeship contract was concluded through migrant networks created during these interactions.[89] For some of the apprentices from the Low Countries, we do not know whether they came together with their masters, or if they were hired in England. Such was the case of John van Gaunt, who was sued in the borough court of Great Yarmouth by a weaver exiled from Bruges, Christian fan the Scelle, for withdrawal from service in 1380.[90] Hiring servants and apprentices from the Low Countries was common not only among weavers. For example, Paul Souter, a Fleming and cordwainer, had two servants, Gosekin and Lamkyn fan Durdraught, whose forenames indicate that they were from the Low Countries.[91] All these cases point to the existence of an established network which allowed young immigrants from the Low Countries to come to England through friendly or family ties to finish their apprenticeship. Of course, a lot of apprentices and servants might have migrated on their own in search of work.

This is probably why Flemish and Brabantine weavers had designated locations in London where they could hire journeymen from the Low Countries. In 1370, they petitioned Edward III with a request to be able to hire journeymen at separate locations. It was decided that the Flemings should hire their journeymen at the churchyard of St Laurence Pounteney, and the Brabantines at the churchyard St Mary Somerset, 'and that the serving-men in that trade, as well of Flanders as of Brabant, should serve indifferently under the weavers of either nation, that is to say, as well under Fleming as Brabanter, who should wish to hire them for competent salary to work in that trade; without any impediment or gainsaying thereof, on pain of imprisonment, etc.'[92] This certainly increased the chances for young newcomers with no family connections in London of finding a job soon after their arrival. Although the evidence here suggests that the immigrant master weavers of London preferred to hire serving-men, if not from the same duchy or county, at least from the Low Countries, this was not the case elsewhere. Newly arrived immigrants did not necessarily work for their compatriots, as in 1375, when Simon de Almaigne, a merchant of Norwich, accused Peter Soot from Zeeland of withdrawal from service under the Statute of Labourers.[93]

88 ERO, D/B 5 CR 24, m. 59. 89 ERO, D/B 5 CR 24, m. 21d.
90 NRO, Y/C4/91, m. 5. 91 NRO, Y/C4/85, m. 3 and NRO, Y/C4/83, m. 6d.
92 *Memorials of London*, ed. Riley, pp. 344–5. 93 TNA, KB 27/459, m. 36.

Apprentices and servants, too, had no problems with working for English masters. We saw in Chapter 2 that in Warwickshire and Bristol newly arrived immigrants from Flanders and Brabant worked for English masters. But this was also the case in Great Yarmouth and Colchester. For example, Galfride Fordele, an Englishman, had two servants originating from the Low Countries. He sued Mankyn van the Pythe for withdrawal from service in 1375, while his other servant, William Yanesson, drew blood from Roland Reys.[94] Another Englishman, Thomas Steel, a tailor, sued his apprentice, John de Ecluse, tailor, for withdrawal from service before the term ended.[95] Similarly, a prominent weaver in Colchester, John Somenour, accused a Fleming, Herman Revele, of leaving his service earlier than agreed.[96]

Migrant networks also served for some as a means to escape the authorities after criminal activity. A weaver from Bruges, John Pacelyn, was banished in 1361 and shortly afterwards settled in Colchester.[97] He was killed in the same town by his compatriot, John Blake, in 1370. What is interesting here is that Blake was aided and abetted by fellow weavers from Bruges, Peter van Tyelte, Giles Bytre, and Giles Berempoot and his wife, Katerina, who were banished from Flanders at the same time as the victim.[98] It seems that the authorities at times wanted to emphasise this aspect of immigrant collaboration. In Great Yarmouth, when Flemings were fined for a minor offence like prostitution, on several occasions it would be added that 'they were also seen harbouring thieves and other malefactors'. We must exercise caution with these statements, as they might not have been true, but the authorities evidently included an additional formulaic phrase in order to justify the fine and present the immigrants' inns as having a bad reputation.

Nevertheless, this aspect of migrant networks permitted the continual mobility of Flemish artisans within England. In 1355, a weaver exiled from Ghent, Seger de Wulf, was nowhere to be found when he was suspected to have been an accomplice in a murder committed by two of his compatriots in Boston.[99] It becomes clear that he had escaped to Lynn, where he was arrested in 1371 when the general order to arrest all banished Flemings was issued by Edward III in retaliation for the

[94] NRO, Y/C4/86, m. 14d and NRO, Y/C4/91, m. 10d. [95] NRO, Y/C4/84, m. 4d.

[96] Benham, *Court Rolls*, vol. III, p.140.

[97] SAB, Groenenboek C, fo. 132. He pleaded twice in the borough court of Colchester during the 1360s. Benham, *Court Rolls*, vol. II, p. 164.

[98] TNA, JUST 2/33A, m. 7.

[99] TNA, JUST 2/67, m. 17. For more on this case, see the sections on Lincoln and Lynn in Chapter 2.

treatment of English merchants in Flanders.[100] De Wulf was only suspected of crime, and not convicted, which might have been the main reason he was allowed to stay in another town in England. This was not the only time that immigrants from the Low Countries moved from Boston to Lynn for similar reasons. In 1368, officials of the King's Bench court issued an order to arrest Hannekyn Blaunchespore, *Ducheman*, for an unspecified crime he had committed in Boston.[101] It seems that he moved to Lynn, where he was arrested ten years later, together with another alien, Nicholas Hammond, for using false coins.[102] Personal ties with other immigrants in both of these towns certainly facilitated the escape of Seger and Hannekyn from the authorities. However, migrant networks also allowed some immigrants to change towns in England for business purposes. For example, in 1360, Copin Godername appears in the borough court of Colchester on several occasions and then disappears.[103] However, in 1363 he was accused of violence towards one Henry Braban in Ipswich, suggesting that he had moved to this town.[104] These examples of mobility both across the Channel and between English cities were certainly made easier thanks to the established networks of immigrants who would facilitate the circulation of information about employment opportunities and smooth the reception of new members of their own community.

The development of migrant networks was fostered through both the working and non-working environments. Meetings in inns and parish churches served certainly to make connections. For example, the house in Colchester of Richard Baker (who might have been a Fleming himself) served various immigrants from the Low Countries as a meeting-place to conclude business deals on seven occasions. The exchange of goods in Richard's house sometimes led to aggressive behaviour. A violent dispute arose in 1382 between Hanyn Myre, Lamsin and Katherine Ungred, and an unnamed Fleming over an unjust seizure of a fardel of cloth.[105] When it comes to the non-working environment, Flemings seem to have been engaged in pastimes mostly in the company of their compatriots. 'Vices' such as playing dice, chess and other games were forbidden in most towns in Europe in the later Middle Ages.[106] Colchester was no exception:

[100] TNA, C 255/4/13. For the context of these arrests, see Chapter 2 and the sections on Lynn.
[101] TNA, KB 27/429, m. 3d.
[102] TNA, JUST 3/168, m. 1d; Fenwick, *Poll Taxes*, vol. II, p. 184.
[103] Benham, *Court Rolls*, vol. II, p. 115. [104] TNA, KB 9/115, m. 7.
[105] ERO, D/B 5 CR 20, m. 6, calendared in Benham, *Court Rolls*, vol. IV, p. 10.
[106] J.-M. Mehl, *Les Jeux au royaume de France: Du XIIIe au début du XVIe siècle* (Paris, 1990); I. Paresys, 'L'Ordre en jeu: Les autorités face aux passions ludiques des Lillois 1400–1668', *Revue du Nord*, 69 (1987), 535–51.

Hanyn van Myre was fined twice for playing dice with other Flemings, once for playing with Laudus van Vynk, and on one other occasion with Thomas Ungered and Clais Taylor.[107] All of these individuals were well-established residents in Colchester and appear in the town's sources regularly for over twenty years, and both through working and non-working activities they certainly strengthened the connectedness between members of their own community.

In order to maintain social order, the authorities of Great Yarmouth and Colchester used the presence of migrant networks. Apart from being compelled to participate in civic duties such as social policing, prominent members of the immigrant community were probably also encouraged to get involved in private disputes between other Flemings and act as pledges and sureties. The town's officials might have considered that dispute settlement between immigrants could be resolved quickly if the involvement of individuals with similar origins was promoted. The roles of pledges or sureties are apparent in three forms in the fourteenth-century records of Great Yarmouth and Colchester: those who pledged that the plaintiff would pursue his or her plea, those who swore to ensure that an individual would appear in court and those who pledged that he or she would maintain good behaviour.[108] The names of pledges were not systematically recorded in private litigation involving immigrants from the Low Countries, but whenever this information is available, in the majority of cases at least one of those who acted in this role was another immigrant. While Flemish and Brabantine litigants did resort to English pledges and sureties, no Fleming or Brabantine is known to have done so for an Englishman. This suggests that the authorities probably preferred to have immigrants from the Low Countries act as pledges for other immigrants, but if none of the members of their community were present at a given court session, an English individual would be assigned.

In late medieval English towns, pledges and sureties were usually leading members of the community who took responsibility for the behaviour of others. In both Colchester and Great Yarmouth throughout the second half of the fourteenth century, individuals who frequently stood as pledges also assumed various roles as town officials. Similarly, within the community of immigrants from the Low Countries, those who stood as pledges were also individuals of good standing and probably trusted by the authorities. The immigrants did not hold office in the municipal government in the fourteenth century, and we cannot

[107] ERO, D/B CR 17, mm. 9d, 10d and CR 20, m. 15d, calendared in Benham, *Court Rolls*, vol. II, pp. 78, 81, 186.

[108] Rodziewicz, 'Great Yarmouth', p. 220.

measure their standing in the same way as the natives', but the length of their permanent residence, as well as the number and types of their appearances in the sources, might be a testament of their reputation. For example, Lippin Sceepstale resided in Great Yarmouth for thirty years after he was exiled from Bruges. Over this time, he appeared 104 times in the borough court, most frequently in private litigation as a plaintiff or defendant, but also in the leet-court for failing to join the tithing. On six occasions, he stood pledge of prosecution, and all these cases involved other immigrant textile workers. For example, in 1378, Lippin and a Flemish fuller, John Wythbrod, were pledges of prosecution for a weaver, Peter fan Skele, in a trespass plea against Henry Hasard and his wife, Maya. As this plea involved an assault between immigrants, it was probably prudent to involve two other members of their own community to ensure that the dispute was resolved fairly and quickly.[109]

Immigrants from the Low Countries were not called upon to act as pledges for other immigrants only: they also took up this role when plaintiffs were merchants from the Low Countries who regularly visited the port of Great Yarmouth. In the case of a shipmaster, William Riqward de Flandre, who brought a plea of detention of chattels against Andrew Braunt, pledges of prosecution were provided by an exiled weaver, William Cappel, and an exiled fuller, John de Langhforde, who resided at Great Yarmouth.[110] We will see in Chapter 4 that Flemish weavers like William Cappel were involved in international trade through the port of Great Yarmouth. The establishment of trustworthy relationships through prior contact with shipmasters and transient merchants might have led to a willingness to act as a pledge for other parties in their disputes.

The second type of pledge or standing bail to ensure that the defendant would appear in court also reveals the cohesion within the immigrant community. When an Englishman, Henry Curteys, brought a plea of trespass against Levin van Gaunt in the court of Great Yarmouth, two immigrants from the Low Countries, John Elys, a weaver, and Derick Cordwainer, 'attached' (pledged) that Levin would appear in court.[111] It seems likely that, as various studies have suggested of village communities, the defendant selected these pledges, but it is also plausible that the municipal authorities would expect more settled members of the immigrant community to take on this role and ensure that the defendants appeared in court when accused by the English.[112] The municipal

[109] NRO, Y/C4/90, m. 4. [110] NRO, Y/C4/73, m. 1. [111] NRO, Y/C4/91, m. 7.

[112] M. Pimsler, 'Solidarity in the medieval village? The evidence of personal pledging at Elton, Huntingdonshire', *Journal of British Studies*, 17 (1977), 1–11, at 3; E. B. Dewindt, *Land and People*

government, however, might have had such a greater influence in the third type of pledging, as the taking of an oath that an individual would maintain good behaviour was almost exclusively done by immigrants for other immigrants. In 1377, for example, Maas de Seyntjones and Jacob Ducheman pledged that John Baker, *Ducheman*, would keep the peace of the king towards Christian Juweler. They also committed to produce John's body in the court under penalty in order to reply to Christian's plea of trespass.[113] In a similar manner, John Gerard, a Dutchman, and William Cappel pledged that John Gerard's servant, William, would behave well and keep the king's peace towards Robert and Lambin de Selande, and that they would produce him if the jury found in Robert and Lambin's favour.[114] In all other cases where such pledges were recorded, the immigrants from the Low Countries who acted in this role were usually well-established residents in England who enjoyed a certain amount of respect within the native population. With this in mind, it seems that it was expected of leading members of the immigrant community that they would ensure good behaviour within their own ranks and thus contribute to maintaining social order in the town.

FLEMISH DISORDER

In these final sections, we will look into the involvement of immigrants in crimes that included violence and what these can reveal about patterns of socialisation and networks.[115] Assault cases extracted from borough and royal courts will be the basis for this examination. In order to maintain social order, local and royal authorities in England resorted to various processes of justice depending on the seriousness of the crime. Minor crimes, including night walking, the carrying of weapons, physical aggression that fell short of felony and all kinds of offence detected by petty policing procedures, were brought to judicial bodies such as the hundred court in Colchester and the leet-court in Great Yarmouth. Allegations of serious felonies such as homicide, rape, grand larceny or abduction were presented in front of the higher jurisdiction courts, most

in Holywell-cum-Needingworth: Structures of Tenure and Patterns of Social Organization in an East Midlands Village 1252–1457 (Toronto, 1972), p. 243.

113 NRO, Y/C4/88, m. 5. 114 NRO, Y/C4/85, m. 3.

115 This section partly owes its title to the late Richard Britnell. During my first visit to the archives in the UK, I was honoured to meet Professor Britnell in person and discuss my findings on Flemings in Colchester. He gave me his own copies of Benham's editions of Colchester's court rolls, and I was very lucky that they contained his notes, which were extremely helpful. Whenever a case of trespass (concerned with physical aggression) appeared that involved Flemings, Britnell had made a note – 'Flemish disorder' – in pencil in the right-hand margin – hence my title.

notably the King's Bench and gaol deliveries.[116] A combination of cases from local and royal legal records where violence towards another individual was alleged will be used here. The relationships between the victim and the perpetrator, as well as his or her accomplices, may display some interesting features about the immigrants' networks.

Immigrants from the Low Countries represented about 10 per cent of all violent offenders in the borough courts of Great Yarmouth (or 28 out of a total of 302) and Colchester (57 out of 518). Flemish litigants opposed members of their own community in the borough court of Colchester (70.2 per cent of the cases), a lot more than they did the English (29.8 per cent). The often violent nature of the pleas had little to do with manifestations of anti-alien hostility or xenophobia, as immigrants from the Low Countries acted eleven times as perpetrators against the English but forty times against their own compatriots, and only six times were they the victims of aggression from natives.[117] Walter le Baker, an immigrant from Ghent, was recorded twice for assault in the borough court rolls between 1357 and 1361. In both cases he had fallen out with fellow Flemish exiles. In 1357, he proceeded against Simon Sporeman, also a Ghentenaar, who had violently attacked Walter's wife, Margery, with a knife.[118] In 1360, Walter himself was accused of assaulting Daniel Flemyng.[119] During the 1350s, the Colchester Flemings thus emerge from the records as a closed community which primarily used the available courts to settle existing and new disputes in its own midst. This was more or less comparable to Great Yarmouth's borough court, where we find evidence of immigrants from the Low Countries committing violence against their own community to a higher extent than against the English – twenty cases out of twenty-eight. Among the twenty cases, on 29 June 1375, Henry fan Buske brought a plea of trespass against Laurence Souter fan Seland, who was eventually found guilty and had to pay damages to the aforementioned Henry.[120] Later on, at the summons of the court leet, it is stated that Laurence Souter had to pay a fine because he did hamsoken[121] and drew blood with a knife from

[116] Britnell, 'Colchester courts and court records', 133–40; Hanawalt, *Crime and Conflict in English Communities*, pp. 32–44.

[117] M. Pajic, 'Xénophobie et intégration: Le cas de la communauté flamande de Colchester 1351–1367', *Revue du Nord*, 98 (2017), 509–31, at 523; Lambert and Pajic, 'Drapery in Exile', 9.

[118] ERO, D/B 5, CR 11, m. 1, calendared in Benham, *Court Rolls*, vol. II, p. 68.

[119] ERO, D/B 5, CR 13, m. 3, calendared in Benham, *Court Rolls*, vol. II, p. 115.

[120] NRO, Y/C4/87, m. 5.

[121] As mentioned in the Introduction, in some places in England 'hamsoken' meant an attack on someone in their house. For the discussion about hamsoken, see Rodziewicz, 'Great Yarmouth', pp. 79–81.

Henry fan Buske in his house.[122] Henry was one of twenty immigrants who had committed assault against other newcomers. In the remaining eight cases of assault involving immigrants from the Low Countries, they acted as perpetrators six times and had only twice fallen victim to the English. A similar pattern was observed by Alwyn Ruddock in late medieval Southampton, and by Martha Carlin in late medieval Southwark, in both of which the number of violent confrontations between foreigners alone far exceeded that between aliens and Englishmen.[123] Although everything indicates that there was a degree of mutual assistance between immigrants from the Low Countries, such as cooperation in the production and marketing processes of cloth-making, as we have seen in previous sections, these activities, together with gambling and drinking, might also be a source of tension between members of their own community. In her examination of crime in fourteenth-century England, Barbara Hanawalt also noted that members of close-knit village communities were more likely to suffer assaults from their neighbours, friends or acquaintances than from strangers or lords.[124]

In the few cases where English people were accused of committing assaults against immigrants, their motivation might have been to assert the social hierarchy. In village communities, attacks on poorer villagers by the richer villagers represented a means for social levelling in which the object was not only an economic gain but also punishment of the poorer members of the community.[125] If for the urban areas under consideration we substitute 'richer villagers' for natives, and 'poorer villagers' for immigrants, one case from Colchester borough court is perfectly illustrative of this situation. In 1365, Henry Duale was attached (compelled) to reply to John Pouchemaker, *Fleming*, who alleged that on the eve of Holy Trinity last Henry had presented himself as a royal official and adjudged that the said John should go to Mont Saint-Michel (*ad montem Sancti Michaelis*), or pay 40s, or otherwise he should die. John claimed that for this reason he sold his goods at a great loss and surrendered his house to his master, which he could not regain except by paying an excess of rent, to the loss of £10. Later in the summons, Henry Duale was found guilty and fined 3s 4d. The bailiffs also added that Henry had on many occasions pretended to have royal power (*regiam potestatem*) and summoned many Flemings before him and subjected

[122] NRO, Y/C4/87, m. 20v.

[123] A. A. Ruddock, 'Alien merchants in Southampton in the later Middle Ages', *English Historical Review*, 61 (1946), 1–17, at 12; Carlin, *Medieval Southwark*, p. 157.

[124] Hanawalt, *Crime and Conflict*, p. 168. [125] *Ibid.*, p. 175.

them to pecuniary or bodily punishment.[126] Henry's main motivation was probably to take advantage of the newcomers, who were still not familiar with the town, but also to assert his social standing vis-à-vis the immigrants.

Whereas not a single Englishman had been accused of settling a dispute with a knife in Colchester since the year the borough court rolls started in 1310, seven Flemish immigrants were so accused between 1351 and 1367. The arrival of a group of people with very different and, in many cases, more violent experiences thus forced the Colchester authorities to reconsider the available judicial infrastructure and to develop new sanctions and procedures. In 1372, three Flemings, who had undertaken not to draw knife or sword in Colchester, according to an ordinance made to that effect with the consent of the Flemings residing in that town, paid fines for breaking the order.[127] A similar proclamation was made in Winchester in 1361.[128] According to a decree from the mayor of London in 1362, it was ordered that no Fleming, Brabanter or Zeelander was to carry a knife within the city.[129] In Great Yarmouth, however, the immigrants were not the only ones to use knives to settle their disputes. In ninety recorded cases that included the use of knives, the English were responsible for the large majority, or sixty-eight cases.

When it comes to cases of homicide recorded in gaol deliveries and coroner's rolls, immigrants from the Low Countries appeared eighty-three times over the period of study. As was the case with those instances of violence recorded by the borough courts of Colchester and Great Yarmouth, these royal records indicate that members of the Flemish community committed murders much more frequently amongst themselves or against the English than they themselves were the victims of deadly attacks from the natives. In sixty-six (or 79.5 per cent) of cases Flemings committed crimes against their own countrymen, and in fifteen (or 18 per cent) against the English, while only twice were the immigrants the victims of English perpetrators.[130] Similar conclusions were recently rendered in the study on aliens in the county of Lincolnshire

[126] ERO, D/B 5, CR 14, m. 12, calendared in Benham, *Court Rolls*, vol. II, p. 170.

[127] Benham, *Court Rolls*, vol. III, p. 13. [128] HRO, W/D1/8, m. 10.

[129] *Letter Book G*, p. 150.

[130] TNA, KB 27/401, m. 26d. In 1360, John Bassyngbourn from Messeden and John Tailor from Chesham stole £20 from 'a certain Fleming' and killed him somewhere around Cheap and disposed of his body in the Thames. The case is only entered as such, and, given the fact that the crime happened around Cheap Ward, the amount stolen, and that the scribes had not even written the name of the Flemish victim, it is therefore quite possible that this Fleming was a transient merchant.

that was based on records from the coroner and gaol deliveries.[131] Informal meetings involving gambling, mixed with alcohol and the availability of tools and weapons, sometimes led to violent behaviour with a fatal outcome (probably on account of cheating, or anger over losses). For example, in 1355, a weaver banished from Bruges, John van Ostburch, was accused of the murder in Norwich of Richard Foyt from Brabant. During the inquiry, the jury found that they had both been drinking in the tavern of a certain John de Goneville. Suddenly, Richard started a dispute and, pulling out a knife, assaulted the aforementioned John. As Richard was the first to pull out a knife, and as he was standing between John and the door, it was impossible for John to escape past Richard and the crowd in the tavern. The only thing left for John to do was to pull out his knife too, which he did, and he managed to stab Richard in the stomach. The jury found John not guilty, because he had acted in self-defence.[132] Not long afterwards, Edward III granted him a letter patent of special pardon for this homicide.[133] Some murders did get even more personal, as John Pouchemaker 'Fandebrusch' of Boston allegedly killed his wife, while Peter fan Reylond, a *webster* from Great Yarmouth, was killed by his son.[134] Personal grudges between family members over property rights or spousal abuse that ended with serious consequences for the parties involved can also be observed amongst English village communities in a small proportion of homicides throughout the fourteenth century.[135]

The number of murders that occurred within the immigrant community over the period of this study might have been motivated by the tensions that arose from business relationships. In York in 1357, a weaver, Rulkin Braban, was accused of the murder of another weaver, Robert Fellyng.[136] Some years later, Thomas Braban, a weaver from Malines who lived in York, was murdered by a merchant, Godfride de Burcelles, *Braban*, clearly a compatriot of his.[137] In London, around the same time, a bailiff of the Flemish weavers in the city, Paul van Wetteryn, killed Lambert Soot, a merchant and shipmaster from Flanders who operated in London in the 1360s and 70s.[138] However, business-related aggression

[131] Kissane and Mackman, 'Aliens and the law in late medieval Lincolnshire', pp. 105–23.

[132] TNA, JUST 3/139, m. 26.

[133] *CPR, 1354–8*, p. 284.

[134] TNA, JUST 2/82, rot. 11d; NRO, Y/C4/84, m. 15. Interestingly, the case of Peter fan Reylond was attached to one of the membranes of the borough court.

[135] Hanawalt, *Crime and Conflict*, pp. 158–68.

[136] TNA, JUST 2/219, rot. 4.

[137] TNA, JUST 2/219, rot. 5. There are a lot more cases of a similar sort concerning murders among Flemish textile workers in Lincolnshire and Yorkshire: see Chapter 2 and sections there on these two counties for more references.

[138] TNA, E 122/70/18, m. 3; *CPR, 1377–81*, p. 366; *CCR, 1364–8*, p. 441.

did not always have a fatal outcome, and the evidence from the borough courts may confirm this. For example, in Great Yarmouth in 1375, Lippin Sceepstale, a weaver, maliciously drew blood with a knife from Herman Fuller.[139] Prior to this, Lippin had been a pledge to prosecute for Herman Fuller in a plea of debt against Gysebright Webster,[140] which might indicate a previous business connection. In Colchester in 1361, a group of weavers from the Low Countries – Stefkin Braban, *webbe*, John his companion, Gerard Webbe, *Braban*, and Nicholas Braban, *webbe* – allegedly assaulted Ralph Pastok.[141] One of Ralph's pledges to prosecute was another immigrant weaver, Levyn Webbe, suggesting that the affair was probably related to cloth-making. As can be seen, even though these cases focus on the immigrants' anti-social behaviour, the occupational structure of victims and perpetrators still depicts a variety of connections with other textile workers, suggesting that the immigrants were representative of active members within a broader network of the English cloth-making industry.

CONCLUSION

After the arrival of the exiles throughout the 1350s, Flemings became the most numerous and the most visible foreign community in late medieval England. The evidence from the various sources presented above suggests that the bulk of the Flemings' social networks remained within the community of their compatriots. Whether this was intentional or even promoted by the natives or local authorities remains somewhat hard to determine. However, there are some indications that municipal authorities might have encouraged the leading members of the immigrant community to take responsibility for the behaviour of other foreign artisans. This was done through the system of pledging, whereby better-integrated immigrants acted as pledges for prosecution or stood bail to ensure the appearance in court of other immigrants. Clustering together led to the creation of 'migrant networks', which certainly facilitated the flow of information between those settled and new arrivals, promoting easier integration and mutual help in general. This generally led to a preference for employing servants from the Low Countries and organising trade around family members or with other compatriots. Indeed, the occupational structure of other immigrants allowed them to cooperate amongst themselves in the process of cloth production, which sometimes led to tensions within the immigrant community.

139 NRO, Y/C4/89, m. 12.
140 NRO, Y/C4/88, m. 4.
141 ERO, D/B 5 CR 13, m. 4, calendared in Benham, *Court Rolls*, vol. II, pp. 134–5.

Cooperation within the migrant networks allowed some groups, like the weavers who settled in London, to create their own guild and formalise their association. However, their business networks were not limited to that and went far beyond their own local community. Some of them developed connections with English wool-growers, drapers and merchants, as well as with foreign merchants, which eventually allowed the immigrant textile workers to control the production process, but also to market their cloth both in English domestic and export markets.

Chapter 4

ECONOMIC ACTIVITIES OF THE IMMIGRANTS FROM THE LOW COUNTRIES: WOOL AND WOOLLEN CLOTH PRODUCTION AND TRADE

INTRODUCTION

In previous chapters we have seen that the occupational structure of most of the immigrants from the Low Countries was linked with the production and trade of cloth, but the question that still remains unanswered is what they actually did once they settled in England. The influence of Flemish immigrants on the development of the English cloth industry during the reign of Edward III has been the subject of several debates amongst historians on both sides of the English Channel. Some historians, like William Cunningham, Thomas Fuller and William Ashley, credited the immigrants' arrival with nothing less than the birth of English cloth manufacture.[1] Conversely, their impact has been severely questioned by Henri de Sagher, H. L. Gray and Herbert Heaton.[2] Overlooked by all of them was the actual evidence that suggested the presence of banished Flemish cloth-workers in the localities where the native textile industry took off. Moreover, in all but one of these works the primary focus was elsewhere, and the obvious lack of research on Flemish migration made it harder to reach convincing conclusions. The purpose of this chapter is to evaluate and quantify the ways in which the immigrants' presence and skills contributed to the development of the

[1] Fuller, *Church History*, vol. II, p. 286; Cunningham, 'The commercial policy of Edward III', 202–3; Ashley, *An Introduction to English Economic History and Theory*, pp. 193–203. These positive views were followed later by Salzman, *English Industries of the Middle Ages*, pp. 133–40, and Lipson, *The Economic History of England*, pp. 391–6.

[2] Amongst the first to posit a negative hypothesis about the impact of Flemish immigrants on the English textile industry were: Gray, 'The production and exportation of English woollens', 13–35, and De Sagher, 'L'Immigration des tisserands flamands', pp. 109–26. Their conclusions were followed by Heaton, *The Yorkshire Woollen and Worsted Industries*, pp. 8–21, and later on Bolton, *The Medieval English Economy*, p. 268, Keene, *Survey of Medieval Winchester*, vol. I, pp. 304–6, and Munro, 'Medieval woollens: The western European woollen industries', vol. I, pp. 228–324, subscribed to them.

cloth industry in fourteenth-century England. In order to do so, the scale of the immigrants' contribution to the industry will be examined through the number of workers, as well as the types of cloth they produced in England. The know-how they exhibited in the host country will be compared with their involvement in the textile industry of their homeland prior to exile. Finally, the chapter will touch upon the immigrants' mercantile activities, and assess how their involvement in the trade in cloth and wool allowed them to increase profits and ensure control over the whole production process.

INVOLVEMENT IN CLOTH PRODUCTION AND TRADE

Over the first half of the fourteenth century, London, Colchester and other English towns where the immigrants from the Low Countries settled met many of the basic requirements for the development of a sustainable export-oriented cloth industry. The production of appropriate types of wool was at a high level, and their supply in towns was cheaper and a lot more secure than in Flanders.[3] Cheap water power for mechanical fulling and redundant grain mills suitable for redeployment as fulling mills were available before 1350. There was sufficient demand, and an ability to compete internationally in the market for cheaper cloths dyed and manufactured to recognised standards. A connected urban system with an intricate road network, including direct connections to London and to the sea, provided easy access to the Continent. These economic and social factors, combined with the lack of skilled labour in the post-plague period, made England the perfect environment for the immigrants from the Low Countries. Whereas some towns were hit harder by plague than others, it is generally acknowledged that England lost about half of its population at the outbreak in 1348–9, with further losses in subsequent waves of pestilence in the second half of the fourteenth century. The signs of recovery from the Black Death, in urban areas, were visible rather quickly. The majority of this growth was the result of immigration, most of which came from surrounding villages.[4] The need for skilled labour is further confirmed by the rapidity with which local authorities accepted the newly arrived Flemish clothworkers into the franchise between 1351 and 1354 in the towns of Lynn,

[3] Poos, *Rural Society*, p. 44.

[4] Britnell, *Growth and Decline*, pp. 95–7; A. Dyer, *Decline and Growth in English Towns 1400–1640* (Basingstoke, 1991), pp. 23–4, 56.

York and London.[5] Most of them, as we will see, had skills and experience in the industry which, over exactly the same years, began to expand spectacularly.

From John Oldland's numerous works on cloth production and trade in London and Richard Britnell's on Colchester, we can reconstruct the whole process of production in the fourteenth century in these two places.[6] For Norfolk, and more precisely the town of Great Yarmouth, there is still no detailed study of the cloth industry before the fifteenth century, although Yarmouth's importance grew so much that it had become one of the biggest industries of the region by the mid fourteenth century.[7] Nevertheless, the sources for Great Yarmouth, combined with the evidence from other English towns where Flemings took up residence, allow us to make some contributions to the story. Apart from the lack of quantifiable data, the most decisive argument for calling into question the impact of Flemish immigration on the development of the English cloth industry is its chronology. Some scholars have stated that even if textile workers from Flanders did settle in England, they did so at times when native textile manufacture underwent no significant changes.[8] However, it is in fact possible to demonstrate that a large-scale cloth industry started to develop at the time of the arrivals from the Low Countries.

In order to evaluate the immigrants' contribution to the growth of the English cloth industry in the second half of the fourteenth century, we must first determine their significance as a proportion of the labour force of the English textile sector as a whole, and then compare this to the evolution of overall cloth production in England. As the extant source material in fourteenth-century England rarely provides population lists systematically organised by occupational structure, establishing a rough estimate of the total number of textile workers is to some extent a difficult task. However, incidental information from the available sources in London, Colchester, York and Great Yarmouth might give us an idea about the size of the labour force in these four towns. Our second task, on the other hand, may be realised somewhat more accurately through the available sources, such as alnage and customs accounts, which offer

[5] In Chapter 2, the admissions of Copin Isaac in Lynn and of several Flemings in York and London between 1351 and 1355 were mentioned.

[6] Oldland, 'London clothmaking'; Oldland, 'Making and marketing woollen cloth in late medieval London', *The London Journal*, 36 (2011), 89–108; Britnell, *Growth and Decline*, p. 75.

[7] The only comprehensive work on Norfolk cloth production in the fourteenth century is that by A. F. Sutton, 'The early linen and worsted industries of Norfolk and the evolution of the London Mercers' Company', *Norfolk Archaeology*, 40 (1987/89), 201–25.

[8] Goose, 'Immigrants', p. 153; Heaton, *The Yorkshire Woollen and Worsted Industries*, p. 16.

yearly figures for the cloth industry's output, thus providing an impression of both the numbers and types of cloth.

By using these figures for the total cloth produced in England, several scholars have attempted to make an estimate of the number of people engaged in the industry. Professor Postan concluded in 1950 that the proportion of people employed in English cloth production at its height in the fourteenth century was insignificant. He claimed that the demand for 50,000 cloths would have created no more than 15,000 full-time jobs, or 0.65 per cent of the working population as estimated from the 1377 poll taxes.[9] In the same year, Eleanora Carus-Wilson corrected this figure and estimated that the English woollen industry, just to produce exported cloth, employed between 17,000 and 20,000 people at the end of the fourteenth century.[10] Although these estimates are valuable, they are somewhat unsatisfactory for the present study. Both are calculated on the assumed domestic demand, and for England as a whole, without mentioning the number of workers in specific urban areas.

At first glance, the poll-tax returns seem like an ideal source for providing an estimate of the people who worked in the textile sector. With nominal lists of working-age population in all three assessments, and more detailed recording of occupations for the return of 1380–1, the poll taxes would seem to represent the perfect basis for such an analysis. They were used in two recent studies to give an impression of the occupational structure of England. In his examination of evidence from the poll taxes to illustrate the economic structure of urban society, Jeremy Goldberg found that the proportion of textile workers in some towns ranged from 5.9 per cent to 23.3 per cent.[11] Some twenty years later, Gregory Clark calculated that 11 per cent of those who paid the subsidy in urban areas between 1379 and 1381 were employed in the textile sector.[12] Unfortunately, the returns, where they are available, with nominal lists for urban areas in which textile workers from the Low Countries were detected, are either missing or contain some limitations. For example, the 1377 assessment for Colchester contains no record of the taxpayers' occupations and is of no use for the purpose of

9 M. Postan, 'Some economic evidence of declining population in the later Middle Ages', *Economic History Review*, 2 (1950), 221–46, at 232.

10 Carus-Wilson, 'Trends in the export of English woollens', p. 177. Additionally, she assumed that if the importation of cloth had been halted and domestic demand had remained the same, there would have been 23,000 to 26,000 more cloth-workers at the end of the century than at the beginning.

11 P. J. P. Goldberg, 'Urban identity and the poll taxes of 1377, 1379, 1381', *Economic History Review*, 43 (1990), 194–216, at 211.

12 G. Clark, '1381 and the Malthus delusion', *Explorations in Economic History*, 50 (2013), 4–15, at 10.

this study. Even though the city of York has two extant returns, both present some difficulties. The 1377 return is damaged, and only a fraction of the names is legible. Later returns, although much more complete and comprehensive, nevertheless lack consistency in the recording of trades. The same problems are exhibited by the returns for Lynn and Southwark, while the nominal assessment of the poll taxes for London and Great Yarmouth are not even extant. The only two places where the occupations of taxpayers were recorded systematically in the 1381 assessment were Oxford and Canterbury, but both towns had not seen any significant immigration of textile workers from the Low Countries. However, the available evidence there may serve as a guide to the proportion of cloth-makers in a medium-sized town. In Canterbury, out of 2,046 assessed individuals, 150 (or 7.3 per cent) were employed in the textile sector. There were forty-four fullers, thirty-five weavers, thirty-three spinners, twenty tailors and eighteen drapers. At Oxford, out of 1,150 taxpayers, the number of those listed as weavers stood at thirty-four, with fifteen as fullers. These figures roughly correspond to the proportions calculated by Goldberg and Clark, but we cannot make much further use of them, given the lack of any significant number of immigrants in these towns.

In order to determine the proportion of immigrants employed within the overall sector in the places under study, without detailed poll-tax returns a different methodology must be followed. An almost uninterrupted set of borough court rolls from Colchester and Great Yarmouth with numerous residents appearing as litigants provides a good starting-point. Extracting those where trade designations are given might be a good way to get an impression of the size of the cloth industry in terms of employment. For example, in Colchester between 1351 and 1381 there were ninety-five individuals whose occupation was described as a weaver or fuller. Flemish weavers outnumbered natives forty-one to seventeen, while the number of native fullers was more than six times higher than immigrant fullers (Table 4.1). In Great Yarmouth, the number of litigants whose occupation was recorded as a weaver or fuller over the same period was sixty-seven. The vast majority of these individuals were of Flemish origin, and they accounted for 96 per cent of all weavers and for 85 per cent of all fullers who appeared in the borough court. These numbers are probably not complete, as most entries failed to provide litigants' occupations. Nonetheless, the evidence we have is sufficient to provide a general impression that the immigrants from the Low Countries probably controlled the town's cloth production.

Another two places where the sources allow us to get an impression of the size of the cloth industry in terms of employment are the cities of

Table 4.1 *Size of the industry in terms of employment 1351–81*[i]

Town	Number of native weavers	Number of alien weavers	Number of native fullers	Number of alien fullers	Total number of individuals assessed for poll tax
Colchester	17	41	32	5	2,955
York	137	42	47	15	3,165
London	40	97	55	5	23,314
Great Yarmouth	2	50	2	13	1,941

[i] *Sources: Register of the Freemen of the City of York, Vol. I: 1272–1558*, ed. Collins; Fenwick, *Poll Taxes*, vol. III; *CPMR*, vols. I and II; *Letter Books G–H*; ERO, D/B 5 CR 10–23; NRO, Y/C4/72–95.

York and London. Throughout the reigns of Edward III and Richard II, the register of admissions to the freedom of the city of York kept a relatively systematic record of the occupations of all new entrants. We saw in Chapter 2 that following Edward III's invitation of 1351, the references to weavers from Flanders and Brabant entering the franchise become regular for the next thirty years. Each year, one or two immigrant artisans became citizens. Two brothers from Ghent – Gerwin Giffard, *webster*, and Levekyn Giffard – did so in 1355, and two fullers, Gerome and Piers de Durdraght, did the same three years later.[13] To get a better perspective on the proportion of alien cloth-workers in York, it has been thought reasonable here to look into their representation within the overall number of textile workers who entered the franchise between 1351 and 1377. This was a period of major change within the English cloth industry, which coincided with an influx of alien textile workers. During the second part of Edward III's reign, 137 weavers and 47 fullers were admitted, of whom aliens represented around 30 per cent of workers in each case. Aliens probably did not initiate the cloth industry in York, but such representation allowed them to have a noticeable effect on manufacture.

One way to observe the size of London's cloth industry would be through the number of master artisans connected to the textile sector who appear in the city's Letter Books and memoranda rolls. Like any other recognised craft in London, each group – native weavers, Flemish weavers, Brabantine weavers and fullers – had to provide annually two to

[13] *Register of the Freemen of York*, ed. Collins, vol. I, p. 53.

four masters who were elected as bailiffs of their trade. Throughout the second half of the fourteenth century, masters of various trades were also solicited to broker an agreement between two guilds, to observe the ordinances, or to ensure the good behaviour of apprentices and journeymen within their own guild.[14] Over the period 1351–81, the number of master weavers, native or alien, to appear in a variety of these situations was 137. As can be seen in Table 4.1, alien weavers constituted two-thirds of all masters of that trade. On the other hand, alien fullers were barely one-tenth of all master fullers who were recorded in the city's sources. This numerical disadvantage was probably the main reason that alien fullers were unable to organise their own guild, as the alien weavers did. These ratios were also reflected in terms of cloth manufacture, as we will see in the following sections, whereby alien weavers and native fullers handled the vast majority of textiles produced in the capital. It must also be added that the total number of master weavers and fullers in London was probably higher than that stated here, which comprises only artisans who appeared in the sources. During the general decline of the industry in the first quarter of the fourteenth century, the weavers of London claimed in 1321 that they had fallen on hard times, as the number of looms fell from 300 to 80.[15] If these were approximate figures for individuals employed as weavers in the first half of the fourteenth century, and taking into account the general growth of the cloth industry from the 1350s, the number of master weavers working in London was probably higher than 137 throughout the second half of the fourteenth century. Nevertheless, these figures sampled here still allow us to illustrate the scope of employment within the textile sector in London.

The alnage accounts, which record the payment of a fee for the measurement and sealing of woollen cloth, are the best source for evaluating the quantities and types of cloth produced by textile workers. Although there is a very good survival rate for particulars and totals, spanning the mid fourteenth to the sixteenth centuries, the accounts available for the period of this study do contain some limitations. Indeed, between 1353 and 1358 the accounts cover all regions of England, but there are no particulars, which survive only for London between 1374 and 1379. Moreover, the entries in the accounts for the totals of cloth brought to the alnager in the 1350s do not take into account types of woollens such as kerseys, straits and other narrow cloths produced in eastern parts of the country, and must be interpreted with care, as they

[14] See, for example, *CPMR*, vol. II, pp. 65–6.
[15] Consitt, *The London Weavers' Company*, p. 185.

understate the number of cloths produced.[16] Some of the alnage accounts from the second half of the fifteenth century in the south-western parts of England were fraudulent and must be used with extreme caution.[17] However, the particulars of alnage accounts from the 1370s in London are free of those failings. This is further confirmed by the fact that most of the individuals who paid the subsidy can be identified in other local sources. The one minor caveat is that there was no single format for keeping these records: some accounts contain more details than others.

The totals of cloths sealed by the alnager make clear that the expansion of England's cloth industry coincides with the arrival of highly skilled Flemish exiles and Brabantine immigrants. In 1353–4, when the alnage records began, there were 638 London-produced cloths, while in 1356–7 and 1357–8 the figure almost tripled and averaged 1,551 cloths.[18] By comparison, cloth-workers in the city of Bristol (excluding Gloucestershire), who had also seen an influx of Flemish weavers, brought 2,118 pieces of cloth to the alnager in 1353–4.[19] A similar picture prevailed in Lincolnshire, where cloth production grew by 45 per cent, and in York, where it grew by 40 per cent, over the five-year period 1353–8.[20] In Norfolk, Suffolk and Essex, it is difficult to make judgments on the basis of these accounts, as their numbers for the 1350s seem to underestimate the total amount of manufactured cloth. It appears that the officials who sealed the cloth (the alnagers) did not take into account the types of cloth, such as straits, russets, kerseys and worsteds, that dominated these regions. The alnagers from these counties thought that these types of cloth were exempted from the levy, as their measurements did not correspond to those that were imposed by statute in 1353.[21] Indeed, if we look at the total amount recorded in the alnage accounts, the first impression is that the amount of cloth manufactured in East Anglia is underestimated. If we are to believe the numbers from the exchequer, it appears that there were only 2,893 pieces of cloth sealed by the alnager in Essex, Hertfordshire, Norfolk and Suffolk together over the period 1353–8.[22] Many indications suggest that the production of Colchester russet, the town's trademark grey-and-brown-shaded cloth, took off after 1350.

[16] Amor, *From Wool to Cloth*, pp. 219–21; Heaton, *The Yorkshire Woollen and Worsted Industries*, p. 69.
[17] Carus-Wilson, *Medieval Merchant Venturers*, pp. 279–91.
[18] Gray, 'The production and exportation of English woollens', 35.
[19] *Ibid.* On the Flemish presence in Bristol and the West Country, see Chapter 2.
[20] Gray, 'The production and exportation of English woollens', 35.
[21] Amor, *From Wool to Cloth*, pp. 219–21.
[22] Gray, 'The production and exportation of English woollens', 35.

Table 4.2 *Quantity and types of cloth brought to the alnager of London 1374–9*[i]

Year	Long cloths	Short cloths	Coloured	Rays
1374–5	973	205		517.25
1376–7	752.5	210.75		1,020
1377–8			1,820	439
1378–9			1,001.5	243

[i] *Source:* TNA, E 101/340/22; E 101/340/23; E 101/340/24.

The number of textile workers, still very low at the beginning of the fourteenth century, went up.[23] Russets and other types of cloth also begin more frequently to be mentioned in the town's borough court records, and it would seem very unlikely that the output of these four regions could have been that low.[24]

In London, the particulars of alnage accounts are extant for the period from 1374 to 1379, with smaller gaps in 1375 and 1376.[25] These are extremely valuable. No particulars survive for this period for other parts of England. All of the surviving London rolls were kept up daily, and contain the names of individuals and the number of cloths sealed by the alnager, as well as the amount of subsidy paid. The alnage accounts covering the years of Edward III's reign distinguish between short and long cloths of the assize, and contain separate membranes for rays and coloured cloth. When all types are combined, we find 1,695¼ cloths sealed by the alnager in 1374–5 and 1,982 in 1376–7 (Table 4.2). These figures would put the annual production of broadcloth in a range similar to that in the late 1350s. Although the particulars for the 1370s provide the names of individuals who paid the subsidy for different types of cloth, no occupations were recorded, and the only way to trace textile workers is through other sources in London. The names of master cloth-workers extracted from the Letter Books and memoranda rolls to estimate the size of the industry were used here to identify the individuals in the alnage accounts.

When it comes to those Flemish weavers who settled in London, it seems that they focused on the production of rays, that is, medium-quality fabrics with striped bands or checks dyed in the yarn, and

[23] J. Cooper, 'Medieval Colchester: The economy', in Cooper (ed.), *The Victoria History*, vol. IX, p. 32.

[24] *Ibid.*

[25] TNA, E 101/340/22; E 101/340/23; E 101/340/24.

coloureds, the most expensive, heavily finished kind of cloth.[26] In both of the particulars of the alnage accounts that have survived for the capital during Edward III's reign, the separate membranes devoted to these types of textile consist almost exclusively of the names of Flemish immigrants.[27] Out of fifty-eight individuals who brought rays to the alnager, forty-eight were textile workers from the Low Countries. Eight of them were people exiled from Flanders in 1351 (Tables 4.3–4.5). John van Dorme, from Ypres, brought eight short rayed cloths and two scarlets, the most luxurious kind of woollen, dyed with kermes (an expensive dye for making scarlets), to the alnager on 13 December 1374. On 28 September 1376 he alnaged nine short rays, and on 17 February 1377 he had another three rayed cloths sealed.[28] John Capelle, an exile from Ghent, paid the fee for six short rays on 12 October 1374 and for another eighteen rayed cloths six days later.[29] John van Loo took fourteen pieces of rayed cloth to the alnager on 2 October 1376.[30] The most numerous exiles in London were the weavers from Ghent who specialised in rays, as will be seen below in this chapter. They obviously brought the specialist weaving and shearing skills required for this type of cloth, which no English producer had at this time.[31] As these cloths are recorded in the alnage accounts as short rays (*panni curti stragulati*), they were probably the type of Ghent cloths known as *strijpte halflakens* (rayed half cloth). This was a popular form of woollen, with a length of 15 to 18 ells, whose standard price could reach £5 3s 4d groot, or 154.9 days' wages for a master mason.[32] Another place in England associated with this type of cloth was Salisbury, which from the mid fourteenth century developed into a centre for the production and marketing of rays as well.[33] This perfectly coincides with the arrival of the exiles, and we saw in Chapter 2 that some of them settled in Salisbury, but the lack of sources for the period of this study makes it difficult to quantify their contribution in this town.

In the surviving accounts for the first two years of Richard II's reign, changes both in terms of the recording and the number of alnaged cloths can be observed. No longer are there separate membranes for rays, and

[26] For the different ranges of cloth on the London market, see Oldland, 'London clothmaking', pp. 24–5, 59–60.

[27] TNA, E 101/340/22, m. 3; E 101/340/23, mm. 5, 5d.

[28] *Ibid., ibid.*

[29] TNA, E 101/340/22, m. 3.

[30] TNA, E 101/340/23, m. 5.

[31] Munro, 'Medieval woollens: Textiles', vol. I, pp. 183, 211.

[32] J. H. Munro, 'Textiles as articles of consumption in Flemish towns 1300–1575', *Bijdragen tot de geschiedenis*, 81 (1998), 275–88, at 283.

[33] J. Chandler, *Endless Street: A History of Salisbury and Its People*, (Salisbury, 1983), pp. 260–2.

Table 4.3 *Quantities and types of cloth alnaged in London by Flemings (those in bold are exiles) 1374–5*[i]

Weaver/Draper	Date	Pieces of cloth	Type of cloth
John Capelle	12 October 1374	6	Short rays
John van Lest[ii]	13 October	5	Short rays
John Marlebeke	13 October	12	Short rays
Lewyn Cokelar	13 October	15	Short rays
John Stretewauwe[iii]	15 October	23	Short rays
John Grotere[iv]	15 October	17	Short rays
John Capelle	18 October	18	Short rays
Giles van Barle	18 October	5	Short rays
Dionysis van den Vivere[v]	6 November	32	Short rays
John Seland	20 November	3	Short rays[vi]
John Dorme	13 December	8	Short rays
Same person	13 December	3	Scarlets
Lambekin Mone	13 December	3	Short rays
Giles van Barle	7 June 1375	26	Short rays
William van Marght	7 June	20	Short rays
Copyn Seland	1 July	48	Short rays
John van Lest[ii]	1 July	22	Short rays
John Bures	12 August	28	Short rays
Copyn Seland	19 August	103	Short rays

[i] *Source:* TNA, E 101/340/22, m. 3.
[ii] One of the Flemings in a delegation who petitioned Edward III in 1364 to confirm the privileges from 1350, see Chapters 1 and 2.
[iii] *Letter Book G*, pp. 65–6: A certain Flemish weaver, Peter Stertewey, appears as surety for the good behaviour of all Flemish weavers residing in London after they organised a strike. Peter and John might have been related.
[iv] He was banished in 1351 from Ghent and was a bailiff of Flemish weavers in 1362, *Letter Book G*, p. 131.
[v] Nijs is a diminutive in Dutch for Dyonisis. This person is actually Nijs van den Vivere, a weaver banished from Ghent in 1351 (Table 2.1). In one case recorded in 1367 in the London plea and memoranda rolls, he appears as Nys van den Vyure, a draper from Ghent. *CPMR*, vol. II, p. 70.
[vi] In the margins is added 'called Medeleys', probably referring to 'medleys', multicoloured textiles made from a mixture of wools and in which red yarns predominate.

the short and long cloths from earlier accounts are now categorised as 'coloured' cloths. At the same time, the number of rays dropped sharply, with only 439 brought to the alnager in 1377–8, falling by almost half a year later to 243 cloths (Table 4.2). Such a nosedive in demand for the

Table 4.4 *Quantities and types of cloth alnaged in London by Flemings (those in bold are exiles) 1376–7*[i]

Weaver/Draper	Date	Pieces of cloth	Type of cloth
Nijs van den Vivere	18 May 1376	18	Rays
Peter van Hese	18 May	12	Rays
John Marlebeke	18 May	12	Rays
John Houdmaker	20 May	4	Rays
Lewyn Cokelar	21 June	8	Short rays
Dyonisis van Vivere	10 August	14	Short rays
Ras Brewer	12 August	15	Short rays
Lewyn Singheem	12 August	6	Short rays
John van Dorme	28 September	9	Short rays
John van Brele	28 September	13	Short rays
Baldewyne Yawer	28 September	17	Short rays
William van de Mule	28 September	43	Short rays
John Marlebeke	30 September	10	Short rays
John Stertewauwe	30 September	14	Short rays
Lewyn Cokelar	30 September	15	Short rays
John van Strate	2 October	3	Short rays
John van Loo	2 October	14	Short rays
William Dotter	13 November	13	Short rays
Giles van Eke	13 November	13	Short rays
Andrew van He	13 November	8	Short rays
Ras Brewer	10 December	8	Short rays

[i] *Source:* TNA, E 101/340/23, m. 5.

type of cloth that the Flemings in London focused on was reflected in the fact that only three Flemish textile workers appear in these two accounts. Copyn Scland alnaged ninety-three rays and twenty-seven coloured cloths between 1377 and 1379; a fuller, Lodewyk Dol, alnaged seven coloured cloths; and John Veleyn brought twenty-one coloured cloths to the alnager over the same period.[34] Eleanor Quinton has already observed that there was decreasing demand for rays in the capital at the end of the fourteenth century, and it seems that the final years of the 1370s marked the beginning of this trend.[35] Throughout the 1360s there

[34] TNA, E 101/340/24, mm. 1–7d. John Veleyn was also a bailiff of the Flemish weavers in London in 1377, *Letter Book H*, p. 77.

[35] Contrary to what is suggested in Quinton, 'The drapers and the drapery trade', pp. 166–7.

Table 4.5 *Quantities and types of cloth alnaged in London by Flemings (those in bold are exiles) 1376–7*[i]

Weaver/Draper	Date	Pieces of cloth	Type of cloth
John Dorme	16 December 1376	20	Short rays
Laurence Maught	16 December	2	Short rays
Giles Meifrot	16 December	12	Short rays
John Brele	8 January 1377	2	Short rays
John Dorme	8 January	3	Short rays
Dyonisis van Vivere	8 January	11	Short rays
Peter Boye	8 January	14	Short rays
John Everyngham	8 January	14	Short rays
John Dorme	18 January	4	Short rays
John Meinfrot	18 January	2	Short rays
William Mews	18 January	12	Short rays
John van Hame	18 January	2	Short rays
Giles van Brele	18 January	Illegible	Illegible
John Stertewauwe	11 February	8	Short rays
John Rasingham	11 February	9	Short rays
Giles van Brele	11 February	7	Short rays
John van Dorme	17 February	3	Short rays
Peter Canyngham	17 February	2	Short rays
John Stratelyn	17 February	3	Short rays
Dyonisis van Vivere	17 February	9	Short rays
Giles Brele	20 February	7	Short rays
Godfrey Blauwere	26 February	13	Short rays
Ras Brewer	26 February	11	Short rays
John Marlebeke	26 February	10	Short rays
Jacob van Loo	6 March	9	Short rays
Baldwyn Yawer	6 March	19	Short rays
William Yager	6 March	18	Short rays
Dyonisis van Vivere	6 March	14	Short rays
Henry Braban	23 March	1	Short rays
Giles Brele	14 April	21	Short rays
Peter Boye	14 April	11	Short rays
John Stratelyn	13 May	5	Short rays

[i] *Source:* TNA, E 101/340/23, m. 5d.

continued to be a domestic market for striped and checked fabrics. In 1362–3, the Royal Wardrobe still bought 108 rayed cloths, a number inferior only to the 201 long and short coloureds purchased that year. Whereas most of these rays were also supplied by London drapers, one Fleming, Jacob Bone from Ghent, sold twenty-eight directly to the court.[36] By 1392–5, the relative importance of rayed cloth had dropped compared with that of long and short coloureds, with 134 pieces bought of the former and 872 of the latter, but it remained the Wardrobe's second most sought-after cloth type.[37] There is some evidence that other wealthy consumers also carried on purchasing rays until at least the end of the fourteenth century, but nothing to suggest a scale of production as seen in the alnage accounts over the period between 1374 and 1376.[38]

It looks as if the Flemish arrivals in London operated their business on the same capitalist basis as they had done back home.[39] The amounts of cloth the Flemings alnaged were consistently very high and exceeded the capacities of individual weavers, whose average output during this period ranged between ten and fifteen cloths a year.[40] By contrast, the other types of woollen recorded in 1374–7 were invariably brought to the alnager by large numbers of English fullers in much smaller quantities (see Table 4.6).[41] The amount of cloth the fullers handled ranged from half a cloth to five cloths at a time. For example, on 18 October 1374, William Moteshunte brought five-and-a-half long cloths to the alnager.[42] For the next eight months covered by the account, he appeared another seven times alnaging between one-half and five-and-a-half cloths of the same type. Although fullers were bringing smaller quantities at a time, as can be seen, altogether they were still alnaging significantly more cloth than any other textile workers (excluding alien weavers in 1376–7). Individually, only four fullers managed to bring more than fifty cloths to the alnager in a single year. William Corner brought fifty-five, John Oumfray brought sixty and William Doder brought fifty, while Simon Gardiner alnaged ninety-three cloths in 1374–5.[43] Other fullers, including alien fullers Lodewyk de Dole and John Flemynge, generally brought from ten to forty cloths a year.[44] While the fullers handled the same quantities of cloth as the alien weavers, it should be stressed that the rays which the latter overwhelmingly focused on were relatively expensive to produce and required specialist skills. The only other group to alnage these types were prominent London drapers such as John Northampton, Roger Abbot, Geoffrey Walderne and Jacob Snow, though they did so

[36] TNA, E 101/394/12. [37] TNA, E 101/402/13.

[38] See, for example, the many fragments of rayed cloth in the late fourteenth-century deposits excavated at London's Baynard Castle. F. Pritchard, 'Patterned cloths from 14th-century London', in P. Walton and J. P. Wild (eds), *Textiles in Northern Archaeology* (London, 1990), vol. III, pp. 155–64, at p. 159.

[39] For the organisation of the Flemish cloth industry, see Stabel, 'Guilds in late medieval Flanders', 208–9.

[40] Munro, 'Medieval woollens: Textiles', vol. I, p. 197.

[41] Oldland, 'London clothmaking', p. 85. [42] TNA, E 101/340/22, m. 1.

[43] TNA, E 101/340/22, mm. 1–3d. [44] See Oldland, 'London clothmaking', pp. 85–7.

Table 4.6 *Number of cloths brought to the alnager of London by different groups of textile workers 1374–7*[i]

Year/type of cloth	Alien weavers	Alien fullers	Native weavers	Native fullers	Drapers
1374–5/long	-	21	3	515	5.5
Short	-	6	-	59	5.5
Rays	397	-	-	-	120
1376–7/long	0.5	11.5	-	405	3
short	4	7.5	1	84	6
rays	663	-	-	-	65

[i] *Source:* TNA, E 101/340/22 and E 101/340/23.

to a much lesser extent than the alien weavers. They were responsible for less than one-third of rays brought to the alnager in 1374–5 and one-tenth in 1376–7. The absence of native weavers from the accounts seems to be related to developments in the London cloth market over the second half of the fourteenth century that favoured alien weavers and allowed a rise in the importance of fullers.[45]

The Black Death had not reduced the demand for the middling- and high-quality types of cloth being produced by Flemish weavers in the capital. The market for luxury, coloured textiles may even have expanded as living standards rose, and substantial quantities could be sold to noble households and the royal court. In 1350–1, the king's Great Wardrobe spent 53.8 per cent of its money for drapery purchases on coloureds.[46] The London drapers, who monopolised these sales to the court, were the only group apart from the Flemish exiles to alnage rays.[47] Throughout the 1350s cloths imported from abroad, which were usually the higher-quality varieties, still constituted the majority of textiles sealed by the alnager in London.[48] By the second half of the 1370s, when the Flemings were alnaging vast quantities of cloth, all but a few of these imports had disappeared.[49] Edward III's policy of encouraging Flemish craftsmen thus seems to have had an effect.

45 M. Pajic, 'The fortunes of urban fullers in fourteenth-century England', *Historical Research*, 93 (2020), 227–51.

46 Oldland, 'London clothmaking', p. 64, n. 14.

47 Oldland, 'Making and marketing woollen cloth', 94. The following three paragraphs are entirely based on Lambert and Pajic, 'Immigration and the Common Profit', 647–8.

48 Oldland, 'London clothmaking', pp. 64–5.

49 TNA, E 101/340/22, m. 3; E 101/340/23, mm. 5, 5d.

The fortunes of London's native weavers contrasted sharply with those of the Flemish exiles. Over the second quarter of the fourteenth century, the city's English cloth-workers had experienced a revival, as they had been able to extricate themselves from the dominance of the burellers,[50] and technological advancement had enabled them to broaden their range from semi-worsteds to cheap, coarse, full woollens. The Black Death did reduce the demand for lower-quality cloth, although not as much as the drop in the population figures might suggest.[51] In 1364, native weavers were also denied the retail sale of their own products, as only drapers now had the right to market cloth in the city. This did not automatically mean that these drapers would buy from local cloth-workers. In 1351, London's exemption from the Statute of York, which, in 1335, had allowed all merchants to trade freely throughout England, was lifted.[52] This enabled provincial weavers, who were able to work with lower costs, to flood the city with their less expensive textiles. While London developed into the kingdom's most important cloth market, its native cloth-workers became uncompetitive. Many moved out of the city to escape payment of the farm to the crown. They elected members to the Common Council, the representative assembly of the city's mysteries, but, as this was dominated by the mercantile guilds, their political influence was limited.[53]

The types of cloth in which the Flemings specialised, where demand was sufficient and provincial competition less fierce, might have solved some of the problems experienced by native weavers, but those problems were too much for them. The production of rayed cloth required specialist weaving and shearing skills, which native weavers did not have.[54] Making coloureds demanded even more specific know-how, mostly in the preparation of the yarn, which, during this period, no English producer had.[55] The natives' lack of capital and control over the complete production cycle also prevented them from following up on the preferences of the end customers, who specified the colours and other features of the rays, and from imposing the very high quality

[50] Burellers were London cloth-workers who dominated drapery in the city in the first quarter of the fourteenth century.

[51] J. H. Munro, 'The origins of the English "new draperies": The resurrection of an old Flemish industry, 1270–1570', in N. B. Harte (ed.), *The New Draperies in the Low Countries and England* (New York, 1998), pp. 35–127, at pp. 67–8.

[52] *Statutes of the Realm*, ed. Luders et al., vol. I, pp. 270–1.

[53] C. M. Barron, *London in the Later Middle Ages: Government and People, 1200–1500* (Oxford, 2004), pp. 220–1; Oldland, 'London clothmaking', pp. 67–78; Quinton, 'The drapers and the drapery trade', pp. 113–17.

[54] Munro, 'Medieval woollens: Textiles', vol. I, pp. 183, 211.

[55] Oldland, 'London clothmaking', pp. 62–3.

standards needed for manufacturing coloured cloth. Flemish weavers may already have been refusing to hire English apprentices and servants, as they would do in the late fifteenth century, in order to avoid the dissemination of their skills.[56]

Given the elevated economic status of many immigrants before their banishment, it is likely that some of them possessed the capital to organise the whole production process. As we will see below, some Flemish weavers were rich enough to be involved in the exportation of wool, which means that they probably bought large quantities. Some of the wool they possessed was in all likelihood contracted out to their fellow Flemings or their families for different stages of the work in the production of cloths they were alnaging. They might have done so through migrant networks, as they did in Great Yarmouth and Colchester, as discussed in Chapter 3. Since the organisation of yarn production and the quality of the yarns were critical to weaving the finest cloths, they probably wanted to entrust this work to someone on whose skills they could count. Indeed, we might say that there is evidence of some sort of putting-out system (see below).

This sophisticated organisation of cloth manufacture in England is mostly associated with clothiers slightly later than the period of this study.[57] In Flanders, the cloth industry was more integrated, and the system, in which the weaver–drapers possessed raw material which was 'put out' to other workers in return for payment, the finished products to be marketed further, developed a lot earlier. The case of Copin Seland, a Flemish immigrant in London, is the best example for the existence of the putting-out system in the second half of the fourteenth century. In 1374–5, he brought 151 pieces of short rays to be sealed by the alnager, and another 68½ rays and 22 coloured cloths in 1378–9.[58] These amounts were higher by far than those of other individuals who appear in these particulars of the alnage accounts. It seems that Copin Seland operated his business on the basis of the domestic putting-out system, and that the cloth-workers who worked for him lived in his house. In 1371, when numerous banished Flemings were arrested in English towns in retaliation for the treatment of English merchants in Flanders, thirty of those who were imprisoned lived with him.[59] Copin was involved in the export of wool, but some of the wool in his possession must have been

[56] J. R. Oldland, 'London's trade in the time of Richard III', *The Ricardian*, 24 (2014), 1–30, at 16.

[57] J. S. Lee, *The Medieval Clothier* (Woodbridge, 2018).

[58] TNA, E 101/340/22, m. 3; E 101/340/24.

[59] For the context of these arrests, see Chapter 2 and the sections on Flemings in Lynn. Copin Seland complained to the authorities that thirty Flemings who had been living with him prior to their arrest had been in prison for more than seven weeks at his cost; see *CCR, 1369–74*, p. 326.

intended for workers who provided him with cloths he was bringing to the alnager.[60] Moreover, he lived in St Swithin's Lane, an area with the highest concentration of cloth-workers in London, which would naturally have made this system of production a lot easier.[61]

Apart from their use in examining business connections, the cases of litigation from various municipal and royal courts may be scrutinised to determine the amount of money that the parties involved handled. This in turn might reveal whether the alien textile workers of London were able to organise the production process themselves. Some immigrants, as we have seen, possessed considerable potential in terms of capital and political leverage even before their arrival in England. For those who settled in London, their gains certainly continued to grow in the same manner. Banished Flemings dealt with London mercers, who, during this period, were among the leading traders in English cloth abroad.[62] In 1364, John van Stene, an exile from Ghent, sued mercers John Peutre and Henry Forester for debts of £23 0s. 3d. and £4 17s.[63] Three years later, Isabela Backer accused John Comber, *Fleming*, of unjustly detaining goods worth 40s.[64] In 1370, John van Semps, who was one of the exporters of wool in 1366, brought a case for a debt incurred in Candlewick Street against a weaver exiled from Ghent, John Mathys, and his wife for goods valued at 100s.[65] At the time of his unexpected death, a weaver from Bruges who had settled in London, Christian de la Bonegarde, had (amongst other things) £40 in English coinage only, which was to be distributed amongst his creditors in 1364.[66] A haberdasher from Zeeland, John Peterson, called Eversword, acknowledged a debt of £120 owed to his brother-in-law, Peter Blowere, a dyer from the Low Countries, who lived in the parish of St James Garlickhythe.[67] All of these cases suggest that the Flemings handled considerable amounts of money, and that they were engaged in substantial mercantile activity.

These conclusions are further reinforced if we take the exiles who settled in England and look into their involvement in the production and

60 *CFR, 1369–77*, p. 167. Copin Seland got a licence for the export of 134 sacks of wool from the port of London in 1372.

61 *Letter Book G*, p. 292.

62 J. R. Oldland and E. Quinton, 'London merchants' cloth exports, 1350–1500', in R. Netherton and G. R. Owen-Crocker (eds), *Medieval Clothing and Textiles* (Woodbridge, 2011), vol. VII, p. 125; A. F. Sutton, *The Mercery of London: Trade, Goods and People, 1130–1578* (Aldershot, 2005), pp. 148–50.

63 *CPMR*, vol. I, p. 279.

64 TNA, CP 40/428, m. 18.

65 TNA, CP 40/417, m. 254; E 122/70/18, m. 5.

66 *Letter Book G*, p. 182.

67 *CPMR*, vol. I, p. 280. The will of Peter's wife is analysed in Chapter 3.

marketing of cloth before the banishment. We have already seen in Chapter 2 that some of the exiles had held important positions within the city governments of Ghent and Bruges throughout the 1340s. However, it is also important to see their potential in terms of capital, as well as the quantities and types of cloth they produced and sold prior to their arrival in England. One of the main features of cloth production and its organisation in Flemish towns was its highly corporate nature, and the textile guilds in Bruges and Ghent were vertically organised structures which consisted of members who ranged from the rich to those of middling income and the poor. At the top of the chain within the textile guilds were the weaver–entrepreneurs, the wealthiest members, who created the so-called guild elite.[68] The latter were able to buy large quantities of wool and then subcontract the production of cloth to other fellow guild members which those elite members would then sell to foreign merchants. Basically, these weaver–drapers controlled the whole cloth production and marketing process. These elite guild members (who came, of course, not only from the textile guilds, but from other guilds as well) were usually chosen as the deans of their respective guilds or as the city aldermen. These positions with political connections gave them lucrative opportunities, such as obtaining contracts to supply cloth on a yearly basis for the city governments of Bruges and Ghent.

Throughout the fourteenth century, the city accounts of Ghent and Bruges recorded expenses related to purchases of cloth as part of the regular compensation for city office-holders and employees.[69] It was purchased regularly, twice a year, for Easter and on the feast of Saint Bavo in Bruges and for the feast of Tournai, and there were regular yearly purchases of cloths for office-holders in Ghent. These accounts are probably the best sources for establishing the types of cloth, their geographical origin and the sellers, as well as the development of fashion tastes in fourteenth-century Flanders.[70] For the city of Bruges, Murray established that from 1331 until 1381 so-called Bruges cloth dominated the purchases of that city, together with cloth from Ghent and the cities of East Flanders, and from Brabant in particular.[71] Conversely, in Ghent, the most dominant were rays, the kind of cloth that Ghent weavers specialised in and were known for on the international markets

[68] S. Hutton, *Women and Economic Activities in Late Medieval Ghent* (New York, 2011), pp. 28–9; M. Boone, *Geld en macht: De Gentsce statfinancien en de Burgondische staatsvorming 1384–1453* (Ghent, 1990), pp. 23–120; Murray, *Bruges*, p. 285.

[69] Murray, *Bruges*, p. 289.

[70] Munro, 'Textiles as articles of consumption in Flemish towns 1300–1575', 277.

[71] *Ibid.*, and see table 7 at 291.

Table 4.7 *Names of Flemish exiles that appear in English sources and the types of cloth they supplied to the city authorities of Bruges in the years preceding the exile 1341–51*[i]

Exile	Types of cloth supplied
Clais Scotelare	Mixed cloths, linings
Peter van Bassevelde	Linings
John Were	Linings
John van der Cappelle	Mixed cloths, linings
John Losekin	Aerzidine cloths[ii]
Peter Sceepstale	Linings
Lamsin Yperlinc	Linings
John van Coukelare	Linings
Peter van de Moor	Linings
John Veltacker	Linings
Lamsin de Vos	Blue cloths
François van Artevelde	Linings
John van Ypre	Linings
Clais Sleepstaf	linings

[i] Dataset based on: SAB, Stadsrekeningen 1341–51.
[ii] Aerzidine cloths were those coloured with a red-based dye containing alum.

Table 4.8 *Names of Flemish exiles that appear in English sources and the types of cloth they supplied to the city authorities of Ghent in the years preceding the exile 1341–51*[i]

Exile	Types of cloth supplied
John van Everyngham	Illegible
Lievin Godhalse	Rays
John Jonkere	Rays
John van Marlebeke	Rays
Lievin Fisker	Rays
Peter van Bassevelde[ii]	Mixed cloths

[i] *Source: De Rekeningen der stad Gent*, ed. De Pauw and Vuylsteke, vol. II, p. 477; *ibid.*, vol. III, pp. 197, 298.
[ii] Peter van Bassevelde was from Bruges and supplied cloths to Bruges as well. This seems to have been a regular occurrence both ways.

throughout the fourteenth and fifteenth centuries. This was also the type of cloth that those who settled in London brought to be sealed by the alnager, as we have seen above.

Those Flemish exiles who appear in English sources after 1351 were of course amongst the prominent suppliers of cloths and linings to the city governments of Ghent and Bruges throughout the 1340s. Again, the most numerous suppliers were those who decided to settle in London following the banishment. Thus, Peter van Bassevelde, Clais Scotelare, Lamsin de Vos, John Were and Lamsin Yperlinc quite regularly supplied cloths and fabric for linings to the city of Bruges from 1342 until 1350.[72] Amongst those who settled in Great Yarmouth and supplied cloth in Bruges before the banishment were the weavers John van der Cappelle, John Losekin and Peter Sceepstale (Table 4.7). No exile in Colchester had supplied either of the two city governments with cloths before the banishment.

Even though the accounts for Ghent are incomplete, the first noticeable thing is that the Flemish weavers from this town produced the same types of cloth as they did later in London. With fragmentary evidence we can only find four exiles who supplied cloths in the years before the banishment, but all of them were contracted to provide rays. Two of them, John van Everyngham and John van Marlebeke, also brought forty-four pieces of rayed cloth to the alnager in London in the course of the account for 1376–7.[73] The remaining two exiles, Levin Godhalse and John Yonkere, who supplied rays for the city authorities in Ghent in the 1340s, do not appear in alnage accounts, but they both held important positions within the guild of Flemish weavers of London on different occasions.[74] Be it for Ghent or Bruges, all those who feature in Tables 4.7 and 4.8 and who supplied cloths to the city were well-connected people who had held high positions in the same years both in city government and within their own guilds. For example, in the year John van Coukelare supplied linings for the feast of Saint Bavo that amounted to £3 groot, he was also a burgomaster of Bruges, while Lamsin de Vos was dean of the weavers' guild when he sold fifteen pieces of cloth of Bruges three years later.[75] Such circumstances might have facilitated the decision to award them with the task of supplying the city with cloth, but this is again a testament to the fact that those exiles who settled in London regularly rubbed shoulders with both political and commercial elites of

[72] All five of them settled in London after the exile: see Tables 2.1 and 2.3 in Chapter 2 for their names and references.

[73] TNA, E 101/340/23, mm. 5, 5d.

[74] *De Rekeningen der stad Gent*, ed. De Pauw and Vuylsteke, vol. II, p. 477. John Jonkere was elected bailiff of the Flemish weavers' guild in London in 1363, and Levin Godhalse brokered the agreement between native and Flemish weavers in 1352. Consitt, *The London Weavers' Company*, p. 188; *Letter Book G*, p. 157.

[75] SAB, Stadsrekeningen 1343–4, fo. 58v, and Stadsrekeningen 1346–7, fos 54r, 57v.

the most important cities in Flanders. By emigrating to London, they lost some of their political grip, but they were certainly able to use their entrepreneurial skills in order to develop new economic relationships with Londoners.

The immigrants from the Low Countries used these abilities to establish business relationships with prominent drapers in London and to maintain active contact with them. In 1367, for example, Arnold Skakpynkyl and Nys van de Vyure (Dionisis van Vivere), weavers exiled from Ghent, sued draper Nicholas Rouse for a debt of £9 19s.[76] In London, most rays and other cloths that the Flemings produced might possibly have been supplied to the Great Wardrobe by drapers, who feature most prominently as the king's purveyors in these accounts.[77] However, some exiles, like John van Dorne or Lievin van Ordingham, were sufficiently wealthy and influential to do it without the middlemen. The former supplied four red cloths and four russets, while the latter sold considerable amounts of cloths of Paris and Hainaut.[78] For these two purchases alone, Lievin van Ordingham was paid £52 1s 3d. What is also interesting is that Arnold Skakpynkyl, Nys van de Vyure and three more exiles are referred to in London sources as either merchants or merchant-drapers, whilst in Ghent sources they were recorded as weavers, which suggests that they were in the top ranks of the weavers' guild in Ghent before the banishment.[79] Indeed, in 1376–7 alone, Nys van de Vyure alnaged sixty-six rays, which is quite a high number of quality cloths, and so it seems natural to confuse him with drapers.[80] These cases, and the number of cloths the Flemish weavers alnaged, imply that the immigrants were regularly commissioned to organise the whole process of manufacture, and might have distributed their cloths to the Great Wardrobe and the international market through the London drapers.[81] Such evidence suggests that most of the Flemish masters might themselves have stopped weaving and that their main task was to provide raw materials, check the quality of cloth after fulling and prepare it for alnage.

76 *CPMR*, vol. II, p. 270. 77 Oldland, 'Making and marketing woollen cloth', 94.

78 TNA, E 101/394/12, E 101/392/3, m. 2.

79 *Cartulaire historique et généalogique des Artevelde*, ed. De Pauw, p. 712. See also *CPMR*, vol. II, p. 67: another exile from Ghent, Laurence de Maught, who appeared in the alnage accounts, sued a London draper, John Noket, in a plea of a £50 debt for linen cloth supplied to John's wife, Isolda.

80 TNA, E 101/340/23, mm. 5, 5d.

81 The roll of expenses of the Great Wardrobe in 1362 shows that the London drapers provided the royal household with rays, which was presumably in part produced by Flemish immigrants resident in London: see TNA, E 101/394/12.

CLOTH PRODUCTION AND THE RETAIL TRADE

Given the nature of the sources used for Great Yarmouth and Colchester, it is a little bit easier to draw a picture of the immigrants' role in the production process and marketing of cloth domestically than it is for London. The whole process from raw wool to completion of one piece of quality cloth lasted around one year.[82] Wool had to be bought, then washed, broken up, carded, spun on spinning wheels, woven, fulled and then sent for finishing with tailors, shearers and dyers.[83] The evidence from numerous sources used for this book suggests that Flemish immigrants were heavily involved in all of these stages. We will see below in this chapter that some Flemish exiles, both weavers and fullers, were involved in the export of wool, which means that they had contacts with wool-growers, and thus acted as middlemen for other immigrants from the Low Countries. Lippin Sceepstale, *webster*, was acquiring wool from both Flemish exiles and from English wool suppliers, as he was involved in cases for debt concerning the sale of wool on two occasions with Clais Makeler and William Ridlington. In 1371, Lippin was accused of a debt of 19s 6d by William Rydlington for wool bought, while in 1379 he brought a plea of debt against an exile from Bruges, Clais Makeler.[84] The next stage of cloth production was done by Flemish women, who probably contracted work via their husbands, other Flemings and English weavers as well. Katherine, wife of Clais Seger, was accused of the theft of dyed wool by a certain John Webbe, who hired her only to break the wool.[85] The occupational structure of female immigrants from the Low Countries, such as Emma Braban, *kempstere*, or Truyde Frowe, spinster, suggests that they were indeed involved in carding and spinning, as we will see in the next chapter.[86] Flemish

[82] W. Endrei, 'Manufacturing a piece of woollen cloth in medieval Flanders: How many working hours?', in E. Aerts and J. Munro (eds), *Textiles of the Low Countries in European Economic History* (Leuven, 1990), pp. 14–23.

[83] G. De Poerck, *La Draperie médiévale en Flandre et en Artois: Technique et terminologie*, 2 vols. (Bruges, 1951), vol. I, pp. 80–116.

[84] NRO, Y/C4/85, m. 1; Y/C4/91, m. 4. William Rydlington was apparently a regular wool supplier in Great Yarmouth. He was also fined for selling wool by false measurements in 1374: see NRO, Y/C4/87, m. 20d. For Clais Makeler's involvement in wool exports, see NRO, Y/C4/88, mm. 12, 12d, 13.

[85] Benham, *Court Rolls*, vol. II, p. 193. See also Benham, *Court Rolls*, vol. III, p. 20, where Margaret van Vynk was hired by John Lancele to break a portion of wool. For more details about the involvement of Flemish women in cloth production, see Chapter 5.

[86] Emma Braban, *kempstere*, who lived in York, brought a plea of trespass against John de Coloyne to the court of the King's Bench, while Truyde Frowe, spinster, and several other Flemish women paid the poll tax in Southwark. See TNA, KB 27/411, m. 9 and Fenwick, *Poll Taxes*, vol. II, p. 562.

weavers both took on piecework and supervised the whole process of cloth-making. John Barremaker was, for example, hired by William Crabbe in order to make a piece of woollen cloth.[87] The number of cases for debt in Great Yarmouth between Flemish weavers and fullers exiled from Bruges suggests that the immigrants contracted fulling tasks both to their fellow countrymen and to native fullers, whilst distributing the finished cloth themselves afterwards.[88] Flemish dyers seem to have been contracted to add the blue and red dyes to the cloth,[89] while the tailors and shearers focused on the manufacture of tunics and chalons, to which they were adding other garments as well.[90]

Even though there were several obstacles, such as entering the franchise in order to be able to trade retail, or other restrictive local by-laws, there is ample evidence that Flemish textile workers were actively involved in the domestic marketing of cloth. We saw in Chapter 2 that at least five of the immigrants who settled in London acquired citizenship, which, according to London's charter granted by Edward II in 1319, was required in order to trade retail in the city.[91] Moreover, the drapers were granted a letter patent in 1364 that excluded dyers, weavers and fullers from trading in cloth, and gave exclusive rights to the enfranchised drapers to buy or sell cloth within the city. Drapers were cut out from from the wool trade in the 1350s, so they wanted to keep the cloth trade in their hands at all costs.[92] Nevertheless, Quinton asserted that in reality it was rather difficult for established drapers to control the sale of both London-produced and provincial cloth, which was more and more present in the city's market.[93] It thus seems that the alien weavers had a way around the restrictions. In 1364, a weaver exiled from Bruges, Peter le Bakere, was fined for selling unfulled cloth to Henry Leberd.[94] In this case the authorities seem to have been more concerned with the stage of production at which the cloth was sold than with the fact that Peter was a foreigner.

In Colchester, there was a by-law that limited the sale of unfulled cloth only to the burgesses of Colchester.[95] However, the lawhundred

[87] Benham, *Court Rolls*, vol. III, p. 198.

[88] For the cases of debt between Peter van de Scelle, weaver, Bernard Gallin, fuller, and Walter Collessad, fuller, during the terms 1354–8, see NRO, Y/C4/75, mm. 2, 6d; Y/C4/76, m. 6.

[89] NRO, Y/C4/73, m. 2d; when John Lister, *Fleming*, was accused of debt by Simon Scot, he was distrained by 3 ells of red cloth.

[90] NRO, Y/C4/80, m. 12d; Everard Tailor, *Fleming*, accused Edmund atte Paston and Katherina his wife of the detinue of a rayed chalon he had produced for them.

[91] *The Historical Charters and Constitutional Documents of the City of London* (London, 1887), pp. 46–7.

[92] Oldland, 'Making and marketing woollen cloth', 95.

[93] Quinton, 'The drapers and the drapery trade', pp. 116–17.

[94] *CPMR*, vol. II, p. 6.

[95] Britnell, *Growth and Decline*, p. 77.

court of Colchester does not mention fines specifically for infractions in connection with the sale of cloth, and we do not know to what extent the by-law was enforced. The only evidence that suggests strangers could face some trade restrictions if they were not citizens is the case of William de Breggis, *Fleming and foreigner*, who was fined for selling a piece of cloth to Robert Chaplain despite the prohibition 'concerning the sale of yarns and cloths of woollen and russet'.[96] The case does not specify the date of the local prohibition which the fine referred to, but it is implied that William was fined for the sale of cloth as a foreigner. Nevertheless, immigrants from the Low Countries were involved in the trade in both yarn and cloth in the town's market. In 1375, for example, John Rovere accused John Backer, a Fleming, of breaking a contract by failing to provide four pieces of 'Flemish cloth'.[97] Ten years later, John Van Rouns was attached to respond to Stephen Baroun in a plea of debt. Stephen claimed that he sold to John Van Rouns yarns of russet and white woollen valued 13s in order for them to be woven, which John had not done within the agreed time frame.[98]

It was in Great Yarmouth that immigrants from the Low Countries faced some restrictive measures in the retail cloth trade. In 1379, for example, Lippin Sceepstale, John Witbrood and William Tailor, Dutchman, were fined for cutting and selling woollen and linen cloth in contravention of the Statute of Gloucester, and for trading as non-burgesses.[99] Rodziewicz asserted that penalties for some residents of Great Yarmouth for trading under the guise of being a burgess while they were not, recorded in the leet-court, represented a public message from the authorities to others not to buy from them.[100] This was probably in some way the main intention of the town officials, but some immigrants from the Low Countries were fined for this infringement year after year throughout the 1360s and 1370s. In her study of nearby Norwich, Penny Dunn also noticed in the town's leet rolls that a lot of weavers were fined for trading as citizens while they were not, and that might have been an incentive for some to take up the freedom eventually.[101] For this particular offence, John Witbrood, fuller, Lippin

[96] ERO, D/B CR13, m. 5, calendared in Benham, *Court Rolls*, vol. II, p. 138.

[97] ERO, D/B 5 CR 17, m. 7, calendared in Benham, *Court Rolls*, vol. III, p. 70.

[98] ERO, D/B 5 CR 25, m. 28.

[99] NRO, Y/C4/90, m. 12. 'William Tailor, Duchman, John Elys, Webster, Paul Souter, Paul Dumburgh, Gerard Souter, Henry van Campe, Jacob Tailor scindunt et vendent panni di linen et lanna contra statute et mercandirant tam quam burgenses et non sunt.'

[100] Rodziewicz, 'Great Yarmouth', p. 8.

[101] Dunn, 'After the Black Death', p. 158.

Sceepstale, weaver, and Jacob Tailor, *Fleming*, were fined on numerous occasions.[102] However, it seems that for both aliens and natives it was quite difficult to obtain the freedom in Great Yarmouth.[103] Some of the immigrants' activity as evidenced in the Great Yarmouth court rolls would hint that they were wealthy enough to acquire the freedom. For instance, in 1368 alone, Lippin Sceepstale lost three cases for debt against William Fuller, Thomas Stalham and Robert Herbert.[104] Overall, he had to pay damages of 23s 22d that year alone, and his goods were assessed to the value at £7 7s 2d (Table 4.10). The amount of money he owed in damages would probably have been enough to pay the fee to enter the franchise. (The fees for a new burgess in Great Yarmouth stood at 26s 8d in late 1460s.)[105] Moreover, he was never offered a pardon by Bruges or the comital authorities, and therefore he had all the more reason to acquire the freedom and facilitate his trade in the town. Nevertheless, it appears that it was impossible to do so, or that Flemish textile workers did not really need to do so. Indeed, Flemish textile workers had the protection of Edward III, which granted them the right to exercise their trade in England, but, as can be observed, for the local authorities this was not enough. Heather Swanson has suggested that in medieval York entrepreneurial organisation was such that it was not always worthwhile for weavers to enter the freedom in order to do business.[106] We have seen earlier, however, that some of the immigrant textile workers from the Low Countries entered the freedom of the cities of York, Colchester and even London, which would definitely make the existence of some limits to accepting new burgesses in Great Yarmouth all the more plausible.

Litigation or fines relating to infringements in the cloth trade can still provide us with an insight into the types of cloth that immigrants from the Low Countries handled. In most cases where the records make this information available, Flemings were associated with woollen cloth (*panni di lana*), which was probably a standard broadcloth of 12 yards or

[102] NRO, Y/C4/81, m. 25d; Y/C4/84, m. 2d; Y/C4/90, m. 12.

[103] B. Lambert and C. Liddy, 'The civic franchise and the regulation of aliens in Great Yarmouth c. 1430 – c. 1490', in McDonald, Ormrod and Tailor (eds), *Resident Aliens*, pp. 125–43. Difficulties similar to those in Great Yarmouth concerning the entry of craftsmen into the franchise were observed by Maryanne Kowaleski in fourteenth-century Exeter: Kowaleski, *Local Markets Exeter*, pp. 101–4.

[104] NRO, Y/C4/83, mm. 9, 10. See also the value of Lippin's seized goods after the arrest in 1371. For the context of the arrest of all banished Flemings in 1371, see the sections on Lynn in Chapter 2.

[105] Lambert and Liddy, 'The civic franchise', p. 139.

[106] H. Swanson, *Medieval Artisans: An Urban Class in Late Medieval England* (Oxford, 1989), p. 36.

more.[107] When a fuller exiled from Bruges, Walter Collessad, was accused of an unspecified debt owed to John Lythkyrk, in order to ensure his appearance in court he was distrained by a piece of woollen cloth he had in his possession.[108] Sometimes, the records capture other details. Such was the case of Lippin Sceepstale in 1384, who was distrained by a white cloth, when he was accused of owing 20s to William Godefeld and Thomas Ber for a piece of woollen cloth.[109] The same year William Yanesson brought a plea of debt of 8s against Peter van ye Ferre, who was then distrained by a tunic, a cloak and two pieces of linen cloth.[110] More evidence of textile workers from the Low Countries producing rays and coloured cloths comes from Yorkshire at the end of the fourteenth century. In 1399, the weavers of York petitioned the king's council to investigate weaving in the countryside around the town, saying that at least 200 men were so occupied, and that in consequence the York guild was finding difficulty in paying its farm. The king's commission decided in favour of the weavers of York, who received the arrears for the payment of their farm from numerous weavers from the countryside. Amongst the fined weavers we find John Brabaner and Henry Brabaner in Helmesley, John Mons, *Brabaner*, in Whitby, John Brabaner in Lethum and Henry Brabaner in Ripon, who were all obliged to pay fines for weaving rays and cloths dyed 'plunket' (i.e. light blue) and blue over the previous twenty years without permission from the corporation of York weavers.[111] The overall evidence from London and other towns suggests that immigrants from the Low Countries were engaged in the production of high-quality cloths such as rays and coloureds, but that they also adapted to the requirements of local production methods and engaged in the manufacture of standard English broadcloths, as well as straits and russets.

There are even indications that a small part of the Flemings' output was exported. Between 1362, the year in which the guild of alien weavers had its first ordinances approved, and 1366, the new category of 'cloth of Flemish manufacture' figured among the exported types of

[107] See, for example, the cases of Clais de Burgh, a weaver, vs John Scipman, and Walter Baker, *Fleming*, vs William Wadesden in Colchester, which were some of the disputes that involved immigrants from the Low Countries and the sale of 'woollen cloth'. ERO, D/B 5 CR 17, m. 12d, calendared in Benham, *Court Rolls*, vol. IV, p. 183.

[108] NRO, Y/C4/75, m. 2d.

[109] NRO, Y/C4/95, m. 6d. Heyne Tailor and Thomas Tailor, *Flemyng*, had also been distrained by white cloth in pleas brought against them a few years earlier. See NRO, Y/C4/84, m. 4 and NRO, Y/C4/85, m. 6.

[110] NRO, Y/C4/95, m. 7d.

[111] *Calendar of Inquisitions Miscellaneous, Vol. VI: Chancery, 1392–99*, pp. 242–8.

cloth in London's enrolled petty customs accounts.[112] Unfortunately, there are no particulars of account that allow us to identify the exporters, but some of the exiles, like John Kempe and Francis Fan Yabek, banished respectively from Ghent and Bruges, were caught by the London searcher for sending two pieces of cloth uncustomed to Flanders in 1362, suggesting that they were indeed involved with cloth exports in London.[113] However, in places where the particulars of customs accounts are extant, we can confirm that Flemish weavers were themselves actively involved in exports of cloth too. On 5 September 1366, a weaver from Bruges, John van Seint Trude, paid the customs in Boston for the export of nineteen cloths without grain (i.e. undyed).[114] After his exile John settled in York but used Boston as his port of preference on this occasion. It was common for other weavers from the Low Countries in York, with a flourishing international business, like Godfrey van Upstall, to travel to Hull in order to load various goods on ships.[115] In Great Yarmouth, a weaver, Peter fan Reylond, loaded woollen cloths, while a fuller, John Witbrood, exported straits and long cloths on several occasions.[116] Cloth produced in England was officially banned from Flanders, and the Flemings' woollens may have been sold in Gascony, the Baltic and Zeeland, the principal markets for English cloth in the fourteenth century.[117]

TEXTILE WORKERS FROM THE LOW COUNTRIES AND THE ENGLISH WOOL TRADE

There is some evidence that the immigrant weavers organised the whole production process themselves, a feature which allowed them to have a more prominent role in cloth-making than the natives. The quantity of cloth they alnaged within a year is indicative of this, as it widely surpassed the number of cloths normally produced by a single weaver. In order to

[112] The original reads 'panni di Flandria'. The translation is Stuart Jenks': *The Enrolled Customs Accounts (PRO, E356, E372, E364), 1279/80–1508/09 (1523/24), Part 4: E356/9, E356/10, E356/11, E356/12, E356/13*, ed. S. Jenks (London, 2006), pp. 1061–5.

[113] *CCR, 1360–4*, p. 356; *CFR, 1356–68*, p. 193. Both exiles were considered as aliens by the English customs administration.

[114] TNA, E 122/7/10, m. 10.

[115] Van Upstall appears on two occasions in Hull as an exporter of madder, hides, wool and other goods. See *Bronnen*, ed. Smit, pp. 359–60, 367, 422–3.

[116] NRO, Y/C4/81, m. 24, Y/C4/88, m. 11; *Bronnen*, ed. Bronnen, p. 322.

[117] Oldland and Quinton, 'London merchants' cloth exports', p. 120. For the Flemish ban on English cloth, see J. H. Munro, 'Industrial protectionism in medieval Flanders: Urban or national?', in H. Miskimin, D. Herlihy and A. L. Udovitch (eds), *The Medieval City* (New Haven and London, 1977), pp. 229–68.

be able to do this, they needed to have their own supplies of wool and enough money to hire carders, spinners, weavers, fullers, dyers and shearers who would work on their cloth. Being involved in the wool trade would more or less mean that both of these requirements would be fulfilled. Only those with enough connections and wealth were able to penetrate this very lucrative trade. Involvement in the export of wool would provide immigrant weavers with a considerable income, but also with wool of their own that they could pass on to other weavers who would work for them.

From the late thirteenth century, the English crown began to exploit the wool trade in order to increase its tax revenue and also to strengthen its political position, as well as to acquire allies on the other side of the English Channel. In Anglo-Flemish relations the taxation of wool and various embargos became very important (if not crucial) for the course of events in the county of Flanders during the 1330s, only a few years before the beginning of the Hundred Years War. In order to finance his war with France, in 1337 Edward III increased the duty on the export of wool from 6s 8d a sack to 40s for denizens and 60s a sack for aliens.[118] For the easier implementation of these tax levies, from 1294 all English wool was supposed to be exported through the system of the staple. The general policy of the wool staple was that all those who wanted to export wool had to transport it to the town, where the staple stood, and at any given time sell it there under the direction of the mayor and merchants of the company of the staple. The main object of the staple was to avoid smuggling and to create a place where buyers, sellers and royal tax collectors could meet to do business.[119] For political and strategic reasons its location moved several times from its introduction at the end of the thirteenth century until its permanent transfer to Calais in 1363.[120] Political developments from the mid fourteenth century on prompted the crown to introduce various regulatory frameworks, which generated documentary evidence that allows us to quantify the involvement of

[118] Lloyd, *The English Wool Trade*, pp. 155–6; for the comprehensive course of events for this increase, see *ibid.*, pp. 144–56.

[119] *Ibid.*, p. 194; Murray, *Bruges*, p. 263.

[120] Edward I and III used the location of the staple to obtain a better bargaining position in the wool trade with Flanders, but also as part of the strategic measures used in the conflict with France. Thus, in 1294, the first staple was established in Brabant; then, in 1313, the staple was moved to Saint-Omer. Bruges became the main centre for the English wool trade on the Continent in 1325, until it moved briefly in 1338 to Dordrecht in Holland. It was transferred back to Bruges in 1340. However, because of political instability in Flanders between 1345 and 1349, it was moved to Middelburg in 1348. From 1353, under the Statute of the Staple, it was held in England for a few years before it was finally transferred to Calaïs in 1363, where it would stay until the final loss of the town to the French in 1558.

Flemish immigrants in the English wool trade throughout the 1350s, 1360s and 1370s.

In order for us to do so, there are several sources that may be used, but the particulars of the customs accounts in Great Yarmouth and London are the best direct source to quantify the involvement of immigrants in the wool trade, as they list the names of the exporters and the amount of wool loaded on ships. Although there are only two surviving rolls of particulars of customs accounts that exclusively recorded wool exports, they are detailed enough to allow us to recognise people from the variety of sources in Great Yarmouth and London, and have an idea of their involvement in the wool trade in the second half of the fourteenth century. The extant particulars for Great Yarmouth cover the period 1353–4, and they were entered in the local borough court rolls.[121] The particulars of the royal exchequer for 1365–6 for London also survive.[122] These are the only two accounts that are detailed enough for us to engage in an in-depth analysis. However, they will be complemented by subsidiary documents from the chancery and the exchequer to provide evidence of the immigrants' involvement in the wool trade throughout the period of this study.

GREAT YARMOUTH'S IMMIGRANTS AND WOOL EXPORTS

Great Yarmouth is one of the few English towns that possesses a good series of local customs accounts, dating from 1331–2 to 1604–5. The membranes of the surviving accounts are attached to court rolls. At their fullest, the customs accounts record the names and provenance of ships and shipmasters, the goods on which customs and dues were charged, and the names of the owners of the cargo. Of course, these accounts are not without limitations. Although there is an uninterrupted series of local customs accounts in the second half of the fourteenth century, a big chunk of the accounts is almost exclusively concerned with herring exports, which was still the main trade and source of the city's income.[123] Commodities like cloth and wool still appear occasionally, but separate sections for these goods are not systematically included. For example, on two membranes with details about fishing exports in the 1352 account, we find four individuals with Flemish names paying the toll for the export of about fifty sacks of wool. When compared with the 638 sacks that were enrolled in the exchequer as the total amount of wool exported by aliens from Great Yarmouth that year, it becomes clear that

[121] NRO, Y/C4/74, mm. 17–19. [122] TNA, E 122/70/18, mm. 1–9d.
[123] Saul, 'English towns in the late Middle Ages', 75–88.

these four individuals were not the only ones who exported wool that year.[124] On many occasions throughout the second half of the fourteenth century, the local particulars, although very valuable, fail to report the entirety of import–export activity in the port. This allows us to establish that immigrants from the Low Countries were involved in the wool trade, such as an exile from Bruges, Richard Perebom, who paid the duty for eleven sacks of wool in 1352, or Clais Houweghe, also from Bruges, for two sacks and 22 stones of wool in 1355, but does not permit an in-depth analysis.[125] However, the particulars of the account for 1353–4 are an exception in this respect and contain separate membranes for wool exports. This account contains the names, quantities of wool or woolfells exported, duty paid, shipmaster and date of exit from the port. Unfortunately, the ships' final destinations were not recorded. Detailed coverage of wool exports in this local customs account was probably due to the establishment of the staple at Norwich the same year. As the outport of preference for Norwich, Great Yarmouth had probably seen numerous deals between merchants, shipmasters and wool-growers concluded directly in its market without the need to pass through Norwich. Wool exports from Great Yarmouth reached a peak in 1353–4, totalling 3,356 sacks.[126] It is, however, worth noting that there are some inconsistencies between the local particulars of the account and the exchequer's enrolled customs accounts for 1353–4. The particulars run from 25 March 1353 until 24 March 1354, while the enrolled customs accounts run from Michaelmas (29 September) 1353 until Michaelmas 1354. Thus, the total exports recorded in the particulars is a bit lower and represents 1,933 sacks, 2,145 stones of wool and 93,887 woolfells. If we apply a simple calculation in order to transfer woolfells and stones into sacks, we get a total of just over 2,406 sacks that were exported by aliens from the port of Great Yarmouth from end of March 1353 until end of March 1354.[127]

The individuals responsible for the export of all 2,406 sacks recorded in the local customs accounts were aliens. According to their names and cities of origin (when mentioned), more than 95 per cent were from the Low Countries, while the remainder were Hanseatic merchants. This is as expected, as the Statute of the Staple from 1353 stipulated that only aliens were allowed to export wool, as will be discussed below. Amongst

[124] E. Carus-Wilson and O. Coleman, *England's Export Trade 1275–1547* (Oxford, 1963), p. 47.

[125] NRO, Y/C4/73, m. 14, Y/C4/75, m. 15.

[126] Carus-Wilson and Coleman, *England's Export Trade*, p. 47.

[127] If 1 stone = 14lb, 1 sack = 364lb and 240 woolfells = 1 sack, then 2, 406 sacks = $\frac{2{,}145*14}{364} + \frac{93{,}887}{240} +$ 1,933.

the 110 individuals with Dutch names who appear in the account, 23 can be recognised as Flemish exiles resident in Norwich, Lynn and Great Yarmouth. They were mostly weavers and fullers, and responsible for 109 sacks (or 4.5 per cent) of wool exports from Great Yarmouth port (Table 4.9).[128] For example, Michael Baleward, a weaver banished from Bruges, exported one sack and 41 stones of wool.[129] Some of the remaining eighty-seven people from the Low Countries in this account might also have been immigrant artisans who had settled somewhere in Norfolk, but unfortunately, as they do not appear in the available sources, their exact profile remains complicated to establish.

Out of the twenty-three exiles who appear in this account, we can say with certainty that only Maas van Rotherdam, from the liberty of Bruges, Clays Bastard and John Dickbush, both from Nieuwpoort, settled permanently in Great Yarmouth.[130] Others seem to have settled in Norwich and other places in Norfolk and just used Great Yarmouth as a port of preference. For example, Coppin Ysaak, an exile from Diksmuide, who settled and became a freeman in Lynn in 1351, as mentioned in Chapter 2, loaded 2 sacks of wool and 1,080 woolfells on three different ships during 1353–4.[131] Moreover, in 1353 all wool in Norfolk was supposed to be bought at the staple, which was established at Norwich, and we have seen that numerous exiles and other textile workers settled in this town. With Great Yarmouth being its outport, and given the importance of the wool trade for Norwich, it seems that some of the Flemish weavers who appear as exporters of wool in this account, like Michael Balward or Colin Edelman, actually settled in Norwich during the 1350s.[132] An interesting feature of this account is the appearance of Flemish fullers as wool-merchants, who benefited from the general rise in cloth production. They exported both wool and woolfells. Lamsin de Yonge loaded 300 woolfells, while Baldwin Feldacker exported 10 stones of wool on ships whose masters were John Blomard and Jacob Claysson.[133] Although these quantities were relatively small, they do confirm some degree of possession of capital and entrepreneurship even amongst the exiled fullers. In comparison, no English fuller is known to have exported wool in any account that

[128] A total of 68 sacks, 101 stones and 7,050 woolfells. [129] NRO, Y/C4/74, m. 18r.

[130] See Chapter 2 and the section on Great Yarmouth exiles. [131] NRO, Y/C4/74, m. 17.

[132] For wool as the major and most interesting trade in Norwich, check Dunn, 'After the Black Death', pp. 217–19. See Chapter 2 for Flemish textile workers in Norwich. The same year, Michael Balward and Colin Edelman appear both as exporters of wool and importers of dyestuffs, and it is noted that they are taking them to Norwich (*versus Norvico* is written in the margins).

[133] NRO, Y/C4/74, m. 17d.

Table 4.9 *Quantities of wool exported by Flemish exiles and other textile workers from the Low Countries as evidenced in the particulars of the customs accounts for Great Yarmouth 25 March 1353–22 March 1354*[i]

Boatmaster and date	Flemish immigrant artisan	Sacks	Stones	Woolfells
Heyneman Claysson 25 March 1353	Jacob Ysaac	1	5	240
	Jacob de Ipre		5	285
	John Abeel			440
John Blomard 4 April 1353	Lambert Yonge			480
Boat called 'Welisar'	William Brokere	1	15	36
Constantin Petrisson 11 July 1353	Jacob Ysaac	1	15	400
	Jacob Couse			
	Jacob de Ipre		12	160
Gerard Henrikson 11 July 1353	Maas de Rotherdam	3	12	
John Smyth 12 July 1353	Michael Baleward		12	
Henry Hughesson 12 July 1353	Nicholas Houweghe	3	18	
Jacob Claysson 18 July 1353	Baldwin Feldacker		10	
John Petrisson 2 August 1353	Clays Bastard	3	3	
	Baldwin Broukere	2	7	
	John Dickbusch	2	18	
Athlardus Simmundesson 7 October 1353	Richard Perebom	11	1	90
Hugo Baselard 15 October 1353	Walter Bastard		3	
Peter Bollard 2 November 1353	John Timerman			100
Hamund Heynesson 6 November 1353	John Abeel	1	7	180
Alardus Simondesson 6 November 1353	Peter de Reylond	6	4	1200
Michael Bakere 20 November 1353	Richard Perebom	13	15	
John Smyth 20 November 1353	Clays Bastard			60

Table 4.9 (*cont.*)

Boatmaster and date	Flemish immigrant artisan	Sacks	Stones	Woolfells
John Adamsson	Michael Baleward		14	
2 December 1353	Jacob Isaak			440
	Nicholas de Palling			280
William Bek 31 January 1354	Giles Hortere			154
Oker Symondesson 7 February 1354	John Boidin	22		
John Peterson February (illegible)	Nicholas Houwegh			420
Baldwin Jonesson 4 March 1354	John Gerlof			340
Peter Jonesson 10 March 1354	Thomas Rotherdam			420
Peter Gillesson	John Dickbush			700
14 March 1354	Michael Baleward	1	15	
	Peter Arnold	5	8	
	Walter Bastard			240
	John Gerlof	1	25	
	John Maynard		20	
	Clays Bastard	1	2	395
	Lambert Veys			269
	William Broker		8	316
	Peter Welmakere			80
Peter Gibbisson	Walter Ingilbrigth			480
22 March 1354	John de Gistele			
	Total:	77	244	7,725

[i] NRO, Y/C4/74, mm. 17–17d.

survives for the second half of the fourteenth century.[134] Flemish fullers in England probably operated their trade as they did in Flanders throughout the fourteenth century, where they worked as wage-earners required to complete a piece of cloth within a specific time frame. This wage was

[134] Pajic, 'The fortunes of urban fullers', 227–51; Dunn, 'After the Black Death', pp. 153, 160–2; P. Nightingale, *A Medieval Mercantile Community: The Grocers' Company and the Politics and Trade of London 1000–1485* (New Haven, 1995), pp. 210–22; Goddard, *Credit and Trade in Later Medieval England 1353–1532* (New York, 2016), pp. 53–5.

composed of 20 per cent of value-added costs, which might determine the difference between a draper's profit or loss.[135] The increase in the manufacture of high-quality broadcloths in England, which coincided with the arrival of Flemish exiles, was probably beneficial to alien fullers. Unlike the serges that English cloth-workers focused on in the first half of the fourteenth century, broadcloths required fulling, and the fullers became an essential part in their manufacture. Enjoying an increase in the number of cloths to work on generated the profits that might have allowed them to seek out other business activities, such as the wool trade.

The presence of Flemish exiles in the particulars of the Great Yarmouth customs accounts for wool exports in 1353–4 is in part justified by the new regulations introduced for the English wool trade by Edward III around the same period. With political developments in Flanders, which automatically worsened the position of English merchants in Bruges at the beginning of the 1350s, the staple was moved to England, and a ban on denizen exports of wool was introduced.[136] In addition, wool intended for export was to be bought only in the staple towns designed by the statute: Norwich, Canterbury, Newcastle, York, Lincoln, Westminster, Exeter, Bristol and Chichester. In other words, English wool-dealers were allowed to trade in wool intended for local cloth production, but if they wanted to send it for export, they were obliged to sell it to aliens.[137] Furthermore, in order to avoid inland staples, such as those at Norwich and Lincoln, most of the wool-growers and middlemen from 1353 started carrying their wool directly to the port of London, where Hanseatic and Italian merchants could bid up the price. These trends pushed most of the Hanseatic merchants to move from their traditional ports of preference on the east coast to London. In this way they avoided transport costs from the staple to the port.[138] This seems to have left room for the resident alien craftsmen. Thus, under these conditions Flemish weavers and fullers in Great Yarmouth and the surrounding towns, such as Lynn and Norwich, obviously benefited from their ambiguous legal situation and direct contact with the wool-growers, local middlemen in England and merchants on the other side of the English Channel to take part in this lucrative trade. Some of this wool might have reached Flanders, its big cities in particular. Indeed, the authorities in Ghent seem to have been aware of the

135 Munro, 'Industrial entrepreneurship in the late medieval Low Countries', pp. 380–4.

136 *Ibid.*, pp. 205–7; *CCR, 1349–54*, p. 506.

137 Munro, 'Industrial entrepreneurship in the late medieval Low Countries', pp. 207–8.

138 Nightingale, *A Medieval Mercantile Community*, p. 207. The names of shipmasters and exporters, as well as the provenance of ships, in the 1353–4 Great Yarmouth particulars are usually from Holland and Zeeland, which goes hand in hand with the trends suggested by Pamela Nightingale.

involvement of the banished rebels in the wool trade in England. Around the same time as these particulars of account, on 10 November 1353 the aldermen of Ghent forbade the dyers of that city from dyeing the wool that was sent to Ghent by the exiles.[139]

While denizens became allowed to export wool from 1357, the port of Great Yarmouth gradually lost importance as a centre for the wool trade over the following two decades. The average number of sacks exported from Great Yarmouth fell from around 1,000 a year throughout the 1360s to about 500 in the 1370s. Moreover, the collectors of the local customs accounts failed to report the names of denizen wool exporters, and at the same time the record of aliens' wool exports is incomplete. Therefore, the local customs accounts and the subsidiary sources from the chancery and the exchequer provide fragmentary evidence that allows us to observe that the immigrants from the Low Countries in Great Yarmouth and Norfolk continued their involvement in the wool trade throughout the 1360s and 1370s, but we cannot engage in any systematic comparison between alien and native textile workers. In 1366, Clays van Lethy, in his response to an investigation by the governor of Calais concerning the export of uncustomed wool, woolfells and hides on his ship, provided the names of individuals on his ship who travelled from Great Yarmouth to Rotterdam. Among the listed merchants were the exiles Peter van Thouroud and Coppin Isaac.[140] It seems that on this occasion, the two of them (Peter and Coppin) exported wool and woolfells directly to Rotterdam, avoiding Calais, thus violating the ordinances of the staple. The records of the cocket seals for the export of wool from 1377 to 1379 show that some of those who appear in the leet rolls exported large quantities of wool and woolfells.[141] On 26 March 1378, Walter Pouchmaker, *alienigena*, paid the cockets for the export of one-and-a-half sacks and 17 stones of wool.[142] Another exile from Bruges, Clais Makeler, who actually settled in Norwich, appears on a few occasions in the particulars of the customs accounts loading wool for exports. In 1376–7 alone he exported 13 sacks, 26 cloves of wool and 789 woolfells on three different ships.[143] Again, the evidence shows that

[139] Nicholas, *The Metamorphosis*, p. 156; *Voorgeboden der stad Gent*, ed. De Pauw, p. 63: 'dat negheen verwere no blauwere gheenrande wulle en verwe no en blauwe die van buten comt, ballinghen toebehorende, up de boete van L lb. ende de wulle verbuert, ende wie dat bevondeu zoude hebben deene eelft van der wullen, ende de here dander eelft.'

[140] *Bronnen*, ed. Smit, document no. 518. Coppin Isaak appears one more time in the Great Yarmouth customs accounts: see NRO, Y/C4/79, m. 8.

[141] TNA, E 122/149/12. Before paying the customs and loading woolsacks on ships, the exporting merchant was supposed to get the cocket seal at the customs collectors.

[142] TNA, E 122/149/12; also in *Bronnen*, ed. Smit, document no. 574, p. 314.

[143] NRO, Y/C4/88, mm. 12, 12d, 13. A 'clove' equals 7lb of wool.

artisans from the Low Countries still managed to take part in the wool trade even when the denizens became allowed to engage in exports, with a lower duty.

The same year, the collectors of customs in the port of Great Yarmouth, Simon atte Gapp and William Elys, launched a random inquiry concerning the export of uncustomed merchandise. They found that some of the textile workers from the Low Countries who appear regularly in the court rolls sold and exported wool without paying customs. Textile workers from the Low Countries resident in Great Yarmouth – namely Lippin Sceepstale, a weaver, John Witbrood, a fuller, John Elys, an alien weaver, Henry fan Campe, John Tailor, alien, William Tailor, alien, and James Tailor, alien – were fined for receiving aliens in their houses and there secretly selling them wool and woolfells. It was added that they also provided help, counsel and aid to their alien buyers on how to carry the wool on board ship by night without paying the customs.[144] This case is interesting because although it does not specify the quantities of wool that the alien textile workers sold or exported, it provides evidence that neatly summarises some of the claims made in this and the previous chapter. It supports the claim that they possessed wool on their own and engaged in the export trade. More importantly, although this case is concerned with illegal activity, it still shows the extent of their knowledge of local market structures and how this was used within their business network. It reveals that in many cases they probably acted as middlemen, or a bridge between alien merchants, local traders and wool-growers.

What we know about the immigrants' wealth might explain their ability to engage in the export of wool and to organise the whole production process of cloth. The only direct evidence of the Flemish craftsmen's actual wealth is the confiscations of their goods after Edward III ordered the arrest of all banished Flemings in England on 26 August 1371, in retaliation for the treatment of English merchants in Flanders. These documents unfortunately survive only for Great Yarmouth, which in a way limits our scope, but still provides precious information. After the order of 1371, the bailiffs and mayors of all port towns were supposed to produce a list with the names of Flemings under arrest and the value of their goods.[145] The bailiffs and mayors of Bristol, London, York and other towns certainly returned these documents to the chancery, but unfortunately they do not survive; however, Great Yarmouth's town

[144] *Calendar of Inquisitions Miscellaneous, Chancery, Vol. IV: 1377–88*, p. 39.

[145] See Chapter 2 and the sections on Lynn, and above in this chapter, for more context for this order.

Table 4.10 *Value of the goods found with exiles at the time of their arrest by the authorities of Great Yarmouth in 1371*[i]

Exile	Value of goods
Lippin Scepestale, weaver	£7 7s 2d
Paul Souter de Ostburg	£14 5s 7d
William Cappel, weaver	£6 3s 8d
John Wythbrood, fuller	£4 1d
Boudyn Wymyn, fuller	£7 3s 7d

[i] NRO, Y/C4/84, m. 1d.

officers attached a copy to the borough court roll (see Table 4.10). The writ is dated three days after the order (29 August 1371) and contains the names of Flemish craftsmen who regularly appeared as litigants in the borough court, and the value of their goods, as well as orders to surrender for those who had still to be arrested.[146]

As can be seen in Table 4.10, the value of the goods was assessed for only five exiled craftsmen, and they ranged from £4 to £14. As for the other twelve exiles named, some of the immigrants under arrest were to make a guarantee of their appearance under pain of penalties ranging between £10 and £20.[147] These were even recorded in the recognizance rolls of the borough court; for example, William Cappel, Jacob Taylor and Andrew Fullere were to act as sureties for the appearance of a fuller exiled from Bruges, Herman van Inkhout.[148] Another fuller exiled from Bruges, Rijke Muske, was released under mainprise from William Cappel and Boudin Wymyn, as he had proved he was a citizen and resident of Dordrecht at the time of arrest.[149] This example demonstrates that the exiled craftsmen did not necessarily return to Flanders once it became possible, but remained highly mobile and moved to places where better employment and entrepreneurial opportunities presented themselves. It is clear that the Flemings belonged to the upper crust of the ranks of urban craftsmen, if we are to compare this evidence with the

146 NRO, Y/C4/84, m. 1d.

147 From the fact that the writ was sent only three days after the order it is clear that it was not possible to assess the goods of all the Flemings in Great Yarmouth. The names of those listed appear frequently in the borough court between 1350 and 1380: Peter fan Skelle appeared under a penalty of £10, as did Christian fan Skelle, William Marholt, Lamsyn Weyneforth, Mathijs Specke, John de Eclo, Herman van Inkouth, John Buk and John Prouvere; while Jacob Taylor appeared under a penalty of £20, as did Arnald Fuller.

148 NRO, Y/C4/84, m. 16. 149 *Ibid.*, m. 16d.

extant evidence from throughout the fourteenth century for English textile workers whose goods were assessed. Christopher Dyer considered that urban craftsmen, who were among the middling rank of townsmen, had possessions of between £2 and £3.[150] For example, William Beltone, who was a bailiff of the weavers of London on several occasions, had all of his goods valued at around £4 in his will of 1390, which would put him below alien artisans from a provincial town.[151] If alien textile workers were wealthier than an artisan who was able to hold office in the capital, it is not surprising that they managed to engage in the wool trade and supervise the production of cloth.

LONDON IMMIGRANTS AND WOOL EXPORTS

The only surviving particulars of the customs accounts for wool exports from London are those for 1365–6.[152] These have already been used in several other studies in order to quantify the involvement of alien merchants, grocers, mercers and drapers in the wool trade from various perspectives.[153] It is important to mention that, unlike the Great Yarmouth local customs accounts particulars, where only aliens' wool exports were recorded, the London particulars enrolled with the exchequer make the distinction between aliens and denizens. They also contain information about the quantities of wool each merchant exported, and the names of ships and shipmasters, as well as on what date the ship left port. Naturally, the final destination of the ships was not recorded, as the policy of the staple at that period meant that wool was assumed to be going to Calais.

Where this account contrasts with the 1353–4 local particulars in Great Yarmouth is the marked dominance of the natives in wool exports from London. The total wool exported from the capital was over 16,000 sacks, of which almost 12,000 belonged to denizens, the second-highest figure ever recorded. The denizen trade was handled by only ninety-two individuals, more than half of whom exported over fifty sacks each. The leading wool merchants were drawn from the trades that controlled the town's government, such as grocers, fishmongers and drapers. The biggest individual export came from a grocer, Nicholas Brembre, with an incredible 1,419 sacks.[154] He was followed by fishmongers John Curteys,

150 C. Dyer, *Standards of Living in the Later Middle Ages: Social Change in England c. 1200–1520* (Cambridge, 1989), pp. 205–6.

151 LMA, MS 9171/1, fo. 203v.

152 TNA, E 122/70/18.

153 Beardwood, *Alien Merchants in England*; Quinton, 'The drapers and the drapery trade'; Nightingale, *A Medieval Mercantile Community*; Sutton, *The Mercery of London.*

154 Nightingale, *A Medieval Mercantile Community*, p. 220.

677 sacks, John Lovekin, 544 sacks, and Edmund Oliver, 470 sacks. Other grocers, such as William Barret or Fulk Horwood, also figured prominently, with 540 and 338 sacks respectively, while, among the drapers, James Andrew stood out, with 91 sacks dispatched from the port of London.[155] The alien shipments were more spread out and were made by 126 individuals. In this group the most prominent was a Florentine merchant, Sivester Nicholas, 409 sacks, followed by his compatriot Jacob Jakemyn, 151 sacks. Other aliens represented in this account seem to have originated from Italian cities and from the Low Countries, and their exports ranged between three and sixty sacks. It is possible that the final destination of their wool exports was the important cloth towns in Flanders. After the establishment of the staple in Calais in 1363, wool was transported from Calais to Bruges by the Italians, while Ghent sent people directly to buy wool at Calais.[156]

The quantities exported by weavers from the Low Countries are a lot lower than what was exported by this group of mercantile elites who controlled the London wool trade. Moreover, those who managed to engage in the export of wool were the leading weavers amongst the alien craftsmen settled in London. William van Carlewick, who was a bailiff of weavers from Brabant in London, exported only 1,440 woolfells, which, when transferred into woolsacks, represents the equivalent of 7 sacks.[157] Two exiles from Ghent, John van Eke and Lievin Fisker, exported only three and eleven sacks respectively in 1365–6 (see Table 4.11).[158] Other alien weavers loaded between one and twenty sacks, no individuals particularly standing out in terms of quantities. This implies that the alien weavers probably acted as middlemen and acquired quantities of raw wool for themselves to distribute to other weavers who worked for them. It seems that the Flemish weavers were more focused on the production and marketing of cloths than on the wool trade, or that they were simply pushed out of the trade by merchants who possessed a lot more capital. The wool trade became increasingly dominated by the London grocers, and just the mere fact that the Flemish weavers managed to take part on a small scale in this profitable trade was quite a success in England over the period of this study.[159] Those who wanted to export wool from London were obliged to have the money to purchase and

[155] Lloyd, *The English Wool Trade*, pp. 251–2.

[156] A case from 1381 brought in one of the London courts against the Venetian merchant Luke Bragardin is a perfect example of how wool was transported and sold to Bruges by Italian merchants during this period: *CPMR*, vol. III, pp. 26–8. For Ghent, see Nicholas, *The Metamorphosis*, p. 139, nn. 9 and 10.

[157] E 122/70/18, m. 5. [158] E 122/70/18, mm. 1, 2.

[159] Nightingale, *A Medieval Mercantile Community*, pp. 219–21.

Table 4.11 *Quantities of wool exported by Flemish exiles and other textile workers from the Low Countries as evidenced in the particulars of the customs accounts for London 8 October 1366–26 September 1367*[i]

Shipmaster and date	Exile	Sacks	Woolfells
John Mone 8 October 1365	William van Wattre	8	
Lambin Sot 8 October 1365	John Dorme	19	
	John Loppere		615
Michael Wale 18 October 1365	Peter Walraven	15	
	John Dorme	1	
George Mesday 18 October 1365	John Dorme	8	1,440
	Peter Walraven		123
	William Dene	14	
	Lievin Fisker	11	
John Loppere 25 October 1365	Matthew Stulpart	9	198
Fabian Erme 8 November 1365	John Dorme	10	
	Peter Wattre	8	
	John Cappelle	3	
John Spaignard 8 November 1365	John van Eke	3	
	Matthew Stulpart	10	
John Vyne 8 November 1365	John Oudenard	18	
John Pierson 11 November 1365	John Oudenard	1	
	John Brest	1	
Henry Dumble 18 November 1365	John Brest	2	
Matthew Everday	John van Stone	9	
	John van Brele	11	
Lievin Pierson 10 February 1366	John Risele	6	
Matthew Everday 22 February 1366	John Jaghere	3	
John Jorne 1 March 1366	John Jaghere	1	
William Sottard 18 April 1366	William van Carlewyk		1,028

Table 4.11 (*cont.*)

Shipmaster and date	Exile	Sacks	Woolfells
William Nere 21 June 1366	Henry Rothe	1	
John Mewesson	John Dorme	13	
26 September 1366	Henry Halling	8	69
Total		193	3,473

[i] TNA, E 122/70/18, mm. 1–9d.

wool ready to transport. Only few London men had enough money to act as middlemen between the provincial merchants and the wool exporters.[160] Once the wool reached London, expenses incurred would include storage. From that point, there were three different taxes to be paid, and only then was the wool ready for export.[161] With all this in mind, the alien weavers seem to have bought wool principally for themselves in order to organise the production of cloth and sold some of their own wool to other weavers, and only then, if they had some left, dispatched the surplus for export.

On the other hand, native weavers were also involved in the wool trade, albeit in a relatively minor role. If we take, for example, those who appeared as master weavers in London sources, only one of them can be found in the accounts for 1365–6. This was John Bennet, who exported 25 sacks and 1,188 woolfells.[162] Although native weavers enjoyed the advantage of being considered denizens, which meant a lower tax on each sack exported, they were unable to penetrate this trade in any considerable way. It seems that the bailiffs of the London weavers' guild had a role somewhat similar to that of the leading alien weavers. Most of the wool brought to London by the native weavers' guild was probably put out to poorer weavers for local cloth production, and only small quantities would be left for export. From the beginning of the fourteenth century the London burellers operated in a similar manner, where they had wool of their own and subcontracted work on manufactured cloth.[163] The London weavers certainly possessed their own wool. On

[160] *Ibid.*, pp. 220–1. Local middlemen bought wool from growers usually after the shearing in June. However, sometimes they made arrangements with manors even before the shearing. Britnell, *The Commercialisation*, pp. 161–2.

[161] Lloyd, *The English Wool Trade*, pp. 62–5. [162] TNA, E 122/70/18, m. 5.

[163] On the burellers, see Oldland, 'London clothmaking', pp. 21–46.

the account for the wool subsidy of 1359–60, which does not provide quantities, Nicholas Hotoft, who was also one of the bailiffs of the London weavers, paid the tallage for export.[164] A bit later on, John Bathe bequeathed £200 to be paid to his wife in wool or cash, suggesting a habit of handling quantities of wool surpassing the needs of a single weaver.[165] Some of the London master weavers who possessed wool probably acted as small entrepreneurs and contracted out the weaving, before selling the cloth to fullers and drapers.

CONCLUSION

The main phases of growth in Colchester's later fourteenth-century cloth industry were probably 1351–6 and 1375–80, and if we look at the evidence in other English towns, we can observe similar trends.[166] The first phase would correspond to the dates of the Flemish rebels' arrival in England after their exile, while the second phase represents a period of total domination of cloth production by the alien cloth-workers, as evidenced by various sources in the capital. In London, they were able to withstand the decline in the city's cloth manufacture, during the first years after their arrival, by substituting quality textiles produced domestically for imported cloth. It is clear that the exiles who settled in London possessed both the capital and the manufacturing skills to be able to contribute to the development of the English cloth industry. In the period between 1375 and 1380, where the particulars of alnage accounts are extant, they were bringing vast quantities of rays to the alnager. By combining these with other sources, it can be observed that the main impact on London textile workers lay in the immigrants' organisational skills. Flemish weavers brought the methods of trade previously established in Flanders, where they possessed the wool and dyestuffs, which they passed on to other workers, supervised the manufacturing process and then marketed the product themselves. This was a production process no native weaver was able to put into practice. The immigrants' success was not only marked by superior manufacturing skills, they were also engaged as exporters of wool, which provided them with an accumulation of capital and raw material such as to enable them to develop some sort of a putting-out system, similar to that of clothiers in the fifteenth century.[167]

[164] TNA, E 122/70/14.

[165] *Parish Fraternity Register: Fraternity of the Holy Trinity and SS Fabian and Sebastian (Parish of St Botolph without Aldersgate)*, ed. P. Basing (London, 1982), no. 97.

[166] Britnell, *Growth and Decline*, p. 182. [167] Lee, *The Medieval Clothier.*

Chapter 5

WOMEN FROM THE LOW COUNTRIES IN ENGLAND AND THEIR ECONOMIC ACTIVITIES

INTRODUCTION

The economic activities of women in late medieval England and the Low Countries have been the subject of historical study stretching back well over a century. The pioneering studies by Annie Abram and Eileen Power posited that women in England played an active role both in industrial activities and in the marketplace during the Middle Ages, and thus established scholarly interest in the economic position of women.[1] Over the years that followed, various aspects of the economic lives of women in late medieval England and Flanders have been studied.[2] Broadly speaking, an overview of the literature suggests that women in urban areas had relatively few problems with being active as artisans or traders, but class, wealth, marriage status and household position, in the end, affected opportunities for women on the labour market. Apart from these factors, the position of women engaged in cloth manufacture also

1 A. Abram, 'Women traders in medieval London', *Economic Journal*, 26 (1916), 276–85; E. Power, 'The position of women', in C. G. Crump and E. F. Jacob (eds), *The Legacy of the Middle Ages* (Oxford, 1926), pp. 401–34.

2 C. M. Barron, 'The "golden age" of women in medieval London', *Reading Medieval Studies*, 16 (1990), 35–58; Goldberg, *Women, Work, and Life Cycle*; S. Bardsley, 'Women's work reconsidered: Gender and wage differentiation in late medieval England', *Past and Present*, 165 (1999), 3–29; J. Bennett, *Ale, Beer and Brewsters in England: Women's Work in a Changing World 1300–1600* (Oxford, 1996); M. K. McIntosh, *Working Women in English Society 1300–1620* (Cambridge, 2005); M. Kowaleski, 'Women's work in a market town: Exeter in the late fourteenth century', in B. Hanawalt (ed.), *Women and Work in Pre-industrial Europe* (Bloomington, 1986), pp. 145–64; Hutton, *Women and Economic Activities*; Murray, *Bruges*; P. Stabel, 'Women at the market: Gender and retail in the towns of late medieval Flanders', in W. Blockmans, M. Boone and T. De Hemptinne (eds), *Secretum Scriptorum: Liber alumnorum Walter Prevenier* (Leuven, 1999), p. 262; M. C. Howell, *Women, Production and Patriarchy in Late Medieval Cities* (Chicago, 1986); M. C. Howell, *The Marriage Exchange: Property, Social Place, and Gender in Cities of the Low Countries, 1300–1550* (Chicago, 1998); E. Bousmar, 'Neither equality nor radical oppression: The elasticity of women's roles in the late medieval Low Countries', in E. E. Kittell and M. A. Suydam (eds), *The Texture of Society: Medieval Women in the Southern Low Countries* (New York, 2004), pp. 109–23.

depended upon general developments in the textile industry. The shift in organisation of the north-western textile industries, from the beginning of the fourteenth century, not only transformed the types of cloth that were produced, but changed the organisational structure too, which in turn affected the opportunities for female workers. In Flanders, throughout the twelfth and thirteenth centuries, women seem to have played an important role in urban textile industries. They had been active in key stages of cloth production, such as weaving, or other finishing crafts (apart from fulling). However, when the textile industry shifted over the fourteenth century towards guild-controlled production of more expensive woollens, job opportunities for unskilled workers and also for women declined. Their involvement as independent workers became rather restricted. They were gradually pushed towards lower-paid, labour-intensive activities in the preparatory stages of cloth production, such as washing, combing, carding and spinning the wool, as well as cleaning woollens at the finishing stages.[3] As no scholars on either side of the English Channel have ever considered the position of immigrant women in the fourteenth century, we are left with several open questions:[4] would this shift in production within urban industries have been one of the push factors? How better off would Flemish women have been if they emigrated to England (alone or with husbands)? The purpose of this chapter is to examine the economic activities of Flemish women in England, with a specific focus on the textile industry and the ways in which women contributed separately from their male compatriots.

IMMIGRANT WOMEN'S PRESENCE IN ENGLAND 1350–1400

The letter patent of 1352, which gave Flemish immigrants the right to plead in English courts, does not make any distinction between the sexes, but it seems that women were granted the same right automatically.[5]

[3] Dumolyn, Puttevils and Stabel, 'Production, markets', p. 95. See also in the same collection: Dumolyn, Dupont, Lambert, Murray, Puttevils and Stabel, 'Production, markets and socio-economic structures II: c. 1320 – c. 1500', pp. 196–267, at p. 254.

[4] More recently several studies have looked into the experiences of immigrant women in late medieval England resulting from an investigation of the alien subsidies in the fifteenth century as part of Mark Ormrod's Arts and Humanities Research Council (AHRC) project, 'England's Immigrants 1330–1550' based at the University of York. J. Bennett, 'Women (and men) on the move: Scots in the English north, 1440', *Journal of British Studies*, 57 (2018), 1–28; Ormrod, Lambert and Mackman, *Immigrant England 1300–1550*, pp. 169–77; B. Lambert, 'Double disadvantage or golden age? Immigration, gender and economic opportunity in later medieval England', *Gender & History*, 31 (2019), 545–64.

[5] *CPR, 1350–4*, p. 232. See also Chapter 1.

They appear in borough and royal courts in numerous pleadings for trespass, debt and breach of covenant, or to pay fines for minor economic infractions, and for probate, either as *femmes soles* (women making business contracts independently from their husbands) or with their spouses (as part of a business partnership or under legal guardianship). Out of a total of 889 pleas brought by or against immigrants from the Low Countries in the borough courts of Great Yarmouth and Colchester, almost a quarter involved immigrant women. These legal actions allow us directly or indirectly to grasp the extent of Flemish women's economic activities. Legal traditions in Flanders provided women with greater autonomy in matters of private law, such as inheritance, property rights, legal guardianship and commercial capacity, compared with other parts of Europe.[6] Indeed, throughout the fourteenth century women were quite active in credit activities and property management.[7] In both England and the Low Countries, any appearance by women in courts had to be, at least in theory, under the legal responsibility, or coverture, of the male head of the household.[8] For single women, it was usually their father who took on this role, and for married women, their husband. Although nothing is specifically mentioned about female immigrants from the Low Countries residing in England and their ability to make contracts, sue or be sued, it seems that coverture applied to them in English courts too. However, this issue becomes more complicated when we look at the court rolls, as scribes did not systematically record the legal or marital status of women, English or immigrants. Teresa Phipps has recently pointed out the inconsistencies in the way that women's identities were recorded and in the way the marital partnership was represented through the litigation of spouses in the borough court across several medium-sized English towns. Indeed, not only did the court clerks omit to record systematically whether women appeared under coverture or as *femmes soles*, they were also not always consistent with the use of descriptors that allow us to determine women's marital status,

[6] J. Gilissen, *Le Statut de la femme dans l'ancien droit belge*, vol. XII, Recueils de la Société Jean Bodin pour l'histoire comparative des institutions (Brussels, 1962), pp. 255–7.

[7] Hutton, *Women and Economic Activities*.

[8] On coverture in England, see T. Stretton and K. Kesselring, 'Introduction: Coverture and continuity', in T. Stretton and K. J. Kesselring (eds), *Married Women and the Law: Coverture in the Common Law World* (London, 2013), pp. 3–23; T. Stretton, 'Coverture and unity of persons in Blackstone's commentaries', in W. Prest (ed.), *Blackstone and His Commentaries: Biography, Law, History* (Oxford, 2009), pp. 111–28; C. Beattie, 'Married women, contracts and coverture in late medieval England', in C. Beattie and M. F. Stevens (eds), *Married Women and the Law in Premodern Northwest Europe* (Woodbridge, 2013), pp. 133–54. For towns in the Low Countries, see Gilissen, *Le Statut de la femme*; Hutton, *Women and Economic Activities*; Bousmar, 'Neither equality nor radical oppression', pp. 109–23.

such as wife, widow, daughter or single woman.[9] Similarly, immigrant women did not escape these same problems, and the presence or lack of these identifiers when they appeared in court does make it hard to establish their legal capacity with any certainty. Although Flemish women might have been constrained in reality by being aliens and sometimes by being single, the bulk of the evidence in England shows that they still made extensive use of judicial instruments to bring their grievances to the authorities. The capacity and ability to plead in borough and royal courts provided immigrant women from the Low Countries with the legal security that enabled them to fully engage in the economic life of the host country.

Like their male compatriots, immigrant women from the Low Countries also settled all over England and were not confined to the capital. Of those whom we can identify with certainty as originating from the Low Countries, the total number of women appearing in a variety of English sources throughout the period of the study is 206 (Table 5.1). Forty-five of them settled in Colchester, thirty-five are known from pleadings in Great Yarmouth borough court and twenty-two in London, while eighty women chose other towns in England as their new place of residence. For at least ninety-eight of them, we can say that they were married and came to England with their husbands, all of whom were of Flemish origin. More than half of the Flemish women found in English sources did not necessarily appear with their husbands. This would imply that many of them may have emigrated to England alone, although it is somewhat difficult to establish whether they were single or just acted as *femmes soles*.[10] This is further confirmed by poll-tax returns, as 86 per cent of Flemings paid the subsidy as a married couple, suggesting that 108 immigrant women who appeared in borough or royal courts alone were not necessarily single. However, even if they were married, it does not mean that they possessed no agency. Betekyn the Duchewoman is a case in point here, because whenever she appeared in the borough court of Great Yarmouth, she did so unaccompanied. Between 1394 and 1401, she regularly paid fines for regrating beer, and on one occasion she was accused of hosting prostitutes.[11] She also

9 T. Phipps, *Medieval Women and Urban Justice: Commerce, Crime and Community in England 1300–1500* (Manchester, 2019), p. 53; T. Phipps, 'Coverture and the marital partnership in late medieval Nottingham: Women's litigation at the borough court ca. 1300–1500', *Journal of British Studies*, 58:4 (2019), 768–86.

10 On problems with labelling women and their marital status within the English late medieval sources, see C. Beattie, *Medieval Single Women: The Politics of Social Classification in Late Medieval England* (Oxford, 2007).

11 NRO, Y/C4/105, m. 11d; Y/C4/106, m. 20d; Y/C4/107, m. 21d; Y/C4/111, m. 18.

Table 5.1 *Number of women from the Low Countries in England 1351–81*[i]

Town	Number of women	Married
London	24	11
Colchester	55	18
Great Yarmouth	47	27
York	15	12
Winchester	4	3
Norwich	4	3
Lynn	5	3
Lincoln	2	2
Boston	1	1
Ipswich	5	4
Southwark	15	0
Coventry	13	12
Hadleigh	1	0
Clare	10	0
Bath	2	2
Oxford	2	0
Bristol	1	0
Total number	206	98

[i] Dataset based on: ERO, D/B 5 CR 9–22; NRO, Y/C4/72–96; *CPMR*, vols. I–II; *Letter Books G–H*; NRO, KL /C 17/6–10; NRO, NCR 5b/10–11; HRO, W/D1/8–15; SRO, C/2/3/1/28–9; Fenwick, *Poll Taxes*.

pursued several debt and trespass cases against both natives and other Flemings resident in Great Yarmouth.[12] In all these instances she appeared alone, and even when it is revealed that she was married, her husband's name is not mentioned. In 1401, when her husband failed to join the tithing, in the presentments of the leet-court he was recorded as Betekyn the Duchewoman's spouse.[13] This is interesting, because only men over the age of 12 were supposed to enroll in a tithing, and this is the only instance over the period of the study where failing to join the tithing was recorded as such. This suggests that through her activity in the marketplace, Betekyn was a lot better known to the authorities than her husband and might have been the one who managed the family business.

Some immigrant women became widows and stayed in England, which provided them with some autonomy. For example, Margaret de

[12] NRO, Y/C4/92, m. 7; Y/C4/104, m. 11d.
[13] NRO, Y/C4/105, m. 11d.

Douai, who paid the poll tax in York, was listed as a widow.[14] Similarly, Margaret de la Bonegarde, wife of a weaver from Bruges named Christian, remained in London after the latter was killed in 1364 by another weaver from Flanders who had settled in England.[15] As Christian's executor she was tasked with settling his remaining debts, amounting to a rather large sum of £40, to several Flemish weavers in London, and she presumably resumed her husband's business on her own.[16] However, this might only have been temporary, as widows (and widowers) usually tended to remarry, as we saw in Chapter 3 with the example of Belia Petersone, who in her will mentioned the family of her second husband.

The reasons for which women from the Low Countries emigrated to England were familial, political and economic. Some of them followed their husbands and parents who had been banished for political reasons. On the lists of exiles, forty-four women were explicitly said to be wives, three to be daughters. Further examination of comital charters of pardon demonstrates that numerous Flemish women were actually exiled for their participation in rebellions. Women would often pass unnoticed and unsuspected in helping the rebels and assisting them to clandestinely enter the city, or in other ways during the revolt.[17] These activities required particular courage, because in some cases, as in Ghent over the period 1350–9, aiding political exiles meant up to fifty years' banishment.[18] One woman from Ghent, a certain Aleit uten Pothijsere, was banished for ten years because she was probably a messenger who kept contact with exiled rebels.[19] However, women sometimes also played more active roles in a rebellion: for instance, one Zoete Soys Zoen was banished for causing bloodshed during the revolt in Ghent, a crime

[14] Fenwick, *Poll Taxes*, vol. III, p. 143.

[15] *Letter Book G*, p. 182; *CPR, 1364–7*, p. 53.

[16] *Ibid.*

[17] L. Demets, 'Spies, instigators, and troublemakers: Gendered perceptions of rebellious women in late medieval Flemish chronicles', *Journal of Women's History*, 33 (2021), 12–34. Our evidence of such assistance in the mid-fourteenth-century revolt is restricted to men. ADN, Série B, 1596, fo. 19r: Peter Houckin, a miller, was banished from Ghent because he had let exiles enter the city and caused new disturbances ('bloedstuertinghe te makene ende toe te bringhene ghewapend was bi nachte ende ooc om de ballinghe in te roupene'). ADN, Série B 1596, fo. 20v: Gillis Bosch from Ghent was banished for a similar offence, 'dat hi heift ghestaen bi daghe ende bi nachte omme dat de ballinghe in te roupene ghebanen van meuten ende beroerte te makene in contrarien van miin here van Vlandren, in contrarien der ruste ende paise van der stede' ('that he has stood about by day and by night and allowed exiles who were banished for rebellion rush into the city and make the tumult against our lord of Flanders, and against the peace and tranquility of the city').

[18] ADN, Série B 1596, fos 17–20r.

[19] *Ibid.*, fo. 21v.

against the city government and the count.[20] Exile was probably not the main push factor, but the economic disruption after the revolt throughout the 1350s and 1360s was certainly one of the reasons for leaving Flanders and Brabant.

IMMIGRANT WOMEN'S ECONOMIC ACTIVITIES – CLOTH PRODUCTION

In terms of occupations, as with their male counterparts Flemish women were engaged mostly in the textile industry, but they were also active in ale-brewing, hostelling and stew-keeping. Of those who worked in the woollen industry, they can be found involved in all aspects of the production and sale of cloth. The extant poll-tax returns for some of the towns in this study only occasionally give us a glimpse of female immigrants' occupations (although, it should be said, this is a general problem with the poll-tax records for any town). Immigrant women appear as servants to immigrant weavers who paid the subsidy, such as an unnamed female servant who was listed with a prominent weaver from Brabant, Godfrey van Upstall, in York, or Isabella, in the service of an exile from Bruges, Cent Kampe, in Colchester.[21] The returns for 1381 in Southwark are a little bit more informative than other sources for the origin of some of the women who worked in the textile sector. For example, Truyde Frowe, *spinestere*, and Mathilda Frowe, *spinestere*, each paid a subsidy of 12d in 1381.[22] Apart from their suggestive surname, used by the London scribes to describe Flemish women, it is also added that they were working as spinners. The extant poll-tax returns in other towns listed women from the Low Countries together with their husbands, but fail to mention their occupational status. Their involvement in the textile industry has to be determined through court records. Sometimes, the court scribes would provide information about the occupations of immigrant women who appeared in various legal actions.

20 *Ibid.*, fo. 20r: on the same folio, her husband, Gillis Soys Zoen, and Jacop Soys Zoen, another family member, were also banished for their involvement in a rebellion 'because they would have organised a riot against the count and the law'. The active role of Flemish women in violence is also reflected in trespass cases in the borough courts. Sometimes, there are additional details about physical aggression between immigrant women. For example, Marieria, wife of Jacob Tailor, *Fleming*, drew blood from Beatrix Coperose with her fist (Benham, *Court Rolls*, vol. II, p. 224); the available tools and weapons were used, as well. In 1367, Marieta, wife of an exile from Ghent, Giles van Molle, was charged with an assault on Joan van Clanemere with knife and stone; Margaret, wife of Hanyn Hancock, was charged with violent assault with an iron candlestick on another Fleming, Peter Jonessone, in 1383; Benham, *Court Rolls*, vol. IV, pp. 131, 185.

21 Fenwick, *Poll Taxes*, vol. I, p. 197; vol. III, p. 135. Presumably both female servants were from the Low Countries.

22 *Ibid.*, vol. II, p. 565.

Such were the cases of Mary de Brussele, *webster*, who was fined by the bailiffs of Lynn for throwing out waste during the night; or of Agnes Dutchwoman, *sempstere*, who appeared in order to testify in favour of another Fleming, William Couper, who was imprisoned for various crimes in Ipswich; or of Emma Braban, *kemstere*, who in the King's Bench accused John de Coloyne from York of an unspecified trespass.[23] Although these three cases are not related to the women's economic activities, they nonetheless reveal that Mary worked as a weaver, Agnes as a seamstress and Emma as a *kempster*, or woman who combed or carded wool.

It is commonly accepted that throughout the late Middle Ages the preparatory stages of cloth manufacture were done by women. More precisely, hard labour was required for the conversion of wool shorn from sheep into yarn for weaving. After the wool had been sorted and washed, it needed to be prepared for spinning by carding if it was a short staple and combing if it was a long staple wool. Most of the time, this was done by women using wooden tools with either short metal hooks or long metal teeth, depending on the type of wool. The fibers were straightened by carding and combing, which also eliminated defective fibers and dirt and separated the shorter from the longer strands. The wool, duly oiled, was then spun into yarn.[24] This was almost invariably done by women, with the spinning wheel. One of the most significant innovations in the cloth-making was the invention of the spinning wheel, which presumably started to be used in the thirteenth century but may have occurred earlier. From the spinners the yarn went on to the weaver.[25] All of this work was realised by women who worked from home on a piece-rate basis, or within the family business unit.[26]

Flemish women in England were hired to wash, break and spin the wool for both native and alien weavers. For example, Margaret van Vynk was hired by a weaver from Colchester, John Lancele, in 1372 in order to break a portion of wool.[27] Her husband was Loy van Vynk, also involved in cloth-making, which suggests that women supplemented the family income by taking piecework with other weavers. They also worked in the first stages of manufacture for particular textile workers as servants. In 1381, in the borough court of Great Yarmouth, Jacob Taylor, *Ducheman*, and his wife, Margaret, accused Diota del Castel, a spinner, of withdrawal

[23] NRO, KL/C17/8; SRO, C/2/3/1/29, m. 2d; TNA, KB 27/411, m. 9.

[24] De Poerck, *La Draperie médiévale en Flandre*, vol. I, pp. 44–55, 61–4.

[25] Munro, 'Medieval woollens: Textiles', vol. I, pp. 181–227.

[26] McIntosh, *Working Women*, p. 212.

[27] Benham, *Court Rolls*, vol. III, p. 20.

from service before the agreed date.[28] Presumably Diota was a young immigrant who had entered the service of a family business. Similar arrangements occurred in other parts of England. For example, John Lyntre, *Braban*, acted as legal guardian in a trespass case that occurred in London in 1366 involving his servant Katherina.[29] Isolda Spinster and Margaret Rokelyn, who both worked for a certain John Braban, were accused of detention of chattels by John Salisbury, who brought his plea before chancery in Herefordshire.[30] Cases like this, where one clothworker, John Braban, had several spinsters working for him, might be related to the beginnings of the organisational structure employed by clothiers later in the fifteenth century.[31]

However, within the urban context and the activities of the textile industry, women seem to have enjoyed more independence. In 1366, Katherine Flemyng came before the bailiffs of Colchester and acknowledged that she had failed to comb 2.5lb of wool worth 4s 2d for Simon Hadleigh, a weaver who had hired her to do so.[32] Indeed, further evidence suggests that many immigrant women engaged in the first stages of cloth-making were solely dependent upon the income from these activities, some of which included the preparation of wool. In Coventry, Margaret Braban, *kempster*, paid a fine for charging too much for combing 1lb of wool.[33] In 1382, Lippin Sceepstale was accused of owing 3s for thread and yarn in a plea brought by Alicia Rolland to the borough court of Great Yarmouth.[34] The amounts these women were paid for these tasks would allow them to sustain themselves on their own if such piecework was found regularly. Moreover, we have seen above that immigrant women from the Low Countries who worked as spinsters were assessed for 12d towards the poll tax at Southwark in 1381, and it seems that these women paid the subsidy alone and were probably single. In the poll taxes of 1377–81, the spinners' per capita contribution was slightly lower than that of weavers and fullers, which means that if weavers and fullers were able to be independent on their wages, we can assume that the earnings of women engaged in this trade would at least allow them to live on their own.

Some of their activities were also in the finishing parts of the cloth-making process. These ranged from stretching cloth on the tenter frame and cleaning woollens (burling) after fulling, to more complex tasks such as tapestry-weaving. In Great Yarmouth in 1377, five white broadcloths

[28] NRO, Y/C4/CR93, m. 2. [29] TNA, KB 27/424, m. 39d. [30] TNA, CP 40/466, m. 23d.
[31] Goldberg, *Women, Work, and Life Cycle*, pp. 118–19.
[32] ERO, D/B 5 CR15, m. 2; incomplete case calendared in Benham, *Court Rolls*, vol. II, p. 188.
[33] TNA, JUST 1/971, m. 1d. [34] NRO, Y/C4/CR93, m. 3d.

were declared to have been stolen. Katherina Bowdin, wife of an exile, John Bowdin, acknowledged before bailiffs that she had received these cloths (from someone whose name has unfortunately faded from the manuscript) in order to put them on the tenter frame, but she denied involvement in the theft.[35] Masters of the trade of tapiters (tapestry-weavers) in London accused Katherine the Dutchwoman of false work because she had used a particular combination of linen and wool to make a tapestry *coster* (a wall-hanging)[36] wrought upon the loom, in the manner of work of Arras – which, according to the ordinances of their trade, was against the rules.[37]

The majority of pleas in judicial records do not provide more details than simply the type of plea, but this still allows us to determine that female immigrants were part of wider cloth-making networks, and worked both with Flemish and native cloth-workers. For example, a certain Sota Flemyng was pursued in the borough court of Colchester for debt and breach of covenant on two occasions in 1379. The first was for an unspecified debt owed to Richard Baude, who was a prominent fuller in Colchester.[38] Also, the same year, she was charged by a weaver, John Keek, with removing certain chattels and goods, most notably wool and threads.[39] John Keek was one of those prominent weavers in Colchester who appeared in several cases throughout the 1370s and 1380s, which suggests he conducted his business with immigrant textile workers from the Low Countries.[40] Individuals of a similar stature were also involved in standing bail or as pledges for female immigrants. Such was the case of a prominent weaver, John Dober, and a fuller, John Sebern, who stood bail for Katherine Flemyng before the bailiffs of Colchester in 1377 to ensure that she paid her fine.[41] As we were able to see in Chapter 3, going by the testamentary evidence women's social and business networks were largely related to textile workers from the Low Countries resident in England. This is also reflected in the litigation in borough courts. For example, a weaver exiled from Bruges, Peter van the Skelle, brought a plea of trespass against a tailor, Henry Hasard, and his wife,

35 NRO, Y/C4/CR88, m. 3.

36 E. Crowfoot, F. Pritchard and K. Staniland, *Textiles and Clothing 1150–1450* (London, 1992), p. 69.

37 *Memorials of London*, ed. Riley, p. 375.

38 Benham, *Court Rolls*, vol. III, p. 192. Richard Baude appears on numerous occasions in the borough court and was also still bringing large quantities of cloth to the alnager during the 1390s, TNA, E 101/342/9, mm. 1–3d.

39 ERO, D/B 5 CR 19, mm. 27 and 27d, incomplete case calendared in Benham, *Court Rolls*, vol. III, p. 202.

40 Benham, *Court Rolls*, vol. III, p. 188.

41 *Ibid.*, p. 144. For John Dober acting as a weaver, see *ibid.*, vol. III, p. 204; while for John Sebern, see Britnell, *Growth and Decline*, p. 76.

Maya, and among the pledges to prosecute were a weaver, Lippin Sceepstale, and a tailor, Jacob Flemyng.[42] A few years earlier, Katerina fan Berghwe accused a weaver, Peter fan Reylond, of detention of chattels, and managed to win her case after an inquiry.[43] When Beatrix Fleming, who had recently settled in Colchester, got license to come to terms with John Kekyn, her pledges were two weavers exiled from Ghent, John Synay and John Fan Loo.[44] As can be seen from these examples, even when the sources do not provide information about the women's occupations, their connections and relationships gravitated around textile workers.

Flemish women in England were also involved in the trade in woollen cloth and clothing. For example, in 1377, Katherine Flemyng was brought to the borough court of Colchester in order to reply to Augustine Plomer, who claimed 7s 6d for cloth sold.[45] At the same time, Gisell de Derham accused Elena, wife of an exiled fuller, John Witbrood, who lived in Great Yarmouth, of detaining a piece of woollen cloth.[46] Such evidence from judicial sources would suggest that, in these cases, husbands were not the legal guardians of their wives, but rather part of husband-and-wife partnerships. The nuclear family had generally become a common feature of north-western Europe in the thirteenth and fourteenth centuries, and both England and Flanders seem to follow this pattern.[47] It was a fundamental economic institution for artisans that served as a means of subsistence and became inextricably linked to commodity manufacturing.[48] In Colchester too, for immigrants engaged in cloth-making who came with their spouses, family also represented the basic business unit. In 1366, for example, a couple, John Pouchmaker, *Fleming*, and Margery, his wife, appeared twice in the borough court for detention of chattels, once as plaintiffs and the second time as defendants. First, they accused another textile worker from the Low Countries, Michael Ballyng, of detaining an item of purchased goods. They claimed that Margery had paid Michael to deliver a purse and a veil, which he did only partially, not providing the second item.[49] In another case, they were accused of owing 2s to Gilbert Wrighte for

[42] NRO, Y/C4/CR90, m. 4. [43] NRO, Y/C4/CR80, m. 12.

[44] Benham, *Court Rolls*, vol. II, p. 7. [45] *Ibid.*, vol. III, p. 146.

[46] NRO, Y/C4/CR84, m. 9d.

[47] J. Luiten van Zanden, S. Carmichael and T. de Moor (eds), *Capital Women: The European Marriage Pattern, Female Empowerment and Economic Development in Western Europe* (Oxford, 2019); P. Stabel, 'Working alone? Single women in the urban economy of late medieval Flanders (thirteenth–early fifteenth century)', in J. De Groot, I. De Vos and A. Schmidt (eds), *Single Life and the City, 1200–1900* (London, 2015), pp. 27–49.

[48] Howell, *Women, Production and Patriarchy*, pp. 9–10. [49] ERO, D/B 5 CR 15, m. 2.

cloth and silk he had delivered to them to make him a purse.[50] This is where the complicated issue of coverture might be observed. It is difficult to assess the proportion of women who worked in partnership with their husbands after they settled in England, but there were twenty-five cases in the borough courts of Great Yarmouth and Colchester that might hint at the existence of such an arrangement. This issue becomes slightly less problematic on the other side of the English Channel. If we look into the account book of money changer Collaert de Marke, who operated his business in Bruges between 1366 and 1377, purchases of cloth from individual weavers were referred to as lists of payments from small drapers, or weavers, among whom were 450 individuals, 184 men, 222 women and 22 husband-and-wife partnerships.[51] This would suggest that if Flemish women were involved in the production and sale of cloth in Flanders together with their husbands, there is no reason to believe that they would not have continued to do so after emigrating to England.

There is ample evidence in the sources of London, Colchester and Great Yarmouth to support the argument that women were selling textiles and clothing there. In London, on 22 January 1367, Margaret Kemestere, *Flemyng* (plaintiff), and Lambkyn Flemyng, weaver, came to terms in a plea of detinue of a furred gyte and kyrtile.[52] Margaret Fraunceys was attached to reply to Katherine Van the Brok on a charge of detention of goods – a silk veil to the value of 5s.[53] In Great Yarmouth, a fuller exiled from Bruges, Baldwyn Wymes, and his wife, Katherine, accused Beatrix fan Oudewater of a debt, who was distrained by a tunic.[54] Their role as market sellers and drapers was also very common in urban areas of the Low Countries.[55]

Because of the high mortality rate due to the Black Death, Caroline Barron concluded that the second half of the fourteenth century represented a 'golden age' for women.[56] She argued that women were able to find work due to the labour shortages, as well as to gain higher wages, as was the case for their male counterparts. Shortly afterwards, Jeremy

50 *Ibid.*, m. 2d.

51 S. Hutton, 'Organising specialised production: Gender in the medieval Flemish wool cloth industry (c. 1250–1384)', *Urban History*, 45:3 (2018), 396.

52 *CPMR*, vol. II, p. 69. A gyte, or kyte, was a kind of dress or gown; and a kyrtile, or kirtle, was a tunic worn by men or women, as we saw in Belia Petersone's will in Chapter 3.

53 Benham, *Court Rolls*, vol. IV, p. 118.

54 NRO, Y/C4/82, m. 1d.

55 Howell, *Women, Production and Patriarchy*; P. Stabel, 'Women at the market: Gender and retail in the towns of late medieval Flanders', in W. Blockmans, M. Boone and T. De Hemptinne (eds), *Secretum Scriptorum: Liberalumnorum Walter Prevenier* (Leuven and Apeldoorn, 1999), pp. 259–76; E. E. Kittell and K. Queller, '"Whether man or woman": Gender inclusivity in the town ordinances of medieval Douai', *Journal of Medieval and Early Modern Studies*, 30 (2000), 63–100.

56 Barron, 'The "golden age" of women', 35–58.

Goldberg came to similar conclusions for late medieval Yorkshire.[57] These conclusions were somewhat brought into question a few years later.[58] Nevertheless, Flemish women, most of whom emigrated in search of a better life, often managed to fare quite well. The evidence from the Court of Common Pleas suggests that they dealt with fairly considerable amounts of goods and money. In 1358, Margaret van West was accused by a prominent Italian merchant, Matthew Noire, of detaining chattels worth £11.[59] A wool merchant from the Low Countries was brought to the Court of Common Pleas by the wife of a weaver exiled from Ghent, John Mattys, to whom he owed 100s.[60] These cases suggest that some immigrant Flemish women played a role in the business of their husbands who were involved in the wool trade.

Immigrant women were also buying wool for the purposes of their family business where husbands are known to have been involved in cloth-making. In Colchester, Margaret, wife of an exile from Bruges, John Skyleman, was charged in 1374 with owing William Somerton 6s 3d for wool sold to her as far back as 1367.[61] Ten years later, Sibilla Van Mersh was accused of owing 18d for wool that her husband, Copin, bought from Thomas Kentish. The plaintiff claimed that she was liable for the debt as she became pledge and guarantor 'when she was sole', the implication seeming to be that after her husband's death she undertook to pay this debt.[62] It seems also that some women bought small portions of wool, presumably in order to prepare the thread themselves and sell it afterwards. A case from Great Yarmouth in 1360, in which Alice fan Tyne accused John Robel of a debt for woollen thread she had sold to him, supports this argument.[63] That Flemish women managed to organise the whole process from buying the wool to making threads themselves should not be surprising, as some of them even exported wool. On the particulars of the customs accounts from 1353 to 1354, three Flemish women appear as exporters. On the boat of John Petrisson, Margery Doumburg loaded 8 stones of wool; Christiana Andrewsdoughter exported 1 stone of wool and 677 woolfells on two different boats; while Isabella Letheyn loaded a cargo with 180 woolfells.[64] We saw in Chapter 3 in Lelia Blawer's will that she had paid off her debts towards John Pape, tailor, and Ghys Deigher, who was a dyer.[65] In Lelia's and

57 Goldberg, *Women, Work and Life Cycle*.
58 Bardsley, 'Women's work reconsidered', 3–29; Bennett, *Ale, Beer and Brewsters*; McIntosh, *Working Women*.
59 TNA, CP 40/397, m. 52d.
60 TNA, CP 40/417, m. 254.
61 Benham, *Court Rolls*, vol. III, p. 66.
62 ERO, D/B 5 CR 25, m. 28.
63 NRO, Y/C4/CR 77, m. 5.
64 NRO, Y/C4/CR 74, mm. 17, 19 and 19d.
65 LMA, MS 9171/1, fo. 137.

some of the other cases cited above, it is clear that these women were widows and continued their late husbands' business. However, there is no evidence as to whether single female immigrants were able to climb the ladder; on the other hand, it was more or less the same for single male immigrants, who arrived in England as apprentices and without established business networks.

The nature of the source material would suggest that it was women's involvement that was the most important in the preparatory stages of cloth manufacture in occupations like carding, combing and spinning. The activities of women engaged in the sale and finishing of cloth are often rendered invisible because of the business partnership with their husbands and coverture. Fortunately, single women who worked in low-pay and low-status jobs due to a lack of guild organisation are more visible. However, even these female textile workers should not be looked upon as lower-level producers. This is principally because significant skills were required in order to prepare threads for weavers and, secondly, because women performed more than half of the labour that went into making woollen cloth. In this sense, Flemish women, with a different set of skills and organisational habits, certainly contributed towards improving cloth manufacture in England. However, we have seen that in the context of business partnerships with their husbands, women were often responsible for the procurement of wool, as well as the sale of cloth, while nonetheless being married. This suggests that their role was certainly important within the family business unit that was engaged in cloth production. Some of them were also involved in the finishing stages of cloth production, such as weaving and sewing. Despite being overshadowed by their husbands because of coverture, it can still be observed that some female immigrants were successful in mercantile activities during their widowhood, when they were able to handle the family trade on their own.

ACTIVITIES OUTSIDE THE CLOTH INDUSTRY

The most widespread activity of women in fourteenth-century England was the production of ale. Brewing was, also, a means to supplement the household income but was certainly not a principal activity, as other members of the household were usually engaged in activities other than brewing.[66] We will see that immigrants from the Low Countries, and their wives in particular, seem to have followed this pattern after their

[66] For the division of labour in brewing, see Kowaleski, *Local Markets*, p. 131; Bennett, *Ale, Beer and Brewsters*, pp. 24–33.

arrival in England over the course of the second half of the fourteenth century. The sessions of the court leet in Great Yarmouth and the hundred court in Colchester contain the names of individuals amerced for the production and sale of beer and ale. The names were recorded in the form of a fine for breaking the assize. In order to keep ale for commercial purposes up to a certain standard, a royal statute, the so-called *assisa panis et cervisie*, was introduced in the thirteenth century, which was intended to regulate the quality, prices and measures of bread and ale.[67] Most of these individuals who 'broke the assize' appear regularly, and it seems that this system of fines worked in fact as a licensing fee to produce and sell ale.[68] In both Colchester and Great Yarmouth brewing ale was mostly associated with women and was the most common economic offence brought to the borough court.[69] We must make an important note that, in the fourteenth century, beer was not produced in England, merely imported (from Holland and Hanseatic towns), and the fines for producing and selling against the assize are strictly related to the production of ale. The English were well aware of the differences between the two, however. Already from the 1350s, the sources make a clear distinction between ale, always recorded with the Latin term *cervisia*, and beer, designated by different variations of the word that came from vernacular German, such as *ber, beer, bier, beere*. (Ale was traditionally produced in England by mixing malt, yeast and boiled water, while beer contained hops, which increased the durability of the beverage.)

As soon as they arrived in England, Flemish women made their mark on the leet-court records as producers of ale. Beatrix Cappel, wife of a weaver exiled from Bruges, William Cappel, was fined five times for brewing and selling ale against the assize during the fifteen years for which the leet rolls survive. It is interesting to note that on the leet roll for the year 1367 it was William Cappel, *Flemyng*, who paid the fine for brewing against the assize, while a year later it was Beatrix who paid the fine.[70] Some Flemish women, like the wives of William de Gaunt and of John Duchman in Colchester, were amerced on a regular basis between 1371 and 1377, as were other women in this town.[71] They probably

[67] *Statutes of the Realm*, ed. Luders et al., vol. I, pp. 199–205.

[68] Kowaleski, *Local Markets and Trade*, p. 132; Bennett, *Ale, Beer and Brewsters*, 162.

[69] Rodziewicz, 'Great Yarmouth', p. 59; also, for more on the organisation of the assize of ale in Colchester, see, Britnell, *Growth and Decline*, pp. 89–91.

[70] NRO, Y/C4/CR81, m. 25d; Y/C4/CR82, m. 16.

[71] Benham, *Court Rolls*, vol. III, pp. 41, 52, 119, 178. The number of women amerced for brewing in Colchester from 1350 until 1450 varied between 150 and 250 individuals; see Britnell, *Growth and Decline*, p. 194.

produced ale principally for domestic consumption and sold the surplus before it soured, while having another primary occupation. Although brewing still served as a secondary occupation for many people, the distinction can still be made between commercial brewers (those who made larger quantities and appeared regularly in the leet-courts with its subsections of 'by-industrial' and 'occasional' brewers) and domestic brewers (who primarily produced ale for their own domestic consumption and periodically paid fines, probably when they made a sufficient surplus to sell ale).[72] The majority of those appearing in presentments for breaking the assize of ale before the fifteenth century were women. One out of ten of these women were aliens, for the most part wives of textile workers from the Low Countries who arrived in England after 1351. Throughout the fourteenth century most female immigrants from the Low Countries in England seem to have been by-industrial brewers who pursued brewing not as a primary occupation, but as a source of intermittent income, involved principally in the production of ale.[73] Actually, we will see that the wives of Flemish exiles who were weavers or fullers usually supplemented the household income with the production of ale and by hosting other merchants from the Low Countries.

Apart from the production of ale, immigrants as well as natives were involved in the retail sale or 'tippling' of beer and ale. This was done in two ways: either in alehouses, or on the streets by hucksters.[74] It seems that there was a clear distinction between those who sold retail and those who produced ale. Indeed, in the towns of Cambridge and Ipswich, brewers would be named separately from tipplers in every leet. In Ipswich, for example, the proportion of tipplers to brewers was five to three throughout the fifteenth century, suggesting that the brewers were probably focused more on the manufacture and sale of their product wholesale.[75] Tippling, or selling ale retail, was done by both men and women. For example, in Great Yarmouth in 1379, Katherina Boydin, Beatrix Cappelle, Aughte Legate, Maas Saint-Johnes and Henry Hasard, a tailor – all immigrants from the Low Countries – were fined for being common regrators of beer and ale.[76]

Hostelling was a service that could basically be offered by anyone who had surplus accommodation in which a visitor could be supplied with a place to sleep, plus the capacity to provide lodgers with food and drink. It

[72] Bennett, *Ale, Beer and Brewsters*, p. 18.

[73] By-industrial brewers were a subsection of commercial brewing. On the division between commercial and domestic brewing, see *ibid.*, p. 19.

[74] McIntosh, *Working Women*, p. 157.

[75] Amor, *Late Medieval Ipswich*, p. 153.

[76] NRO, Y/C4/CR90, m. 12.

was not uncommon for hostels to act as taverns for the sale of drink. Holding a tavern, and selling ale and beer while practising another occupation, were not uncommon for the Flemish community living in Great Yarmouth. Again, Beatrix Cappel as well as Aughte Legate were active in tavern-keeping.[77] Other Flemish residents in Great Yarmouth, like Lippin Sceepstale, Henry Hasard, John Taylor, *Fleming*, and William Taylor, *Fleming*, were accused on several occasions of having held unlawful taverns where they sold beer and ale.[78] As most of them had other occupations, hostelling was probably a seasonal occupation. During the herring fair, many fishermen and merchants from the Low Countries would visit the town, and lodging as well as food and drink were essential for the enlarged population.[79] Many of these merchants stayed in one of the hostels held by immigrants from the Low Countries. The latter, as they became established in their new place of residence, offered valuable knowledge of the local market and acted as a broker between international merchants, artisans, wool-growers and others.

Thanks to these contacts, some of the ale produced by Beatrix Cappel found its way onto the international market as well. Indeed, on 20 December 1367, her husband, William Cappel, exported six barrels of ale on the boat of John Othelard from *Newhaven* (Nieuwehaven in Holland).[80] It is possible that Beatrix exported this ale herself, but William's name was the one entered, as he had legal responsibility. It seems plausible that Flemish women exported ale themselves, since on the same boat Margaret, wife of Clays Lanternemaker, also exported eight barrels of ale.[81] Other Flemish craftsmen who exported ale were John Gerard, cordwainer, and John Witbrood, fuller. In 1375, the former loaded forty-eight barrels, and the latter three lasts of ale for export.[82] Given the quantities they sold, it is quite possible that they acquired this ale from other producers, both English and Flemish. They might have sent it to Holland and Zeeland, as the demand for English ale was still high during the late fourteenth century.[83]

Even though ale production was dominated by them, women did not work completely alone, but were assisted by the whole household. Female servants probably helped with various tasks needed to brew the ale.[84] In this environment, single Flemish women probably worked alongside other women who produced ale. For example, in the 1370s

[77] NRO, Y/C4/CR89, m. 12d. [78] NRO, Y/C4/CR90, m. 12d; CR91, m. 10d.

[79] N. Kerling, *Commercial Relations of Holland and Zeeland with England from the 13th Century to the Close of the Middle Ages* (Leiden, 1954), pp. 89–90.

[80] NRO, Y/C4/CR81, m. 23. [81] *Ibid.* [82] NRO, Y/C4/CR87, m. 14.

[83] Kerling, *Commercial Relations*, pp. 217–18. [84] Bennett, *Ale, Beer and Brewsters*, pp. 24–5.

Flemish immigrant Katherine Cornbyter was a servant at the house of Richard Evessing, who held a tavern as well.[85] Richard's wife, Agnes, paid the assize of ale on several occasions,[86] and therefore one can assume that Katherine Cornbyter was also helping with making, serving and selling the ale. In 1381, in Colchester, Alice van Polt was charged with an assault on Idonea Fleming in the house of Richard Baker. Although this case is concerned with trespass, it reveals indirectly that Richard Baker held a tavern and that both Idonea and Alice worked for him.[87] It seems that Richard Baker's tavern in his house attracted other Flemish residents in Colchester for their leisure activities or business meetings, which would occasionally turn into disputes. In 1380, Arnold Flemyng and Outre Camber were both fined for drawing knives on one another in Richard's house.[88] Richard Baker might have been a Fleming himself, as there were other immigrants bearing the same surname who had settled in Colchester in previous years; however, it is never explicitly stated that Richard was a Fleming.[89]

Apart from being involved in the production and sale of ale, immigrants from the Low Countries were also importing and selling beer.[90] From litigation in the borough court of Great Yarmouth we can observe that beer was present in England from at least the 1350s, which is three decades earlier than previous studies have suggested.[91] In the second half of the fourteenth century the retail distribution of beer was overwhelmingly controlled by Flemish immigrants. For example, already in 1358, Margaret fan Outraght accused Mace fan Rotterdame of detention of chattels: she claimed that six barrels of beer left at Mace's house by one Robert Houdestoc were missing.[92] Mace fan Rotterdame was an exile from the liberty of Bruges, and, as we were able to see in Chapter 4, he was involved in the wool and cloth trade. One can note, therefore, that exiled Flemish textile workers were not involved exclusively in the sale

85 Benham, *Court Rolls*, vol. III, p. 5. 86 *Ibid.*, vol. IV, p. 90. 87 *Ibid.*, p. 120.

88 *Ibid.*, p. 58.

89 An exile from Ghent, Walter de Backer, settled in Colchester after the banishment, as well as a certain John Baker, *Fleming*. See *ibid.*, vol. II, pp. 68, 115.

90 M. Pajic, '"Ale for an Englishman is a natural drink": The Dutch and the origins of beer brewing in late medieval England', *Journal of Medieval History*, 45 (2019), 285–300.

91 Kerling, *Commercial Relations*, p. 114. The only earlier evidence comes from Norwich in 1290, when a man was fined for 'selling Flemish ale privily'. The name is suggestive, but there are no other examples in the surviving borough courts before the mid fourteenth century. Moreover, hopped beer was introduced to Flanders only after the 1350s, as has been shown by Erik Aerts, *Het bier van Lier: De economische ontwikkeling van de bierindustrie in een middelgrote Brabantse stad einde 14de–begin 19de eeuw* (Brussels, 1996). For these examples, see: *Leet Jurisdiction in the city of Norwich during the XIIIth and XIVth Century: With a Short Notice of Its Later History and Decline, from Rolls in the Possession of the Corporation*, ed. W. Hudson (London, 1892), p. 43.

92 NRO, Y/C4/76, m. 4d.

and production of cloth and wool. They obviously had contacts with merchants from across the English Channel who would bring beer to them in order for it to be sold retail to both their compatriots and the English.

In the sale of beer, both male and female immigrants were involved. In Norwich, six out of seven people fined for tippling beer in 1391 were aliens.[93] The leet roll of 1369–70, for example, contains the names of twenty-nine individuals who appeared among the regular amercements for brewing ale against the assize. There were twenty-five women who paid fines and, at the bottom of the section listing people who had paid an amercement for brewing ale, four male names were written. The latter were actually immigrants from the Low Countries: Lippin Sceepstale, *webster*, Jacob Fleming, Walter Pouchmaker, and Boudewyn Fuller, *Fleming*. It is specifically added that they sold beer retail. Lippin and Walter paid a fine of 12d, while Boudewyn and Jacob paid heavy fines of 2s each.[94] Their customers were probably other immigrants from the Low Countries. A year later, Heyne fan Campe brought a plea of debt against another Fleming, John Pouchmaker, for two barrels of beer.[95] In another case, a Flemish woman, Alice Pouchmaker, took twelve barrels of beer to the city of Norwich which had arrived at the port of Great Yarmouth on a ship from Vlaardingen.[96]

Overall, it seems that during the 1360s and 1370s immigrant textile workers from the Low Countries used ale production and the sale of beer only to supplement their incomes. They also used these activities to serve the merchants who lodged at their hostels/taverns. This was a perfect way to keep close contact with foreign merchants who held capital and increase the chances of marketing their cloth to a wider customer base. However, taverns were not only about business and networking: some illegal activities took place there too, as we will see in the following sections.

WOMEN AND PROSTITUTION

The role of female immigrants, and especially of Flemish women, in prostitution and sex work is already well established in the literature. Indeed, in contemporary chronicles and literary sources, women from

[93] NRO, NCR 5b/11, m. 3d. John Prikker, Henry Wylde, John Donsell, Walter Goldsmith, John van Lere and Floritius Taylor, are all described explicitly as 'aliens', while John Trewlove was probably an Englishman. These are also calendared in *Leet Jurisdiction Norwich*, p. 73, but the information is a lot more complete in the original manuscript.

[94] NRO, Y/C4/84, m. 2d: *tabernant ber contra statute.*

[95] NRO, Y/C4/89, m. 3.

[96] NRO, Y/C4/91, m. 12d: *exeunt versus Norwico.*

the Low Countries residing in England were associated with paid sex and brothels. While describing the events that took place in London during the Peasants' Revolt of 1381, the *Anonimalle Chronicle* mentions the destruction of a brothel in Southwark occupied by Flemish women.[97] In his *Pardoner's Tale*, Chaucer speaks of Flemish 'Stywes' and 'tavernes',[98] while Langland makes reference to Purnelle of Flanders, a *frow* and prostitute, in a tavern scene in Piers Plowman.[99] The existing historiography on medieval prostitution in England suggests that women immigrants from both the English countryside and overseas were especially liable to turn to sex work. Migrants were very well represented among prostitutes in medieval Winchester, as has been suggested by Derek Keene.[100] Maryanne Kowaleski argued that, in the market town of Exeter, women were driven into sex work because of their limited commercial opportunities and lack of legal rights in common law. She notes that prostitutes in the court records of Exeter were typically poor, unmarried women and immigrants.[101] In a detailed study of women's activities in Yorkshire, Jeremy Goldberg argued that a number of women accused of prostitution bore the surname 'Scott', and that this may indicate that local prejudices denied northern migrants access to regular employment.[102] More generally, Ruth Karras has observed that in English towns many prostitutes were indeed immigrants, and most prominent amongst them were those from the Low Countries, who might also be brothel-keepers as well as prostitutes.[103] She concluded that all the factors suggested above that could drive women to prostitution – un- or underemployment, lack of family support – affected women of all ages and origins, though some more than others.[104] As far as Flemish women are concerned, it seems that they turned to prostitution for exactly these same reasons. Lack of employment opportunities during the revolts and wars in fourteenth-century Flanders provided an incentive for single women to emigrate and look for work in other European towns. Immigrant women from the Low Countries active as sex workers are attested in Florence, Venice, Dijon, Avignon

97 *The Anonimalle Chronicle, 1333 to 1381: From a MS. Written at St Mary's Abbey, York*, ed. V. H. Galbraith (Manchester, 1927), p. 140.

98 *The Canterbury Tales: Fifteen Tales and the General Prologue*, ed. V. Amos Kolve and G. Olson (New York, 1989), p. 195.

99 *William Langland, Piers Plowman*, ed. E. Salter and D. Pearsall (London, 1967), p. 89.

100 Keene, *Survey of Medieval Winchester*, p. 392.

101 Kowaleski, 'Women's work in a market town', pp. 145–64, p. 154.

102 Goldberg, *Women, Work and Life Cycle*, p. 152.

103 R. Karras, *Common Women: Prostitution and Sexuality in Medieval England* (Oxford, 1996), pp. 56–7.

104 *Ibid.*

and Cologne.[105] The proximity of the English and Flemish coasts led to continual contact between mercantile communities, with numerous ships calling at the ports regularly. However, in England, even with the Black Death, jobs that women could find were still very low paid; therefore, supplementing income with prostitution and sex work seems to have become an option for some.

FLEMISH WOMEN IN THE CONTEXT OF THE REGULATION OF PROSTITUTION IN ENGLISH TOWNS

Even though it was not legally tolerated, as in many other European towns, the authorities of Colchester, Great Yarmouth and London considered prostitution not a crime, but a dishonorable activity instead.[106] Through various by-laws, proclamations and ordinances, as elsewhere in Europe, the civic authorities tried in various ways to establish control over this activity. In this endeavour, some towns on the Continent went as far as to create public brothels in an attempt to oversee paid sex.[107] The authorities in English towns tended to regulate the locations where prostitutes could operate and prescribed specific clothing in order to distinguish the 'women of bad repute' from 'good and noble dames and damsels'. In fourteenth-century London, it is stipulated in an ordinance from 1393 that prostitutes should be segregated in one street, Cock's Lane. The same ordinance mentions Flemish women specifically, suggesting again that they were numerous in this trade:

whereas many and divers affrays, broils, and dissensions, have arisen in times past, and many men have been slain and murdered, by reason of the frequent resort

[105] J. Rossiaud, *Amours vénales: La prostitution en Occident, XIIe–XVIe siècles* (Paris, 2010), p. 117; F. Irsigler and A. Lassotta, *Bettler und Gaukler, Dirnen und Henkler: Randgruppen und AuÖenseiter in Köln, 1300–1600* (Cologne, 1984), p. 204; R. Trexler, 'La Prostitution florentine au XVe siècle: Patronages et clientèles', *Annales ESC*, 36 (1981), 983–1015, at 991.

[106] Karras, *Common Women*, pp. 5 6; Karras, '"Because the other is a poor woman she shall be called his wench": Gender, sexuality and social status in late medieval England', in S. A. Farmer and C. B. Pasternak (eds), *Gender and Difference in the Middle Ages* (Minneapolis, 2003), p. 219. More generally on contemporary views of prostitution: J. Rollo-Koster, 'Prostitutes', in M. Schaus (ed.), *Women and Gender in Medieval Europe: An Encyclopaedia* (New York, 2006), pp. 675–8; K. Mummey, 'Prostitution: The Moral Economy of Medieval Prostitution', in R. Evans (ed.), *A Cultural History of Sexuality in the Middle Ages* (Oxford, 2010), pp. 165–80.

[107] G. Ravancic, 'Prostitution in late medieval Dubrovnik: Legislation, practice, and prosecution', in C. Mielke and A.-B. Znorovszky (eds), *Same Bodies, Different Women: 'Other' Women in the Middle Ages and the Early Modern Period* (Budapest, 2019), p. 101; Irsigler and Lassotta, *Bettler und Gaukler*, p. 180; A. Roby, *La Prostitution au Moyen Âge: Le commerce charnel en Midi toulousain du XIIIe au XVIe siècles* (Villemur sur Tarn, 2020), pp. 83–93; J. Page, *Prostitution and Subjectivity in Late Medieval Germany* (Oxford, 2021), pp. 65–111.

of, and consorting with, common harlots, at taverns, brewhouses of hucksters, and other places of ill-fame, within the said city, and the suburbs thereof; and more especially through Flemish women, who profess and follow such shameful and dolorous life:—we do by our command forbid, on behalf of our Lord the King, and the Mayor and Aldermen of the City of London, that any such women shall go about or lodge in the said city, or in the suburbs thereof, by night or by day; but they are to keep themselves to the places thereunto assigned, that is to say, the Stews on the other side of Thames, and Cokkeslane; on pain of losing and forfeiting the upper garment that she shall be wearing, together with her hood, every time that any one of them shall be found doing to the contrary of this proclamation.[108]

In both Colchester and Great Yarmouth no such ordinances or proclamations survive; however, from the fines imposed on prostitutes and bawds in the court rolls of these towns it can be observed that the authorities tended to impose rules on prostitution similar to those drawn up in the London ordinance. In Great Yarmouth, as in the capital, prostitutes were forced into living at a location outside the city walls (called the Denes – see Map 4, Chapter 2).[109] In 1395, Lucebet Gimptressone, an immigrant from the Low Countries, was fined for 'worldly and bad behaviour' and sent to live with other such women outside the city walls in the Denes.[110] This location was also associated with lepers, who were supposed to live there too, suggesting that prostitutes were considered as equally undesirable for the community as lepers were.[111] It was even feared that through prostitutes leprosy would spread rapidly throughout society.[112] In Colchester, there was a by-law that assigned 'le Berislane' as a place where prostitutes were supposed to congregate. For example, in 1379, Katherine Kytlyng and Agnes Terry were fined for being common harlots and for living outside 'le Berislane', against the custom of the town.[113] Also, when a Flemish immigrant, Alice Chlovekin, was fined for being a prostitute, it is stated that she is 'living outside the old appointed place for such in the borough of Colchester'; presumably the bailiffs were referring to 'le Berislane'.[114] Setting aside that both cases suggest that there was a location assigned to prostitutes, the first example makes clear that the town possessed some kind of ordinance that was

[108] *Memorials of London*, ed. Riley, p. 535. [109] Rodziewicz, 'Great Yarmouth', p. 98.

[110] NRO, Y/C4/105, m. 6d; see also Rodziewicz, 'Great Yarmouth', p. 98.

[111] Rodziewicz, 'Great Yarmouth', p. 98.

[112] C. Rawcliffe, *Leprosy in Medieval England* (Woodbridge, 2006), p. 284.

[113] *Court Rolls Colchester*, ed. Benham and Jeayes, vol. III, p. 177; in 1374, two other women, 'Littlemalin' and Alice Fairealsen, were fined for being common harlots and living outside 'le Berislane'. ERO, D/B 5 CR, m. 1, calendared in Benham, *Court Rolls*, vol. III, p. 53.

[114] Benham, *Court Rolls*, vol. III, p. 186.

supposed to be enforced. Like the Denes in Great Yarmouth, 'le Berislane' (nowadays Vineyard Street) is just outside the city walls in Colchester, not so far away from St Botolph's Priory (see Map 3, Chapter 2).[115]

Apart from locations, the London ordinance also laid down that prostitutes were to have their garments and hoods forfeited if they were outside the appointed locations. Although the ordinance does not specifically mention striped hoods, a proclamation was issued twice by the city's officials, in 1351 and 1382, that women of bad repute, if within the franchise, were supposed to wear a hood of ray only.[116] The striped hood was also common in fourteenth-century Great Yarmouth. Several female immigrants from the Low Countries were either ordered to wear a striped hood or were fined for not wearing one.[117] There is no evidence of such a rule in fourteenth-century Colchester, but as other English towns had a similar rule, it would not be surprising if the Colchester authorities did not make use of it.[118] However, when it comes to the other side of the Channel, for example in Bruges, there was no distinctive clothing prescribed for prostitutes as there was in England.[119] In Paris, by contrast, prostitutes' clothing was very strictly regimented in order to distinguish 'les femmes de mauvaise vie des femmes honnêtes'.[120]

In terms of imposing punishments on Flemish women engaged in sex work, slight differences occur between Colchester and Great Yarmouth. On two occasions, when the bailiffs of Colchester brought Flemish prostitutes to the lawhundred court, pecuniary fines were imposed. Alice Chlovekin was fined 2s, and Sara Malin was fined an unknown amount.[121] In Great Yarmouth, the usual punishment for prostitutes was to 'abjure the town'. Thus, in 1368, Trude van Heys and Giselle Blok were publicly accused of prostitution, and their fine was to abjure the town, presumably to go to the Denes.[122] Fines were also imposed on those who provided accommodation and/or clients for prostitutes, the so-called procurers or bawds. For example, Thomas Clerk and Katherine Crane, both immigrants in Great Yarmouth in 1367, were fined 6d and 12d respectively for receiving prostitutes during the night at their

115 Cooper (ed.), *The Victoria History*, vol. IX, p. 22.

116 *Memorials of London*, ed. Riley, pp. 267, 458.

117 NRO, Y/C4/105, m. 6v; Y/C4/90, m. 12; Y/C4/96, m. 9d. See also Rodziewicz, 'Great Yarmouth', p. 98.

118 Karras, *Common Women*, p. 19.

119 Murray, *Bruges*, pp. 328–9.

120 Geremek, *Les Marginaux parisiens*, p. 246.

121 Benham, *Court Rolls*, vol. III, pp. 104 and 186. For Sara Malin, it is recorded simply that she was fined, but the amount is faded and completely illegible.

122 NRO, Y/C4/82, m. 16d.

homes.[123] Unfortunately, in Colchester even though the hundred court mentions people who were fined for harbouring prostitutes with their clients, the amount is specified only once. In 1375 'Littlemalin'[124] was fined 6d for being a common harlot and receiving married priests at her place.[125] The low amount of the fine and the fact that the same Littlemalin had been fined the previous year as well suggest that the bailiffs of Colchester might have used fines for prostitution as a sort of licensing fee. This practice of a fine as a 'licensing fee' was suggested by Karras, as she observed that in some other English towns over the same period the same persons were fined repeatedly every year.[126]

FLEMISH ALEHOUSES, BROTHEL-KEEPING AND PROSTITUTION

Taverns where ale and beer were served were places associated with prostitution, and were visited by both occasional and regular prostitutes, who might have had arrangements with the owners to steer potential customers their way in order to share the profits.[127] Occasional prostitutes could meet potential customers there, since the taverns would have had private rooms available.[128] The tavern and the sale of ale and beer seem to have gone hand in hand with prostitution in Great Yarmouth. In 1379, Robert Northich and Emma Somenour, who both appear to be English, were accused of receiving prostitutes, and also paid an amercement for brewing ale the same year.[129] A similar case is that of Bartholomew Meller and William Porter, who were accused of receiving Clarice Soyt, a prostitute from the Low Countries, and Hannekin de Durdraught in their taverns by night. In the same session of the leet-court, Mathilde Meller, Bartholomew's wife, paid the amercement for producing and selling ale.[130] The taverns held by immigrants from the Low Countries were also associated with hosting prostitutes. In 1380, a Flemish woman, Aughte Legat, was fined for receiving prostitutes and other malefactors, but also for holding a tavern and selling beer contrary to the assize.[131] William Tailor, *Fleming*, was fined twice, in 1380 and in

[123] NRO, Y/C4/81, m. 25.

[124] Suggestive nicknames were quite usual in the English records, apparently adopted by the prostitutes themselves for the sake of exoticism. See Karras, *Common Women*, p. 56.

[125] Benham, *Court Rolls*, vol. III, p. 69. For other examples of fines imposed on people for receiving harlots and their clients in Colchester, see *ibid.*, p. 53.

[126] Karras, *Common Women*, pp. 22–3.

[127] *Ibid.*, p. 72. For taverns connected with prostitution, see Karras, 'The regulation of brothels in later medieval England', *Signs: Journal of Women in Culture and Society*, 14 (1989), 399–433, at 407. See also Bennett, *Ale, Beer and Brewsters*, pp. 140–1.

[128] Karras, *Common Women*, p. 71.

[129] NRO, Y/C4/87, m. 20.

[130] NRO, Y/C4/89, m. 12d.

[131] NRO, Y/C4/89, m. 12d.

the following year, for being a common regrator of beer and a receiver of prostitutes and thieves in his tavern.[132] Both William Tailor, *Ducheman*, and Aughte Legat, along with some other Flemish residents, were also fined in 1379 for being common regrators of beer in their taverns and for being night vagrants.[133] Taverns where sex for pay took place might have also served as locations that facilitated adultery. For example, in 1398, Mayken and Trewe, *Duchewomen*, were fined for being common prostitutes and bawds hosting the wives of other men without the knowledge of their husbands.[134] Although they were fined for hosting prostitutes, this seems to suggest that they provided a place where married individuals could meet to cheat on their spouses. On the other side of the Channel, a similar offence would be to hold a 'bad hostel', 'malvais hostel' in French or 'quader herberghe' in Dutch.[135] One of the noticeable features in Great Yarmouth is that the same people would repeatedly be fined for receiving prostitutes, which suggests that the town's authorities to some extent tolerated this activity. In any case, the link between the tavern and prostitution can clearly be observed. The tavern would in a way represent a perfect cover for prostitution, since the owner would usually have rooms available where newly arrived young female immigrants could stay and also provide other work for the brothel-/tavern-keeper if the latter had no customers, such as helping with producing and serving beer.

The tavern was not the only place associated with prostitution in England. Medieval bath houses, also called stews, were often places where this kind of service might have been provided. However, bath houses and stews were not necessarily associated with sex work.[136] The place in England where stews were most connected to prostitution was Southwark, the suburb of London belonging to the bishopric of Winchester. In both judicial records and literary sources, the stews of Southwark were often associated with violence and promiscuous behaviour. Of course, the fourteenth-century Flemish immigrants would have not escaped this stereotype. In 1378, Eborardus fan Combe, *Fleming*, was accused in the court of the King's Bench of the murder of Gilbert ate Nasse. After the inquiry, the jurors heard testimonies that the aforementioned Eborardus came to the stews and murdered Gilbert with a knife. The jurors added that the aforementioned Eborardus was a known

[132] NRO, Y/C4/91, m. 10d; Y/C4/92, m. 14d: 'William Tailor, Fleming est communis hospitator et receptor latronem et meretriicorum et aliorum malefactorum ad nocumento vicinus etc ideo in misericordia.'

[133] NRO, Y/C4/89, m. 12d. [134] NRO, Y/C4/109, m. 20d.

[135] ADN, Série B 1596, fo. 25r.

[136] D. Boisseuil, 'Le Bain dans les sociétés occidentales à la fin du Moyen Âge', *Studi Storici*, 55 (2014), 365–84.

murderer, and that he had already murdered six men in London, both English and Flemish, and that one Beatrice Fustian, called 'Blake Bete', had been aiding and abetting him in Gilbert's murder. Eventually, Eborardus was found guilty and hanged.[137] Even though it is not explicitly stated, the suggestive nickname added to the Beatrice who helped him suggests that she might have been the keeper of a stew that operated as a brothel. Indeed, contemporaries suggested that stews functioning as brothels were usually kept by women, more precisely by Flemish women. According to the *Anonimalle* chronicler, the Southwark stew-house attacked during the Peasants' Revolt in 1381 was run by Flemish women.[138] The sixteenth-century chronicler John Stow explained that 'English people disdayned to be baudes. Froes of Flandres were women for that purpose.'[139]

The poll-tax particulars of Southwark show indeed that some Flemish women were probably employed as prostitutes. These returns include four people listed with the occupation *stewmonger* or hosteler, all of them having female servants with explicitly Flemish names, such as Aughte Frowe, who was a servant of Yenan Walshman.[140] One of them, Petrus Davy, a hosteler, paid 5s and his wife, Sote (Zoete), paid 2s poll tax. Because of her name, we can conclude that his wife was Flemish, and in this context she might have been in charge of women.[141] Ten years later, Petrus Davy would again be connected to stew-keeping. In 1391, the men of Southwark from the parish of St Olave petitioned the king to request the destruction of the brothels in their town, as they had become places of sin and hotspots for crime, to the extent that married women and the servants of good men became unable to go around the town without being troubled.[142] The petitioners then go on to name the landlords and tenants of these stews, among whom John Mokkyng, vintner, figured as a landlord and Petrus Davy as his tenant. There were ten other individuals on this list, including Christian Fleming of Southwark, who was a tenant of John Capel of Fenchurch Street; and John Toryn, a Flemish dyer, with his subtenant, Vincent de Toryn, at the stew held by John Southcote; as well as Gilkin Flemmyng, who was listed after a landlord, Robert Power, and may have been his tenant.[143] An interesting feature of this list is that it is composed only of men, but also that it implicates immigrants from the Low Countries in stew-keeping.

[137] TNA, KB 27/470, m. 16d (rex).
[138] *The Anonimalle Chronicle, 1333 to 1381*, ed. Galbraith, p. 140.
[139] Cited in Karras, 'Brothels', 415–16. [140] Fenwick, *Poll Taxes*, vol. II, p. 564.
[141] *Ibid.*, p. 559. [142] TNA, SC 8/73/3626. [143] TNA, SC 8/73/3627.

In London, it seems that stew-keeping was not reserved only for men. Apart from the 1393 ordinance cited above, there is one piece of direct evidence that links Flemish women with the stew-house. In her will of 1385, Lelia Blawer, wife of the late Flemish dyer Peter Blawer, bequeathed amongst other things 'le stuwhous' in the street called Medelane near the River Thames in the parish of St James Garlickhythe to her brother, John Ewersward, an immigrant from the Low Countries and a haberdasher of London.[144] We have seen mentions in administrative sources and chronicles of Flemish women active as prostitutes, but this document provides the first known direct evidence for Flemish women as stew-keepers in fourteenth-century London. Lelia came from a rather well-off background, as both her husband and brother were quite successful, which suggests in turn that her operation of the stew-house shared the same characteristics with those in some Flemish towns. Jelle Haemers has recently shown that brothel-keepers in major cities of the Low Countries were wealthy women who enjoyed relative freedom.[145] In 1422, a Fleming, Gerard Clayson, and his wife were indicted as receivers and maintainers of harlotry in their stew-house in the London ward of Cripplegate Without, suggesting that immigrants from the Low Countries were involved in stew-keeping well into the fifteenth century.[146]

We do not know much about the clients of Flemish prostitutes in England, but we can assume that they consisted of those men to whom marriage and sex were out of reach: young servants, transient merchants who would have visited towns without their wives, or priests.[147] For example, in Colchester, according to the fragmentary evidence, the most significant clientele seems to have been the clergy. Out of ten fines from 1352 to 1384 for prostitution or procuring, five of them involved priests. For example, Henry Fens and his wife were fined for receiving married priests and harlots at night.[148] In some cases, the town clerks are not so explicit as with Henry Fens and his wife. For instance, in 1373, William, chaplain of the parish of St Mary, was fined for being a night vagrant and a violent person. Just underneath on the same roll, Thomas Underwood was fined for harbouring William.[149] It is clear that the chaplain was visiting prostitutes, even though it is not explicitly stated. We can assume that both Henry Fens and his wife and Thomas Underwood probably

144 LMA MS 9171/1, fo. 137.

145 J. Haemers, 'Women and stews: The social and material history of prostitution in the late medieval southern Low Countries', *History Workshop Journal*, 92 (2021), 29–50.

146 *CPMR*, vol. IV, p. 154.

147 Karras, *Common Women*, pp. 76–81.

148 Benham, *Court Rolls*, vol. III, p. 53.

149 *Ibid.*, p. 31; for William, see also *ibid.*, p. 17.

did not hold a brothel per se, but instead acted as intermediaries between the priests and prostitutes. Two other places in England where the evidence suggests that the most frequent visitors of prostitutes were clerics were Exeter and York.[150] Kowaleski even found a case in the borough court of Exeter where a prostitute brought a plea of debt against a priest for 'services' provided – and won.[151] We do not have much information about the clients of Flemish prostitutes in fourteenth-century London and Great Yarmouth, but, given the structure of the population and the international economic activity, we can assume that the bulk of the customers would have been young apprentices and, of course, merchants visiting without their wives.

There is not much within the source material to go on in order to determine the background of female immigrants from the Low Countries engaged in sex work, but it seems that they were somewhat integrated into town life. For example, Lucebet Gimpetersone was apparently a prostitute, as she appeared in the borough court of Great Yarmouth in that capacity. In 1395, she was fined and sent to live in the Denes.[152] Such public punishment before the community present at the court leet would presumably have undermined respect for Lucebet. The stigma to which she was subject would probably have affected the possibility of finding a jury who would have been in her favour, in case she ever wanted to bring pleas to the borough court or find any alternative employment. Unfortunately, the source material does not allow us to find out whether Lucebet was able to do so. Apart from this mention, she appeared in court only once more, when she was accused of owing 8s to Robert Everton for 12 ells of woollen cloth.[153] This happened only a few months after she was ordered to abjure the town and, on top of that, the case does not provide further details that would allow us to determine whether she was involved in some activity connected to cloth production or if she was just buying cloth. However, a more clear-cut example was found by Rodziewicz of an Englishwoman, Katherine Chenkode, who was fined on one occasion for being a prostitute, but who had also been able to plead in the borough court and had some family members in the town.[154] It seems that reintegrating from sex work to cloth-working, in this case, was possible, and that many female immigrants might have

[150] Kowaleski, 'Women's work in a market town', p. 154; Goldberg, *Women, Work and Life Cycle*, p. 145.

[151] Kowaleski, 'Women's work in a market town', p. 154.

[152] The decision of the leet-court is recorded as a note from August 1395 in the form of a charter attached to NRO, Y/C4/105, m. 6d.

[153] The plea is recorded in December 1395: NRO, Y/C4/105, m. 6d.

[154] Rodziewicz, 'Great Yarmouth', pp. 278–80.

engaged in prostitution to sustain themselves on their own until an opportunity arose in some other activity.

CONCLUSION

This chapter has shown that even though Flemish women were mostly engaged in the first stages of cloth production, their involvement in the world of work went beyond this role, demonstrating that immigrant women played an important role in urban economies. We have seen that they also complemented the household income with the production of ale and sale of beer. Some of them were not just followers of their husbands but dared to leave the Low Countries alone and single in search of employment. It is clear that women who came with their husbands were in a slightly better position, be it in cloth or ale production. Some of them managed to bring wool or ale for export. Given the legal structure, female immigrants enjoyed some independence and protection, but the fact that it was impossible for single women to acquire freedom and an apprenticeship in crafts pushed some of those who emigrated alone into ending up as servants or even prostitutes. Nevertheless, the fact that they were ready to leave everything while single provides us with a profile of the immigrant other than the stereotypical one of the young single man.

Chapter 6

ANTI-FLEMING SENTIMENT AND THE PEASANTS' REVOLT OF 1381

INTRODUCTION

The body of evidence from local sources illustrates that immigrants from the Low Countries were able to become an integral part of the social, economic and cultural structure of the towns where they settled and spent most of their time in England living and working in peaceful coexistence with their native-born neighbours. Expressions of marked xenophobia or physical attacks by the local population were rather rare, and it seems that throughout the second half of the fourteenth century immigrant artisans were treated with some degree of toleration. Only a few documented disturbances are known, which were limited to London and to a large extent concerned verbal abuse and complaints about the administrative privileges granted to aliens. Yet infrequent observable abuse and violence committed by natives against foreigners might have hidden the fact that some friction existed. Some violent outbursts were just impossible to contain. Such was the case with premeditated attacks against Italian merchants in London by native mercers in 1357 and 1369, one of which included loss of life.[1] In the same manner, ten years later, a Genoese merchant, Janus Imperial, was assassinated by two apprentices under the instructions of leading London merchants.[2] In all of these

[1] *Memorials of London*, ed. Riley, pp. 302–3. In 1369 Nicholao Sarducci was accused of inflating the price of silk in the capital. Eighteen months later he was killed in a brawl with three mercers, all of whom were eventually pardoned. Sutton, *The Mercery of London*, pp. 115–17.

[2] Janus Imperial had been intending to discuss making Southampton the main port for Genoese exports, which threatened the monopoly on the wool trade held by the grocers of London. During the trial, a young grocer, John Algor, confessed that he and John Kirkeby had been instructed by leading London merchants such as Nicholas Brembre, William Walworth, Richard of Preston and John Philipot to start a brawl with the Genoese merchant. However, the role of these reputable citizens was never investigated. Paul Strohm argued that such a cover-up of their involvement in the assassination was based on hatred of foreigners and xenophobia. P. Strohm, 'Trade, treason, and the murder of Janus Imperial', *Journal of British Studies*, 35 (1996), 1–23; Nightingale, *A Medieval Mercantile Community*, pp. 259–61.

examples, the underlying motive for violent acts by natives was to protect their economic interests by intimidating foreigners. Similar organised violent attacks, albeit on a much larger scale, took place in 1381 during the Peasants' Revolt, when a number of immigrants from the Low Countries were killed by rebels in London, as well as in various places in East Anglia. While it is difficult to relate the murder of this specific group to the more general concerns that inspired the participants in the Peasants' Revolt, which centered upon the abolition of villeinage, the specifics of English labour legislation and the right to rent land at low rates, the bloodshed was important enough to be recorded soon afterwards and in later accounts both by chroniclers and in administrative sources such as the Letter Books of the city of London.[3]

While these reports are helpful for reconstructing the main course of events, as will be discussed in the following sections, unfortunately none of the medieval authors elaborated on the attackers' reasons for turning against the Flemings. However, several hypotheses have been proposed by scholars who have looked into this topic over the past century. The most widely accepted views on the massacre of June 1381 are those that take into account the economic context of the Flemish presence in fourteenth-century London. Already in 1898, in his introduction to André Réville's unfinished work on the Great Rising, Charles Petit-Dutaillis suggested that the victims in Vintry Ward were weavers from the Low Countries living and working in the city. The perpetrators appear to have been London's native cloth-workers, disgruntled with the competition from the newcomers from abroad.[4] It is true that London's native and alien cloth-workers also had a history of often violent opposition. Between 1337 and 1381, proclamations ordering English weavers to stop molesting their Flemish colleagues had been issued on at least seven occasions.[5] However, these generic proclamations do not specify how far the violence against Flemings actually went, or if it resulted in loss of life. In his *Bond Men Made Free*, Rodney Hilton expanded on Petit-Dutaillis' ideas by adding a class-conflict viewpoint. The killings could have been a culmination of continuous fighting between alien and native master weavers, or between the Flemings and

3 For the most detailed accounts, see *The Anonimalle Chronicle, 1333–1381*, ed. Galbraith, p. 145; *The Westminster Chronicle, 1381–1394*, ed. L. C. Hector and B. F. Harvey (Oxford, 1982), pp. 6–9; *The St Albans Chronicle: The Chronica Maiora of Thomas Walsingham*, ed. J. Taylor, W. R. Childs and L. Watkiss, 2 vols. (Oxford, 2002–11), vol. I, pp. 430–1; *Memorials of London*, ed. Riley, p. 450.

4 Réville, *Le Soulèvement*, pp. xlvii–viii.

5 *Letter Book F*, p. 190; *CCR, 1339–41*, p. 103; *CCR, 1343–6*, p. 486; *Letter Book G*, pp. 109, 112, 150; *CCR, 1369–74*, p. 91.

their English employees.[6] Caroline Barron and, in her wake, Alastair Dunn also argued that the onslaught was made on Flemish textile workers whose presence had jeopardised the livelihoods of the city's English artisans.[7] Drawing from the comments on the events by Geoffrey Chaucer in the *Nun's Priest's Tale*,[8] Derek Pearsall concluded that the assault was the result of both economic rivalry between native and Flemish craftsmen and fear of a foreign military invasion.[9]

Other studies focused more on xenophobia and upholding of 'national' identity as the main motivation for these attacks. In a recent study, Erik Spindler claimed that the rebels asserted their English identity by opposing and violently excluding those who were nearest to, but different from them, the Flemings.[10] Len Scales argued that the idea of removing other racial groups was far more important to and visible in medieval thought than we assume and hence did not need further explanation in light of the historical silence regarding the motives of the 1381 killers.[11] These conclusions were somewhat more nuanced in Samuel Cohn's work. He concurred with views that hatred of foreigners was the main driving factor by stressing that the number of artisans from the Low Countries who were killed far surpassed the number of lawyers, landlords and royal officials, groups the rebels proclaimed were responsible for high taxation, losses in France and other main causes of the revolt. However, Cohn also added that such slaughter of foreign artisans by native artisans was not a typical feature of urban revolts throughout late medieval Europe.[12]

The purpose of this chapter will be threefold: to revisit the economic arguments advanced by Hilton and others by considering them in their full political context; to provide an account of the identity of the attackers and the Flemings who were killed in East Anglia and London by drawing on documentary and prosopographical work; and to evaluate

[6] R. H. Hilton, *Bond Men Made Free: Medieval Peasant Movements and the English Rising of 1381* (London, 1973), pp. 195–8.

[7] C. M. Barron, *Revolt in London, 11th to 15th June 1381* (London, 1981), p. 6; C. M. Barron, 'Introduction: England and the Low Countries, 1327–1477', in Barron and Saul (eds), *England and the Low Countries*, pp. 1–28, at p. 13; A. Dunn, *The Great Rising of 1381* (Stroud, 2002), p. 90.

[8] L. D. Benson (ed.), *The Riverside Chaucer* (Boston, MA, 1987), p. 260.

[9] D. A. Pearsall, 'Strangers in late fourteenth-century London', in F. R. P. Akehurst and S. Cain Van D'Elden (eds), *The Stranger in Medieval Society* (Minneapolis and London, 1997), pp. 46–62, at p. 58.

[10] Erik Spindler, 'Flemings in the Peasants' Revolt, 1381', in H. Skoda, P. Lantschner and R. Shaw (eds), *Contact and Exchange in Later Medieval Europe: Essays in Honour of Malcolm Vale* (Woodbridge, 2012), pp. 59–78.

[11] L. Scales, 'Bread, cheese and genocide: Imagining the destruction of peoples in medieval Western Europe', *History*, 92:307 (2007), 284–300.

[12] S. Cohn, *Popular Protest in Late Medieval English Towns* (Cambridge, 2012), pp. 288–9.

the effects of the massacre on the immigrant community and immigration in England after 1381. First, this chapter will reconstruct a three-decade-long quarrel between native and alien weavers in London which culminated in the murder of Flemings during the Peasants' Revolt. This will be linked to the capital's native cloth-workers' dissatisfaction with the government's economic immigration policy. Convinced that the immigrants' activities benefited the common profit of the realm, the crown remained deaf to the concerns of London's native weavers, who claimed that the work of exiled Flemish cloth-workers in the city encroached on their privileges. Then, attention will be turned to the available judicial records in order to develop the biographies and prosopography of both the attackers and the victims in East Anglia. Finally, the years after the revolt will be examined from the perspective of old and new immigrants, both of which groups seem to have been affected. As most immigrant textile workers resident in England were aware of the killings, questions concerning how immigrant textile workers went about their lives and work after June 1381 will also be examined. At the same time, news of the massacre had certainly reached the Low Countries too, and it seems to have dissuaded other weavers and fullers from further emigration to England. It will be argued that although the rebels' official intention during the revolt was not to reduce the importance of immigrant textile workers in England, or to prevent new arrivals from emigrating, eventually the killings did have these effects.

FLEMINGS AND THE PEASANTS' REVOLT OF 1381 IN LONDON

Disputes over the payment of the poll tax between local communities and the royal commissions in the English counties of Essex and Kent set off a violent rebellion at the end of May 1381 that quickly spread to other parts of the country and became known as the Peasants' Revolt.[13] The rebels, who came from a variety of social backgrounds and were driven by diverse resentments, reached the city of London on 13 June, and attacked several symbols of royal authority and other forms of power. According to several chronicles and administrative sources, acts of violence against the Flemish community living in the capital took place at different locations as soon as the rebels entered London and on the following day. Whereas their reports allow us to reconstruct the main course of events, some contemporary accounts provide more details than

[13] The bibliography on the revolt is extensive. A good introduction is R. H. Hilton and T. Aston (eds), *The English Rising of 1381* (Cambridge, 1984). The key primary sources are translated in R. B. Dobson, ed., *The Peasants' Revolt of 1381* (London, 1983).

others about the attacks on foreigners. The first recorded attack on Flemings took place on 13 June in Southwark. It is reported by the *Anonimalle Chronicle* that on their way to the city across London Bridge, 'the commons of Kent broke down a brothel, occupied by Flemish women who had farmed it from the mayor of London'.[14] It is not clear whether this incident included any fatalities, but the chronicler is the only source to report these attacks on the immigrants. We have seen in the previous chapter that Southwark and especially the area around the River Thames were associated with sex workers from the Low Countries, and they might have been the primary targets of this attack.[15]

The same day, outside the London wall, a group of immigrants from the Low Countries were allegedly killed at Clerkenwell.[16] Almost a year after the revolt, the king's commission accused one Richard Gardiner from Holborn of coming with a crowd of rebels to Clerkenwell and killing seven Flemings who had taken refuge in the priory of the Hospital of St John of Jerusalem. However, Gardiner was able to produce a letter of pardon and get himself exonerated, which neither confirms nor denies that he was a perpetrator. None of the chroniclers referred to this incident, and the King's Bench, the only place where it was recorded, does not provide many details. The names of the victims were marked unknown, as well as their occupations, and therefore we can only guess who these Flemings were.[17] Nevertheless, some evidence suggests that immigrant craftsmen from the Low Countries had settled just north of the city in Middlesex, and some of them might have been the victims. In 1377, an order was issued for the capture of Giles Webbe, *Flemyng*, who had allegedly committed trespass and extortion, together with Thomas Brewer from St John's Street in Clerkenwell.[18] Chris Fletcher has suggested that these rebels certainly targeted the Clerkenwell priory for its association with the treasurer of England, Sir Robert Hales, which might have been the main interest of the investigation at the King's Bench and the reason the scribes did not record the names of those Flemings killed.[19]

[14] *The Anonimalle Chronicle, 1333–1381*, ed. Galbraith, p. 140.

[15] Because of the statement by the chronicler that the brothel was farmed from the mayor, Spindler proposed that the attack might have been directed against the mayor, William Walworth. Spindler, 'Flemings', p. 61.

[16] Réville, *Le Soulèvement*, p. 203.

[17] 'venit cum magna multitudine felonice et proditorie ad domum Sancti Johannis apud Clerkenwell et ibidem interfecit septem homines vocatos Flemynges, quorum nomina ignorantur'. TNA, KB 27/485, m. 13 rex.

[18] TNA, KB 27/468, m. 13d rex.

[19] C. Fletcher, 'Justice, meurtre et *leadership* politique dans la révolte anglaise de 1381', *Cahiers de Recherches Médiévales et Humanistes*, 34 (2017), 61–86, at 79.

It was the following day, Friday 14 June, that the biggest expression of organised violence towards any immigrant community took place in the city of London in the fourteenth century. The degree of brutality of this event was probably impressive enough to explain why it was recorded by all the main contemporaries, who provide a more or less unanimous account: in addition to the killings of several political figures, numerous Flemings were dragged out of churches and houses in the city's Vintry Ward, near the Thames, and were beheaded on the spot. According to the *Anonimalle Chronicle*, after the attack on the Tower of London, the commoners proclaimed that 'whoever could catch any Fleming or other aliens of any nation, might cut off their heads'. He then specifically reports the massacre of more than thirty-five Flemings, pulled from the church of St Martin Vintry and beheaded in the street.[20] This chronicle is the closest to the 'official' account of the killings, recorded in the city's Letter Book H, which also specifies that 'the great massacre of Flemings' happened in Vintry Ward.[21] This is consistent with the evidence presented in Chapters 2 and 3, which illustrates that the immigrant weavers from the Low Countries lived in parishes near the River Thames and even had a fraternity in the church of St Martin Vintry.[22] Jean Froissart's and the monk of Westminster's accounts are compatible with the *Anonimalle Chronicle*, but offer a slightly more dramatic portrayal. They state that the rebels beheaded any Fleming they could find, without specifying how many of them were killed, concluding with a vivid picture: 'for you could see heaps of dead bodies and corpses lying in the squares and other places'.[23] Finally, Thomas Walsingham provided broadly the same narrative, with somewhat different details. He reports that, on the second day of the revolt in London, 'many men, both Flemings and Englishmen, were executed for no real cause but only to satisfy the cruelty of the domineering rustics'. But when he describes the incident, he goes on to say that thirty Flemings were killed at Austin Friars church, and seventeen others were taken out from an unspecified parish church and executed in the open street.[24] The main feature that comes across from these key contemporary accounts is the rebels' hatred of Flemings.

A similar tone was conveyed by later chroniclers and poets in their interpretation of these events during the revolt. According to one

20 *The Anonimalle Chronicle, 1333–1381*, ed. Galbraith, p. 140.

21 *Memorials of London*, ed. Riley, p. 450.

22 See Chapter 3 and the bequest to the fraternity of *Cortrike* in the will of Peter Smyth de Flandre.

23 *The Westminster Chronicle*, ed. Hector and Harvey, pp. 6–9.

24 *The St Albans Chronicle*, ed. Taylor, Childs and Watkiss, vol. I, p. 430.

fifteenth-century chronicler, the perpetrators used the inability to pronounce the shibboleth 'bread and cheese' to single out Flemish people.[25] The massacre was also (as mentioned above) revisited by Chaucer in his *Nun's Priest's Tale*, where he likened the shouts of the mob as they chased the Flemings to the din of farmyard workers as they chase a fox: 'Certes, he Jakke Straw and his meynee, Ne made nevere shoutes half so shrille, Whan that they wolden any Flemyng kille, As thilke day was maad upon the fox.'[26] As even the most concise amongst the commentators found it necessary to highlight that all the victims originated from Flanders, it seems safe to assume that they did not end up being accidental casualties of an angry mob but were specifically targeted. However, the problem is that both the official account and the chronicles do not tell us much about the identity of the victims, or the reasons for attacking them, apart from latent xenophobia. The judicial records are also not helpful in this regard. For example, Roger Boye from Ickham in Kent was accused of murdering three Flemings on 14 June 1381 in London, but the names of the victims are not provided.[27] Nevertheless, the available judicial records after 1381 provide us with the names of Londoners who were suspected to have joined the rebels from Essex and Kent. By identifying the perpetrators and examining their relationships prior to the revolt, we might get an idea as to whether Flemings were targeted because they were textile workers.

Among the most important sets of records relating to the revolt that can allow us to identify the rebels in London are the returns to Mayor Walworth's commission made by the aldermen and preserved on the plea and memoranda rolls of the city. On 14 August 1381 the city officers compiled a list of 201 Londoners suspected to have participated in the revolt and stated the occupations of seventy-five of them. There were artisans from various industries, but the most numerous were those from the textile sector, comprising fifteen weavers, eleven tailors, eight fullers, six dyers and two shearers.[28] Their social status was also mixed and included not only experienced artisans, like William Pygas and Thomas Pynnok, who were masters and became bailiffs of the guild of native weavers in the following years, but also recently freed apprentices, like

25 *Chronicles of London*, ed. C. L. Kingsford (Oxford, 1905), p. 15.

26 Dobson, *The Peasants' Revolt*, p. 387. For more details on Flemings in Chaucer, see M. Hanrahan, 'Flemings', in P. Brown (ed.), *A New Companion to Chaucer* (Hoboken, 2019), pp. 151–66.

27 TNA, KB 9/43, m. 19. See also H. Eiden, *'In der Knechtschaft werdet ihr verharren. . .': Ursachen und Verlauf des englischen Bauernaufstandes von 1381* (Trier, 1995), p. 249 n.

28 *CPMR*, vol. II, p. 289; *Rotuli Parliamentorum*, vol. III, p. 113.

John Bateman.[29] On 20 March 1387, seven of these weavers – Richard Bone, *webbe*, William Harowe, *webbe*, Henry Nasse, *webbe*, William Pygas, *webbe*, John Nook, *webbe*, William Pypar, *webbe*, and Thomas Wolf, *webbe* – were offered an amnesty by the mayor.[30] Two out of the eight suspected fullers (William Caux and Richard Skeet) were among thirty-six 'best men of the mystery' who had attached their names to broker the approval of the ordinances of fullers in 1376.[31] The fullers might have also been jealous of the alien weavers' dominance in the city's cloth industry. Although the fullers were able to be in charge of the production of regular broadcloths, as evidenced in Chapter 4, they probably wanted to take a more prominent role in the production and sale of the more expensive rays and coloureds, which were almost entirely controlled by alien weavers. However, prior relationships between native and alien weavers suggest that, of all the groups of textile workers, it was the native weavers who were by far the most motivated to use the general turmoil of the revolt to express their frustration with the presence of artisans from the Low Countries. As we will see below, native weavers were unhappy that Flemings were allowed to form their own guild, something that they considered infringed upon their privileges. What was even more frustrating, even though they appealed to the king on several occasions between 1352 and 1381, the crown either ignored their complaints or outrightly supported the position of the Flemings.

During this period the native cloth-workers' political failures resulted in physical aggression against their Flemish colleagues. On 11 April 1377, Katherine, the English wife of a Flemish weaver, Gilbert Strynger, sued London weaver Richard Bone in the King's Bench for the murder of her husband. Bone was summoned to appear in person on 18 November 1377. He did not show up and, after failing to do so twice more, he was outlawed.[32] On 19 April 1379, however, Bone bought a royal pardon for the murder and had his penalty cancelled. Although the writ delivered by the Privy Seal Office, which was usually based on the supplicant's petition, specified that Strynger was a Fleming, the entry on the King's Bench plea rolls did not do so.[33] In the context of the rivalries between the two groups of workers, Bone found it expedient to emphasise his victim's origins in order to obtain mercy. On 23 June 1381, two years

[29] *Letter Book H*, pp. 97, 315, 337, 369; LMA, MS 9171/1, fo. 60. John Bateman had been freed four years earlier by the master weaver Richard Bolle.

[30] *Letter Book H*, p. 315.

[31] *CPMR*, vol. II, p. 37. The six other fullers were Simon Gerard, William Gatesby, John Trigg, William Plomer, John Bentele and Thomas Crawe.

[32] TNA, KB 27/469, m. 50.

[33] TNA, C 81/460/430. See also *CPR, 1377–81*, p. 340.

later and only nine days after the massacre of the Flemings, the same Richard Bone (together with several other London weavers) would acquire another pardon, this time for his participation in the Peasants' Revolt.[34]

Let us now look more closely at the relationships between native and Flemish weavers during the decades that preceded the revolt. Soon after the arrival of the exiled cloth-workers, native weavers were unhappy with their presence and tried to impose obstacles to their activity. Already in 1352, native weavers had expressed their displeasure in a petition to the king, in which they complained that foreign textile workers were active outside their (the natives') guild and did not contribute to their farm. The London weavers claimed that this was in violation of their privileges, established by a royal charter granted to them in 1155.[35] In order to avoid having the matter debated in parliament, Edward III brought representatives from both parties instead to the court of the exchequer, where the issue was discussed. The weavers of London brought their 1155 charter and a 1347 decree passed by their city's court of aldermen which stated that all weavers working in London and Southwark should be subject to the same laws as native weavers.[36] The jury found these claims reasonable, but added that, over the previous thirty years, the guild of natives had made additional orders and ordinances concerning the work of weavers that were to the detriment of the wider population. For that reason, the jury decided in favour of the Flemings, saying that by virtue of the 1337 statute which promised them unlimited franchises, alien weavers are not to be 'burdened or troubled' by the guild that they do not belong to.[37]

It seems that this decision did not calm things down. Already the same year, the Flemish textile workers petitioned the king and the council, alleging that the guild of native weavers was still harassing them, contrary to the privileges granted to them by the statute of 1337 that permitted alien weavers to work in England. As a remedy to their problems, in the same petition, the Flemings demanded the right to choose two of their own men to oversee their labour and settle disputes within their own community. The crown's response, which is written on the dorse of the document, is incredibly unambiguous:

[34] *CPR, 1385–9*, p. 280. See also John L. Leland, 'Aliens in the pardons of Richard II', in J. S. Hamilton (ed.), *Fourteenth-Century England* (Woodbridge, 2006), vol. IV, pp. 140–1.

[35] For the text of the privileges, see Consitt, *The London Weavers' Company*, pp. 180–1.

[36] For this ruling of 1347, see *Letter Book F*, p. 173.

[37] TNA, E 13/76, mm. 97–8d. The entry contains the original text of the natives' petition and its endorsement. For a full transcription, see *Firma Burgi, or an Historical Essay concerning the Cities, Towns and Buroughs of England*, ed. T. Madox (London, 1726), pp. 283–7.

Because this petition touches the common profit of all the realm of England and of the lands specified in it, our lord the king, with the assent of the prelates, earls and barons, and other great men in this full parliament, grants for himself and his heirs to all and singular alien cloth workers ... who then resided in this kingdom ... and should thereafter come and abide there and follow their craft ... that they may safely abide in the realm under the king's protection, and may freely follow their craft; without being answerable to the members of the guild of weavers of London, natives, or of other cloth-workers of this realm, or liable to pay any sums of money by reason of such guild.[38]

Not only did the king's decision protect Flemish textile workers from being subsumed by the guild of native weavers, Edward III hinted that attracting foreign cloth-makers had become a part of his political programme. With the adoption of the rhetoric of the 'common profit of the king and kingdom', immigrant textile workers were being presented as beneficial for the whole realm, which fact far exceeded the narrow interests of London weavers.[39] On 8 February 1352, the king's decision was enacted on the patent rolls, which extended the rights of alien textile workers granted to them by the statute of 1337.[40]

The crown's decision seems to have pushed the two groups into finding some common ground. Only eight months after the letters patent were issued, representatives of London's native and alien cloth-workers reached agreement on several issues. The English weavers acknowledged the Flemings' freedom to work in the city and promised no longer to attempt to incorporate them within their guild. The Flemish textile workers were prepared to contribute to the annual farm to the exchequer and agreed to a joint supervision of their looms. They would also refrain from undertaking further legal action against their English colleagues.[41] The agreement implied the de facto recognition of the alien weavers as a separate guild, and, as we saw in Chapter 3, the names of the bailiffs of the Flemish guild were recorded regularly in the city's Letter Books.[42] The compromise was not the only indication of a rapprochement during these years. In 1356, exile John Kempe from Ghent even obtained the citizenship status he needed to sell retail in the city by joining the guild of

38 TNA, SC 8/110/5463. See also *PROME*, vol. V, pp. 62–3.

39 For strategies used in political discourse throughout the fourteenth century in order to frame the debate about the material prosperity of the kingdom, see W. M. Ormrod, '"Common profit" and "the profit of the king and kingdom": Parliament and the development of political language in England, 1250–1450', *Viator*, 46 (2015), 219–52.

40 *CPR, 1350–4*, p. 232.

41 LMA, CLA/023/DW/01/80/184. For a full transcription, see Consitt, *The London Weavers' Company*, pp. 188–91.

42 *Letter Book G*, pp. 2, 16, 48, 104, 131, 237; *CPMR*, vol. II, p. 84.

native weavers. Three of his sureties were John Payn, Richard atte Boure and John Bennet, London cloth-workers who had brokered the 1352 agreement.[43] The two groups were also cooperating to stop collective actions that threatened both guilds. Inspired by the greater opportunities for labourers in post-plague England, Flemish journeymen, among whom were the exiles John and Peter Pape, and John Tybes, refused to work for less than 7d a day and in 1355 threatened to physically attack their own bailiffs. The mayor ordered a joint committee of native and alien weavers, including the banished Giles Ripegast, Henry van the Rothe, John van Somergham and John atte Were, to negotiate about appropriate wages. In the end, the traditional enmity between both groups prevented them from reaching a compromise, and the matter was not settled.[44] However, the 'truce' did not last for long. A series of proclamations by the king and the city's office-holders suggests that native weavers, instead of looking for political solutions, turned to the intimidation of immigrant textile workers by physical violence.

In June 1355, the king addressed a writ to the mayor and sheriffs of London, telling them to intervene. The text referred explicitly to the immigration of the exiles, condemning the molestation of the 'men of Flanders . . . banished from those parts for adhering to the king'.[45] Four years later, in two similar proclamations, Edward III had again to forbid physical aggression against those from the Low Countries pursuing their business in both the city and the suburbs.[46]

The violence between local and immigrant cloth-workers during the 1360s was briefly overshadowed in the majority of the sources by internal issues within the guild of foreign weavers in London. Conflicts between Flemings and Brabanters, as well as between Flemish masters and journeymen, raged for a number of years. As the number of textile workers from Flanders and Brabant in the city grew throughout the 1350s, so did their importance. In 1362, they were strong enough to have their ordinances approved by the city's mayor and aldermen. At this stage, the ordinances were approved as those of 'alien weavers', and representatives both of Flemish and Brabantine weavers attached their names to oversee these rules.[47] However, as we saw in Chapter 3, Brabantine weavers would manage to separate themselves from Flemish weavers in 1366 and have their own men supervising their trade. From that moment onwards, the city's Letter Books would record the bailiffs of the English, Brabantine and Flemish weavers separately every year. In addition to the

43 LMA, CLA/023/CP/01/80, m. 4d.
44 *CPMR*, vol. I, p. 248.
45 *Letter Book G*, p. 42; *CCR, 1354–60*, p. 221.
46 *Letter Book G*, pp. 109, 112.
47 *Memorials of London*, ed. Riley, pp. 306–8, 332.

conflict with Brabantine textile workers, collective actions continued to occur throughout the decade.[48] In 1366, the bailiffs of the Flemish weavers, Baldwyn Gyles and Gerard atte Hyde, were committed to prison for failing to inform the mayor and aldermen about their compatriots who had instigated a strike.[49] Probably because of the issues both with Brabantine and native masters, the bailiffs of the Flemish weavers' guild had a hard time keeping servants and journeymen under control.

At the same time, fear of the Londoners' aggression had not completely disappeared either. In 1362, the mayor issued a decree that forbade Flemings, Brabanters and Zeelanders from being armed.[50] In a climate of violent rivalry between various groups of textile workers, the immigrants might have felt so unsafe that they constantly carried knives and other weapons with them. In a petition from 1370, the Flemings and Brabanters demanded to have separate places for meetings and hiring journeymen in order to avoid any public display of violent confrontation.[51] Disunity between immigrant groups and their fights around the city might have resulted in a climate more favorable to anti-Flemish concerns and made it easier for the natives to 'justify' their assaults. Indeed, around the same period, these assaults effectively returned. Having 'heard by frequent report of several that evil and insult is by the people of the said city daily inflicted on the ... men and the merchants [of Flanders] dwelling there and coming thither', Edward III once again attempted to calm things down.[52]

To assume that the frequent attacks by London weavers in the city's streets over the course of the 1350s and 1360s, which were discussed in parliament, were motivated by a general anti-alien sentiment, or even resentment over losing business to Flemings, would be an easy conclusion. The situation is more complicated than that, and to fully grasp the challenges faced by the local textile workers it is essential to take into account the developments in the London cloth market during the second part of the fourteenth century. As explained in Chapter 4, immigrants from the Low Countries conquered most of London's luxury cloth market. Between 1351 and 1381, they controlled the production and marketing of rays and coloureds, high-quality types of cloth, demand for which steadily increased after the Black Death and a general rise in standards for consumers. Although native cloth-workers rose in importance in comparison with the first quarter of the fourteenth century, they were still working for the London drapers, who controlled the retail

48 Consitt, *The London Weavers' Company*, pp. 43–9; Good, 'Alien clothworkers', pp. 12–15.

49 *CPMR*, vol. II, pp. 65–6.

50 *Letter Book G*, p. 150.

51 *Memorials of London*, ed. Riley, pp. 345–6.

52 *CCR, 1369–74*, p. 91.

trade in the capital.[53] This subordinate position to the drapers prevented them from gaining enough capital to be able to organise the whole production process themselves. At the same time, the Flemings' separate guild prevented native weavers from acquiring specialist skills in the production of higher-quality types of cloth. This explains, at least in part, why London weavers pursued the supervision of the guild of alien cloth-workers with such determination: with the Flemings' incorporation would come their expertise, their capital and their unique selling proposition. The incorporation of a group of immigrant workers who had fared much better could have given them access to new sections of the market and have ameliorated their problems with the payment of the farm. For this to have happened, they needed the support of Edward III. Yet the English king, who claimed to work for the common profit of his entire realm, continued to ignore the legitimate claims of native weavers and preferred to court the Flemings.

THE PETITIONS WAR OF 1376–1378

A series of developments in the second half of the 1370s gave the native textile workers additional reasons to believe that they could find a political solution to their issues. Firstly, as the monarch's health deteriorated, he lost the power to handle the mounting discontent in the realm, which erupted dramatically in the so-called Good Parliament of 1376.[54] This was to seriously affect Edward III's capacity to continue his steadfast support for the guild of Flemish artisans. Secondly, a general growing public displeasure with a sizeable presence of foreigners in the realm started to develop from 1371.[55] Finally, the use of petitions became more accessible to wider communities, which provided the London weavers with another opportunity to make their grievances heard.[56]

In a petition from 1376, the native weavers of London reiterated the argument they had made in the 1350s. They reminded the king that his ancestors had granted them a charter that gave their guild the sole right to practise their craft in the city, but Edward III had allowed Flemings, Brabanters and other aliens that had newly come to England to do the

53 Although they elected members to the Common Council, their political influence was very limited: see Barron, *London in the Later Middle Ages*, pp. 220–1; Oldland, 'London clothmaking', pp. 67–78; Quinton, 'The drapers and the drapery trade', pp. 113–17.

54 G. Holmes, *The Good Parliament* (Oxford, 1975), pp. 100–58; W. M. Ormrod, *Edward III* (New Haven, 2011), pp. 524–76.

55 Lambert and Ormrod, 'Friendly foreigners', 15–16.

56 G. Dodd, *Justice and Grace: Private Petitioning and the English Parliament in the Late Middle Ages* (Oxford, 2007), p. 146.

same. They requested either the abolition of the aliens' charter of 1352 or the cancellation of the obligation to pay their yearly fee.[57] In response, the Flemish weavers petitioned the new monarch and his council, demanding the confirmation of their 1352 charter in order to be able to practise their trade under the king's protection.[58] As in 1352, when the first dispute between the two groups was deferred to the court of the exchequer, the crown decided once more to avoid having the issue debated in parliament. This time, the Flemings and Brabanters' 1352 charter was to be investigated in the court of chancery.[59] Even though this was not an uncommon procedure, it seems obvious that the crown was not particularly keen on addressing the criticisms of its economic immigration policy in parliament.[60]

In anticipation of a verdict from chancery, both groups tried to find additional support. The Flemings quickly turned to Richard II's uncle, John of Gaunt. They pleaded for his assistance in a petition, in which they recounted how English cloth-workers were attempting to have the aliens' charter granted by John's father, Edward, abolished in chancery.[61] John of Gaunt had a lot of power in the kingdom during his nephew's minority, despite being barred from the regency council.[62] The Flemings must have been aware of this and considered that he would look favourably on their request. Political language was another battleground in the petitions war. The Flemings cleverly highlighted the larger significance of their argument by adopting the crown's own rhetoric of immigration for the common profit in their requests both to Richard

57 TNA, SC 8/43/2127. Two identical petitions were submitted to the new king, Richard II, later in the year, implying that no decision had been reached by Edward III, who passed away in June 1377. TNA, SC 8/123/6147; SC 8/143/7128.

58 TNA, SC 8/143/7122.

59 TNA, SC 8/123/6147. The decision is recorded on the dorse of this petition presented by the native cloth-workers.

60 For the deferral of petitions outside parliament, see Dodd, *Justice and Grace*, pp. 82–5. The same period was marked by a growing anti-alien atmosphere, and native weavers were probably driven by this sentiment. During the Bad Parliament of January to March 1377, for instance, a request to expel all French residents was even granted. It seems, however, that the bill concerning alien weavers found much less support. *PROME*, vol. VI, pp. 48–50. See also Lambert and Ormrod, 'Friendly foreigners', 15–17.

61 TNA, SC 8/102/5061. The petitions in TNA's SC 8 series are undated, and so dates need to be derived from internal and contextual evidence. G. Dodd, 'Parliamentary petitions? The origins and provenance of the "ancient petitions" (SC 8) in the National Archives', in W. M. Ormrod, G. Dodd and A. Musson (eds), *Medieval Petitions: Grace and Grievance* (York, 2009), pp. 15–16. This request refers to the procedure in chancery, and so should be dated after the native weavers' petitions and before the end of the investigation in March 1380.

62 G. Dodd, 'Richard II and the fiction of majority rule', in C. Beem (ed.), *The Royal Minorities of Medieval and Early Modern England* (New York, 2008), pp. 103–59.

II and John of Gaunt.[63] In the earlier petition they asked for confirmation of their privileges, 'so they could use their mystery so well for the profit of the realm as for themselves'.[64] In the later one, the very last words were to reassure John that they were interested only in the 'profit of the realm'.[65] While others during this period avidly adopted the idea of the 'common profit', the native weavers never did so in a way that served the interests of the kingdom as a whole.[66] They insisted on highlighting how the denial of their earlier petitions had caused 'the great impoverishment of their estate', demonstrating a greater concern for their own profit.[67]

The English weavers tried to put pressure on the foreigners to back down by mobilising support on the political front, but also by violent action on the streets of London. In the same petition of 1377–8, the immigrant weavers claimed that because of the privileges granted to them in 1352, the English had 'murdered, wounded, and horribly trampled down' some of their members.[68] The Flemings do not specify the date of these attacks, but it is safe to assume that some of them happened early in the reign of Richard II. In October 1377, when parliament decided to introduce stricter control of the wages earned by servants and that no alien in England should run a hostel, native cloth-workers attempted to use this decree to their own benefit.[69] They turned to the London Common Council, requesting a ban on alien weavers from being hostel-keepers, but also to place the regulation of foreign servants' wages under the natives' guild. They made it clear who the real targets of their attacks were by using language that was more direct than that used earlier, and that was indicative of rising frustration: 'the foreigners and strangers being for the most part exiled from their own country as notorious malefactors, and unwilling to place themselves under the rule of the free weavers'. The Common Council made clear to the weavers that no changes could be made until malpractices were actually observed.[70] The assembly, which was dominated by the mercantile elite and had no desire to limit competition among the city's

63 The Flemings had already petitioned the mayor of London 'for the common profit of the land and of the city and for the saving of their said trade' in 1362. *Memorials of London*, ed. Riley, p. 306.

64 TNA, SC 8/143/7122.

65 TNA, SC 8/102/5061.

66 W. M. Ormrod, 'The Good Parliament of 1376: Commons, communes and "common profit" in fourteenth-century English politics', in D. Nicholas, B. S. Bachrach and J. M. Murray (eds), *Comparative Perspectives on History and Historians: Essays in Memory of Bryce Lyon (1920–2007)* (Kalamazoo, 2012) pp. 179–82.

67 TNA, SC 8/123/6147.

68 TNA, SC 8/143/7122.

69 *PROME*, vol. VI, pp. 36–7, 38.

70 *Letter Book H*, p. 94.

manufacturers, showed only a limited amount of sympathy for the specific issues of the local weavers.[71]

On 4 March 1380, fourteen months before the rebellion, the outcome of the chancery investigation was enacted on the patent rolls. The native cloth workers' concerns were once more denied, and the Flemish weavers' rights, notably their freedom to work outside the Londoners' guild, were upheld.[72] The two groups reached some sort of agreement on several issues, but it was once again completely disregarded. Conflicts persisted over the following hundred years.[73] Only in 1497 did London's native and alien weavers come to a 'final peace' and unite in one guild.[74]

While none of the source material that covers the events of the Peasants' Revolt of 1381 directly linked the killings of Flemings in London with the guild of native weavers, it is obvious from their relationship throughout the years leading up to the rebellion that local textile workers were the only ones who had an interest in intimidating foreign artisans in such a way. The king's support for immigrant textile workers shattered the native Londoners' attempts at finding a political solution, and the turmoil in the city over several days in June 1381 was a great opportunity to turn things in their favour. However, as we will see below, even though they managed to reduce the importance of foreign artisans in the city, the consequences would be detrimental to them too.

FLEMINGS AND THE PEASANTS' REVOLT OF 1381 IN EAST ANGLIA

Although the Vintry Ward massacre was highlighted by all chroniclers, they fail to mention any slaughter of Flemings outside London.[75] It is the judicial records relating to the revolt which reveal that such incidents took place in East Anglia. Killings of Flemish residents were recorded at Great Yarmouth and Lynn in Norfolk, and at Colchester, Maldon and Manningtree in Essex. As we will see, however, premeditated, organised violence was on a much smaller scale than in the case of the Vintry Ward massacre.

71 P. Nightingale, 'Capitalists, crafts and constitutional change in late fourteenth-century London', *Past and Present*, 123 (1989), 3–35, at 17–24.

72 *CPR, 1377–81*, p. 452.

73 In 1406, for example, the guild of native cloth-workers complained again that the Flemish weavers did not pay their farm. *PROME*, vol. VIII, pp. 399–400.

74 Consitt, *The London Weavers' Company*, pp. 58–60.

75 A. Prescott, 'Judicial records of the Rising of 1381', unpublished Ph.D. thesis, Bedford College, University of London (1984), p. 117.

The revolt in Essex started at the end of May in Brentwood and spread rapidly to Coggeshall, Chelmsford and other places in the county. The rebels' grievances focused on any symbols of royal authority, as they aimed 'to destroy divers lieges of the King and his common laws and lordship ... and to have no other law in England but those they themselves made to be ordained'.[76] The general insurrection in Essex witnessed the destruction of records and attacks on royal officials. The rebels rapidly took control of Essex, and one group marched on London and took part in the incidents there.[77] In addition to the destruction of manorial and fiscal records in the county, members of the Flemish community were targeted as well. According to the confessions of two insurgents, on 16 June 1381 one John Thechere beheaded a Fleming at Manningtree, under the orders of John Hardyng.[78] There is no further information about the victim in this case, but John Hardyng was granted a pardon in 1386 for his involvement in the rebellion.[79] At the same time, Segoos Webbe from East Mersea was incited by Richard Coventry from Maldon to behead a Flemish weaver, John Preme, who also resided at Maldon.[80] This is the only case so far where the Flemish victim is named and his occupation is stated. He might have been an exile from the Liberty of Bruges, Jan Prems, who had plied his craft in Maldon for several years.[81] It appears that Richard and Segoos were part of the same group of rebels whose main goal was to loot and steal across the county, and the killing was probably done to settle a preexisting dispute.[82] John was not the only immigrant from the Low Countries who chose to settle in Maldon. For example, seven years before the rebellion, Torinus Flemyng and Henry van Drene, *Flemyng*, were indicted for the murder of Giles Braban, which hints at the existence of an immigrant community of artisans in this town.[83] The immigrants certainly interacted with the natives prior to the revolt, and Richard Coventry might have had some personal grudge against John Preme and used the turmoil of the revolt to 'resolve' the issue.

The town of Colchester was not touched by the rebellion as heavily as the rest of the county, but some disturbances were documented. The town was apparently a gathering-place for rebels from the surrounding

[76] Quoted in H. Eiden, 'Joint action against the "bad" lordship: The Peasants' Revolt in Essex and Norfolk', *History*, 83:267 (1998), 5–30, at 11.

[77] *Ibid.*, 12–13.

[78] Réville, *Le Soulèvement*, p. 216; TNA, KB 27/485, m. 5 rex.

[79] Réville, *Le Soulèvement*, p. 217.

[80] TNA, KB 145/3/6/1.

[81] *Cartulaire historique et généalogique des Artevelde*, ed. De Pauw, p. 731.

[82] TNA, KB 145/3/6/1: Segoos and Richard were accused of entering the houses of John Gildersburg and John Sewale and carrying off goods (gold and silver) worth 140s.

[83] TNA, JUST 2/35/5, m. 3.

villages, who joined with the insurgents from Colchester and left for London on 13 June 1381.[84] Those who stayed in Colchester attacked the moot hall and St John's abbey on 16 June 1381.[85] The main goal of this attack was to find the borough records in order to destroy them, but it seems that they did not manage to do so. However, the borough court sessions in Colchester were not held for five weeks after the rebellion.[86] These disturbances were actually recorded in the hundred session of the borough court in October 1381. John Forde of Brightlingsea, William Pakke, Henry Henkyn and John Broke were fined for entering by force the abbey of St John's and carrying off its rolls and muniments.[87] At the same session, William atte Appelton was charged with having threatened to burn the rolls and muniments of the treasury, which were now missing. He denied the charge but was found guilty by the jury and sent to prison.[88] Of these accused men, William atte Appelton and William Pakke can be identified as fullers in the borough court, where they appeared in litigation that concerned the trade in cloth during the years preceding the revolt.[89] This is consistent with Herbert Eiden's analysis of the rebels' occupational structure in Essex, which noted that one of the characteristics was the high proportion of rebels working in the textile sector.[90]

The remainder of the disturbances recorded in Colchester were concerned with violence against Flemings. In 1382, a resident of Colchester, Adam Michel, was excluded from the general amnesty granted by parliament for being one of those who murdered Flemings during the time of the troubles in Colchester, between the end of May and November 1381.[91] This implies that he was probably indicted straightaway after the revolt, and that his guilt was indeed proven. It was only in 1385 that he was granted a pardon by King Richard II for the murder of Flemings.[92] The letters patent actually specify that he was one of the ringleaders of the revolt in Essex, and that this was the reason he was excluded from the general amnesty in 1382. This may, in fact, be brought into question indirectly through a case at the borough court of Colchester related to disturbances arising from the revolt. On 30 December 1381, Walter Baker was charged with a violent assault on Laurence Cobeler at le Southsherde on Sunday 16 June; Laurence

[84] Cooper (ed.), *The Victoria History*, vol. IX, p. 22. [85] Benham, *Court Rolls*, vol. IV, pp. 52, 56.
[86] *Ibid.* [87] *Ibid.*, p. 52; ERO, D/B 5 CR 21, m. 1d.
[88] Benham, *Court Rolls*, vol. IV, pp. 52, 56; ERO, D/B 5 CR 21, mm. 2, 4.
[89] Benham, *Court Rolls*, vol. III, pp. 43, 183; vol. IV, pp. 56, 72.
[90] Eiden, 'Joint action against the "bad" lordship', 26. [91] TNA, KB 27/502, m. 4d rex.
[92] *CPR, 1381–5*, p. 551.

claimed that Walter injured his left arm with a bow and arrow.[93] In his defence, Walter said that he was put up to it by Adam Michel and a weaver, John Wright, a claim that was disputed by Laurence Cobeler, who replied that Walter had acted independently from Adam Michel and that 'he did so through his own wickedness'.[94] Although the scribes have unfortunately not provided further information about the victim and perpetrator here, elsewhere in the court rolls both Laurence Cobeler and Walter Baker appear as Flemings and might have been the same individuals as the men in the 1381 case.[95] This would then make it a case of trying to settle a personal disagreement during wider disturbances. However, this does not solve the problem of those unnamed Flemings who were allegedly killed by Adam Michel and a group of rebels associated with him. If we look at his prior dealings with immigrants in the borough court, there is nothing to suggest that there had been an ongoing dispute between natives and foreigners such as there was in London. Adam was twice in direct contact with immigrants from the Low Countries before the revolt. In 1367, he was a pledge to prosecute for John Bailly, a Fleming, in a case of trespass against Henry Duale and was also accused of debt by William de Gaunt in respect of a sale of wax.[96] However, even if there had been no observable violence on Adam's part prior to the revolt, that does not mean that there was no resentment of foreigners.

The revolt in Norfolk started on 14 June in Thetford, when the rebels threatened the mayor and other residents with fire if they did not pay them.[97] The revolt spread in the following days to Lynn, Norwich and other towns in the county, spreading to around 150 localities mentioned in the sources as being touched by the general insurrection.[98] Both Réville and Walsingham have argued that there was no other county where simultaneous acts of the rebellion were so widespread or the participants so numerous as in Norfolk.[99] What distinguished the county of Norfolk from other parts of England was that the main goal of the rebels during the first days of insurrection was theft.[100] No murders or ransacking took place in the west part of the county; the rebels took both money and goods from the people they considered wealthy and

[93] Calendared in Benham, *Court Rolls*, vol. IV, p. 66, but the case is a lot more detailed in the manuscript: ERO, D/B CR 21, m. 12d.

[94] *Ibid.*, 'quod fecit per maliciam suam propram'.

[95] Walter Baker appears on a few occasions in cases where he sold cloth. See Benham, *Court Rolls*, vol. IV, p. 183.

[96] *Ibid.*, vol. II, p. 167. [97] Réville, *Le Soulèvement*, p. 85. [98] *Ibid.* [99] *Ibid.*, p. 84.

[100] *Ibid.*, p. 86. For events in Norfolk during the revolt, see also Eiden, 'Joint action against the "bad" lordship', 5–30.

politically influential, under the threat of murder.[101] This situation changed when the mob reached Lynn and joined with local rebels who were already in the process of pillaging the town. When the revolt started in Lynn, on 17 June 1381, there were around thirty rebels, all of them local craftsmen. The main concern of these rebels in Lynn was to find traitors.[102] For them, the Flemings apparently fell into that category. Indeed, John Spanye, cordwainer, Thomas Colyn, tailor, John Whetweng, weaver, Henry Cornish, glover, Walter Prat, glover, and John Pynchebeck, tailor, all from Lynn, were indicted for the murder of Hankyn Flemyng, which allegedly happened on 18 June 1381.[103] The following day, the same group of craftsmen, led by a cordwainer, John Spanye, started moving towards a village near Lynn called Snettisham.[104] They were indicted because they 'incited the people of that vill to rise up against the peace of the lord king [and] to seek men of Flanders, so as to kill and decapitate them'.[105] In 1383, John Spanye was granted a royal pardon. It was claimed that he had been a chief captain during the revolt and had killed a man of Flanders of unknown name, but the the bishop of Norwich, Henry Despencer, claimed that he was not guilty, but the victim of slander.[106] As in London, we may note that the rebels from urban areas were mostly artisans. Herbert Eiden has argued that the number of participants from the clothing sector in Norfolk was noticeably high, and he managed to identify thirty-four of them.[107] What is interesting here is that this group from Lynn specifically targeted Flemings both in Lynn and in Snettisham. Moreover, from their occupations one may also note that they were active in the same crafts in which immigrants from the Low Countries were the most numerous: cordwainers, tailors and weavers. Therefore, under the excuse of looking for traitors, they might just have wanted to get rid of competition.

On 19 June 1381, the insurrection reached Great Yarmouth. The evidence from the available judicial records and secondary sources suggests that there were no rebels from the town itself. Great Yarmouth was attacked by two groups of rebels from the surrounding villages in Norfolk and from the neighbouring county of Suffolk.[108] Both Prescott and Reville have argued that Great Yarmouth and its townsfolk

101 M. Muller, 'Conflict and revolt: The bishop of Ely and his peasants at the manor of Brandon in Suffolk c. 1300–1381', *Rural History*, 23:1 (2012), 1–19.

102 Réville, *Le Soulèvement*, p. 96.

103 TNA, KB 9 166/1, m. 73.

104 See also Réville, *Le Soulèvement*, pp. 96–7.

105 TNA, KB 9/166/1, m. 67: 'incitavit homines dicte ville ad surgendum contra pacem domini Regis ad querendum homines patrie de Flaundres ad eos occidendos et decapitandos'.

106 *CPR, 1381–5*, p. 272. See also Réville, *Le Soulèvement*, p. 162.

107 Eiden, 'Joint action against the "bad" lordship', 28.

108 Réville, *Le Soulèvement*, p. 109.

suffered a lot in the revolt, since the rebels were interested only in destroying the privileges of this town. Indeed, in 1379, at the parliament of Gloucester, Great Yarmouth had received trading privileges that were resented by the surrounding towns. The port town was given a charter which stipulated that no one, apart from the people of Great Yarmouth, could buy or sell goods in seven places surrounding the town. Moreover, it granted them jurisdiction over the port at Kirkley Road in Suffolk and control of the sale of herring.[109] Basically, the charter gave to the burgesses of Great Yarmouth the monopoly over trade in its surrounding area, touching both the villages in east Norfolk and in neighbouring Suffolk. Therefore, it does not seem strange that this town was attacked by two groups of rebels, one coming from Norfolk and the other from Suffolk.

The town was penetrated on Tuesday, 18 June 1381 by the group from Suffolk, led by a knight, Roger Bacon. First and foremost, the rebels' demand of the Great Yarmouth officials was to surrender the aforementioned charter of privileges. Naturally, the rebels tore it into pieces, so that no one could claim these monopolistic privileges again.[110] By this time (18 June), the troops of Roger Bacon were joined by those led by Geoffrey Lister, a dyer and infamous leader of the revolt in Norfolk.[111] They went to the houses of the customs collectors, Hugh Fastolf and William Elys, and took the rolls of the customs accounts that they had on them, as well as £600 in cash.[112]

As in London, the rebels broke into a local gaol and released the prisoners. When they broke into Great Yarmouth's prison there were four inmates, three Flemings and one native: Copin Sele de Cirice (Zieriksee), John Rosendale, Copin Ysang and John Cook de Coventry. According to the indictment, under the orders of Geoffrey Lister the group beheaded the three Flemings and let John Cook go free.[113] Obviously, the Flemings were specifically targeted here as well.

109 *Rotuli Parliamentorum*, vol. III, pp. 94–5; Reville, *Le Soulèvement*, p. 109; Prescott, 'Judicial records', p. 99.

110 Réville, *Le Soulèvement*, pp. 109–10; Prescott, 'Judicial records', p. 99.

111 On Lister, see Réville, *Le Soulèvement*, pp. 100–2.

112 *Ibid.*, p. 111; Prescott, 'Judicial records', p. 99.

113 TNA, KB 9/166/1, m. 83 : 'Predicti Rogerus Bacoun, Galfredus Lyster, et socii sui, predicti vi et armis contra pacem dominum Rege, die mercuris proximo ante festum Sancti Johannis Baptisti anno supradicto, gaolam domini regis in dicta Jernemouth felonice fregerunt et prisones, videlicet Copyn Sele de Cirice, Copyn Ysang, Johannem Rosendale, extraverunt et decapitaverunt et Johannem Cook de Coventry liberaverunt.' The same text is recorded at TNA, KB 9/166/1, m. 88; TNA, KB 145/3/6/1. Also, in Réville, *Le Soulèvement*, p. 110 n, there is a transcript of the last document; the only thing is that Réville made a minor mistake and transcribed mercuris (Wednesday) as martis (Tuesday).

This is one of the rare documents where the exact names of the Flemings murdered are reported. Andrew Prescott has argued that the execution of the three prisoners was carefully reported, since the town was liable for any escapes from the prison due to negligence.[114] In this case, it provides us with names that we can trace in the court rolls of Great Yarmouth and gives some background to the Flemings murdered during the revolt.

The three foreigners in question appear only a few times in the court rolls of Great Yarmouth before 1381, but unfortunately the pleadings do not provide many details about their occupations or relationships with the natives. The three of them appeared in February 1380 in the same session of the petty pleas in trespass cases accusing the same group of people – William Bever, John Pitcherew, John Deyerop and Jacob Johneson de Dordrecht.[115] The cases did not continue in later sessions, which suggests that they were settled outside court. The only further information known about these three individuals is that Copin Sele was from Zieriksee, Copin Ysang from Dordrecht and John Rosendale from Brabant. A few indications suggest that they might have been involved in the cloth industry. On 29 December 1378, on the boat of Henry Claissone from Vlarding, Copin Ysang exported 5 ells of broadcloth, alongside William Bever, who exported 3½ sacks of wool. William, whom all three victims were to accuse of trespass just over a year later, was himself a Fleming, a wool-dealer, and certainly a resident of Great Yarmouth.[116] The evidence here suggests that the victims were probably residents of Great Yarmouth: not only did they stay long enough to get indicted, captured and then imprisoned (albeit for an unknown reason), they were also already present and active in trade two years before the revolt. This unfortunately does not explain whether they had any disputes with the rebels who ransacked the prison in Great Yarmouth. While the attacks on Flemings in Essex could be linked to prior personal disputes, it seems that the foreigners killed at Great Yarmouth were targeted for being foreigners.

THE AFTERMATH

After a month of major disturbances, the Peasants' Revolt of 1381 did not result in any general improvement of the lives of the poorer classes, but it did have unintended consequences for alien artisans. It seems that the massacre of Flemings in London marked a turning-point in the lives of immigrant textile workers from the Low Countries who remained in

114 Prescott, 'Judicial records', p. 99.
115 NRO, Y/C4/91, m. 4.
116 *Bronnen*, ed. Smit, doc. 576, p. 319.

England. Most of the indicators that have been used throughout this book to show their importance for the development of the English cloth industry started to go into reverse immediately after 1381. The decline of their significance within the trade was visible both in terms of numbers and status.

In London, this is possible to observe through the number of masters elected as bailiffs of the alien weavers' guild. As explained in previous sections, with the support of the crown alien weavers were granted the privilege of forming their own guild in 1352 and acting separately from the association of native weavers. As with any other recognised craft in London, from that moment onwards their ordinances were approved by the mayor and aldermen, which allowed them to regulate the work of other alien weavers by themselves. The names of the masters elected annually to observe these ordinances were recorded regularly in the city's Letter Books.[117] The number of masters presented by craft associations in London varied from two to six:[118] the richer and more important the craft, the higher the number of masters. For example, trades that dominated the political and economic life of the city, such as grocers, drapers or mercers, presented six masters annually, while tanners, hurrers (hat-makers or -dealers) or cappers (cap-makers) each presented two.[119] Apart from the dyers, who presented between two and four, other textile workers, such as fullers or shearers, elected two masters each throughout the second half of the fourteenth century. Because of the ongoing dispute over the associations of weavers in London presented above, a compromise was found between native weavers, Brabantine weavers and Flemish weavers, who each elected two masters annually to observe the ordinances. For the first fifteen years after the approval of the alien weavers' ordinances in 1352, the bailiffs were elected exclusively from the ranks of Flemish exiles. But the increase in immigration of textile workers from the Duchy of Brabant in the 1360s provided the Brabantine weavers with the numerical strength to impose their own two representatives in 1366. This arrangement would last until 1381. In the years following the revolt, only two masters, one Fleming and one Brabanter, were elected to represent 'foreign' weavers. While the number of elected masters being halved clearly represents a loss of political importance, there are some indicators that the overall number of alien weavers also dropped. Between 1352 and 1381 there was a good rotation among alien weavers, no master being elected more than once as bailiff (Table 3.5). This changed drastically from 1381 on, and the office

117 *Letter Book G*, pp. 2, 16, 48, 104, 131, 237; *CPMR*, vol. II, p. 84.
118 Barron, *London in the Later Middle Ages*, p. 207. 119 *Letter Book H*, p. 41.

began to revolve around only a small number of individuals. For example, Peter Egelyn, Peter Van Braughin, Ralph Clofhamer, John Van Severne and some other alien weavers were all elected as bailiffs more than twice.[120] This strongly suggests that the pool of masters to draw upon had been considerably reduced after the revolt.

A lack of textile workers from the Low Countries is even more visible in the borough court rolls in Colchester and Great Yarmouth. Some of the prominent members of the immigrant community did not leave England after 1381, but apprentices and younger immigrants who could have taken up their role became less visible. A good few might have moved to the countryside, or even returned back across the Channel. The key figures amongst the textile workers from the Low Countries that we can find in various legal disputes during the years preceding the revolt, such as James Pappe, John Van Rouns and Paul Barremaker in Colchester, or John Witbrood and Lippin Sceepstale in Great Yarmouth, continue to appear in the court rolls for several years after the massacre. However, following their disappearance from the sources sometime around the end of the 1380s, presumably after they had passed away, their businesses seem not to have been taken over by other Flemings. As was presented in Chapter 2, an increase in new textile workers with Dutch names in the borough court rolls may be observed throughout 1350–70. This was not the case throughout the 1380s, and the profile of the newcomers started to change. Most of them now appearing in the leet-court, such as John Gerard, cordwainer, Deric fan Delft, patyn-maker, Albright Cordwainer and Heyne fan Campe, were involved rather in the leather industry and were less numerous than the cloth-makers who had arrived between 1350 and 1370.[121] It should be borne in mind that immigration from the Low Countries did not totally stop after 1381, but there was an overall decrease of new artisans, and especially of those engaged in cloth-making. Towards the very end of the fourteenth and the beginning of the fifteenth century, it would be beer-brewers from the Low Countries who would emigrate to England and play an innovative role similar to that of the Flemish weavers by introducing a new product (in this case, beer) to the English market.[122]

The loss of numerical strength also meant a loss of significance in the production and trade of cloth. In Chapter 4 it was shown that, of all the textile workers in London, it was immigrant weavers from the Low Countries who were bringing the biggest quantities of cloth to the

[120] *Ibid.*, pp. 77, 152, 170, 202, 274, 318, 346, 356, 369.
[121] NRO, Y/C4/100, m. 13; Y/C4/101, m. 11d; Y/C4/102, m. 10d.
[122] Pajic, 'Ale for an Englishman', 285–300.

alnager in the 1370s. These accounts do not survive in the capital for later periods, but the particulars are available for the towns of Colchester and York for some of the years during the 1390s. Out of 3,256 cloths of assize brought to the alnager in the city of York in 1394–5, only 3 were sealed by an immigrant weaver, Godfrey Van Upstal.[123] He was one of those immigrants from the Low Countries who had lived in York since at least 1375, when he was admitted into the franchise, but he is also the only individual with a Dutch name who appears in this account. A similar picture prevails in Colchester. Only one Fleming, Henry Lyndholte, was amongst 189 individuals who paid the alnage subsidy between 1395 and 1397.[124] Henry might have been the son of the Flemish fuller John Lyndholte, who appeared regularly in the borough court of Colchester between 1365 and 1384. In both Colchester and York more than half of the cloth in the alnage accounts was alnaged by a small group of men, consisting of mercers and drapers. Heather Swanson was able to positively identify sixty-six mercers and twenty-six drapers from York who brought cloth to the alnager. Some of them individually alnaged more than thirty cloths. Conversely, only fifteen weavers or tapiters can be found, and they never accounted for more than three cloths individually.[125] In the accounts for Colchester some fullers can be identified, but sales were dominated to a large extent by those who monopolised municipal power.[126] It seems that the weavers from the Low Countries who had dominated the cloth industry in terms of numbers, skills and output did not lose their position to native fullers or weavers, but rather to drapers and other mercantile elites. The native cloth-workers, instead of improving their own position to the detriment of the foreigners, managed only to help the elites increase their dominance and cement the fullers and weavers into a subordinate position for the remainder of the late Middle Ages.

CONCLUSION

The chronicles and official accounts report that there were some fifty Flemings who were murdered by the rebels in London, and across various places in Norfolk and Essex. The names are recorded of only four of the victims (in Great Yarmouth and Maldon), while the others were simply reported as 'men or *frows* of Flanders', which does not allow

[123] *The Early Yorkshire Woollen Trade: Extracts from the Hull Customs Rolls and Complete Transcripts of the Ulnagers' Rolls*, ed. J. Lister (Cambridge, 2013), p. 92.

[124] TNA, E 101/342/9, m. 10d.

[125] Swanson, *Medieval Artisans*, p. 36.

[126] Britnell, *Growth and Decline*, p. 127.

us easily to conclude why Flemings were targeted. However, the massacre of thirty-five to forty Flemings in Vintry Ward provides reason to believe that these Flemish victims were probably for the most part weavers who had settled in England during the reign of Edward III. Firstly, most of the immigrants from the Low Countries in London were weavers, and they had settled in parishes around the River Thames where the incident took place. There was, secondly, also the ongoing dispute with native weavers about the chartered freedoms and privileges in the capital. Native weavers found that the king's grant allowing aliens to organise their own guild violently clashed with their own exclusive right to control drapery production in London. From 1352 onwards, native weavers resorted to parliament, the usual channel of political communication, to convince the crown of the need to obtain the incorporation of the Flemish cloth-makers into their (the natives') guild. But the English king, arguing that the unhindered work of the immigrants benefited the common profit of the whole realm in a way that transcended the interests of any particular group of workers, remained deaf to the natives' concerns for over two decades and consistently blocked every attempt at discussion, even when other requests to restrict the activities of alien residents were granted. These frustrations effectively escalated into the bloody massacre of Flemings in the capital in June 1381.

The killing of Flemings also took place at Great Yarmouth and Lynn in Norfolk, and Colchester, Manningtree and Maldon in Essex, but on a much smaller scale than in London. In all cases where these incidents are documented, they are individual murders and not instances of organised violence as in London. This would suggest that some of the killings of Flemings in East Anglia were settlings of personal grudges, which would not exclude as a motive resentment at the presence of foreigners in these areas. What is certain is that the mass killing of foreigners across different parts of the country had an effect both on those immigrant textile workers who remained in England and on those who planned to come from the Low Countries after 1381. Over the last two decades of the fourteenth century, immigrant cloth-workers lost importance in terms both of numbers of workers and their proportion of the output of cloth. It was not only that their numbers dropped: the constant inflow of other immigrants from across the Channel was also reduced. It seems that news about the massacres discouraged other immigrants from coming to England. While the immigration of textile workers was not officially on the agenda of the rebels, the message that they conveyed through the killing of foreigners was definitely received on the other side of the Channel.

CONCLUSION

The aim of this book has been to examine the impact of the immigrant community on the economy of England and the development of its cloth industry. The main hypothesis was to show that Flemish and Brabantine immigrants had an influence on the development of the English textile industry, which grew exponentially from the mid fourteenth century. I thus undertook to refute the interpretations of several economic historians, such as Herbert Heaton, Henri de Sagher, H. L. Gray, Henry Johnson, May McKisack, Eleanora Carus-Wilson, Jim Bolton, Derek Keene and John Munro, who had concluded in the second half of the twentieth century that this immigration had not contributed to England's economic development.[1] These scholars claimed that the number of textile workers from the Low Countries who came to England had probably been insignificant (some of them estimated that the number was not higher than 200 artisans), and thus incapable of making any impact on the English cloth industry. However, we have seen throughout the book that at least 1,200 artisans immigrated to England between 1351 and 1381.

Yet this study has also gone beyond economic questions and touched upon issues of social integration and cultural influence as well. The reason that we have been able to do so is because the number of Flemish immigrants was a lot higher than previously thought, and the rich evidence they left behind provides us with a representative sample of individuals, allowing us to investigate the life stories of a cross-section of these immigrants in a manner that properly reflects their social diversity (place of origin, gender and status), networks (family, household, community), geographical dispersion (taking in the provincial and rural, as well as the metropolitan, experience), and their distinctive economic and

[1] See Introduction and Chapter 2.

social contributions. From the great variety of sources both in England and on the Continent, we have been able to determine that favourable economic conditions in the second half of the fourteenth century in England, such as the availability of high-quality wool, established urban networks, the crown's immigration policies and a labour shortage due to the Black Death, together made it possible for thousands of men and women from the Low Countries to come and settle in various towns of the kingdom. At the same time, the political situation on the other side of the English Channel went hand in hand with these developments in England. Those Flemish textile workers who decided to side with the English king at the beginning of the Hundred Years War, and turn against the Francophile count, were subsequently exiled 'for eternity'. Some of them already enjoyed contacts with the English capital and some coastal towns prior to emigration, but most of the immigrants, the more humble artisans, found themselves in an environment that was completely new from any point of view. This must have been especially true of those who settled in Colchester, as the town's borough courts had seen no Fleming before 1351.

The exile of well-to-do weaver–drapers from Flanders' most important textile centres reduced employment opportunities for other textile workers in the county, which forced some of them to emigrate to England on a voluntary basis as well. Indeed, because of the vertical structure of Flemish urban guilds, poorer weavers worked for richer weavers who controlled production and sale. After the exile of the elite from the weavers' guild, who were also the ringleaders of the rebellion, many poorer weavers must have followed them to England in order to have work. This emigration was not limited to weavers only, as had been thought in previous studies. They were the most numerous amongst the immigrants and the exiled rebels, but textile workers engaged in other, related crafts followed their path as well. A lack of employment opportunities must have been the primary reason for leaving Flanders, but it is possible that some of the fullers, shearers and tailors were part of the exiled weaver–drapers' wider network before the banishment, and that they fled to England together.[2] The exiles and other immigrants from the Low Countries were followed not only by their wives but also by single

[2] Some of the first letters patent that were granted to individual textile workers from the Low Countries allowing them to set up their trade in England mention that they will come 'with their men, servants and apprentices', suggesting that master weavers probably had several artisans working for them at any one time, *CPR, 1330–4*, p.161; Nicolas Appelman obtained protection for himself and 'other dyers and fullers in his company', *CPR, 1334–8*, p. 500.

women, who played an important role both in English cloth-making and the marketplace.

It is still difficult to determine the exact way the immigrants from the Low Countries chose which towns in England to settle in on a longer-term basis, but some patterns might be observed here. We have seen that Great Yarmouth attracted the highest number of immigrants who originated from Bruges and other coastal towns from the Low Countries. Close contacts prior to 1351[3] between merchants and fishermen from Great Yarmouth and the Zwin estuary towns played an important role here. Business partnerships from before the exile were probably a determining factor in the decision to settle in this port town, and in Norfolk in general. The same goes for Ipswich and other places in Suffolk, along with towns in Lincolnshire such as Boston and Lincoln, whose trade with Bruges dates back as far as the twelfth century.[4] Information flows about the possibility of economic engagement in these regions probably came directly from the mercantile community and mariners. But we have seen as well that the immigrants from the Low Countries would not hesitate to change their locations in England, once the economic or personal situation in the initial destination became unfavourable.

It is obvious that London, as the capital, presented better employment opportunities and so attracted the highest number of immigrants. However, it seems that London was reserved principally for immigrants of better standing from Ghent, Bruges and Ypres. We have seen that those who settled in London fared a lot better than those in other English towns from both an economic and political point of view. The exiles in London produced higher-quality cloths and were the only ones among those who settled in urban areas in England to obtain ordinances from the crown and organise themselves into a guild separate from that of the English weavers. The situation was similar in the county of Norfolk, where the existence of an established cloth industry (in the towns of Norwich, Lynn and Great Yarmouth) that was already known in European markets attracted numerous textile workers from the Low Countries. Very quickly after their arrival, the immigrants created business partnerships with wool-growers from the region and organised the whole process of cloth manufacture themselves.

When it comes to Colchester, it is unlikely that this was a principal choice of the immigrants. Colchester's cloth-making industry was still in its early stages of development before the 1350s, and it was certainly not

[3] Kerling, *Commercial Relations*, pp. 125–9.

[4] Bailey, *Medieval Suffolk*, p. 158; M. Bailey, 'Technology and growth of textile manufacture in medieval Suffolk', 13–20.

on the European map as a textile centre during the biggest wave of influx of Flemish textile workers in 1351. Those who settled in Colchester probably made their decision once they were already on English soil. Colchester was the first urban area on the east coast between the ports of Maldon and Manningtree and the city of London. Flemings who disembarked at these two Essex ports might have planned to go on to London, but eventually they stayed in Colchester after they realised that the guild-regulated and highly restrictive textile workforce in the capital would be quite an obstacle to the search for a better life. Conversely, Colchester's lack of formal associations and rather loose regulations concerning the newly arrived cloth-workers presented them with better possibilities for economic integration. Other towns, particularly those with an established infrastructure for developing cloth manufacture, like Coventry, Bristol, York and Salisbury, also saw a steady influx of immigrants from the Low Countries during the second half of the fourteenth century. Although the number of surviving sources for these towns is rather low, they still confirm a pattern of continual migration and effectively complement our story.

Immigrants from the Low Countries seem to have had good personal relationships with their compatriots and even formed their own fraternities. However, even though they were a tight-knit community, they clustered together in neighbourhoods where native textile workers also lived, and seem to have worshipped in the same parish churches as their native counterparts. These English neighbours were, for the most part, their business partners, and the fact that they were surrounded by them resulted in the immigrants integrating to a large extent in a manner that resembled the English lifestyle. For example, this is particularly visible in the ways in which immigrants from the Low Countries made bequests to parish churches and fraternities frequented by natives. We can also observe that their production methods were slightly changed once they had settled in England in order to fit in with the rules of the market. For example, immigrant weavers in Colchester had no problems working on russets.[5] This flexibility in lifestyle and adapting to English rules probably helped a good deal in increasing the immigrants' success in cloth production.

In terms of manufacture, the immigrants certainly brought skills and introduced new types of cloth. The most important type here would be the production of rays, which in turn enhanced the development of different production techniques. For example, weavers from the Low

[5] See Chapter 4 and the case between Stephen Baroun and John van Rouns.

Countries certainly had to employ the services of native fullers, shearers and dyers, since the immigrant labour force engaged in this craft probably could not meet the demand for the number of cloths they produced. This in turn increased the quality of production and the ability of native cloth-workers to become more competitive on the domestic market as well. The immigrants' greatest contribution, however, was that they had brought with them not only the craft skills but also the practices in the organisation of manufacturing that would later be imitated by English clothiers in the fifteenth century.[6]

Another important novelty of this study is the examination of the role of immigrant women in the English cloth industry. Women represented around 14 per cent of all immigrants from the Low Countries who appear in the sources. We can confirm that half of them came to England with their husbands, as evidenced by the payment of the poll-tax returns of married couples, or by their appearance in court records as part of husband-and-wife business partnerships. Female immigrants, like their male counterparts, were mostly engaged in the production and sale of cloth. Because of the nature of the sources, where women are hidden behind coverture, the evidence suggests that immigrant women from the Low Countries predominantly worked in the preparatory stages of cloth production, such as washing, combing, carding and spinning the wool, and that some of them also earned their living as weavers or seamstresses. However, the extent of immigrant women's involvement in the sale of cloth as well as the purchase, export and distribution of wool, especially during widowhood, suggests that they had an important role in managing the family business and were not limited to lower-paid activities only.

Some of the exiles returned to Flanders when general pardons were offered in 1359, and we saw in Chapter 1 that, as in other revolts, this only produced a new wave of rebellions and again a return to England.[7] It was less common for exiles to return to Flanders than one might expect. The surviving wills of immigrants suggest that no return had been considered in most cases. Only those who possessed political leverage and a guaranteed position as an officer of the guild were particularly likely to return to Bruges or Ghent. Others, even if they did return, would generally come back to England after a short while. We must take into account the fact that some of these textile workers

[6] Lee, *The Medieval Clothier.*

[7] For the pattern of pardoned exiles throughout the fourteenth century being able to regroup after returning to the Continent and organise a new rebellion before being banished again, see Dumolyn and Pajic, 'Enemies of the count and of the city'.

were probably exiled at a very young age, and so their formative years would have been in England. If some of them spent their time in England from the age of 19 to 29, the uprooting from their home county must have been quite profound, and the possibility of return equally difficult. However, we have seen that those who came to England kept in contact with Flanders through the mercantile networks, and, sometimes, their relatives were sent to serve apprenticeships with them in England.

The massacre of Flemings in London in June 1381 must be placed in the context of English weavers' growing discontent over the previous decades. The natives' guild had tried in vain to reach a political solution for its problems with the Flemish cloth-workers for over thirty years; the attacks happened only months after its latest attempt had been rejected by the crown. One of the reasons the rebels targeted Flemings during the revolt of 1381 was the fact that those involved in the textile industry were the most numerous and the most visible group of aliens to live in England. A couple of years before that, in 1379, a new revolt occurred in Flanders, commonly known as the Ghent War.[8] Initially, a lot of rebels, mostly textile workers, were again exiled, but there is no evidence that these rebels emigrated to England to the same extent that their compatriots had done in 1351. The tragic events of 1381 in London had the effect of reducing the numbers and importance of textile workers from the Low Countries in England. This is visible in the decrease in the number of cloths they produced, and in the number of masters, as well as in the lack of newcomers from the Low Countries who worked in the textile sector. The massacre of Flemings in 1381 during the Peasants' Revolt certainly did not entirely stop the influx of immigrants in later periods, as the recently finished project at the University of York testifies.[9] The presence of immigrants in general, and of those from the Low Countries in particular, remained steady over the entire fifteenth century. What changed, however, was that textile workers became a lot less numerous. Artisans were present, but they were now engaged in the production of beer and ale, as well as in the leather industries. We might therefore consider that this pioneering movement, the fourteenth-century emigration of Flemish textile workers, opened the door for other groups to come to England, as in a way it pushed the royal authorities to see the economic potential, and to reframe their immigration policies accordingly.

[8] R. Demuynck, 'De Gentse oorlog 1379–1385: Oorzaken en Karakter', *Handelingen der Maatschappij voor Geschiedenis en Oudheidkunde te Gent*, New Series, 5 (1951), 304–18.

[9] See www.englandsimmigrants.com and other outputs of the project.

Appendix 1

LIST OF REBELS BANISHED FROM BRUGES 1351, 1361, 1367, 1369

The translation below is compiled from the cartulary called Groenenboek, held at the city archives in Bruges. These are the copies of documents from 1351, 1361, 1367 and 1369, written in a fifteenth-century hand, containing the names of people who were banished after the disturbances during the aforementioned years. The original list with the names of rebels exiled in 1351– fols 110–18 – also survives in the city archives (SAB, Politieke charters 1e reeks, no. 497). Three other waves of banishments from the 1360s are recorded only in Groenenboek. The total number of rebels banished from Bruges in these lists is 1,042. These documents are connected with the list of pardons granted to about 1,500 rebels exiled from Flanders in 1359 and transcribed in *Cartulaire des Artevelde*, pp. 711–34. Numerous individuals from the Bruges list below appear there too, but we can see straightaway that not all textile workers exiled from Bruges were offered pardons.

SAB, GROENENBOEK C, FOS110R–118R, COPIED FROM SAB, POLITIEKE CHARTERS 1E REEKS, NO. 497

[Original in Middle Dutch:] On the fourth day of October 1351, the count himself, his council and the aldermen of Bruges proclaimed the following people enemies of the count, of the city and of the commons. They were expelled for eternity from all the count's lands because they made alliances with foreign countries, and should anyone within the county house them or help them he will be considered in the same manner.

Michiel van Assenede dictus vat
Lauwers Waye
Robrecht de Rouc
Willem Bateman
Pieter seer Aernouds
Jan Dadelare
Pieterkin Streeckaerd
Jan de But dictus van Leke
Lammin de Jonghe
Jan van Aeltre
Jan van Langhevoorde
Pieter van Heurssele

Jan Moenaerd
Pieterkin van Zwevesele
Jan van Gavere dictus Helsene
Jacob van Ziessele
Loy van Lenscote
Claeis van Zeerkengheem
Lamsin de Keyser
Gillis de Pape
Jan van Trieren
Colaerd de Kelsiedere
Gillis de Coning
Joris de Rovere
Aernout vanden Wielkine
Moenin de Vos
Pieter Wijt
Baudet van Lake
Jan Wormhont dictus Buekelare
Hannin Uuten Riede
Hannin Biesebout met ere hand
Lamsin van Keyheem
Lamsin Feys
Jan Veldacker die bailgiu was
ten Houtschen
Gheeraerd van Lo
Joos de Keiser
Jacob van Winghene filius Jan van Winghene
Jan van Winghene filius Jan van Winghene
Clais van Winghene filius Jan van Winghene
Lamsin Haghelsteen
Jan vander Rehaghe
Willem Diederix
Christiaen Sceefbeen
Jan vanden Dike de vulre
Zegher Castelein
Jan Tinke
Wouter van Ansame
Jacop van den Driesche
Gillis Roodsaerd
Jan Ghentelin
Jan de Zot de Jonghe
Clais Laudaet
Pieter vande Rehaghe
Jacop Cortebrugghe
Lamsin de Vos
Jan Scone Jans
Jacop Veys
Jan van Coukelare f. veraghetcn

Gillis van Coudebrouc
Jacop Witte Bolle
Gillis Hooft f. ser Wouters
Gillis Lam
Pieter Gabbaerd
Bernaerd Gallin
Jan Roodsaerd Doude
Jacop vanden Abele
Jan Duetel
Heinric vanden Muelne
Christiaen Locgaerd
Pieter de Terningmakere
Boudin Snidewind
Wouter Vizael
Pieter Ybeloot
Pieter Spore dictus Moyt
Jan de Werd Doude
Henric Vluegaerd
Rignaerd Gallin
Boudin Wenins
Olivier Veldacker
Jan van Orscamp dictus man
Jan van der Mane
Jan van den Hoghenweghe
Maertin zijn broedere
Jacop van Beernheem (Claikin Beernehem, poorter is pardoned)
Pieter Uten Wissele
Jan de Waerd de Jonchere
Wouter Dommel
Willem de Vriend
Gillis Hooft disercoopere
Jan van Cranenburch
Jan Moyt
Lauwers Moyt
Symoen Dabt
Hannin Mansel
Mathijs vander Scuere
Pieter Puetin
Gillis Brantin
Michiel Balewaerd
Jan Maertin de Wevere
Hannin van Spaengen
Pieter Beyaerd
Clais Dedding
Coppin van Lo
Coppin vanden Driesche
Jan van Lisseweghe de ionghe

Jan aderic de ionghe
Jan van Ghent
Jan van Sinte Cruus de Jonghe
Jan Melgewaerd vanden berghe
Jan van Lo
Pieter van Sceepstale dictus leestkin
Pieter Knye (Maes 1359)
Joos Hemelrike
Gheerkin van den Eechoute
Jan Potterkin
Pieter Joye
Willem de Maerscalc
Coppin van Oudenburch
Coppin Lam Willems
Jan de Knuut
Gheerkin Immeloot
Hannekin Rycquaerds
Andries Joiaerd
Pieter van der scelle
Martin vander Scelle
Christiaen Bertolf
Heinric de Meyere
Christiaen Pec
Meeus de Hoyere
Jan van Artrike de Meseeus
Hannin vander Helpe dictus Grave
Fierin Bibau
Hannekin vander Duve
Jan Loud
Jan van Oudenburch sonder Zorghe
Pieter van Zwevesele
Hannin Moenins de Boetere
Jacop de Coc de Boetere
Hannin van den Steene de Wevere
Gillekin de Melkere dictus Aermeziele
Hannekin Dobbelrose
Jan f. Clais Maes
Boudin van Trieren
Clais de Crudenare
Willem de Coning
Jan Everaerd de Makelare van Colen
Wouter Bulc
Jan de Crudenare
Meeus vander Leye
Jacop Bonthond
Lauwers de Hond de Wulleslare
Pieterkin de Smet der Stede Gaersoen Was

Jacob Dabt
Jan Gallin
Pauwels Bode vander Vischmaerct
Jan van Male de Vulre
Jacop de Deken
Pieter Gallin f. Jans
Jan van Ypre f. Jacops
Jan van Oudenburch de Selversmit
Pieter van Ghistele die Scaerwettere
Boudin Bret
Hannin van Biervliet
Coppin van Ghent
Jan van Ghent
Coppin Willaerd
Hannekin de Mandemakere
Hannin de Beere
Coppin van den Walle de ionghe timerliede
Jan vanden Walle de Jonghe timerliede
Coppin Benne
Jan van Assenede de Bonte
Jacop Sobbe
Jan Duvekin
Michiel Cornelis
Jan Beerhout f. Claus
Gillis van Bassevelde dictus Maes
Jan Ravens f. Martins
Pieter Aechte
Lamsin Winne dictus Muelnare
Jan Zelverin
Theeus Vande Rehaghe
Clais de Kersghietere Doude
Jan Vizael
Jan van Arssebrouc
Alaerd De poortere dictus Rikebake
Heynekin Quintin
Lammekin Vanden Riede
Jan vanden Riede
Jacop Sine
Sentkin de Scuetelare
Arnoud de Buf
Rike Musche
Jan Boele
Pieter Denaerd
Jan de Veltere
Elond Bune
Danin vanden Velde
Michiel van Stuutvelde

Roeger Coopal of Clapal
Gillis van Wackene
Jan Cricke Doude
Jan Oem Willems
Clais Oem Willems
Wouter Blijfhier
Jan Caepoud Doude
Jan Caepoud de Ionghe
Lauwers Vluegaerd
Hannin van Oostburch
Aernoud Broeder
Ghijs van Lo
Pieter Diederic f. Jans
Naes Karstinman
Hannin de Keyser f. Clais
Lauwers Roodsaerd
Pieter van Coolkercke de Scerre
Clais van Zeland
Lamsin de Coning
Jan Minne f. Jans
Willem van Axele
Lamsin Veys
Willem Varshinc
Gillis Moerhinc
Rike Gallin
Lippin van Slipen
Colin Edelman
Tideman de Vos
Pieter Boomgaerd
Hannin Laudaet
Jan Teunis
Kielaerd Tinke
Boudekin Veldacker
Jan de Man f. Seer Pieters
Wouter de Keyser
Pieter Everaerd
Wouter Laudaet
Pieter Refin
Hannin de Doelre f. Hueghs
Jan vander Lanterne
Diederic Ketelhoed
Franse van Jabbeke
Christiaen vander Scelle
Hannekin Sarrasijn f. Maes
Gherard vande Dwerstrate
Jan van Oudenburch f. Jans
Willem Lam

Jan van Ansebeke f. Clais
Pieter Veltacker
Pieter van Maerkijs
Jan van Pedsebrouck
Zegher van Poelvoorde
Jan Care
Lamsin de Sceppere
Willem van Oorscamp
Claikin de Bedelare
Jan de Moor f. Jans
Lauwers zijn Broeder
Wouterkin Moordonc
Coppin Steen de Wevere
Lippin Teurnekin graenwere tauwer
Jan Coene graenwere tauwer
Jan van Bredene graenwere tauwer
Coppin de Vriese graenwere tauwer
Wouter de Verse
Jan vander Niewerpoort, Scheerder
Ghildolf vander Houte Scheerder
Ghiselin van Vinct Scheerder
Claikin vanden Driesche dictus
Royaelkin
Michiel Lauwers
Joos van den Dike
Hannekin de Vos f. Jans
Hannin van Cortrike
Pieter upt Hoghe
Coppin Tienpond
Jan de Clerc de Hudevettere
Jacop van Jabbeke Doude CleetCoopere
Willem Cosijn
Jan de Besemmakere
Hannin dictus Paedse
Jan van der Naelde
Pieter vanden Vivere
Wouter Landaet
Willem vander Lo wevere
Pieter de Gast wevere
Jan de Vinc de Witledertau-Were
Coppin van Vinc sijn broeder
Boudekin Veltacker de Vulre
Claikin van Asschen de Vulre
Jan de Rode f. Meester Pieters van Zunnebeke
Hannin Corthals
Hannin Spinrocke
Claekin van Cruninghem wulleslare

Roegear Fallaes wulleslare
Jacop de Coning de Hudevettere
Jacop Wouterman
Willem de Walcherling
Pieter Hancke
Martin Karstinman de Strikere
Willem vanden Hille Doude
Jan Pelewelling
Willan de Bey
Clais de Wankere
Michiel van Oudenburch
Jan Aderic Doude
Jan van Oudenburch Dictus van Colemiers
Pieter Hildebrant dezwerteledertauwere
Jan van Praet
Jan Stoorm de Wijnmetere
Jan van Lopheem
Jan Reingoot
Jan de Rode
Pieter Wouters
Gille de Hond
Jan van Zoetenay
Herreman van Hinchoud
Rike Curre
Wouter Coolsaet
Jan Quareid
Wouter de Haerst
Gillis de Mueselare
Jacop vander Rehaghe
Joos Heeme
Symoen de Wide
Pieter van Scaerpenessen
Jan Dommel f. Wouters
Clement van Coukelare
Coppin van Vinct dictus van Zeverne
Renier Chapelain
Jan Rose
Meeus Moenin
Andries Blondekin
Pieter Gallin
Groote Michiel
Wouter Hooft f. Ser Jans
Pauwelin Matte
Ghildolf Joosep
Clais Daniels
Jacop de Grant
Clais de Meestere

Pieter de Bul
Pieter de Mommelare
Jan Bolleman
Jan van Wackene
Pieterkin Streckaerd
Clais de Zoutere
Martin Coopmans f. Ser Martins
Joris Bortoen
Jan van Bassevelde f. Clais
Clais Coopman f. Martins
Coppin Danijd
Jan de Moor
Jan de Drussate
Michiel Rose
Christiaen de Mesmakere
Hannakin van Coolkercke f. Wouters
Jan de Grant
Coppin Daniels
Pauwels van Muelnebeke
Michiel van Muelnebeke
Martin van Jabbeke
Lammekin Bredebolle
Renier de Lombaerd
Jan Rose
Gillis Stankin de Vulre
Magherman Seer Jans knape van
Couckelare
Maes Aderic
Hannin Heile
Hannin van Zeland
Wouter de Ruddere
Moenin Meestercoc
Hine van Zwevesele
Coppin van Zwevezele f. Claren
Jan Melgewaerd
Hannin Sarrefijn f. Jans
Robin Loddier
Pieter van den Driessche
Hannin Aloud
Mewelin Daens
Willekin Vander Cappelle
Clais Paelding
Boudin van Ardenburch
Willem van Praet
Willem Drinkaluut

The number of named exiles adds up in total III^{c} LXXXIII [383]

Appendix 1

SAB, POLITIEKE CHARTERS 1E REEKS, NO. 497

The above 383 names that appear in the fifteenth-century copy of Groenenboek are also recorded in the charter collection of the Bruges municipal archives called 'Politieke charters', and in the same order. However, the following names are to be found only in the latter document:

Pieter le Pape
Jaqueme Bollin
Quintin Dankaerd
Jehan le Vos f. . . .
Hannekin le Vos ses fier
Jehan vandenbourgh f. Jan
Jehan Spore
Jehan le Stier
Pieter de Ste Crois le Jouene
Hannekin Clai
Hannekin de Courtray
Hannekin le Ruddere f. Huon
Pieter Medinoghe de Jonghe
Sandres Crayc Sanders
Jan Aderic de Vielx
Willemme Checouke
Jehan de Zomerghem
Heinryc van Gotheem
Gheraerd li Roys
Pieter Everaerd
Leurenc le Scotelare
Pieter Hildebrand
Jehan Baes
Jehan le Clerc
Thumas Stalpt
Jehan de Praet
Jehan Quacthano f. Jehans
Jehan le Landshere
Jehan de Liere
Jehan li Sages dictus Ostburgh
Baudin de Colkerke f. Levins
Franch Snieuien
Lamsin dele Lys
Lexis le Sceppere
Pieter f. Langheghcraerds
Jehan Adelaerd
Wautier de Leke
Robin de Mons
Jehan de Lo
Willaume Uten Coten

Vroomkin de Straten le Jouene
Willaume de Siesele dictus Hellenaghe
Pieter Dardembourgh
Jehan Denys
Pieter Pool
Arnoud Pool
Caprike li Foulon
Willaume Gherolf
Jaqueme Gherolf
Jehan Gherolf
Jehan le Lappe
Lonis Le Bourghque
Jehan de Dudsele f. Jehan
Clai le Riemakere Dictus Leu
Stasin Banin li Vielx
Stasin Banin li Jouene
Thumas Knie
Jehan de la Chapele
Jehan Ballinq li Foulon
Clai Cheneye
Pieter Boudz le tisseran
Jakene Weynins
Nicole Weynins
Wille Dele Bussce
Nicoles Ackerman
Jehan Hulle li Foul
Jehan le Rochlare
Pieter de Zevencote
Pieter de Sante Croys
Jehan Wullepond
Wauter Loue li Fourier
Hanin de Gand
Willem Adelaerd Li Tisseran
Pieter Ruebin Li Foul
Coppin Gallin Li pissonier
Jehan Massemijn
Jehan Dansebeke f. Sire Gille
Jequeme de Stachille li Vielx
Weynin f. Arnoul
Pol de Leffinghe
Lamsin Yperlinc

[Original in French:] The following people are banished by law and by judgment of the aldermen of the city of Bruges on the grounds that they have caused rebellions and conspiracies in the said city and the county of Flanders against the count and against the city:

Jehans Maldehem li fevre
Lamsin li Ruems li cordouanier
Jehans van der Holst dit Baraed
Jehans de Varsenare fevre
Jehans Melghewaerd tisserans
Daniel Leire cordouanier
Jehans Oestelmare cordouanier
Gossins Splecce cotourier
Jaquemes Veys tisserans
Lamsin Sceperre tanere
Pierres Wouter tanere conleriers
Jehan de le Zwijnehaghe tisserans
Pierres li Roi Viesvarier
Jehans du Croissant tonderes
Gillis Lam
Gillis Berempoet tisserans
Jehan Everart cordouanier
Clais Zweije hurhuies
Jaquemes de le Vmege conelier
Michiel Cornelis houihies
Joris Duvekin houhies
Gilles Ghijs barbier
Clais li Vos parmentier
Jehans Losekin tiserans
Jehans Ravens fil Martins hourhies

On the IX day of September LXI

Willems du Pont
Jehans Berout fils Nicolai houchies
Boudins li Grise houchies
Gerard de Lo tonderes
Andreus Houikere cordouanier
Gillis de Breda cordouanier
Pierres de Risele cordouanier
Jehans de Wachtere cordouanier
Jaqueme de Lo
Lamsin Cornelis houchiers
Woutre Vule
Jehans f. Gillis dict. Slonaert
Jehan du Dam tailleur
Lamsin le Lievre tailleur
Jehans Maes filius Pieron tisserans
Jaqueme van Naelde bastard tisserans
Willem le Jaghere foulon et barbier
Gillis Veldacker folons
Pierres Tollin cordouanier
Pol de Assenede

On the XIIII day of September LXI

Jehans Godevard tisserans ou folons
Woutre Moocgher folons
Johan de Sperille cordouanier
Michiel Ponriment cordouanier
Tristrans Ghijs barbier
Pierres de Thielt tisserans
Philips de Lewe fever
Jehans Daens cordouanier
Colin Duvekin houchier
Pierres le Mor seman fevre
Jehan de Naelde
Jehan Rapegheer cordouanier
Lievin le Hert meedeghereeder
Daniel le Mol barbier
Pierres le Smit f. Pieter tisserans
Christian Hildrichem condour
Jehan le Walsche canderlier
Jaqueme Drieghe canderlier
Pierres du Fosset canderlier
Pierres li Cuiet conletier
Lamsin d Colkerke dit scuerzac folons
Loy van den Oede anketonier
Anthonie Grant Christian faiseur de bourses
Amand de Assche folons
Jaqueme de Saint Crois fevre
Willem Cousijn Kendeilleur
Jehan de oostborch dit le sag candelier
Jehan Rose candelier
Jehan du Fosset candelier
Jehan van de velde
Jaqueme de Tielt fevre
Lamsin de Sainte Crois fevre
Jehan Poitevine
Robin Melleward candelier
Willem Balleke dit de Lichtervelde
Jehan de Ronde cordouanier
Ghildolf Roel houchies
Henri de Ghelre cordouanier
Francois de Brune cordouanier
Pierres Strite cordouanier
Jehan le Roi fil Gherard cordouanier
Jehan le Chien
Clais Strobant cordouanier
Jehan Rijx tisserans
Jehan de Lo tisserand
Jehan le Meestre tisserand

Lippin van Sceepstale tisserand
Clais de Wisant tisserand
Michiel de Stitvelde dit Stupart tisserand
Willems de Hofstede boulanger
Henri du Mond boulanger
Willems du Ham boulanger
Jehan le Blawere boulanger
Jaquemes le Carpentier boulanger
Jehan Wijtsghate cordouanier
Jehan de le Tour tanneur
Michiel de le Mote fevre

On 28 September 1361, each banished for six years

Jehan de Mendonc
Nicoles de Colkerke poingier
Willem de Miesport fasent dank
Andrier de le Cappelle cordouanier
Pierres Teises
Lamsin de Wachtere
Pol Bode
Ormone Cranekin
Clais Pas
Jehan Vranke
Maes de Coppenolle
Clais Wenis fil Piters houchier
Clais Wenis fil Clais houchier
Gabriel de Maldeghem
Jehan de Buurt
Theeus de Zomergheem
Clais le Makelare f. Clais
Mestre Jehan Jomineel dit de le Crois barbier
Jehan Brandijs candelier
Willems vallet Jehans de Maldegheem fevre
Philips de Wissighem
Feins van der Matte tisserans
Jehan Pacelin tisserans
Pierres Aloud folons
Andrieu Bodekin
Giselin Coudscuere folon
Willems Adighem folon
Jehan de Redelem f. Marote tisserans
Jehan Aket tondeur a grande forche
Lamsin Gheleman
Jaqueme Lam tisserans
Willems Coudscuere
Jehan Daens tisserans
Copin Baderel

Michiel Goethrouc dit bon enfant
Pierres Wadepoel
Heine de Caestre vieswarier
Lievin de Bare
Phillip Canon conletier
Jehan de Caetselare tisserans
Clais van den Weghe lanie
Willem de Wyt couletrer
Jehan le Zelverin
Jehan le Vos tisserans
Pierres de Namur folon
Pol du Vos tailleur de draps
Daniel van den Wale faiseur danketons
Hannin Moens faiseur des bourses
Hannin le Bitre
Woutier le Vieswairier
Giles le Mostre couletier
Jehan de Leke f. Marie
Jehan Loscart broutrier
Theeus Brouteur
Coppin le Pappe
Pierres du Chelier
Coppin de le Chappelle tisserans
Jehan de Daverlo tisserans
Katherine Zorgheloos
Jehan de Breede
Gilles Wideleman
Willems de Kieldracht
Jehan van den Vorne
Pierres le Fevre lanie tisserans
Willems Calfnel
Mestre Jehan le Bliec barbier
Simon de Baillene
Jehan Michiel vallet Michiel de le Motte
Jehan Goetghenoot tisserand
Jehan de le Mote tisserand
Jehan de Capelle dit le conte tisserand
Pierres Frere tisserand
Hannekin de Cappellebrouc tisserand
Jehan le Brouckere tisserand
Pierres Spore dit Moye tisserand
Clais Brand cordouanier
Jehan Nulanamie?
Cent Kempe
Pierres de Drivere cordouanier
Lievin de Ichtighem
Jehan Collin

Jehan de Cupre cordouanier
Jehan Wuitghate
Jehan Dec
Willem de Zuttere cordouanier
Pacelin de Oudembourg
Jehan Flameng tisserans
Wouter Ruwersinere vis
Jehan Bile vis
Gillis de Werd tisserans
Jehan le Werd tisserans
Jehan Moyt poigneur de maisons
Theeus Frere folon
Pierres Namur folon
Lamsin Colkerke folon
Jehan le Blondere folon
Gillem Everard
Jehan f. Riquard cordouanier
Pieterkin de Sceepstale
Jehan de Marc boulangier
Jehan Lotin boulangier
Pierres Tasin fondeur de candeilles
Leuxis ou Leuxens de Mots fevre
Pierres le Onghereede mannier
Henry de Heyman
Jehan Muike
Coppin de Bassevelde dit porteur de Koessins
Clais Tibelin tisserans
Jehan de Tielt chanetier
Pierres le Lepelare
Pierres le Gentil
Wulfrant de Saint Jaqueme
Pierres de Saint Amand
Jaqueme foundeur de Klokes
Lamsin le Wachtre f. Pierron faiseur de pots destain
Jehan Labbe

On XXVIII (month missing) LXIIII for disturbances (van tensemente)

Jehan le Chien tisserans
Jehan Hameman tisserans
Jehan le Blawere
Gherard Clot ou Cloot tailleur de draps
Jehan de Rumbeke boulangier
Riquart Staltin tailleur de draps
Jehan de Grawelinghe boulangier
Boudekin Grijse f. Boudin
Jehan Bollekin fondeur de candeilles
Wouter Coolzaet folon

Andrieu Blondekin lanie folon
Wautier le Mercier
Ruebekin de le Wale
Jehan de le Wale
Willem Colpart
Jehan f. Boudin
Godevart le Cnoc
Alaerd f. Henry fasaint les bourses
Jehan Losekin f. Jaqueme Losekin tisserans
Jehan de Ghistele tisserans
Thieri de Maldeghem tisserans
Jehan de le Sachele fondeur de bol
Jehan de Pape sommeur de klokes
Ormone Frere
Coppin de Oudembourgh
Coppin Deboud
Jehan Walop
Jehan de Vrien ? foulon
Jakeme Coene carpentier
Jehan Trise dit boulangier
Jehan Hoyere broeder Jans
Jehan le Teghelare
Guille Guiselin
Jehan Scilleman
Guille le Tensere
Woutier le Haerst teinturier
Josses Slipen
Pol Stolpart tisserans
Willem de Ruesselare fevre
Jehan le Jomme soient le Vos
Jehan Veltaker
Gilles de Daverlo cordouanier
Clais Coppiere f. Jehans
Jehan de Thoroud qui fu begars
Woutier de le Mine cordouanier
Pierres de Thoroud tisserans
Simon de Smontere
Jaqueme Brant cordouanier
Willem Keyt cordouanier
Simon Tolfin tisserans
Pierres Calewart cordouanier
Pierres Tollin cordouanier
Jehan Danid cordouanier
Elisabette femme Jehan Oosterman
Coppin le Barbier de Saint Omer
Jehan de Maldegheem cordouanier
Henry de Maldigheem

Guille Rose tisserant
Jaqueme Dulle cordouanier
Boudin Tuesaet cordouanier
Pol le Ruts
Guille de Drayere
Jehan ver Johan
Jehan le Vos
Pierres Cortebrueghe f. Jehan
Jehan Zeeman cordouanier
Christian le Stamere cordouanier
Pierres le Guester cordouanier
Lievin vallet de Jehan Oosterman
Guille Bijl porteur de carbons
Coppin Wautier Weits
Jehan de Boodt
Coppin de Thueet faiseur du [?]
Gherkin Vanghelin
Guille Casin
Philips Colpart
Pierres Moordost
Gillis Slimpin
Hectoor de Wachtere machon
Jehan le But machon
Jehan le Vos dit Veys
Jehan Reiment
Belle Goedinghes
Jehan de Saint Trude
Lem le Mersier
Philip Oste
Willem van den Hille f. Wautier
Jehan Diere
Henri le Grise
Lamsin Goetweet
Ormone de Dordrecht dit Mont
Gilles de Hasebrouc
Jehan de Merendre
Jehan le Ruevelmakere
Pieter Maes
Hanse qui ot le fille Jorge Heldebolle
Lamsin Crippinc viswarier
Gillis de Keyheem
Sohier du Vos tondeur de Gand
Jehan le Simersake fevre
Daniel Mande
Michiel le Mol
Sohier del Atre
Andreu le Hamer f. Jehan

Laurens Smalaert
Manassis Ruevolin
Jehan le Vos porteur du poisson
Coppin Losscart
Pierres le Frison
Coppin de Assenede houchier
Jehan Maes tisserans
Jehan Munekin manier
Jehan le Raed f. Simons
Christian Ribout tailleur de draps
Pierres Markijs folon
Leurens le Man f. Pieron
Wouter Colzaet folon
Clais Muilaert folon
Meeus Melgeward folon
Loy van den Oede faiseur danketous
William de le Lepe
Pierres de Calkere mester descole
Pierres Gerard carpentier
Jehan le Bitere viswarier
Jehan Piereman maronier
Jaquemes de Ledeghe carpentier
Jehan Buf tisserans de lin
Pieres Lormier
Jaqueme le Boulangier tisserans
Pierres de Graweninghe boulangier
Thierri de Wy tailleur de draps
Daniel van den Walle faiseur de danketons
Henin de Zelande
Boudin de Grave ommireur de cordes
Pierres le Vos viswarier
Jehan Stelart
Guille le Ruede
Pierres le Hardere
Jehan de le Wastine le mercier
Jehan le Weerd tailleur des bourses
Jehan de Ruede cordouanier
Jehan Wampnet folon
Oernoul Sohier dit cormuit
Coppin Musebek mannier
Pierres de Loden maronier
Pierres de le Hane f. Ernoul van Lichtervelde
Jehan Wanimot foulon
Ghiselin Coudescuere foulon
Jehan de Strates bastart
Lievin del Angele faiseur de pourpoing
Hannekin le Marissal

The number of individuals named above adds up to iiiC LXXI [371]
Collacionne...

The individuals here named are the enemies of the count, of the city and of the commons and are expelled for eternity from Flanders. Their return within the lands of Flanders would only be possible by the will and consent of the count, of his cities and of his common lands. Acted and approved on XX day of August 1367 by the aldermen Jan van Risele and Joris van Tielt

Clais van Coolkerke de schilder
Willem Meuwerpoort de porpointstickere
Andries de Cappelle cordouanier
Pieter Trise de handscoenwerker
Lamsin de Wachtere
Arnout Cranekin vander Vismaerkt
Jan Vranke
Maes van Coppenholle
Clais Weins
Clais Weins vleeshouwers
Gabriel van Maldengheem
Jan van Buict
Hannekin van Dudsele de peinre
Meester Jan Tomineel dictus van der Cruse baerdmakere
Jan Brandijs de Ketelare
Willem Jans Knape van Maldegheem smeds
Philips van Wisheem
Theeus van Zomeergeem
Feins van der Matte wever
Jan Pacelin wever
Pieter Aloud vulre
Andries Bodekin
Ghiselin Coudscuere
Willem van Adegheem vulre
Jan van Hoedeleem f. Maro
Jan Aket scerer
Lamsin Gheyleman
Jacop Lam wever
Willem Coudscuere
Jan Daens wever
Coppin Badereel wulleslaer
Michiel Goedjonc doctus Goedkint wulleslaer
Pieter Waedpoel
Heine van Caestre houdcleercopere
Lievin de Baerd
Philip Cannoen makelare
Willem Wyt makelare
Jan van Catselare wever
Clais van den Weghe doude
Jan de Zelverinc

Jan van den Busche wever
Pieter van Namen vulre
Pauwels van den Busche sceper
Danijn van den Walle culcstriker
Hannin Moens buersemakere
Hanin de Bitre
Woutre doude Graeuwereker
Gillis de Meestre makelare
Jan van Leke f. ver Marien
Jan Losshaert cardewaghemeruder
Theeus de Pijnre
Coppin de Pape de peinre
Pieter uten Kelnare
Coppin van der Cappelle wever
Jan van Daverlo wever
Catheline Zorgheloos
Jan de Breede
Gillis Wideleman
Willem van Kieldracht
Jan van den Vorne
Pieter de Smit doude wever
Willem Calfnol f. Willems riemakkere
Meester Jan de Wioc baerdmaekere
Symoen van Belle
Jan Michiel knape van den Walle
Jan Goedghenoot wever
Hanin van den Walle wever
Jan van der Cappelle wever
Pieter Broeder wever
Hannekin van Cappellebrouc wever
Jan de Brouckere wever
Pieter Spore dictus Moye wever
Clais Brand cordouanier
Jan Mulamene
Cent Kempe
Pieter de Divere cordouanier
Lievin van Jchtenghem
Hannin Tollin
Jan de Cuppre cordouanier
Jan van den Wintgate
Jan Dec
Willem de Zuttre cordouanier
Pasin van Oudenburch
Jan Vlaminc wever
Wouter Ruwescnere oudwercker
Hanin Bile oudwerker
Gillis de Weerd wever

Jan de Weerd wever
Hannin Moite
Theeus Broeder vulre
Peter van Namen vulre
Lamsin van Coolkerke vulre
Jan de Blonder vulre
Gillis Everard
Jan f. Riquards cordouanier
Pieterkin van Sceepstale
Jan Maet backer
Jan Lotin backer
Pieter Casin keersegnieter
Lueris of Laurens de Smit van Mot
Pieter Donghereede molinar
Heine van Heiman
Heine Muike
Coppin van Bassevelde dictus de carsdragher
Clais Tibelin wever
Jan van Tielt oudstromakere
Pieter de Lepelare
Pieter van Edelmic
Wullfrand van Sint Jacobs
Pieter van St Andries
Jacop de Clorchnote
Lamsin de Wachter f. Pieters
Jan de Abt
Jan Walop
Jan van Vuren vulre
Gillis Gherard vulre
Jacop Coene
Jan Trise dictus de baker
Jan de Hoyere f. broeder Jans
Jan de Teghelare
Willem Ghiselin
Jan Schileman
Willem de Toyzere
Willem de Haerst barbier
Joos van Slipen
Pauwels Stalpart wever
Willem van Ruesselare smit
Jan de Jonghe zagher
Jan Veltacker
Gillis van Daverlo cordwainer
Clais Coppin f. Jans
Jan van Thoroud de begare was
Wouter van den Mude cordouanier
Pieter van Thoroud wever

Simon de Smontre
Jacob Brand cordwainer
Willem Keyt cordwainer
Moenin Tolfin wever
Pieter Calewaert cordvainer
Pieter Collin cordouanier
Jan Danijt cordouanier
Lijsebette Jan Oostermans wijf
Coppin de Baerdmakere van St Omaers
Jan van Maldegheem cordouanier
Heyne van Maldegheem
Willem Rose wever
Jacop Dulle
Boudin Toyzart cordouanier
Pauwels Cuts smit
Willem de Drayere
Jacob Scone Jan
Jan de Vos lormier
Pieter Cortebrueghe f Jans
Jan Zeeman
Christian de Scavere cordouanier
Pieter de Guestre cordouanier
Lievin Jan Oostermaers knape
Willem Byl de cooldraghere
Coppin Woutier Weits
Jan de Boodt
Coppin van Treet de scoenmakere
Gherkin Vanghelin
Willem Casin
Philip Colpaert
Pieter Moordhoost olislaegher
Gillis Slimpit machon
Ortour de Wachtre machon
Jan de But machon
Jan de Vos dictus Veys strodecker
Jan Clement stroodecker
Jan van Sinte Truden
Lievin de Moorseman
Lippin Oste
Willem van den Hulle f. Wouters
Jan Diere
Heyne de Grijse
Lamsin Goodweet
Aernout van Dordrecht dit mont
Gillis van Hasebrouc
Heyne van Moorendre
Hannin de Ruewelmakere

Pieter Maes wiltwercker
Anse du Joris Heldebolle dochter hadden
Lamsin Knippin huidevetter
Gillis van Keygheem peinre
Zegher van den Busche van Gent Nayere
Jan van Simmersacker
Coppin de Hond
Clais Sleepstaf
Hannin Oste de cordouanier
Jan de Wilde de scrivere
Clais Coppin de huidewercker
Jacop Hooft f. Jacops

The number of people written on the roll above iC xvii [107]
Another roll of exiles

Boudin Wemmis
Rike Musche
Bernaerd Gallin
Hannin de Vriend f. Willems
Hannin Dankaert handscoemaker
Hannin de Zot kindscoemaker
Aernoud de Zwijnarde
Coppin de Popinghen
Hannin van Assenede f. Pieters
Quintin de Jchtinghem
Jan Capegheer cordouanier
Hannin van Wingheene
Jan Weits
Jan van Thoroud
Pieterkin de Neve
Willem de Neve
Gossin de Jchtingheem cordouanier

All banished for six years from Flanders for disturbances [*van tensemente*] on xxiiii day of January 1369 Lxix

Appendix 2

LIST OF PEOPLE BANISHED FROM DIXMUIDE WHO WERE OFFERED A PARDON IN 1361

This document is preserved in the departmental archives in Lille. Most of these names match the names of rebels from Dixmuide, banished in 1351 for their involvement in the general rebellion and who were offered a pardon in 1359 (*Cartulaire historique et généalogique des Artevelde*, ed. De Pauw, pp. 711–34). It follows from this that numerous exiles did not want to return from England in 1359 and that another general amnesty was proposed in 1361.

SOURCE REFERENCE: ADN, SÉRIE B, 1566, FOLS 21–2

14 February 1361

The following people from Dixmuide, who were previously banished from Flanders for rebellion, are granted grace by the count under condition that they take an oath never to rebel again against the count or to make alliances with the deans of weavers. Given by Janne den Corenlose, Clays Voet, Pieter Bonin, Lamsin de Rassche, Pieter den Keiser, Jan de Vassere, Pieter Gherolf, Clais Sconepape, Jan Relm, Jacop den Suut, Jacop van Roeselare, Willem de Breden ende Clais Brant, aldermen of Dixmuide on xiiii February 1361.

Teerst

Clais Pacelin
Clais van der Beke doude
Hannin Balkaerd
Coppin Balkaerd
Gillis Relm
Clais de Bune
Pieter Sprint
Hannin van Leide
Clais van Leide
Tierin Naghel
Christian Heem
Anthinis van de E
Claikin Pottin
Collin Adaem

Jan Ysac
Paulin van den Boongaerde
Andries Mane
Moenin van den Boongaerde
Forteneus van Zuduit
Michiel Molensteen
Rogier de Vassere
Jan Anfoort
Jan de Cupere de wevere
Frans Palm
Jacop van Zuduut
Jan de Suucht bi der Halle
Jan Kielm
Jan Kielm f. Pieters
Loy de Ionghe
Tierkin Tars f. Tierins
Hannekin Tars f. Jans
Jan van Cleerken
Jan van Cleerken de bastaerd
Gillis de Tolnare
Jan Boideman de parmentier
Jan Boideman de scoenmalere
Willem de Bomere
Lauwers de Bomere
Clays Witte
Arnoud Bone
Clays de Laye
Hannoot de Laye
Frans Baudaerd de bastaerd
Clays Baudaerd f. Jans
Willem van Sinthomaers
Willem Boodsaerd de bastaerd
Gillekin Boorsaerd f. Gillis
Gariet de Baertmakere
Jan Zeghers
Frans Lodewijc
Jake Bake
Willem de Ionghe
Barnabas de Vleeshouwere
Martin Cools
Clays van Cleerken
Kerstiaen Sconepape
Lammin Verachten
Willem de Buit f. Willem die met heet Vuxkin
Jan Bone
Lammekin de Keyser
Kerstiaen f. Lammin Zoets

Lievin f. Lammin Zoets
Vedast Masiin
Frans de Darsschere
Wouterkin Mane
Coppin van den Boongarde
Willem Clays
Gillis Slabbaerd
Andries van den Heymeldale
Hannin de Vulre
Jan de Kaesmakere
Jan van Viven f. Frans
Lammin Coudinc
Coolkin Coudinc
Willem Josep
Jan de Kaesmakere de wevere
Jan Lermin de vulre
Pieter Alwillems
Pieter de Wulf
Ruebin Sterus
Gille de Vos
Lammin de Vos
Jan Godseide de wevere
Jan Godzede de wulre
Jacop de Wulp
Andries Coren
Clays de Pottre
Hannekin de Pottre f. Clays
Jan Pinin
Michiel de Kerke
Frans Gosemarijn
Pieter de Visch
Franskin Michiel
Hannekin Michiel
Pieterkin de Raed
Jan de Madre zuduut
Jan de Drayere
Coppin de Drayere
Claikin Muesin
Martin de Vannemakere f. Martins
Willem Kitte f. Frans
Gille Noyd
Pieter van Viven
Willem de Hane
Claikin Troppineel
Hannin van Lonnen f. Maes
Andries de Hauwere
Gille Courtoys

Pieter Courtoys
Loy van Zarren
Gillis Gherard doude
Clais de Hukere de ionghe
Willem van Greweninghe doude
Hannin van Greweninghe f. Joris
Pieter Lauwerin
Thierin Lauwerin
Jan Balde
Hannekin Adaem
Jacop van Tielt
Pieter Cuerdin
Willekin Bernaers
Willekin Kite f. Jans
Jan Kite f. Jans
Jan Bemoot
Jan Lodewijc de verwere
Rogier Anstim
Clays Noid
Willem Dauwelin
Franskin de Vos f. Frans
Claikin de Brauwere
Coppin de Brauwere
Willem Bootsaerd
Jan Cansteel f. Willem
Kerstiaen Cansteel f. Willem
Willem Cansteel f. Willems
Zegher van Loo
Jan de Gheel de ionghe
Jan Saelgeman gheheten blaisoen
Hannekin Saelgeman f. Zuernits
Coppin Honesschegille
Jan Baselis
Jacop de Cammere
Jan Coren
Kerstiaen Lievier
Hannin Pluenis
Jan Palm
Jacop Eleboud f. Clays
Clay Eleboud f. Clays
Drokin Gillis
Willem Barenkin
Gherkin de Burarc
Kerstiaen Andries
Clays van den Moere
Jan Marteel
Willem Tant

Jan de Brune vulre
Andries van Lovene
Clays van Lovene
Jan van Haringhe
Jan Follin doude
Willem de Donimere
Hannoot de Madre
Jan de Madre
Clays Plateel
Thierin de Juede
Lammin de Visch
Gillis Dallin
Bernaerd de Moelnare
Jan de Baenst
Willem Lauwerin
Jacop Lemmin
Willem de Voghel
Willem Aelmare
Jan de Cupere vulre
Pieter Armoen
Andries Keren
Meus de Hertoghe
Ende Jan Kere

Appendix 3

TESTAMENT OF BELIA [MABILIA], WIDOW OF (1) JOHN PETRESSONE CALLED 'EVERSWERD', CITIZEN AND HABERDASHER OF LONDON; AND (2) JOHN OTEMELE, DATED 7 APRIL 1391, PROVED 15 MAY 1391

LMA, MS 09171/001, fos 235v–236r
(Commissary Court of London wills, Register 1, fols 235v–236r)

[*FOLIO 235V*]

In the name of God, amen. I, Belia, who was the wife of John Petressone, called 'Everswerd', late citizen and *haberdasshere* of London, being sound in mind and in my good memory, the 7th day of April, AD 1391, 14 Richard II, establish, make, and ordain my present testament in this manner:

Firstly, I leave and commend my soul to God, and to the blessed Mary his mother, and to all the saints, and my body to be buried in the church of St Martin Orgar *iuxta Candelwykstrete*, London, namely, annexed to the body of the said John, late my husband. To the new work of the said church, 40d. To the high altar of the said church, for my forgotten oblations, 3s 4d. To the light of the Holy Cross on the high beam in the same church, 12d. To the old work of the church of St Paul, London, 3s 4d. To the Carmelite friars of *Fletestrete*, London, 3s 4d for a trental for my soul. I leave £4 sterling to be done and distributed among paupers for my soul and for the souls of my husbands, of our parents, and of all those to whom I am bound, and of all the faithful departed.

To Katherine my sister, £16, six silver spoons, one mazer, one feather-bed, two pair of sheets, 2 chalons, 2 *pelughes* (pillows), and cloths for my body, and all my kerchiefs, except for the cloths and veils bequeathed below. To William Mummard my kinsman, 60s sterling, and to each of his children, 6s 8d. To Katherine, wife of the said William Mummard, one *kertel* [kirtle] of red colour, and one *courtepi* [a short cloak] of *sangueyn* [red].[1] To Margaret the wife of John van Seuerne, one of my best veils [*vnum capitergium de optimis meis capitergijs*].[2] To John son of the said John van Severne, my godson, 6s 8d.

To a certain one called Fulkwyk [*cuidam vocato Fulkwyk*] a veil made from a thread in the manner of work of Paris [*vnum capitergium meum de parysthred*].

[1] William Mummard might have been related to Michael Mommart, a Flemish immigrant who had been living in London since at least 1362 and who passed away in 1370. *Letter Book G*, p. 182; Fitch, *Index Archdeaconry Court*, vol. I, p. 260.

[2] John Fanasseverne was elected and sworn in as the bailiff of the Flemish weavers in 1375, *Letter Book H*, p. 17.

To William *atte Dragon*, 13s 4d, so that he may supervise what good and faithful administration be done of my goods. To Richard Meryweder, 6s 8d on the same condition.

[In the left margin of the above page the scribe has, without further explanation, added]

habet ac
facta est
collacio

[*FOLIO 236R*]

To the kinsmen [*cognatis*] of John Otemele, my second husband, 40s sterling to be divided among them, on condition that they hold themselves well contented for their part concerning the goods of the same John Otemele, otherwise they will have nothing by my legacy.[3]

In the same manner I leave 4 marks sterling to be divided among the kinsfolk of the said John Petressone lately my husband [*gentes de parentel' dicto Johannis Petressone nuper mariti mei*], so that they hold themselves well contented for their part concerning the goods of the same John Petressone, otherwise they will have nothing by my legacy.[4]

The residue of all my goods, chattels and debts, wheresoever they be, I leave wholly to John Olyuer, my kinsman and apprentice, without any inventory to be made thereof, to bury my body and to pay my debts wherein I am bound, and to do for me as he would wish that I would do for him in the same case [*et ad faciend' pro me sicut vellet quod fecerem pro illo in eodem casu*]. I leave to the same John Olyuer all my terms to come of my house [*mansionis mee*] in which I dwell in *Candelwykstrete*, London.[5] I also leave and remit to the same John Olyuer all my terms to come of his apprenticeship. I pardon Alice Balewalke of 6s 8d of the debt that she owes to me.

Of this my testament I make and constitute the said John Olyuer my executor, and as his supervisors the said William *atte Dragon* and Richard Meryweder.

In witness whereof I have put my seal to this present testament. Given at London, the day and year aforesaid.

This present testament was proved before us, president of the London consistory at London, 17 Kal. June, AD 1391 [15 May 1391]. And administration of all the goods and of all things concerning the testament of the deceased was committed to the executor named in the testament. In witness whereof, the seal of the Official of London was appended to these presents. Given at London, the day and year abovesaid.

[END]

[3] John Otemele stood surety for the bailiffs of the Flemish weavers in London in 1366, *CPMR*, vol. II, pp. 65–6.

[4] In 1385 the couple is mentioned in the will of Lelia, widow of Peter Blawer, who passed away that year, and so Belia married her second husband before that; see Appendix 4.

[5] It seems that her second husband, John Peterson, bought this house in Candlewick Street in 1375; *CPMR*, vol. II, p. 209.

Appendix 4

TESTAMENT OF LELIA, WIDOW OF PETER BLAWER, CITIZEN AND DYER OF LONDON, DATED 13 OCTOBER 1385, PROVED 7 JANUARY 1386

LMA, MS 09171/001, fs 225v–226r
(Commissary Court of London wills, Register 1, fols 225v–226r)

[*FOLIO 225V*]

In the name of God, amen. I, Lelia, who was the wife of Peter Blawer, dyer of London, being sound in mind and in my good memory, the 13th day of October, AD 1385, 9 Richard II, establish, make and ordain my present testament in this manner:[1]

Firstly, I leave and commend my soul to God, and to the blessed Mary his mother, and to all the saints, and my body to be buried in the church of St James Garlickhythe next to my husband, if possible, for 2s 6d paid for the work of the said church, or wherever God may otherwise arrange. Also, to the high altar of the said church, for my forgotten oblations, 40d. Also, bequests to master clerk 12d and subclerk 6d. Also, I bequeath to the fraternity of blessed Mary at the abbey St Mary Graces by the Tower of London, 22d. Also, to Guydo Flaccard, 40d. Also, to John de Pape, who was my tailor, 2s 6d. Also to a certain Gys Deigher, 2s. Also I bequeath 40s sterling to John Dankart, my relative, who is living with my brother, John Ewersward.[2] The residue of all my goods, chattels and debts, wheresoever they be, I leave wholly to Mathilde, my daughter, and if something should happen to her while still a minor, I leave all these goods to John Ewersward, my brother, and John Dankart, my relative, guardians of said Mathilde, together with the goods entrusted to them.[3] Of this my testament I make and constitute the said John, my brother, my executor and Mabila, his wife, the administrator of all my goods. In witness whereof I have put my seal to this present testament. Given at London, the day and year aforesaid. I also leave all my ventures in my house together with the Stew house [*le Stuwhous*] in Medelane in the parish St James Garlikhythe to my brother, John Ewersward.

1 Peter Blower/Blawer, dyer, had passed away a year earlier. His will was proved in the London Archdeaconry Court but survives there only as an entry in the table of contents; the earliest extant wills in Register 1 commence in November 1393. Fitch, *Index Archdeaconry Court*, vol. I, p. 40.

2 The Latin is *cognato meo*, which can also mean her brother-in-law, or just a relative.

3 Her husband Peter Blawer and her brother John Ewersward seem to have done some business deals in partnership, *CPMR*, vol. II, p. 284.

This present testament was proved before us, 'Presidente Cons*istorio*[?]' at London, 7 Kal. January, AD 1385. And administration of all the goods and of all things concerning the testament of the deceased was committed to the executor named in the testament 'in forma iuris et per eundem admissa'. In witness whereof, the seal of the Official of London was appended to these presents. Given at London, the day and year abovesaid.

[END]

SELECT BIBLIOGRAPHY

MANUSCRIPT SOURCES

London: The National Archives

CP 40: Court of Common Pleas. Terms consulted: CP 40/389, 390, 397, 402, 405, 414, 417, 426, 428, 440 (1350–90).

C 255: Chancery files – miscellaneous files and writs (1371–2).

E 13: Exchequer's Court (1350–90).

E 101: Exchequer, King's Remembrancer: Various accounts (alnager's accounts), London, Colchester, Winchester, York E 101/340/ 22; E 101/340/23; E 101/342/9 (1373–98).

E 101: Exchequer, Various accounts: Roll of Expenses of the Great Wardrobe, E 101/394/12 (1362–3), E 101/402/13 (1392–5).

E 122: Exchequer, King's Lord Treasurer: Customs accounts, particulars – Boston, London.

E 356: Exchequer, King's Lord Treasurer: Customs accounts (wool and cloth subsidy).

JUST 1: Justices itinerant, Assize Rolls (1350–1400).

JUST 2: Justices itinerant, Coroner's Rolls. Consulted for various counties (1350–1400).

JUST 3: Justices itinerant, Gaol Delivery Rolls. Consulted for various counties (1350–1400).

KB 9: King's Bench indictments. Terms consulted: KB 9/29, 115, 141, 166/1 (1350–80).

KB 27: King's Bench Court. Terms consulted: KB 27/372, 373, 376, 377, 381, 388, 389, 390 391, 392, 394, 396, 400, 401, 405, 406, 407, 409, 410, 411, 412, 414, 415, 416, 417, 418, 419, 421, 422, 423, 424, 425, 426, 427, 428, 429, 430, 431, 436, 437, 438, 439, 440, 441, 442, 443, 444, 445, 446, 447, 459, 466, 485 (1350–90)

KB 145: King's Bench files, *Precepta Recordum* related to the Peasants' Revolt of 1381.

KB 146: King's Bench files, *Panella* related to the Peasants' Revolt of 1381.

SC 2: Manorial Courts. Clare 'Burgus': SC 2/203/55–61; Sudbury: SC 2/204/4 (1350–77).

SC 8: Special Collections, Ancient Petitions.

Select Bibliography

London Metropolitan Archives

Court of husting:
CLA/023/CP: Court of Common Pleas
CLA/023/DW: Deeds
Archdeaconry Court Wills:
MS 9051/1
Commissary Court of London Wills:
MS 9171/1

Canterbury Cathedral Archives

CCA-U15/16/35: Manorial Court Hadleigh

Norfolk Record Office

Borough Court Rolls of Great Yarmouth 1351–90
Y /C4/72–96.
Court Leet Rolls of King's Lynn 1352, 1359, 1375, 1379
KL /C 17/6–10.
Court Leet Rolls of Norwich 1374, 1390
NCR 5b/10–11.

Essex Record Office

Borough Court Rolls Colchester 1351–84
D/B 5, CR 9–25.

Hampshire Record Office

Borough Court Rolls Winchester 1351–77
W/D1/8–15.

Suffolk Record Office (Ipswich Branch)

Borough Court Rolls: Petty Rolls Ipswich 1377–81
C/2/3/1/28–9.

Ghent: State Archives

Fonds: Gent: Oorkonden der graven van Vlaanderen
Fonds: Saint-Genois

Select Bibliography

Ghent: City Archives

The Courts of Aldermen
Serie 301 (Keure)
Serie 330 (Gedele)

Bruges: City Archives

Oud Archief, Groenenboek C
Politieke charters 1e reeks, no. 497
Stadsrekeningen: 1340–67

Brussels: General Archives of the Realm

Rekenkamers: Rolrekeningen, 839–47.
Oorkonden van Vlaanderen 1e reeks

Lille: Archives départementales du Nord

Série B, cartulaires: 263, 1562, 1566, 1595, 1596.

PRINTED SOURCES

Annals of Ghent, ed. H. Johnstone (London, 1951).

The Anonimalle Chronicle, 1333 to 1381: From a MS. Written at St Mary's Abbey, York, ed. V. H. Galbraith (Manchester, 1927).

Bronnen tot de geschiedenis van den handel met Engeland, Schotland, en Ireland, ed. H. J. Smit, 2 vols. (The Hague, 1942).

Calendar of the Close Rolls Preserved in the Public Record Office, 61 vols. (London, 1892–1963).

Calendar of the Fine Rolls Preserved in the Public Record Office, 22 vols. (London, 1911–62).

A Calendar of the Freemen of Lynn, 1292–1836, Compiled from the Records of the Corporation of the Borough by Permission of the Town Clerk (Norwich, 1913).

Calendar of Inquisitions Miscellaneous, 8 vols.: I–VII (London, 1916–68); VIII (Woodbridge, 2003).

Calendar of Letters from the Mayor and Corporation of the City of London, circa A.D. 1350–1370, Enrolled and Preserved among the Archives of the Corporation at the Guildhall, ed. R. R. Sharpe (London, 1885).

Calendar of Letter-Books of the City of London. A–L, ed. R. R. Sharpe (London, 1905).

Calendar of the Patent Rolls Preserved in the Public Record Office, 55 vols. (London, 1891–1916).

Calendar of the Plea and Memoranda Rolls Preserved among the Archives of the Corporation of the City of London at the Guildhall, ed. A. H. Thomas and Philip E. Jones, 6 vols. (Cambridge, 1926–61).

Calendar of Wills Proved and Enrolled in the Court of Husting London AD 1258–1688, ed. R. R. Sharpe, 2 vols. (London, 1890).

Cartulaire de Louis de Male, Comte de Flandre. Decreten van den Grave Lodewyck van Vlaenderen, 1348 à 1358, ed. T. de Limburg-Stirum, 2 vols. (Bruges, 1898).

Cartulaire historique et généalogique des Artevelde, ed. N. De Pauw (Brussels, 1920).

Chronicles of London, ed. C. L. Kingsford (Oxford, 1905).

Codex diplomaticus Flandriae inde ab anno 1296 ad usque 1325, ed. Th. De Limburg-Stirum (Bruges, 1879), vol. I.

Comptes de la ville d'Ypres de 1267 à 1329, ed. G. Des Marez and E. de Sagher (Brussels, 1909–13).

Corpus chronicorum Flandriae, ed. J. De Smet, 4 vols. (Brussels, 1837–65).

The Court Rolls of the Borough of Colchester, ed. W. G. Benham and H. I. Jeayes, 4 vols. (Colchester, 1921–41).

De Dynter E., *Chronicon ducum Brabantiae*, ed. P. F. X. de Ram, 3 vols. (Brussels, 1854–60).

De Klerk J. et An., *De Brabantsche Yeesten ofrymkronyk van Braband*, ed. J. F. Willems and J. H. Bormans, 3 vols. (Brussels, 1839–69).

De Rekeningen der stad Gent: Tijdvak van Jacob Van Artevelde 1336–1349, ed. N. De Pauw and J. Vuylsteke, 3 vols. (Ghent, 1874–85).

Van Duyse, P. and E. De Buscher, *Inventaire analytique des chartes et documents appartenant aux archives de la ville de Gand* (Ghent, 1867).

The Early Yorkshire Woollen Trade. Extracts from the Hull Customs Rolls and Complete Transcripts of the Ulnagers' Rolls, ed. J. Lister (Cambridge, 2013).

The Enrolled Customs Accounts (PRO, E356, E372, E364), 1279/80–1508/09 (1523/24). Part 4: E356/9, E356/10, E356/11, E356/12, E356/13, ed. S. Jenks (London, 2006).

Firma Burgi, or an Historical Essay concerning the Cities, Towns and Buroughs of England, ed. T. Madox (London, 1726).

Fitch M., *Index to Testamentary Records in the Commissary Court of London, Vol. I: 1374–1488* (London, 1969).

Index to Testamentary Records in the Archdeaconry Court of London, Vol. I: 1363–1649, Guildhall Library (London, 1979).

Foedera, conventiones, literae et cujuscunque generis acta publica, ed. T. Rymer, 10 vols. (The Hague, 1745, reprint Farnborough, 1967).

Gentsche stads- en baljuwsrekeningen, 1280–1336, ed. J. P. Vuylsteke and A. van Werveke (Ghent, 1900).

Gentsche stads- en baljuwsrekeningen, 1351–1364, ed. A. van Werveke and H. van Werveke (Brussels, 1970).

The Historical Charters and Constitutional Documents of the City of London (London, 1887).

Inventaire analytique des chartes et documents appartenants aux archives de la ville d'Ypres, ed. I. Diegerick, 6 vols. (Bruges, 1853–68).

Inventaire des archives de la ville de Bruges, Section I: Inventaire des chartes, ed. L. Gilliodts-Van Severen, 9 vols. (Bruges, 1871–85).

Inventaires mobiliers et extraits des comptes des ducs de Bourgogne de la maison de Valois (1363–1477), ed. B. Prost and H. Prost, vol. II (1902–13).

Jamees, A., *Brugse poorters opgetekend uit de stadsrekeningen, Deel 1: 1281–1421* (Handzame, 1974).

L'Estrange, J., *Calendar of the Freemen of Norwich, from 1317 to 1603*, ed. W. Rye (London, 1888).

Leet Jurisdiction in the City of Norwich during the XIIIth and XIVth Century: With a Short Notice of Its Later History and Decline, from Rolls in the Possession of the Corporation, ed. W. Hudson (London, 1892).

Memorials of London and London Life, in the 13th, 14th, and the 15th Centuries, Being a Series of Extracts, Local, Social and Political from the Early Archives of the City of London AD 1276–1419, ed. H. T. Riley (London, 1868).

Munimenta Gildhallae Londoniensis: Liber Albus, Liber Custumarum et Liber Horn, ed. H. T. Riley (Rolls Series, 1859–62).

Nouveaux Comptes de l'argenterie des rois de France au XIVe siècle, ed. L. Douët d'Arcq (Paris, 1851).

The Oath Book or Red Parchment Book of Colchester, ed. W. G. Benham (Colchester, 1907).

The Parliamentary Rolls of Medieval England, ed. C. Given-Wilson et al., 16 vols. (Woodbridge, 2005).

The Poll Taxes of 1377, 1379, and 1381, ed. C. C. Fenwick, 3 vols. (Oxford, 1998).

Records of the Borough of Leicester, ed. M. Bateson, 2 vols. (London, 1899–1901).

The Records of the City of Norwich, ed. W. Hudson, and J. C. Tingey, 2 vols. (Norwich, 1906 and 1910).

Recueil des documents relatifs à l'histoire de l'industrie drapière en Flandre, ed. G. Espinas and H. Pirenne, 3 vols. (Brussels, 1909).

The Red Paper Book of Colchester, ed. W. G. Benham (Colchester, 1907).

Register of the Freemen of the City of York, Vol. I: 1272–1558, ed. F. Collins, Surtees Society no. 96 (Durham, 1897).

Registres aux sentences des échevins d'Ypres, ed. P. De Pelsmaeker (Brussels, 1914).

Rotuli Parliamentorum 1278–1503, 6 vols. (London, 1832).

The St Albans Chronicle: The Chronica maiora of Thomas Walsingham, ed. J. Taylor, W. R. Childs and L. Watkiss, 2 vols. (Oxford, 2003).

The Statutes of the Realm: Printed by Command of His Majesty King George the Third: In Pursuance of an Address of the House of Commons of Great Britain; from Original Records and Authentic Manuscripts, ed. A. Luders et al., 11 vols. in 12, Record Commission (London, 1810–28, reprint London, 1963).

Voorgeboden der stad Gent in de XIVe eeuw (1337–1382), ed. N. De Pauw (Ghent, 1885).

The Westminster Chronicle, 1381–1394, ed. L. C. Hector and B. F. Harvey (Oxford, 1982).

Yorkshire Sessions of the Peace 1361–1364, ed. B. Putnam (Cambridge, 1939).

SECONDARY WORKS

Amor, N., *From Wool to Cloth: The Triumph of the Suffolk Clothier* (Bungay, 2016).

Late Medieval Ipswich: Trade and Industry (Woodbridge, 2011).

Ashley, W., *An Introduction to English Economic History and Theory, Part II: The End of the Middle Ages*, 10th edn (London, 1925).

Auweele, D. van den, 'De brugse gijzelaarslijsten, 1301, 1305 en 1328: Een komparatieve analyse', *Handelingen van het Genootschap voor Geschiedenis te Brugge*, 100 (1973), 105–67.

Bailey, M., *Medieval Suffolk: An Economic and Social History 1200–1500* (Woodbridge, 2007).
'Technology and growth of textile manufacture in medieval Suffolk', *Proceedings of the Suffolk Institute Archaeology and History*, 42 (2009), 13–20.
Baker, J. H., *An Introduction to English Legal History*, 3rd edn (London, 1990).
Balard, M. and A. Ducellier (eds), *Migrations et diasporas méditerranéennes (Xe–XVIe siècles)* (Paris, 2002).
Bardsley, S., 'Women's work reconsidered: Gender and wage differentiation in late medieval England', *Past and Present*, 165 (1999), 3–29.
Barron, C. M., 'The "golden age" of women in medieval London', *Reading Medieval Studies*, 16 (1990), 35–58.
London in the Later Middle Ages: Government and People, 1200–1500 (Oxford, 2004).
Revolt in London, 11th to 15th June 1381 (London, 1981).
Barron, C. M. and Nigel Saul (eds), *England and the Low Countries in the Late Middle Ages* (London, 1998).
Bautier, R.-H., 'La Place de la draperie brabançonne et plus particulièrement bruxelloise dans l'industrie textile du Moyen Âge', *Annales de la Société Royale d'Archéologie de Bruxelles*, 51 (1966), 31–63.
Beardwood, A., 'Alien merchants and the English crown in the later fourteenth century', *The Economic History Review*, 2 (1930), 229–60.
Alien Merchants in England: Their Legal and Economic Position, 1350–77 (Cambridge, Mass., 1931).
Beattie, C., *Medieval Single Women: The Politics of Social Classification in Late Medieval England* (Oxford, 2007).
Bennett, J., *Ale, Beer and Brewsters in England: Women's Work in a Changing World 1300–1600* (Oxford, 1996).
Berben, H., 'Une Guerre économique au Moyen Âge: L'embargo sur l'exportation des laines anglaises, 1270–1274', in *Études d'histoire dédiées à la mémoire de Henri Pirenne* (Brussels, 1937), pp. 1–17.
Billot, C., 'L'Assimilation des étrangers dans le royaume de France aux XIVe et XVe siècles', *Revue Historique*, 270 (1983), 273–96.
Blockmans, W., B. De Munck and P. Stabel, 'Economic vitality: Urbanisation, regional complementarity and European interaction', in B. Blondé, M. Boone and A-L. Van Bruaene (eds), *City and Society in the Low Countries 1100–1600* (Cambridge, 2018), pp. 22–58.
Boffa, S., *Warfare in Medieval Brabant* (Woodbridge, 2004).
Boisseuil, D., 'Le Bain dans les sociétés occidentales à la fin du Moyen Âge', *Studi Storici*, 55 (2014), 365–84.
Bolton, J. L., *The Alien Communities of London in the Fifteenth Century: The Subsidy Rolls of 1440 and 1483–4* (Stamford, 1998).
The Medieval English Economy 1150–1500 (London, 1980).
Boone, M., 'Armes, courses et assemblées et commocions: Les gens de métiers et l'usage de la violence dans la société urbaine flamande à la fin du Moyen Âge', *Revue du Nord*, 395 (2005), 7–34.
'Le Comté de Flandre dans le long XIVe siècle: Une société urbanisée face aux crises du bas Moyen Âge', in M. Bourin, G. Cherubini and G. Pinto (eds), *Rivolte urbane e rivolte contadine nell'Europa del Trecento* (Florence, 2008), pp. 17–47.

'La Construction d'un républicanisme urbain: Enjeux de la politique municipale dans les villes flamandes au bas Moyen Âge', in D. Menjot and J.-L. Pinol (eds), *Enjeux et expressions de la politique municipale (XIIe–XXe siècles)* (Paris, 1997), pp. 41–60.

Geld en macht: De Gentsce statfinancien en de Burgondische staatsvorming 1384–1453 (Ghent, 1990).

Gent en de bourgondische hertogen 1384–1453: Een social-politieke studie van een stats-vorming process (Brussels, 1990).

'Social conflicts in the cloth industry of Ypres (late 13th – early 14th centuries): The Cockerulle reconsidered', in M. Dewilde, A. Ervynck and A. Wielemans (eds), *Ypres and the Medieval Cloth Industry in Flanders: Archaeological and Historical Contributions* (Zellik, 1998), pp. 147–55.

'Une Société urbanisée sous tension: Le comté de Flandre vers 1302', in R. C. Van Caenegem (ed.), *1302: Le Désastre de Courtrai: Mythe et réalité de la bataille des éperons d'or* (Antwerp, 2002), pp. 27–77.

Boone, M. and H. Brand, 'Vollersoproeren en collectieve actie in Gent en Leiden in de 14e en 15e eeuw', *Tijdschrift voor Sociale Geschiedenis*, 19 (1993), 168–93.

Boone, M. and W. Prevenier, *La Draperie ancienne des Pays-Bas: Débouchés et stratégies de survie XIVe–XVIe siècles*, Actes du colloque tenu à Gand le 28 avril 1992 (Louvain, 1993).

'Le Rêve d'un état urbain (quatorzième et quinzième siècles)', in J. Decavele (ed.), *Apologie d'une ville rebelle: Histoire, art, culture* (Antwerp 1989), pp. 81–105.

'Les Villes des Pays-Bas méridionaux au bas Moyen Âge: Identité urbaine et solidarité corporative', *Bulletin du crédit communal*, 183 (1993), 25–42.

Boone, M. and I. Schoups, 'Jan, Johan en alleman: Voornaamgeving bij de Gentse ambachtslieden (14de–15de eeuw), symptoom van een groepsbewustzijn?', in J. De Zutter, L. Charles and A. Capiteyn (eds), *Qui valet ingenio: Liber amicorum Johan Decavele* (Ghent, 1996), pp. 39–54.

Boone, M. and P. Stabel, *Shaping Urban Identity in Late Medieval Europe* (Garant, 2000).

Bottin, J. and D. Calabi (eds), *Les Étrangers dans la ville: Minorités et espace urbain du bas Moyen Âge à l'époque moderne* (Paris, 1999).

Bourdieu, P., 'Le Capital social: Notes provisoires', *Actes de la Recherche en Science Sociale*, 31:1 (1979), 2–3.

Langage et pouvoir symbolique (Paris, 2001).

Bourdieu, P. and Loïc Wacquant, 'The organic ethnologist of Algerian migration', *Ethnography*, 1 (December 2000), 173–82.

Bowden, P. J., *The Wool Trade in Tudor and Stuart England* (London, 1962).

Bridbury, A. R., *Medieval English Clothmaking: An Economic Survey* (London, 1982).

Briggs, C., *Credit and Village Society in the Fourteenth Century* (Oxford, 2009).

'Manor court procedures, debt litigation levels, and rural credit provision in England, c. 1290–1380', *Law & History Review*, 24:3 (2006), 519–58.

Britnell, R. H., 'Colchester courts and court records, 1310–1525', *Essex Archaeology and History*, 17 (1986), 133–40.

The Commercialisation of English Society 1000–1500, 2nd edn (Cambridge, 2009).

Growth and Decline in Colchester 1300–1525 (Cambridge, 1986).

'The towns of England and northern Italy in the early fourteenth century', *Economic History Review*, 44 (1991), 21–35.

Brown, A. and J. Dumolyn (eds), *Medieval Bruges c. 850–1550* (Cambridge, 2018).
Buylaert, F., J. Dumolyn, G. Dupont, J. Haemers and A. Ramandt, 'Political power and social groups 1300–1500', in A. Brown and J. Dumolyn (eds), *Medieval Bruges c. 850–1550* (Cambridge, 2018).
Caenegem, R. C. van, *Geschiedenis van het Strafrecht in Vlaanderen van de XIde tot de XIVde eeuw* (Brussels 1954).
(ed.), *1302: Le Désastre de Courtrai: Mythes et réalités de la bataille des éperons d'or* (Antwerp, 2002).
Campbell, B., *The Great Transition: Climate, Disease and Society in the Late Medieval World* (Cambridge, 2016).
Carlin, M., *Medieval Southwark* (London, 1996).
Carus-Wilson, E. M., *Medieval Merchant Venturers: Collected Studies* (London, 1954).
'Trends in the export of English woollens in the fourteenth century', *The Economic History Review*, 3:2 (1950), 162–79.
'The woollen industry', in E. Miller and S. Pollard (eds), *Cambridge Economic History of Europe: Trade and Industry in the Middle Ages* (Cambridge, 1987), vol. II, pp. 613–90.
'The woollen industry before 1550', in E. Crittall (ed.), *The Victoria History of the Counties of England: A History of the County of Wiltshire*, vol. IV (London, 1957).
Cavaciocchi, S. (ed.), *Le migrazioni in Europa, secc. xiii–xviii. Atti della venticinquesima settimana di studi, Istituto internazionale di storia economica F. Datini, 1993* (Florence, 1994).
Childs, W., 'The English export trade in cloth in the fourteenth century,' in R. H. Britnell and J. Hatcher (eds), *Progress and Problems in Medieval England: Essays in Honour of Edward Miller* (Cambridge, 1996), pp. 121–47.
Chorley, P., 'The cloth exports of Flanders and northern France during the thirteenth century: A luxury trade?', *The Economic History Review*, 40 (1987), 349–79.
'English cloth exports during the thirteenth and early fourteenth centuries: The continental evidence', *Historical Research*, 61 (1988), 1–10.
Clark, P., *European Cities and Towns* (Oxford, 2009).
Cohn, S. K., *Lust for Liberty: The Politics of Social Revolt in Medieval Europe, 1200–1425: Italy, France and Flanders* (Cambridge, Mass., 2006).
Popular Protest in Late Medieval English Towns (Cambridge, 2012).
Consitt, F., *The London Weavers' Company* (Oxford, 1933).
Cooper, J. (ed.), *The Victoria History of the Counties of England: A History of the County of Essex: The Borough of Colchester*, vol. IX (London, 1994).
Crowfoot, E., F. Pritchard and K. Staniland, *Textiles and Clothing 1150–1450* (London, 1992).
Cunningham, W., *Alien Immigrants to England* (New York, 1897).
'The commercial policy of Edward III', *Transactions of the Royal Historical Society*, New Series, 4 (1889), 202–3.
The Growth of English Industry and Commerce during the Early and Middle Ages, 5th edn (Cambridge, 1922).
D'Alteroche, B., *De L'étranger à la seigneurie à l'étranger au royaume (XIe–XVe siècles)* (Paris, 2000).
Davies, M., 'Lobbying parliament: The London livery companies in the fifteenth century', *Parliamentary History*, 23 (2004), 136–48.

Davis, J., 'Market courts and lex mercatoria in late medieval England', in M. Allen and M. Davies (eds), *Medieval Merchants and Money: Essays in Honour of James L. Bolton* (London, 2016), pp. 271–90.

Medieval Market Morality: Life, Law and Ethics in the English Market Place (Cambridge, 2011).

Debrabandere, F., *Verklarend Woordenboek van de Familienamen in België en Noord-Frankrijk*, 2 vols. (Brussels, 1992).

Demets, L., 'Spies, instigators, and troublemakers: Gendered perceptions of rebellious women in late medieval Flemish chronicles', *Journal of Women's History*, 33 (2021), 12–34.

De Poerck, G., *La Draperie médiévale en Flandre et en Artois: Technique et terminologie*, 2 vols. (Bruges, 1951).

Dept, G.-G., *Les Influences anglaise et française dans le comté de Flandre au début du XIIIe siècle* (Ghent and Paris, 1928).

De Sagher, H., 'L'Immigration des tisserands flamands et brabançons en Angleterre sous Edouard III', in W. Ashley and P. Berghmans (eds), *Mélanges d'histoire offerts à Henri Pirenne par ces anciens élèves et ses amis à l'occasion de sa quarantième année de l'enseignement à Université de Gand* (Brussels, 1926), pp. 109–26.

De Sturler, J., *Les Relations politiques et les échanges commerciaux entre le duché de Brabant et l'Angleterre au Moyen Âge: L'Étape des laines anglaises en Brabant et les origines du développement du port d'Anvers* (Paris, 1936).

Dobson, R. B., 'Aliens in the city of York during the fifteenth century', in J. Mitchell (ed.), *England and the Continent in the Middle Ages, Studies in Memory of Andrew Martindale*, Harlaxton Medieval Studies VIII (Stamford, 2000), pp. 249–66.

'The General Survey 1300–1540, in D. M. Palliser (ed.), *The Cambridge Urban History of Britain* (Cambridge, 2008), pp. 273–90.

Dodd, G., *Justice and Grace: Private Petitioning and the English Parliament in the Late Middle Ages* (Oxford, 2007).

'Richard II and the fiction of majority rule', in C. Beem (ed.), *The Royal Minorities of Medieval and Early Modern England* (New York, 2008), pp. 103–60.

Doumerc, B., 'L'Immigration dalmate à Venise à la fin du Moyen Âge', in S. Cavaciocchi (ed.), Le migrazioni in Europa, secc. XIII–XVIII. Atti

della venticinquesima settimana di studi, Istituto internazionale di storia economica F. Datini, 1993 (Florence, 1994), pp. 325–34.

Ducellier, A., 'Les Albanais dans les Balkans et en Italie: Courants migratoires et connivences socio-culturelles', in S. Cavaciocchi (ed.), Le migrazioni in Europa, secc. XIII–XVIII. Atti della venticinquesima settimana di studi, Istituto internazionale di storia economica F. Datini, 1993 (Florence, 1994), pp. 233–70.

Dumolyn, J., 'Economic development, social space and political power in Bruges, c. 1127–1302', in H. Skoda, P. Lantschner and R. L. J. Shaw (eds), *Contact and Exchange in Later Medieval Europe: Essays in Honour of Malcolm Vale* (Woodbridge, 2012), pp. 33–58.

'Guild politics and political guilds in fourteenth-century Flanders', in J. Dumolyn, J. Haemers, H. R. Oliva Herer and V. Challet (eds), *The Voices of the People in Late Medieval Europe: Communication and Popular Politics* (2014), pp. 15–48.

'The legal repression of revolts in late medieval Flanders', *The Legal History Review*, 68 (2000), 479–521.

Dumolyn, J., and G. Dupont, B. Lambert, J. M. Murray, J. Puttevils and P. Stabel, 'Production, markets and socio-economic structures II: c. 1320 – c. 1500', in A. Brown and J. Dumolyn (eds), *Medieval Bruges c. 850–1550* (Cambridge, 2018), pp. 196–267.

Dumolyn, J. and J. Haemers, 'Patterns of urban rebellion in medieval Flanders', *Journal of Medieval History*, 31 (2005), 369–93.

Dumolyn J. and M. Pajic, 'Enemies of the count and of the city: The collective exile of rebels in fourteenth-century Flanders', *The Legal History Review*, 84:3–4 (2016), 461–501.

Dumolyn, J., J. Puttevils and P. Stabel, 'Production, markets and socio-economic structures I: c. 1100 – c. 1320', in A. Brown and J. Dumolyn (eds), *Medieval Bruges c. 850–1550* (Cambridge, 2018), pp. 86–120.

Dupont, G., 'Van Copkin, over Coppin naar Jacob: De relatie tussen de voornaamsvorm en de leeftijd van de naamdrager in het Middelnederlands op basis van administratieve bronnen voor het grafschap Vlaanderen, einde 14de – midden 16de eeuw', *Naamkunde*, 33 (2001), 111–218.

Durkheim, É., *De la Division du travail social: Livre I,* 8th edn (Paris, 1967).

Dyer, C., *An Age of Transition? Economy and Society in England in the Later Middle Ages* (Oxford, 2005).

'A golden age rediscovered: Labourers' wages in the fifteenth century', in M. Allen and D. Coffman (eds), *Prices, Money and Wages* (London, 2014).

Standards of Living in the Later Middle Ages, Social Change in England c. 1200–1500 (Cambridge, 1989).

Eiden, H., *'In der Knechtshcaft werdet ihr verharren. . .': Ursachen und Verlauf des englischen Bauernaufstandes von 1381* (Trier, 1995).

'Joint action against the "bad" lordship: The Peasants' Revolt in Essex and Norfolk', *History*, 83:267 (1998), 5–30.

Endrei, W., 'Manufacturing a piece of woollen cloth in medieval Flanders: How many working hours?', in E. Aerts and J. Munro (eds), *Textiles of the Low Countries in European Economic History* (Leuven, 1990), pp. 14–23.

Epstein, S. R., and M. Prak (eds), *Guilds, Innovation, and the European Economy, 1400–1800* (Cambridge, 2008).

Espinas, G. *La Draperie dans la Flandre française au Moyen Âge* (Paris, 1923).

Les Origines du droit d'association dans les villes de l'Artois et de la Flandre française jusqu'au début du XVIe siècle (Lille, 1941–2).

Favresse, F., *L'Avènement du régime démocratique à Bruxelles pendant le Moyen Âge (1306–1423)* (Bruxelles, 1932).

Fejic, N., 'Les Catalans à Dubrovnik et dans le Bassin adriatique à la fin du Moyen Âge', *Anuario de Estudios Medievales*, 24 (1994), 429–52.

'Les Espagnols à Dubrovnik', in D. Menjot, J-L. Pinol (eds), *Les Immigrants dans la ville: Insertion, intégration, discrimination (XIIe–XXe siècles)* (Paris, 1996), pp. 83–90.

Španci u Dubrovniku u srednjem veku (Belgrade, 1988).

Fleming, P., 'Identity and belonging: Irish and Welsh in fifteenth-century Bristol', L. Clark (ed.), *The Fifteenth Century, Vol. VII: Conflicts, Consequences and the Crown in the late Middle Ages* (Woodbridge, 2007), pp. 175–93.

Fletcher, C., 'Justice, meurtre et *leadership* politique dans la révolte anglaise de 1381', *Cahiers de Recherches Médiévales et Humanistes*, 34 (2017), 61–86.
Franceschi, F., *'Oltre il tumulto': I lavoratori fiorentini dell'arte della lana fra Tre et Quattrocento* (Florence, 1993).
'I tedeschi e l'arte della lana in Firenze fra Tre et Quattrocento', in G. Rossetti (ed.), *Dentro la città stranieri e realtà urbane nell'Europa dei secoli XII–XVI* (Naples, 1989), pp. 278–90.
Fris, V., *Les Origines de la réforme constitutionnelle de Gand* (Ghent, 1907).
Fuller, T., *The Church History of Britain: From the Birth of Jesus Christ until the Year M.DC.XLVIII*, 6 vols. (Oxford, 1845).
Gauvard, C., *'De grace especial', crime, état et société en France a la fin du Moyen Âge*, 2 vols. (Paris, 1991).
Préface, in H. Zaremska, *Les Bannis au Moyen Âge* (Paris 1996).
Geremek, B., *Les Marginaux parisiens aux XIVe et XVe siècles* (Paris, 1976).
Gilissen, J., 'Le Statut des étrangers à la lumière de l'histoire comparative', in *L'Étranger, recueils de la société Jean Bodin pour l'histoire comparative des institutions*, vol. I (Brussels, 1958).
Given-Wilson, C., 'The problem of labour in the context of English government, c. 1350–1450', in J. Bothwell, P. J. P. Goldberg and W. M. Ormrod (eds), *The Problem of Labour in Fourteenth-Century England* (York, 2000).
Goddard, R., *Credit and Trade in Later Medieval England 1353–1532* (New York, 2016).
Goddard, R. and T. Phipps (eds), *Town Courts and Urban Society in Late Medieval England, 1250–1550* (Woodbridge, 2019).
Goldberg, P. J. P., 'Urban identity and the poll taxes of 1377, 1379, 1381', *Economic History Review*, 43 (1990), 194–216.
Women, Work, and Life Cycle in a Medieval Economy: Women in York and Yorkshire c. 1300–1520 (Oxford, 1992).
Good, J., 'The alien clothworkers of London, 1337–1381', in L. E. Mitchel, K. L. French and D. L. Biggs (eds), *The Ties That Bind: Essays in Medieval History in Honour of Barbara Hanawalt* (Farnham, 2011).
Goodman, A., *John of Gaunt: The Exercise of Princely Power in Fourteenth-Century Europe* (Harlow, 1992).
Goose, N. 'Immigrants and English economic development in the sixteenth and early seventeenth centuries', in N. Goose and L. Luu, (eds), *Immigrants in Tudor and Early Stuart England* (Brighton, 2005), pp. 136–60.
Goose, N. and L. Luu (eds), *Immigrants in Tudor and Early Stuart England* (Brighton, 2005).
Gray, H. L., 'The production and exportation of English woollens in the fourteenth century', *Economic History Review*, 39:153 (1924), 13–35.
Griffiths, R. A., 'The island of England in the fifteenth century: Perceptions of the peoples of the British Isles', *Journal of Medieval History*, 29 (2003), 177–200.
Haemers, J., 'Women and stews: The social and material history of prostitution in the late medieval southern Low Countries', *History Workshop Journal*, 92 (2021), 29–50.
Hanawalt, B., *Crime and Conflict in English Communities 1300–1348* (Cambridge, Mass., 1979).

'Of Good and Ill Repute': Gender and Social Control in Medieval England (Oxford, 1998).
Hanrahan, M., 'Flemings', in P. Brown (ed.), *A New Companion to Chaucer* (Hoboken, 2019), pp. 151–66.
Hatcher, J., *Plague, Population and the English Economy, 1348–1530* (London, 1977).
Hatcher, J. and E. Miller, *Medieval England: Towns, Commerce and Crafts 1086–1348* (London, 1995).
'Unreal wages: Long-run living standards and the "Golden Age" of the fifteenth century', in B. Dodds and C. D. Liddy (eds), *Commercial Activity, Markets and Entrepreneurs in the Middle Ages: Essays in Honour of Richard Britnell* (Woodbridge, 2011), pp. 1–24.
Heaton, H., *The Yorkshire Woollen and Worsted Industries from the Earliest Times up to the Industrial Revolution*, 2nd edn (Oxford, 1965).
Heers, J., *Gênes au XVe siècle* (Paris, 1961).
L'esilio, la vita politica, la società nel medioevo (Naples, 1995).
Hilton, R., *Bond Men Made Free: Medieval Peasant Movements and the English Rising of 1381* (London, 1973).
Hilton, R. and T. Aston (eds), *The English Rising of 1381* (Cambridge, 1984).
Hoerder, D., *Cultures in Contact: World Migrations in the Second Millennium* (London, 2002).
Holbach,R., *Frühformen von Verlag und Grossbetrieb in der gewerblichen Produktion (13.–16. Jahrhundert)* (Stuttgart, 1994).
Holmes, G., *The Good Parliament* (Oxford, 1975).
Howell, M. C., *Commerce before Capitalism in Europe 1300–1600* (Cambridge, 2010).
Houtte, A. van, *An Economic History of the Low Countries, 800–1800* (London, 1977).
The Marriage Exchange: Property, Social Place, and Gender in Cities of the Low Countries, 1300–1550 (Chicago, 1998).
Women, Production and Patriarchy in Late Medieval Cities (Chicago, 1986).
Hutton, S., *Women and Economic Activities in Late Medieval Ghent* (New York, 2011).
Irsigler, F. and A. Lassotta, *Bettler und Gaukler, Dirnen und Henkler: Randgruppen und AuÔenseiter in Köln, 1300–1600* (Cologne, 1984).
Johnson, H., *The History of the Worshipful Company of the Drapers of London*, 3 vols. (Oxford, 1914).
Jordan, W. C., *From England to France: Felony and Exile in the High Middle Ages* (New Jersey, 2015).
Karras, R. M., *Common Women: Prostitution and Sexuality in Medieval England* (Oxford, 1996).
'The regulation of brothels in later medieval England', *Signs: Journal of Women in Culture and Society*, 14 (1989), 399–433.
Keechang, K., *Aliens in Medieval Law: The Origins of Modern Citizenship* (Cambridge, 2000).
Keene, D., 'Metropolitan values: Migration, mobility and cultural norms, London 1100–1700', in L. Wright (ed.), *The Development of Standard English, 1300–1800: Theories, Descriptions, Conflicts* (Cambridge, 2000), pp. 93–114.
Survey of Medieval Winchester, 2 vols. (Oxford, 1985).
Kerling, N. J. M., 'Aliens in the county of Norfolk, 1436–85', *Norfolk Archaeology*, 33 (1965), 200–15.

Commercial Relations of Holland and Zeeland with England from the 13th Century to the Close of the Middle Ages (Leiden, 1954).

Kim, K., *Aliens in Medieval Law: The Origins of Modern Citizenship* (Cambridge, 2000).

Kissane, A., *Civic Community in Late Medieval Lincoln: Urban Society and Economy in the Age of the Black Death, 1289–1409* (Rochester, 2017).

Kissane, A. and J. Mackman, 'Aliens and the law in late medieval Lincolnshire', in N. McDonald, W. M. Ormrod and C. Tailor (eds), *Resident Aliens in Medieval England* (Turnhout, 2017).

Kittell, E. E. and K. Queller, '"Whether man or woman": Gender inclusivity in the town ordinances of medieval Douai', *Journal of Medieval and Early Modern Studies*, 30 (2000), 63–100.

Kowaleski, M., *Local Markets and Regional Trade in Medieval Exeter* (Cambridge, 1995).

'Town courts in medieval England: An introduction', in Goddard and Phipps (eds), *Town Courts and Urban Society*, pp. 17–42.

'Women's work in a market town: Exeter in the late fourteenth century', in B. Hanawalt (ed.), *Women and Work in Pre-industrial Europe* (Bloomington, 1986), pp. 145–64.

Lambert, B. and Ormrod W. M., 'Friendly foreigners: International warfare, resident aliens and the early history of denization in England, c. 1250 – c. 1400', *English Historical Review*, 130 (2015), 1–24.

'A matter of trust: The royal regulation of England's French residents during wartime, 1294–1377', *Historical Research*, 89 (2016), 208–26.

Lambert, B. and M. Pajic, 'Drapery in exile: Edward III, Colchester and the Flemings, 1351–1367', *History: The Journal of the Historical Association*, 99:338 (2014), 733–53.

'Immigration and the common profit: Native cloth-workers, Flemish exiles and royal policy in fourteenth-century London', *Journal of British Studies*, 55:4 (2016), 633–57.

Lee, J. S., *The Medieval Clothier* (Woodbridge, 2018).

Leland, J. L., 'Aliens in the pardons of Richard II', in J. S. Hamilton (ed.), *Fourteenth-Century England*, vol. IV (Woodbridge, 2006).

Liddy, C. D., 'Urban conflict in late fourteenth-century England: The case of York in 1381', *English Historical Review*, 118 (2003), 1–32.

Lipson, E., *The Economic History of England. Part I: The Middle Ages*, 5th edn (London, 1929).

Lloyd, T. H., *Alien Merchants in England in the High Middle Ages* (Brighton, 1982).

The English Wool Trade in the Middle Ages (Cambridge, 1977).

Lucas, H. S., *The Low Countries and the Hundred Years' War, 1326–1347* (Ann Arbor, 1929).

Lucassen, J., and L. Lucassen (eds), *Globalising Migration History: The Eurasian Experience (16th–21st Centuries)* (Leiden, 2014).

Lucassen, J., and L. Lucassen *Migration, Migration History, History: Old Paradigms, New Perspectives* (Bern, 1997).

Luiten van Zanden, J., S. Carmichael and T. de Moor (eds), *Capital Women: The European Marriage Pattern, Female Empowerment and Economic Development in Western Europe* (Oxford, 2019).

Luu, L., *Immigrants and Industries of London 1500–1700* (London, 2005).
Maddern, P., *Violence and Social Order: East Anglia 1422–42* (Oxford, 1992).
Massey, D. S., J. Arango, G. Hugo, A. Kouaouci, A. Pellegrino and J. E. Taylor, 'Theories of international migration: A review and appraisal', *Population and Development Review* 19:3 (1993), 431–66.
Mathorez, J., *Histoire de la formation de la population française: Les étrangers en France sous l'ancien régime*, 2 vols. (Paris, 1919–21).
McDonald, N., W. M. Ormrod and C. Tailor (eds), *Resident Aliens in Medieval England* (Turnhout, 2018).
McIntosh, M. K., 'The benefits and drawbacks of "femme sole" status in England 1300–1630', *Journal of British Studies*, 44 (2005), 410–38.
Working Women in English Society 1300–1620 (Cambridge, 2005).
McKisack, M., *The Fourteenth Century, 1307–1399* (Oxford, 1971).
Menjot, D., 'Introduction: Les gens venus d'ailleurs dans les villes médiévales: Quelques acquis de la recherche', in C. Quertier, R. Chilà and N. Pluchot (eds), *Arriver en ville: Les migrantes en milieu urbain au Moyen Âge* (Paris, 2013), pp. 15–32.
Menjot, D. and J.-L. Pinol (eds), *Les Immigrants et la ville: Insertion, intégration, discrimination (XIIe–XXe siècles)* (Paris, 1996).
Miller, E., 'The fortunes of the English textile industry during the thirteenth century', *Essays in Economic History Presented to Professor M. M. Postan, Economic History Review*, 18 (1965), 64–82.
Moal, L., *L'Étranger en Bretagne au Moyen Âge: Présence, attitudes, perceptions* (Rennes, 2008).
Morawska, E., 'The sociology and historiography of immigration', in V. Yans McLaughlin (ed.), *Immigration Reconsidered: History, Sociology, and Politics* (Oxford, 1990), pp. 187–240.
Muller, M., 'Conflict and revolt: The bishop of Ely and his peasants at the manor of Brandon in Suffolk c. 1300–1381', *Rural History*, 23:1 (2012), 1–19.
Munro, J. H., 'Anglo-Flemish competition in the international cloth trade 1340–1560', *Centre européen d'études bourguignones*, 35 (1995), 97–60.
'The "industrial crisis" of the English textile towns, 1290–1330', in M. Prestwich, R. H. Britnell and R. Frame (eds), *Thirteenth-Century England* (Woodbridge, 1999), vol. VII, pp. 103–42.
'Industrial energy from water-mills in the European economy, 5th to 18th centuries: The limitations of power', in S. Cavaciocchi (ed.), *Economia e energia secc. XIII–XVIII. Atti della trentaquattresima settimana di studi a cura di Simonetta Cavaciocchi* (Florence, 2002), pp. 248–55.
'Industrial entrepreneurship in the late medieval Low Countries: Urban draperies, fullers, and the art of survival', in Paul Klep and Eddy Van Cauwenberghe (eds), *Entrepreneurship and the Transformation of the Economy (10th–20th Centuries): Essays in Honour of Herman Van Der Wee* (Leuven, 1994), pp. 377–88.
'Industrial protectionism in medieval Flanders: Urban or national?', in H. Miskimin, D. Herlihy and A. L. Udovitch (eds), *The Medieval City* (New Haven and London, 1977), pp. 229–68.
'Industrial transformations in the north-west European textile trades, c. 1290 – c. 1340: Economic progress or economic crisis?', in Bruce M. S. Campbell (ed.),

Before the Black Death: Studies in the 'Crisis' of the Early Fourteenth Century (Manchester and New York, 1991), pp. 110–48.
'Medieval woollens: The western European woollen industries and their struggles for international markets, c. 1000–1500', in D. Jenkins (ed.), *The Cambridge History of Western Textiles*, 2 vols. (Cambridge, 2003), vol. I, pp. 228–324.
'Medieval woollens: Textiles, textile technology and industrial organisation, c. 800–1500', in D. Jenkins (ed.), *The Cambridge History of Western Textiles*, 2 vols. (Cambridge, 2003), vol. I, pp. 181–227.
'The origins of the English "new draperies": The resurrection of an old Flemish industry, 1270–1570', in N. B. Harte (ed.), *The New Draperies in the Low Countries and England* (New York, 1998), pp. 35–127.
'The rise, expansion, and decline of the Italian wool-based cloth industries, 1100–1730: A study in international competition, transaction costs, and comparative advantage', *Studies in Medieval and Renaissance History*, 9 (2012), 45–207.
'Symbiosis of towns and textiles: Urban institutions and the changing fortunes of cloth manufacturing in the Low Countries and England 1280–1570', *Journal of Early Modern History*, 3 (1999), 1–74.
Textiles, Towns and Trade: Essays in the Economic History of Late Medieval England and the Low Countries (Hampshire, 1994).
'Three centuries of luxury textile consumption in the Low Countries and England, 1330–1570: Trends and comparisons of real values of woollen broadcloth (then and now)', in Katherine Vestergard and Marie-Louise B. Nosch (eds), *The Medieval Broadcloth: Changing Trends in Fashions Manufacturing and Consumption* (Oxford, 2009), pp. 1–73.
'Urban regulation and monopolistic competition in the textile industries of the late medieval Low Countries', in E. Aerts and J. Munro (eds), *Textiles of the Low Countries in European Economic History* (Leuven, 1990), pp. 41–52.
Wool, Cloth and Gold: The Struggle for Bullion in Anglo-Burgundian Trade 1340–1478 (Brussels and Toronto, 1972).
Murray, J. L., *Bruges, Cradle of Capitalism, 1280–1390* (Cambridge, 2005).
Musson, A. and W. M. Ormrod, *The Evolution of English Justice* (London, 1999).
Nicholas, D., 'The English trade in Bruges in the last years of Edward III', *Journal of Medieval History*, 5 (1979), 23–61.
Medieval Flanders (London, 1996).
The Metamorphosis of a Medieval City: Ghent in the Age of Van Arteveldes, 1302–1390 (Lincoln, 1987).
Town and Countryside: Social, Economic and Political Tensions in 14th-Century Flanders (Bruges, 1971).
The Van Arteveldes of Ghent: The Varieties of Vendetta and the Hero in History (Ithaca, 1988).
Nightingale, P., 'Capitalists, crafts and constitutional change in late fourteenth-century London', *Past and Present*, 123 (1989), 3–35.
A Medieval Mercantile Community: The Grocers' Company and the Politics and Trade of London 1000–1485 (New Haven, 1995).
Oldland, J. R., *The English Woollen Industry, c. 1200 – c. 1560* (Abingdon, 2020).
'The finishing of English woollens 1300–1550', in R. Netherton and G. Owen-Crocker (eds), *Medieval Clothing and Textiles*, vol. III (Woodbridge, 2007).

'Making and marketing woollen cloth in late medieval London', *The London Journal,* 36(2011), 89–108.

Oldland, J. R.and E. Quinton, 'London merchants' cloth exports, 1350–1500', in R. Netherton and G. R. Owen-Crocker (eds), *Medieval Clothing and Textiles*, vol. VII (Woodbridge, 2011), pp. 111–40.

Ormrod, W. M., '"Common profit" and "the profit of the king and kingdom": Parliament and the development of political language in England, 1250–1450', *Viator*, 46 (2015), 219–52.

Edward III (London, 2011).

'The Good Parliament of 1376: Commons, communes and "common profit" in fourteenth-century English politics', in D. Nicholas, B. S. Bachrach and J. M. Murray (eds), *Comparative Perspectives on History and Historians: Essays in Memory of Bryce Lyon (1920–2007)* (Kalamazoo, 2012), pp. 169–88.

'The Peasants' Revolt and the government of England', *Journal of British Studies*, 29 (1990), 1–30.

Ormrod, W. M., B. Lambert and J. Mackman, *Immigrant England 1300–1550* (Manchester, 2018).

Page, J., *Prostitution and Subjectivity in Late Medieval Germany* (Oxford, 2021).

Pajic, M., '"Ale for an Englishman is a natural drink": The Dutch and the origins of beer brewing in late medieval England', *Journal of Medieval History*, 45 (2019), 285–300.

'Flemish rebels in exile: Their perception in 14th-century London and the creation of new identities', in T. Silec and A. Stazzone (eds), *Peuples conquérants, peuples conquis: Perceptions identitaires au Moyen Âge en Europe (Ixe–XVe siècle)*, volume issu du colloque international du Centre d'Études Médiévales Anglaises Paris Sorbonne (7–8 novembre 2014), *Bulletin des Anglicistes Médiévistes* (2015), pp. 187–206.

'The fortunes of urban fullers in fourteenth-century England', *Historical Research*, 93 (2020), 227–51.

'Xénophobie et intégration: Le cas de la communauté flamande de Colchester 1351–1367', *Revue du Nord* (2017), 509–31.

Palmer, J. J. N., 'England, France, the papacy and the Flemish succession, 1361–9', *Journal of Medieval History*, 2 (1976).

Park, R., 'Human migration and the marginal man', *American Journal of Sociology*, 33 (1928), 881–93.

Pearsall, D., 'Strangers in late fourteenth-century London', in F. R. P. Akehurst and S. Cain Van D'Elden (eds), *The Stranger in Medieval Society* (Minneapolis and London, 1997), pp. 46–62.

Peeters, J. P., 'De produktiestructuur der Mechelse lakennijverheid en de ambachten van wevers en volders van 1270 tot 1430', *Handelingen van de Koninklijke Kring voor Oudheidskunde, Letteren en Kunst van Mechelen*, 88 (1984), 93–158.

Peregrine, H. (ed.), *Freedom of Movement in the Middle Ages: Proceedings of the Twentieth Harlaxton Symposium* (Donington, 2007).

Peyregne, A., ' Les Émigrés gascons en Angleterre (1453–1485)', *Annales du Midi*, 66 (1954), 1–15.

Phipps, T., *Medieval Women and Urban Justice: Commerce, Crime and Community in England 1300–1500* (Manchester, 2019).

Piore, M. J., *Birds of Passage: Migrant Labor in Industrial Societies* (Cambridge, 1979).
Pirenne, H., *Histoire de Belgique dès origines à nos jours,* 5th edn, 4 vols. (Brussels, 1928).
Le Soulèvement de la Flandre maritime de 1323–1328: Documents inédits (Brussels, 1900).
Poos, L. R., *A Rural Society after the Black Death: Essex 1350–1525* (Cambridge, 1991).
'The social context of the Statute of Labourers enforcement', *Law and History Review*, 1 (1983), 27–52.
Portes, A. and J. Walton, *Labor, Class, and the International System* (New York, 1981).
Postan, M., 'Some economic evidence of declining population in the later Middle Ages', *The Economic History Review*, 2 (1950), 221–46.
Prevenier, W., 'La Bourgeoisie en Flandre au XIIIe siècle', *Revue de l'Université de Bruxelles*, 4 (1978), 407–28.
Quertier, C., R. Chilà and N. Pluchot (eds), *Arriver en ville: Les migrantes en milieu urbain au Moyen Âge* (Paris, 2013).
Quicke, F., *Les Pays-Bas à la veille de la période bourguignonne, 1356–1384: Contribution à l'histoire et diplomatique de l'Europe occidentale dans la seconde moitié du XIVe siècle* (Brussels, 1947).
Rawcliffe, C., *Leprosy in Medieval England* (Woodbridge, 2006).
Reith, R., 'Circulation of skilled labour in late medieval and early modern central Europe', in S. R. Epstein and M. Prak (eds), *Guilds, Innovation and European Economy 1400–1800* (Cambridge, 2009), pp. 114–42.
Réville, André, *Le Soulèvement des travailleurs d'Angleterre en 1381* (Paris, 1898).
Ricciardelli, F., 'Exile as evidence of civic identity in Florence in the time of Dante: Some examples', *Reti Mediaevali*, 5 (2004), 1–15.
Roby, A., *La Prostitution au Moyen Âge: Le commerce charnel en Midi toulousain du XIIIe au XVIe siècles* (Villemur sur Tarn, 2020).
Rogghé, Paul, 'Gemeente ende Vrient: Nationale omwentelingen in de 14de eeuw', *Annales de la Société d'Emulation de Bruges*, 89:3–4 (1952), 101–35.
Rose, S., *The Wealth of England: The Medieval Wool Trade and Its Political Importance 1100–1600* (Oxford, 2018).
Rosser, G., *The Art of Solidarity in the Middle Ages: Guilds in England 1200–1500* (Oxford, 2015).
'Crafts, gilds and the negotiation of work in the medieval town', *Past and Present* (1997), 3–31.
Rossiaud, J., *Amours vénales: La prostitution en Occident, XIIe–XVIe siècles* (Paris, 2010).
Rubin, M., *Cities of Strangers: Making Lives in Medieval Europe* (Cambridge, 2020).
'Small groups: Identity and solidarity in the late Middle Ages', in J. Kermode (ed.), *Enterprise and Individuals in Fifteenth-Century England* (Gloucester, 1991), pp. 132–50.
Ruddick, A., *English Identity and Political Culture in the Fourteenth Century* (Cambridge, 2013).
Ruddock, A. A., 'Alien hosting in Southampton in the fifteenth century', *The Economic History Review*, 16 (1946), 30–7.
'Alien merchants in Southampton in the later Middle Ages', *English Historical Review*, 61 (1946), 1–17.
Sabbe, J., *Vlaanderen in opstand 1323–1328: Nikolaas Zannekin, Zeger Janszone en Willem de Deken* (Bruges, 1992).

Salzman, L., *English Industries of the Middle Ages: Being an Introduction to the Industrial History of Medieval England* (London, 1913).

(ed.), *The Victoria History of the Counties of England: A History of the County of Warwick: Knightlow Hundred,* vol. VI (London, 1951).

Sassen, S., *The Mobility of Labor and Capital: A Study in International Investment and Labor Flow* (Cambridge, 1988).

Saul, A., 'English towns in the late Middle Ages: The case of Great Yarmouth', *Journal of Medieval History*, 8 (1982), 75–88.

Sayad, A., *L'Immigration ou les paradoxes de l'altérité* (Brussels, 1991).

Scales, L., 'Bread, cheese and genocide: Imagining the destruction of peoples in medieval Western Europe', *History*, 92:307 (2007), 284–300.

Sellers, M. 'Social and economic history', in W. Page (ed.), *The Victoria History of the Counties of England: A History of the County of York* (London, 1907), vol. III, pp. 435–86.

'Textile industry', in W. Page (ed.), *The Victoria History of the Counties of England: A History of the County of York* (London, 1907), vol. III, pp. 406–29.

Shaw, C., *The Politics of Exile in Renaissance Italy* (Cambridge 2000).

Simmel, G., 'Excursions sur l'étranger', in G. Simmel, *Soziologie: Untersuchungen über die Formen der Vergesellschftung,* herausgegeben von Otthein Rammstedt (Frankfurt am Main, 1992), pp. 764–71.

Spindler, E., 'Flemings in the Peasants' Revolt, 1381', in H. Skoda, P. Lantschner and R. Shaw (eds), *Contact and Exchange in Later Medieval Europe: Essays in Honour of Malcolm Vale* (Woodbridge, 2012), pp. 59–78.

Stabel, P., *Dwarfs among Giants: The Flemish Urban Network in the Late Middle Ages* (Louvain, 1997).

'Guilds in late medieval Flanders: Myths and realities of guild life in an export-oriented environment', *Journal of Medieval History,* 30 (2004), 187–212.

Stark, O., 'Migration decision making: A review article' *Journal of Development Economics,* 14 (1984), 251–9.

Starn, R., *Contrary Commonwealth: The Theme of Exile in Medieval and Renaissance Italy* (Berkeley 1982).

Strohm, P., 'Trade, treason, and the murder of Janus Imperial', *Journal of British Studies,* 35 (1996), 1–23.

Sutton, A. F., 'The early linen and worsted industries of Norfolk and the evolution of the London Mercers' Company', *Norfolk Archaeology*, 40 (1987/89), 201–25.

The Mercery of London: Trade, Goods and People, 1130–1578 (Aldershot, 2005).

Swanson, H., *Medieval Artisans: An Urban Class in Late Medieval England* (Oxford, 1989).

Te Brake, W., *A Plague of Insurrection: Popular Politics and Peasant Revolt in Flanders, 1323–1328* (Philadelphia, 1993).

Thoen, E., 'Immigration to Bruges during the late Middle Ages', in Simonetta Cavaciocchi (ed.), *Le migrazioni in Europa secc. XIII–XVIII. Atti della venticinquesima settimana di studi 3–8 maggio 1993* (Florence, 1995), pp. 335–53.

Thrupp, S. L., 'Aliens in and around London in the fifteenth century', in A. E. J. Hollaender and W. Kellaway (eds), *Studies in London History Presented to Philip Edmund Jones* (London, 1969), pp. 251–75.

The Merchant Class of Medieval London 1300–1500 (Chicago, 1948).

'A survey of the alien population in England in 1440', *Speculum*, 32 (1957), 262–73.

Tillott, P. M. (ed.), *The Victoria History of the Counties of England: A History of the County of York: The City of York* (London, 1961).

Tolbert, C. M., P. M. Horan and E. M. Beck, 'The structure of economic segmentation: A dual economy approach', *American Journal of Sociology*, 85 (1980), 1095–116.

Tönnies, F., *Community and Association (Gemeinschaft und Gesellschaft)*, trans. C. P. Loomis (London, 1955).

Trexler, R., 'La Prostitution florentine au XVe siècle: Patronages et clientèles', *Annales ESC*, 36 (1981), 983–1015.

Tucker, P., *Law Courts and Lawyers in the City of London, 1300–1550* (Cambridge, 2007).

Twycross, M., 'Some aliens in York and their overseas connections', *Leeds Studies in English*, 29 (1998), 359–80.

Uytven, R. van, 'La Draperie brabançonne et malinoise du XIIe au XVIIIe siècles: Grandeur éphémère et décadence', in M. Spallanzani (ed.), *Produzione, commercio e consumo dei panni di lana* (Florence, 1976), pp. 85–97.

'The fulling mill: Dynamic of the revolution of industrial attitudes', *Acta Historiae Neerlandica*, 5 (1971), 1–14.

'De omvang van de Mechelse lakenproductie vanaf de 14de eeuw tot de 16de eeuw', *Noordgouw*, 5 (1965), 1–22.

'Peter Couthereel en de troebelen te Leuven van 1350 tot 1363: Kritische nota over de persoon van een hertogelijk ambtenaar en zijn rol in de politieke geschiedenis van Brabant en Leuven', *Mededelingen van de Geschied- en Oudheidkundige Kring voor Leuven en Omgeving*, 3 (1963), 63–97.

Vale, M. G. A., *The Origins of the Hundred Years War: The Angevin Legacy, 1250–1340* (Oxford, 1996).

Vandermaesen, M., 'Brugse en Ieperse gijzelaars voor koning en graaf,1329–1329: Een administratief dossier', *Handelingen van het Genootschap voor Geschiedenis Brugge*, 130 (1993), 119–44.

'De rekening der Brugse gijzelaars 1328/29–1338/41', *Handelingen van het Genootschap voor Geschiedenis Brugge*, 115 (1978), 1–16.

Varenbergh, E., *Histoire des relations diplomatiques entre le comté de Flandre et l'Angleterre au Moyen Âge* (Ghent, 1868).

Veale, E., *The Fur Trade in the Later Middle Ages* (Oxford, 1966).

Verbruggen, J. F., *The Battle of the Golden Spurs: Courtrai, 11 July 1302* (Woodbridge 2002).

Het gemeenteleger van Brugge van 1338 tot 1340 en de namen van de weerbare mannen (Brussels, 1962).

1302: Opstand in Vlaanderen: De Guldensporenslag (Brussels 1977).

Vlaanderen na de Guldensporenslag: De vrijheidsstrijdvan het graafschap Vlaanderen, 1303–1305 (Bruges, 1991).

Verbruggen, R., *Geweld in Vlaanderen: Macht en onderdrukking in de Vlaamse steden tijdens de veertiende eeuw* (Bruges, 2004).

Victor, s., *La Construction et les métiers de la construction à Gérone au XVe siècle* (Toulouse, 2008).

Vuylsteke, J., 'Goede Disendach, 13 januari 1349', *Handelingen van de Maatschappij voor Geschiedenis en Oudheidkunde te Gent*, 1 (1894), 9–47.

Wallerstein, I., *The Modern World System, Capitalist Agriculture and the Origins of the European World Economy in the Sixteenth Century* (New York, 1974).
Waugh, S., *England in the Reign of Edward III* (Cambridge, 1991).
Weber, M., *Economy and Society*, trans. G. Roth and C. Wittich (New York, 1968).
Wedemeyer, Moore E., *The Fairs of Medieval England: An Introductory Study* (Toronto, 1985).
Werveke, H. van, 'De koopman-ondernemer en de ondernemer in de Vlaamsche lakennijverheid van de late middeleeuwen', *Mededeelingen van de Koninklijke Academie voor Wetenschappen, Letteren en Schoone Kunsten van België, Klasse der Letteren*, 8 (1946), 5–26.
'Der flandrische Eigenhandel im Mittelalter', *Hansische Geschichtsblätter*, 61 (1936), 7–24.
'Westeuropese munstelsels in de tweede helft van de veertiende eeuw', *Handelingen der Maatschaapij voor Geschiedenis en Oudheidkunde te Gent*, 27 (1973), 241–7.
Winter, A., 'Population and migration: European and Chinese experiences compared', in P. Clark (ed.), *The Oxford Handbook of Cities in World History* (Oxford, 2013).
Wyffels, C., 'De Vlaamse handel op Engeland voor het Engels–Vlaams konflikt van 1270–1274', *Bijdragen voor de geschiedenis der Nederlanden*, 17 (1963), 205–13.
'Nieuwe gegevens betreffende een XIIIde eeuwse "democratische" stedelijke opstand: De Brugse "Moerlemaye" (1280–81)', *Bulletin de la Commission Royale d'Histoire*, 132 (1966), 37–142.

UNPUBLISHED DISSERTATIONS AND THESES

Bolton, J. L., 'Alien merchants in England in the reign of Henry VI, 1422–61', unpublished B.Litt. thesis, University of Oxford (1971).
Bradley, H., 'The Italian community in London, 1350–1450', unpublished Ph.D. thesis, University of London (1992).
Colson, J., 'Local communities in fifteenth-century London: Craft, parish and neighborhood', unpublished Ph.D. thesis, Royal Holloway London (2011).
Dunn, P., 'After the Black Death: Society and economy in late fourteenth-century Norwich', unpublished Ph.D. thesis, University of East Anglia (2003).
Linsley, C., 'Nation, England and the French in Thomas Walsingham's *Chronica Maiora* 1376–1420', unpublished Ph.D. thesis, University of York (2015).
Oldland, J. R., 'London clothmaking, c. 1270 – c. 1550', unpublished Ph.D. thesis, Royal Holloway and Bedford New College, University of London (2003).
Prescott, A., 'Judicial records of the Rising of 1381', unpublished Ph.D. thesis, Bedford College, University of London (1984).
Quinton, E., 'The drapers and the drapery trade of late medieval London, c. 1300 – c. 1500', unpublished Ph.D. thesis, University of London (2001).
Rodziewicz, J., 'Order and society: Great Yarmouth, 1366–1381', unpublished Ph. D. thesis, University of East Anglia (2008).
Saul, A., 'Great Yarmouth in the fourteenth century: A study in trade, politics and society', unpublished D.Phil. thesis, University of Oxford (1975).
Soloman, E., 'La Condition juridique des étrangers dans les législations anciennes et le droit moderne', unpublished Ph.D. thesis, University of Paris (1844).

INDEX

Royal and aristocratic names: The names of kings are alphabetised by their given name, glossed with the country and date of their reign: Edward III, King (England, 1327–77). Members of the aristocracy are alphabetised by their given name (usually with a descriptive term) and are glossed with their title and lifespan: Louis of Male (Louis II, Count of Flanders, 1330–84).

Page locators in bold represent references to table or maps.

For EU product safety concerns, contact us at Calle de José Abascal, 56–1°, 28003 Madrid, Spain or eugpsr@cambridge.org.

www.ingramcontent.com/pod-product-compliance
Lightning Source LLC
LaVergne TN
LVHW050758061126
851857LV00012B/609
* 9 7 8 1 1 0 8 7 3 3 6 2 5 *